Palgrave Socio-Legal Studies

Series Editor
Dave Cowan
School of Law
University of Bristol
Bristol, UK

The Palgrave Socio-Legal Studies series is a developing series of monographs and textbooks featuring cutting edge work which, in the best tradition of socio-legal studies, reach out to a wide international audience.

More information about this series at
http://www.palgrave.com/gp/series/14679

Senthorun Raj · Peter Dunne
Editors

The Queer Outside in Law

Recognising LGBTIQ People in the United Kingdom

palgrave
macmillan

Editors
Senthorun Raj
Keele University
Newcastle-Under-Lyme, UK

Peter Dunne
University of Bristol
Bristol, UK

Palgrave Socio-Legal Studies
ISBN 978-3-030-48829-1 ISBN 978-3-030-48830-7 (eBook)
https://doi.org/10.1007/978-3-030-48830-7

Cover credit: johnwoodcock/GettyImages

This Palgrave Macmillan imprint is published by the registered company Springer Nature Switzerland AG
The registered company address is: Gewerbestrasse 11, 6330 Cham, Switzerland

Acknowledgements

This project began its life as a conversation over cups of tea at the end of the Socio-Legal Studies Association Conference in Newcastle in April 2017. As legal scholars who use very different methodological approaches in our work but who are both deeply invested in LGBTIQ rights, we wondered what might be gained if we tried to combine our different approaches (as queer as they might be together!) to address current issues facing LGBTIQ people in the United Kingdom. From that brief chat, *The Queer Outside in Law: Recognising LGBTIQ People in the United Kingdom* was born. In realising this project, we have received support from a number of individuals and institutions, without whose generosity, advice and support, we would not have been able to produce this book.

At the beginning of the project, we benefited greatly from the support, advice and mentorship of Professor Dave Cowan, who championed this project and who provided invaluable advice as we navigated the proposal review. We received extremely helpful comments and encouragement from three anonymous reviewers. Their insights were beneficial as we structured the project, and they have undoubtedly enhanced the final collection.

While completing this project (2017–2020), we have benefited from the support of a number of educational institutions. Since 2017, Senthorun Raj has been a lecturer at Keele University, which has been immensely generous in contributing to the edited collection—particularly through their funding and hosting of an authors' workshop in June 2018. Peter Dunne began the project as a Ph.D. student at Trinity College Dublin and took up an academic position at the University of Bristol Law School in 2017. The authors are very appreciative of the contribution of all three institutions, both for their support of this project and the authors' wider research activities.

Since the initial stages of the collection, we have benefited from the exceedingly professional, supportive and patient partnership of the editorial staff at Palgrave Macmillan. We could not have asked for better guidance and assistance on this project, and we are immensely grateful for their knowledgeable and understanding advice throughout. In particular, we owe a significant debt of gratitude to Josie Taylor, Liam Inscoe-Jones and Hemapriya Eswanth.

We are grateful to our families (for putting up with us!), and to the numerous friends and colleagues who have supported and encouraged this work. In particular, we would like to thank Professor Chris Ashford and Professor Stephen Whittle for their contribution, support and advice in bringing this edited collection to fruition. Our final thanks go to the amazing and fabulous authors, who have contributed to this edited collection. It has been a deep honour working with you over the past three years. We are consistently inspired by your commitment to excellence and your collegiality. Thank you for being part of this project!

Contents

Queering the Outsides of Legal Gender and Sex

Notes on Contributors

Felicity Adams is a Ph.D. Candidate and Graduate Teaching Assistant at Keele University. Felicity's doctoral work challenges the rationale of "Gender-Responsive" penal strategies and technologies from a Queer perspective and renews the case to adopt a Queer-abolitionist politic as an alternative to the carceral nation.

Eddie Bruce-Jones is a Reader at Birkbeck College. His research interests include comparative anti-discrimination law, human rights and rights critique, international refugee law, legal theory, prison studies, "culture" and colonialism.

S. Chelvan is a barrister at 33 Bedford Row Chambers in London. He is a refugee advocate, specialising in LGBTI asylum cases. His advocacy and research interests span migration law, public law and international human rights law.

Sharon Cowan is a Professor of Feminist and Queer Legal Studies at Edinburgh University. Her research focuses on gender, law and sexuality, including transgender legal issues, and queer legal theory; criminal law, particularly projects on sex work, sexual offences, domestic violence and criminalisation theories; medical law and ethics, particularly reproductive issues; and asylum and refugee law.

Peter Dunne is a Senior Lecturer at the University of Bristol Law School and an Associate Member of Garden Court Chambers. He researches the intersections of law, sexual orientation, gender identity and sex characteristics.

Fabienne Emmerich is a Lecturer in Law at Keele University. She works in the field of penal sociology and is interested in the way gendered power relations in prison produce governable and ungovernable subjects and at the same time how prisoners engage in varying resistance practices to create counter or alternative subject positions.

Fae Garland is a Senior Lecturer in Criminal Law and Evidence at the University of Manchester. She researches across a broad range of subjects, including gender, children, domestic violence, family law and property law.

Kay Lalor is a Senior Lecturer at Manchester Metropolitan University. Her research focuses on the growth of LGBT/SOGI rights activism in international legal arenas. She recently completed a three-year Leverhulme Early Career Fellowship for the project *International Relations and LGBTI Rights: Conditionality, Diplomacy and Activism.*

Senthorun Raj is a Lecturer in Law at Keele University. He researches ideas of emotion, gender and sexuality across various sub disciplines of law. His recently published monograph, *Feeling Queer Jurisprudence: Injury, Intimacy, Identity* (2020), draws on the analytic and political dimensions of queer, alongside the analytic and political usefulness of emotion, to navigate legal interventions aimed at progressing the rights of LGBT people.

Flora Renz is a Lecturer at the University of Kent. Flora's research is concerned with the legal regulation of (trans)gender identities and sexuality in society and broader questions focusing on the interface between structural inequalities, law, gender, sexuality and emotion.

Mitchell Travis is an Associate Professor in Law and Social Justice at the University of Leeds. Mitchell's research focuses on a range of different issues that are underpinned by a theoretical commitment to feminist theory and the legal humanities. His work focuses on intersex embodiment, vulnerability and legal personhood.

Queering Outside the (Legal) Box: LGBTIQ People in the United Kingdom

Senthorun Raj and Peter Dunne

1 Introduction

In recent years, there has been significant social, political and academic debate on lesbian, gay, bisexual, transgender, intersex and queer (LGBTIQ) rights in the United Kingdom (UK). More than fifty years after partial decriminalisation of male same-sex intercourse in England and Wales, and with growing, yet contested,[1] awareness of gender and sexual diversity, many commentators have observed the supposedly swift expansion of sexual orientation and gender identity protections in this jurisdiction. From marriage equality to legal gender recognition, and from explicit non-discrimination guarantees to inclusive foreign policies, laws in the UK are frequently cited as a model

[1]Editorial, "The Guardian View on the Gender Recognition Act: Where Rights Collide" *Guardian*. October 17, 2018, https://www.theguardian.com/commentisfree/2018/oct/17/the-guardian-view-on-the-gender-recognition-act-where-rights-collide.

S. Raj (✉)
Keele University, Newcastle-Under-Lyme, UK
e-mail: s.raj@keele.ac.uk

P. Dunne
University of Bristol, Bristol, UK
e-mail: pd17563@bristol.ac.uk

S. Raj and P. Dunne (eds.), *The Queer Outside in Law*, Palgrave Socio-Legal Studies,
https://doi.org/10.1007/978-3-030-48830-7_1

of global "best practice" for protecting the rights and freedoms of LGBTIQ communities.[2]

Challenging such narratives of unidirectional progress, this edited collection explores the concept of the "queer outside" in UK law. Through seven substantive chapters, the collection uncovers the myriad ways in which UK law and policy continues to distort, marginalise, suppress and erase queer identities. Despite highly publicised movements for reform, there are still large sections of the UK's queer population who remain untouched by legal advancements. Queer asylum applicants, some intersex, transgender and non-binary populations, and LGBTIQ persons within the criminal justice system remain—despite recent progress—in many ways strangers to the law. The various contributions to this collection identify the often unseen lacunas in existing legal protections, and they ask whether and how UK policy makers can establish more inclusive queer rights frameworks.

The collection also analyses how assimilating queer experiences into pre-existing legal structures has obscured, re-moulded and, ultimately, excluded those queer lives, which transgress heteronormative and cisnormative[3] social conventions. Whether intentionally or not, the processes through which UK law and policy acknowledges binary trans individuals, and seeks to advance intersex rights, have not only ignored the reality of lived experience; they have even reproduced and further entrenched the marginalisation of bodies, sexualities and genders which stretch beyond commonly accepted social norms. The contributions to this collection address the unforeseen consequences of moving inside legal protection and reflect upon the potential benefits of choosing to remain an "outsider" in UK law.

As we write this introductory chapter, the UK has recently exited from the European Union, after 47 years of membership, and is now facing a global pandemic. The question of Brexit has exhausted political and legal commentators over the past five years. As editors of the collection, a key issue for us, but one which has received comparatively little attention, is

[2]See Leslie Moran, "What Kind of Field Is 'Law, Gender and Sexuality'? Achievements, Concerns and Possible Futures", *Feminist Legal Studies* 17 (2009): 309, 310. This has also been considered in the context of legislative debates, see Carl Stychin, *A Nation by Rights: National Cultures, Sexual Identity Politics, and the Discourse of Rights* (Philadelphia: Temple University Press, 1998); Carl Stychin, *Governing Sexuality: The Changing Politics of Citizenship and Law Reform* (Oxford: Hart, 2003); Carl Stychin, "Same-Sex Sexualities and the Globalization of Human Rights Discourse", *McGill Law Journal* 49 (2004): 951. For a discussion of the transnational activist mobilisation of law and policy, see Ryan Thoreson, *Transnational LGBT Activism: Working for Sexual Rights Worldwide* (Minneapolis: University of Minnesota Press, 2014).

[3]"Cisnormativity" refers to a belief in the normality, appropriateness and generality of identifying with the gender that one is assigned at birth.

how the UK's relationship to the EU has influenced (and may still potentially impact) the lives of sexual and gender minorities.[4] In many ways, the EU has been positioned as the quintessential legal "outsider"—shaping (and, according to some politicians, corrupting) the "inside" of UK law and policy. Yet, the "outside" influence of the European Union has also played a vital role in advancing LGBT[5] rights in this jurisdiction. It has established minimum guarantees,[6] which the UK government has been required to respect and, until 31 December 2020, it will retain a floor of protection under which the UK Parliament cannot legislate.[7] Thinking about the complexity of the UK and the European Union's entanglements around LGBT(IQ) rights, catalysed partly by Brexit, has allowed us to approach broader issues about sovereignty, alliance, rights, and in/exclusion by pulling into view what is inside and outside the parameters of state law.

This edited collection brings together a number of queer lawyers and legal scholars to reflect upon how the above socio-legal issues and parameters manifest in their work and to consider the impacts, which law has on the lives of LGBTIQ people in the UK. In preparing their chapters, we asked each of the contributors to consider three overarching questions. First, what does it mean to be "queer" when pursuing inclusion in a legal system? Second, why might those (queers) who are relegated to the "outside" of law wish to remain there? Finally, how does law feature in the construction of what it means to be "queer" and an "outsider"? The chapters in this edited collection reveal how our authors have understood and responded to these questions against a broad range of backgrounds, including asylum processes, legal gender recognition, criminal justice and equality law.

This introductory chapter briefly explains how, as editors, we have understood and addressed key ideas in this collection—including our approach to "queerness" (Part II), "law" (Part III) and the notion of the "outside" (Part IV). Drawing upon the extensive literature in this field, the chapter acknowledges the contested constructions to which these concepts have been subject

---

[4] See Carmelo Danisi, Moira Dustin and Nuno Ferreira, "Queering Brexit: What's in Brexit for Sexual and Gender Minorities?," in *Gender and Queer Perspectives on Brexit*, edited by Moira Dustin, Nuno Ferreira and Susan Millns, 239–272 (London: Palgrave Macmillan, 2019).

[5] We use "LGBT" rather than "LGBTIQ" here because the rights of intersex and queer people generally have not been incorporated or explicitly addressed (yet) through laws in the UK. See Fae Garland and Mitchell Travis' contribution [Chapter 7] in the collection.

[6] See e.g. *P v S and Cornwall* Case C-13/94 [1996] ECR I-2143; Council Directive 2000/78/EC of 27 November 2000 establishing a general framework for equal treatment in employment and occupation; Directive 2006/54/EC of the European Parliament and of the Council of 5 July 2006 on the implementation of the principle of equal opportunities and equal treatment of men and women in matters of employment and occupation (recast) (see particularly Recital 3 to the Preamble).

[7] See Jonathan Cooper et al., "Brexit: The LGBT Impact Assessment", *Gay Star News*, April 2018, https://research-information.bris.ac.uk/files/154151661/PETER_DUNNE_PURE_VERSION.pdf.

and reflects upon how such shifting interpretations can enrich our exploration of law. In the final section, Part V, we set out a roadmap for the seven chapters which are to follow; dividing these contributions into two broad themes: (i) colonising, protecting, and punishing queer outsiders in law; and (ii) queering the outsides of legal gender and sex. Part V gives a brief overview of the main topics and concerns to be addressed in the contributions to this collection.

2 Framing Queer(ness)

This collection engages theoretically and empirically with what it means to be both "queer" and an "outsider" within the context of "law". These key terms, while dynamic and generative of various critical debates in the chapters that follow, warrant some initial (loose) definitions.

The chapters in this collection take a capacious approach to theorising what queer can and might mean. Despite its vernacularisation as a personal identification (e.g. "I am queer!"), queer also carries a history of social stigma, one that is weighted by the marginalisation and alienation of those who fail to conform to social expectations of sex(uality) and gender.[8] Yet, the negative affect associated with the word also carries possibilities of reimagining how we might live in the world. Eve Sedgwick notes that queer refers to:

> ...the open mesh of possibilities, gaps, overlaps, dissonances and resonances, lapses and excesses of meaning when the constituent elements of anyone's gender, of anyone's sexuality aren't made (or can't be made) to signify monolithically.[9]

Sedgwick's definition, or more precisely partial illustration, of queer as a personalised and politicised challenge to normative categories of gender and sexuality is central to the grammar of much queer scholarship.[10] She evokes how queer can register as a person, an issue, a practice, a tactic and a form of play that troubles social normativity. In particular, she draws attention to how queer is an "outside"—a space of "excess"—that refuses containment within

[8] Heather Love, *Feeling Backward: Loss and the Politics of Queer History* (Cambridge: Harvard University Press, 2009), 2.

[9] Eve Sedgwick, *Tendencies* (Durham: Duke University Press, 1993), 8.

[10] Robyn Wiegman and Elizabeth Wilson, "Introduction: Antinormativity's Queer Conventions", *Differences* 26, no 1 (2015): 1, 1. Queer theory has various disciplinary and theoretical commitments, particularly relating to what it means to engage with "the social". For a brief but insightful discussion of this debate in queer theory, see Robyn Wiegman, "Sex and Negativity; or What Queer Theory Has for You", *Cultural Critique* 95 (2017): 219.

a specific set of social norms. We take Sedgwick's theorisation as a departure point in our collection to think about how queer can refer to specific identifications or sexual object choices or gendered ways of living that exist outside social conventions that emerge from cisnormative heterosexuality.[11] But, queer also exceeds confinement to personal identity categories. It is an analytic positionality and strategy of critique that exposes how subjects, issues, identities and relationships that do not conform to (hetero)normative ideas of reproduction, nationhood, productivity and domesticity are divested of social value and cast as outside the zone of national and sexual belonging.[12] Each chapter in this collection further explores these different registers of queer analysis and engages the varied possibilities of queer politics in law.

It is important to highlight that our use of "LGBTI" as an organising tool, alongside "queer", is also loose and contested in this collection. The use of any acronym to encapsulate various non-conforming sexes, genders and sexual orientations is fraught with epistemological, political and ethical challenges. As Ryan Thoreson observes in the context of transnational human rights advocacy and activism, terms which denote specific sexual and gender identities do not always "translate" across jurisdictions nor do those different "LGBTIQ" identity groups see their rights aspirations or political commitments in the same terms.[13] Identities are also always "intersectional"—gender and sexuality cannot be conceived outside other socio-political modes of categorisation such as race, class, disability and religion.[14] Our edited collection does not seek to resolve the tensions which animate these rich conversations. Instead, we focus on making space to bring together some tensions within queer critiques of law by examining specific intersections of LGBTIQ people and legal claims made for LGBTIQ people in the UK. This collection aims to

---

[11]Heteronormativity is a term to describe the ways in which heterosexuality is naturalised and presumed as socially inevitable. See Judith Butler, *Gender Trouble: Feminism and the Subversion of Identity* (New York: Routledge, 1990) and Alex Sharpe, *Sexual Intimacy and Gender Identity 'Fraud': Reframing the Legal and Ethical Debate* (Abingdon: Routledge, 2018).

[12]David Bell and Jon Binnie, *The Sexual Citizen: Queer Politics and Beyond* (Cambridge: Polity, 2000), 13–15. See also Ian Barnard, *Queer Race: Cultural Interventions in the Racial Politics of Queer Theory* (New York: Peter Lang, 2004); Lauren Berlant, "Starved" in *After Sex? On Writing since Queer Theory,* edited by Janet Halley and Andrew Parker, 79–90 (Durham: Duke University Press, 2011); Richard Collier, "Straight Families, Queer Lives? Heterosexual(izing) Family Law," in *Sexuality in the Legal Arena,* edited by Carl Stychin and Didi Herman, 164–178 (London: The Athlone Press, 2000); Lee Edelman, "Ever After," in *After Sex? On Writing since Queer Theory,* edited by Janet Halley and Andrew Parker, 110–119 (Durham: Duke University Press, 2011); David Eng, *The Feeling of Kinship: Queer Liberalism and the Racialization of Intimacy* (Durham: Duke University Press, 2010); Judith Halberstam, *The Queer Art of Failure* (Durham: Duke University Press, 2011).

[13]Thoreson, *Transnational LGBT Activism,* 4–8.

[14]For a discussion of intersectionality as a mode of legal analysis, see Kimberlé Crenshaw, "Mapping the Margins: Intersectionality, Identity Politics, and Violence Against Women of Color" *Stanford Law Review* 43, no 6 (1991): 1241.

show how particular individuals who self-identify with, or might be grouped by legal institutions or activists as, "LGBTIQ" are positioned as "queer" on the "outside" of law in the UK because they turn away from pursuits of recognition and belonging. Yet, as some individuals turn towards the law (such as the institutions of courts and parliaments) to advance claims for legal recognition or inclusion, they have to enter the "inside" of legal systems.[15] We take this paradoxical encounter as a productive moment to think about how we, as legal scholars and activists, can further current law reform conversations about how best to address the lives of LGBTIQ people in the UK. We do this looking at what it means to be a queer outsider without seeking to neatly resolve the paradoxical positions generated by turning away from, while turning towards, law.

Each chapter uses different variations of the "LGBTIQ" terminology, depending on the legal, theoretical, activist, personal and political contexts they engage. Each contributor has made a careful decision when it comes to terminology to foreground the challenges of thinking, legislating, litigating and organising for marginalised sexual and gender groups without being tokenistic or dismissive of the different issues facing disparate populations within these groups.

3 Stretching Law

In this collection, we understand "law", like queer, through varied conceptual registers. We begin with the oft cited premise that law is a system of rules, norms and regulations made by authorised state institutions (courts, parliaments and governments).[16] As Max Weber notes, law is commonly understood from an external perspective as a coherent and calculable form of "authority".[17] However, we do not limit our framing of law to positive rules and formal structures—we explore how law materialises as a fluid expression of governance, authority and power.

Michel Foucault, writing more broadly about the nature of power and authority, offers an alternative to the Weberian approach of thinking about law. His work emphasises an approach to law in terms of governance.

[15] Sara Ahmed, *Willful Subjects* (Durham: Duke University Press, 2014), 8.

[16] Positivist legal scholarship characterises law as a system of unique social rules. For example, legal philosopher HLA Hart insists on the need to distinguish between law and morality: law as it is, and law as it ought to be. See HLA Hart, *The Concept of Law*, 2nd Edition (Oxford: Oxford University Press, 1994), 88–90.

[17] Simona Andrini, "Max Weber's Sociology of Law as a Turning Point of His Methodological Approach", *International Review of Sociology* 14, no 2 (2004): 43, 145.

Foucault's work allows us to see that the law is implicated in an array of intersecting social norms and forms of knowledge that are not reducible to a single fixed institution, and that law is not easily observable from an external distance. That is: the authority we associate with law is an effect of the knowledge that we use to construct it, rather than an inherent condition that precedes the existence of law.[18] Foucault fundamentally alters more "common sense" understandings of autonomy and enforceability in law by decentralising the role of the state or sovereign as the locus of governance.[19] As Mariana Valverde observes, governance is a highly differentiated process, working across different spatial, affective and jurisdictional scales.[20] Law, as a means of governance, is a social instrument created and transformed by social actors (judges, lawyers, politicians, etc.) working across different registers (courts, litigation, parliamentary debates, etc.) and temporal states (permanence, transition, flexibility, etc.).[21]

Law is also performative social practice: speaking about authority, power and governance in law is the means by which those underlying values are created. As James Boyd White notes, the "ideal" way to understand law is as a reader of culture or a social critic who brings purpose, context and other disciplines to bear on conversation.[22] By committing to purposive and contextual approaches to critical (social) reading and analysis, law cannot be reduced to formal or positivist qualities associated with fixed institutional states. Law is an ever-expanding set of social conversations with a pedagogical function that provides a specific set of rhetorical tools that can be used to address disputes.[23] Moreover, to give a fuller account of law, we need to be attentive to that which is cast as "outside" of it: the "non-legal" marks political and social possibilities that might be reached (if such reaching is desired and pursued).[24]

[18]Michel Foucault, *The History of Sexuality (Volume 1): The Will to Knowledge* (New York: Random House, 1978), 19.

[19]Leonard Hammer, *A Foucauldian Approach to International Law: Descriptive Thoughts for Normative Issues* (Aldershot: Ashgate, 2007), 9.

[20]Mariana Valverde, *Chronotopes of Law: Jurisdiction, Scale and Governance* (Abingdon: Routledge, 2015), 66.

[21]Law and regulation are constituted by processes of temporality. See Emily Grabham, *Brewing Legal Times: Things, Form and the Enactment of Law* (Toronto: University of Toronto Press, 2016), 34.

[22]James Boyd White, "Law as Language: Reading Law and Reading Literature", *Texas Law Review* 60 (1981): 415, 415.

[23]Ibid., 435.

[24]Fleur Johns explains in detail why non-legality is a structuring device of (international) legal thought. She urges us to focus on the "something else" of law in order to think more critically about the violation, rejection, creation, and suspension of norms. See Fleur Johns, *Non-Legality in International Law: Unruly Law* (Cambridge: Cambridge University Press, 2013).

The contributions to this collection "recognise" law in terms of its formal properties (jurisprudential doctrines, statutory provisions, bureaucratic decisions), diverse actors (litigants, lawyers, judges, bureaucrats, parliamentarians) and varied territorial articulations (sovereignty, devolution, jurisdiction, crown). Echoing Valverde, the authors think about law across its various spatial and temporal registers.[25] These seven chapters seek to cross different spaces and timescales of law— momentary debates in parliament, fast-tracked decision-making processes in the Home Office, ongoing isolation of prisoners—in order to think through the different ways in which LGBTIQ people in the UK encounter the law and come to be inside and/or outside it.

As a final reflection on the question of "law", it is important to specify the jurisdictional boundaries and application of this edited collection. As the title suggests, the seven contributions to this project seek to explore (and reveal) the queer outside of law as it applies across the UK. For certain legal questions, including the immigration practices discussed herein, the UK operates as a single jurisdictional entity, with common policies applying irrespective of geographical position. As such, when Eddie Bruce-Jones (Chapter 3) and S. Chelvan (Chapter 4) critique the stereotyped, racist and homophobic norms which underpin UK asylum policy, they are highlighting systemic failures, which can correctly be characterised as UK-wide phenomena. Similarly, the recent Government Equalities Office "Call for Information" on Variations in Sex Characteristics (Chapter 7) sought relevant evidence from individuals living and working in all parts of the UK.

Yet, for other issues addressed in this collection—including family law, education, health care and criminal law—the UK is divided into separate legal jurisdictions, with individual courts and tribunals in England and Wales, Northern Ireland and Scotland. The power to legislate in these areas has also been, to different extents, devolved—to the Scottish Parliament in Holyrood, the Welsh Parliament (Senedd Cymru) in Cardiff and the Northern Ireland Assembly (Tionól Thuaisceart Éireann) in Belfast. As such, when speaking about queer experiences and readings of law, there is a need to be aware of the precise jurisdictional context at play. In Chapter 5, for example, when writing about queer individuals within prison borders, Fabienne Emmerich and Felicity Adams acknowledge that they are drawing upon policies and lived experiences within the *English* criminal justice system.

In adopting the language of *UK law*, we as the editors do not seek to simplify or downplay the complex jurisdictional interplays which define the modern legal system in Great Britain and Northern Ireland. While, in many

[25] Valverde, *Chronotopes of Law* 17.

ways, this edited collection does draw upon and critique broader frameworks, which impact the lives of LGBTIQ persons throughout the UK, we also acknowledge that certain rules discussed within the seven chapters are limited in their jurisdictional reach. In addition, we are aware that there may be situations where there remains uncertainty as to whether a particular rule or policy is appropriately presented as "inside" UK law. In Chapter 6, for example, Flora Renz discusses the binary nature of legal gender recognition rules. While the Gender Recognition Act 2004 applies in all three UK jurisdictions, there have historically been subtle differences between England and Wales, Scotland and Northern Ireland, and the Scottish Government has recently announced proposals to adopt an alternative legislative structure.[26] Although the judicial review in *R (on the application of Christie Elan-Cane) and Secretary of State for the Home Department*[27] might ultimately lead to UK-wide non-gendered passports, the applicant specifically instituted proceedings in the English and Welsh courts. Similarly, in Chapter 8, the "gender reassignment protections" in s. 7 of the Equality Act 2010 apply equally to England, Wales and Scotland. Yet, Sharon Cowan (in Chapter 8) is explicit in emphasising the unique ways in which equality law is experienced in Scotland; and it is useful to remember that separate LGBT non-discrimination rules still apply in Northern Ireland.[28]

4 Queer Insiders and/or Queer Outsiders

Legal paradoxes and dramatic shifts in legal reforms bring to the fore a number of socio-legal challenges: laws still do not fully include LGBTIQ people and, even where formal legal equality has been achieved, social inclusion and economic justice remain elusive. Legal scholars and activists who are working to secure the lives and intimacies of LGBTIQ people need to evaluate claims of state recognition as the "goalposts" of "inclusion" begin to shift.[29] Yet, some queers celebrate the absence of legal inclusion altogether—staying outside the proverbial goalposts—as an opportunity for queer liberation from oppressive, (hetero)normative systems of laws. For scholars like Jin Haritaworn, Adi Kuntsman and Sylvia Posocco, claims for

[26] Gender Recognition (Reform) Scotland Bill 2019.

[27] [2018] EWHC 1530 (Admin).

[28] Employment Equality (Sexual Orientation) Regulations (NI) 2003; Equality Act (Sexual Orientation) Regulations (NI) 2006; Sex Discrimination (Gender reassignment) Regulations (N.I.) 1999; Sex Discrimination (Amendment of Legislation) Regulations 2008.

[29] Robert Leckey, "Introduction: After Legal Equality" in *After Legal Equality: Family, Sex, Kinship*, edited by Robert Leckey, 1–22, 12 (Abingdon: Routledge, 2015).

legal visibility and protection are sustained by "death zones" (such as the capitalist economic system) that entrench poverty, isolation and inequality.[30]

Opposition to law cannot be reduced to a binary. It is not simply a matter of us, as critical legal scholars or lawyers, to either embrace or reject law reform. The scholarly tensions or concerns about law reform are unevenly distributed across a range of sub-disciplines of law, including criminal law, refugee law, family law and anti-discrimination law. Some LGBTIQ people enjoy the comfort of being cradled by relationship recognition, while others continue to agitate against (hetero)normative forms of kinship that stifle non-normative identities, families, and communities. Some queers demand to be inside the law (such as people seeking protection as refugees or LGBTIQ-inclusive prison reform), while others (such as anti-border activists and prison abolitionists) seek justice from the outside (of state borders and carceral systems).

The paradoxical tensions of LGBTIQ people being "inside" and "outside" law have generated considerable critical legal scholarship. In *After Legal Equality*, Robert Leckey invites legal scholars to consider the "after" of formal legal equality following the achievement of same-sex marriage (which had been held out by a number of gay and lesbian people as the "final frontier" of legal equality).[31] He particularly focuses on how we might reimagine care, kinship and sexual ethics in response to the realisation of formal equality. Leckey's intervention also exposes how some LGBTIQ communities and activists understand law reform in a temporal register: it is a linear story of progress. We move from being repudiated as sexual or gender "outlaws" criminalised by the state to welcomed "inlaws" who reaffirm the (hetero)normativity of the state.[32]

Alternatively, Libby Adler suggests that we (as legal scholars) might want to embrace a "queer critical legal studies" approach that asks us to move beyond our emotional attachments to narratives of legal progress or formal equality to consider the problematic persistence of "LGBT equality" discourses. In doing so, she urges readers of her work to think about how discourses of legal inclusion produce LGBT identities and shape the (re)distribution of resources.[33] For Adler, the emphasis on legal inclusion or recognition risks

---

[30]Jin Haritaworn, Adi Kuntsman and Sylvia Posocco, "Introduction," in *Queer Necropolitics*, edited by Jin Haritaworn, Adi Kuntsman and Sylvia Posocco, 1–27, (Abingdon: Routledge, 2014).

[31]Leckey, "Introduction: After Legal Equality," 1–22.

[32]The "progressive" story of law reform is characterised by specific emotional styles that resonate (even though they vary) across jurisdictions. See Senthorun Sunil Raj, *Feeling Queer Jurisprudence: Injury, Intimacy, Identity* (Abingdon: Routledge, 2020).

[33]Libby Adler, *Gay Priori: A Queer Critical Legal Studies Approach to Law Reform* (Durham: Duke University Press, 2018), 6.

undermining social policy initiatives to redistribute resources in a way to best support marginalised communities. We (as LGBTIQ people) might, for example, focus critical and activist energies on asking the state to redistribute economic or social resources rather than aspiring for it to grant us equal recognition.[34] Dianne Otto suggests that a queer analysis of law can allow scholars, activists and lawyers to "take a break" with demands for equal rights or sexual assimilation into state institutions and encourages us to pursue pleasures, diversities and fluidities that disrupt binary understandings of sex, gender and sexuality.[35]

The analytic manoeuvres outlined above do not require us (as scholars, activists or lawyers) to subscribe to an interpretation of legal inclusion as a means of either LGBTIQ protection or punishment. Queers do not have to be either inside or outside law. Cynthia Weber notes that LGBTIQ people occupy an "and/or" position in relation to the state. They can be "normalised" by the state (when governments grant some forms of anti-violence legal protection or relationship recognition) and/or "perverted" at the same time (when governments shore up traditional family values by punishing or policing sexual non-normativity).[36] Weber's work speaks to how queers emerge in state narratives in consistently contradictory ways—or, as Sedgwick would suggest, they refuse to signify monolithically.

As legal scholars working with, not just for, LGBTIQ people, "the queer outside in law" is precisely the analytic register in which to explore the persisting contradictions of legal recognition and inclusion. On the one hand, this phrase points to queer "outsiders" that remain in excess of law's reach (such as non-monogamous couples or non-binary individuals). On the other, the "queer outside in law" denotes the ways in which queer outsiders have been brought into law to be governed (such as LGBTIQ prisoners or refugees). These discursive constructions happen simultaneously and structure the ways in which LGBTIQ people are recognised, protected and/or punished within and outside the law.

This edited collection seeks to intervene in current socio-legal debates about LGBTIQ legal recognition in the UK by making analytic room to reflect on the tensions between inclusion/exclusion, law/non-law and queer/non-queer in terms of legal recognition, protection and punishment. In

[34]Dean Spade offers a detailed elaboration of how a critical (trans) politics can challenge the physical, verbal, symbolic, and discursive violence enacted by public institutions (prisons, hospitals, social service providers, etc.). See Dean Spade, *Normal Life: Administrative Violence, Critical Trans Politics & The Limits of Law* (Brooklyn: South End Press, 2011).

[35]Dianne Otto, "Introduction: Embracing Queer Curiosities," in *Queering International Law: Possibilities, Alliances, Complicities, Risks,* edited by Dianne Otto, 1–11, (Abingdon: Routledge, 2017).

[36]Cynthia Weber, *Queer International Relations* (Oxford: Oxford University Press, 2016), 16.

essence, we take up the elastic spatial dimensions of queer and law, discussed above, to highlight the ways in which queers continue to create and/or trouble both social and legal conceptions of inclusion, exclusion, queerness and justice. LGBTIQ people's encounters with law—for recognition, protection and/or punishment—shape and reshape the boundaries of law.

5 Collection Overview

No single edited collection can hope to do justice to the myriad questions raised by such a broad conjunction as the "queer outside in law". This is true for a number of reasons, not least considerations of space, and is equally applicable even for a collection, which is grounded in a select number of jurisdictions. At the outset, we acknowledge the numerous additional issues—such as the legal invisibility of trans youth or queers with disabilities and the assimilationist, censuring consequences of marriage equality—which would also fit within (and enhance) the contours of our enquiry.

Yet, even with this limitation on the scope of the collection, the seven substantive chapters—by bringing together socio-legal scholars working with different aspects of L/G/B/T/I/Q rights claims, in different spaces of law and scales of jurisdiction—present a dynamic discussion to further theoretical debates, activist agendas and law reform initiatives. The contributors focus on how (and, in some cases, whether) queer legal scholarship and activism offer important lenses to interpret and reframe human rights law, especially when pursuing affirming outcomes in situations where the law renders gender and sexuality salient.[37] As editors, we subscribe to the idea that LGBTIQ law reform agendas must prioritise the voices of the most marginalised populations (recognising the interconnections of gender and sexuality with race, class, disability, migration status and geography) and develop legal strategies that attend to their "life-shaping encounters with law".[38] To that end, the collection brings together chapters, which engage with queer, feminist, postcolonial and human rights literatures to consider the disparate ways in which LGBTIQ people interact with, and also produce, social and legal spaces of recognition, protection and punishment. The chapters sometimes use competing conceptualisations of queer, and foreground the tensions in different forms of critical legal scholarship, to demonstrate how queer legal

[37] Damian Gonzalez-Salzberg, *Sexuality and Transsexuality Under the European Convention on Human Rights: A Queer Reading of Human Rights Law* (Oxford: Hart, 2019), 185.

[38] Adler, *Gay Priori*, 215.

scholarship cannot be easily condensed into a single mode of legal analysis nor embraced as a simple framework for law reform.

The edited collection is divided into two parts. The first part of the book (Kay Lalor; Eddie Bruce-Jones; S. Chelvan; Fabienne Emmerich and Felicity Adams) explores the colonial underpinnings of "legal progress" for LGBTIQ people by looking at the racialising and geographical dimensions of protection and punishment facing LGBTIQ individuals within, and outside, the UK. In their four chapters, these contributors address how transnational activism, border politics and carceral systems shape the terms by which LGBTIQ populations are brought inside or pushed outside law (for recognition, protection and/or punishment). In the second part of the collection (Flora Renz; Mitchell Travis and Fae Garland; Sharon Cowan), we turn to the complex, gendering dynamics of recognition and resistance as they apply to the lives of trans, non-binary and intersex people. The authors draw attention to how pursuits of legal gender recognition, formal equality, access to health care and demands to prohibit the "othering" of intersex people redraw the boundaries of who is inside or outside the law.

In Chapter 2, Kay Lalor deftly introduces the role of paradoxes in shaping LGBTIQ rights discourse in (trans)national political spaces. Specifically, she explores a recent UK House of Commons debate about "Global LGBT Rights" as a way to think about the potentialities and paradoxes of pursuing LGBT rights both at "home" and "abroad". Lalor draws on postcolonial and queer theory in order to think about how the UK has deployed diplomatic and other resources to support decriminalisation and LGBTIQ rights protections in Commonwealth and other states, often placing itself in opposition to laws that were first enacted by British colonial regimes. She notes how the apparent opposition between the positions of the British Empire and the modern UK state masks more continuous international dynamics of queer boundary marking. Racialised figurations of queerness have long contributed to the demarcation of spaces as "civilised/uncivilised", "developed/developing" and "centre/periphery", consolidating international hierarchies in which the UK still seeks to play a central role. Thus, the queer legacy of colonialism is one in which queerness is variously regulated and rejected, deployed and denied, stabilising and disruptive. In tracing this paradoxical positioning of queerness across different spaces and temporalities, Lalor shows us that it is important to interrogate the ongoing role of the past within the present and suggests that contending with this past might assist future efforts towards justice.

In Chapter 3, Eddie Bruce-Jones expands on a postcolonial conception of queerness and a paradoxical conception of legal inclusion to confront the ways in which LGBTIQ people who seek asylum are policed within state borders at the same moment they claim protection within those borders. Bruce-Jones offers a careful cartography of refugee legal recognition to render the geopolitical arrangement of "safety" (refugees finding protection within the UK) and "danger" (refugees experiencing persecution outside the UK). Those who seek asylum on the basis of sexual orientation for example, have to demonstrate the authenticity of their sexuality and persecution by reproducing ethnocentric, colonial stereotypes about sexual shame, cultural consumption and (western) sexual freedom. This legal demand places a specific burden on the person seeking asylum within the zone of legal recognition: they must produce a coherent, linear and fixed account of their (homo)sexuality to be treated as credible. Yet, in doing so, the refugee adjudication system casts LGBT people who offer accounts of their fluid sexualities as "queer" and positions them outside the zone of legal relevance and recognition (which can lead to their removal). Bruce-Jones' articulation of the problematic nature of legal recognition invites us, as legal activists and academics, to think about what is at stake when we reify a border policing regime that enables violence against non-citizens while protecting a few people who have the capacity to leave their country and request protection. While acknowledging the importance of turning towards law to provide safety for those who flee persecution, Bruce-Jones shows what might be gained by turning away from law—looking outside it—in order to better support LGBTIQ people who are denied safety and visibility.

However, turning away from law carries enormous risks for those who are vulnerable to persecution both within and outside the law (and the UK). In Chapter 4, S. Chelvan offers a more prescriptive analysis of reform to UK law and immigration bureaucracy in order to create space within refugee law for "queer outsiders" who seek asylum. Drawing on his advocacy work with Aderonke Apata, a Nigerian lesbian who fought for asylum in the UK for thirteen years, Chelvan shows how a new mode of bureaucratic engagement with people who seek asylum on the basis of their sexual orientation could ensure that the law adequately protects LGB people. For Chelvan, asking people about their differences (D), the way those differences are stigmatised (S), the extent to which the person experiences shame about those differences (S) and how those differences led to harm (H) is the best approach. Taking the Home Office to task for their prurient and homophobic questioning and adjudication of LGB people who seek asylum, Chelvan offers the DSSH model as a more empathetic way to evaluate protection claims. Chelvan suggests that rather than expect people to submit their lives to stereotype-based or identity-based questions, immigration decision-makers need to make room for asylum seekers to tell their own stories about what it means to be queer and persecuted. This would bring "queer outsiders" inside the space of legal recognition and protection.

In Chapter 5, we turn to an arena of punishment rather than protection—prisons—to explore how LGBTIQ prisoners are excluded from society through inclusion in violent carceral systems. Fabienne Emmerich and Felicity Adams consider prisons as spaces of punishment sustained beyond the law, at the capillaries of power. They are deeply gendered institutions that enforce a gender binary and perpetuate heteronormative gender performativity. These confinement spaces produce a dynamic of exclusion/inclusion for LGBTIQ prisoners, who both challenge gendered binaries and are subject to others. They are deemed both vulnerable and threatening. In short, they are considered "difficult" prisoners. The purpose of their chapter is to explore the inclusion/exclusion of LGBTIQ people with a focus on three areas: inclusion of the other: gender recognition; exclusion of the other: the segregation (solitary confinement) of the vulnerable; and erasure of the other: non-recognition of intimate relationships. With a focus on prisoners' rights jurisprudence and policies in these areas, Emmerich and Adams critique gender-normative and heteronormative conceptions that underpin the discourse of prisoners' rights. In doing so, they invite us to consider why turning away from "inclusive prisons" to abolishing carceral confinement altogether can help queer people flourish.

As we transition to the second half of the collection, Chapter 6 invites us to reflect upon the complex relationship between law, identity and the politics of recognition. In their contribution, Flora Renz explores legal gender options beyond male and female and considers the potential for a broader, more inclusive understanding of gender under UK law. Renz outlines the current process for amending one's identity status through the Gender Recognition Act 2004—identifying key points of critique, such as mandatory diagnosis and the so-called "real life experience" requirement. Although the law in all three UK jurisdictions acknowledges certain gender identities, its leaves as "outsiders" those whose gender stretches beyond binary explanations. Such legal exclusion contradicts how many individuals live their gender, and it renders UK law increasingly unresponsive to trans and non-binary populations. Drawing upon judicial and parliamentary materials, Renz investigates recent proposals to expand the gender recognition framework. They note persistent retreats into medicalisation and a general failure to acknowledge the social (as opposed to merely private life) dimensions of non-binary gender options. While jurisdictions, such as Australia and Germany, have enacted alternative gender options, both regimes are conceptually and pragmatically flawed, and may not constitute workable blueprints for reform in the UK. In particular, there may be reason to believe that, rather than reducing marginalisation, additional identity categories will merely reinforce the primacy of male and female options. Renz acknowledges that conversations around non-binary recognition encourage us to re-examine the objective utility of all gender regulation; while it might not yet be time to de-gender UK law, liberation from gender status might ultimately be preferable to the inevitably under-inclusive processes of categorisation which have thus far been proposed.

In Chapter 7, Fae Garland and Mitchell Travis problematise the automatic (and unquestioning) inclusion of intersex experiences "inside" broader lesbian, gay, bisexual, trans and queer advocacy movements. Their contribution draws from the findings of a small-scale empirical research project, which the authors conducted with intersex rights activists both in the UK and farther afield. The authors seek to identify how intersex is being constructed by (and to) domestic policy makers and legislators and to reveal who is responsible for constructing the terms of intersex-focused political debates. In doing so, they illustrate how a more nuanced approach is required by law in relation to contemporary intersex movements. Chapter 7 strongly suggests that a solely queer or LGBT*I*Q framing will be an ineffective mechanism through which to incorporate the experiences of intersex individuals. Garland and Travis explore core themes throughout their contribution—including bodily autonomy, identity appropriation and resource division. Their research highlights how intersex people navigate their status as outsiders in terms of both law and activism. For many individuals, inhabiting the space of outsider, while by no means ideal, is necessary in order to communicate their needs without being co-opted or misconstrued by queer and LGBT activists or policy makers. Chapter 7 exposes an underlying tension within the strategies that outsiders can use to instigate legal change relating to the narratives of inclusion/exclusion and queer/non-queer. In the context of intersex populations, these tensions result in an increasingly polarised schism—with the potential risk of undermining future, progressive law reform.

Finally, in Chapter 8, Sharon Cowan explores the intersections of law, identity and discrimination. Like Garland and Travis, her contribution also draws from a larger, four-year empirical project—documenting trans narratives of equality in Scotland, Canada and the United States. In this chapter, Cowan focuses specifically on responses from participants in the first of those jurisdictions. Through the lens of legal consciousness, and using a "femiqueer" perspective, Cowan considers the ways in which trans people in

Scotland talk about their everyday experiences of discrimination. She presents original findings that increase our understanding of the lives of trans people in that part of the UK and contributes to socio-legal theoretical literature by suggesting a new strand of "legal consciousness". Chapter 8 adds to our knowledge of how trans people themselves see the role and relevance of law in their lives: by examining both practical and conceptual understandings and experiences of equality, by contributing to the legal consciousness literature in introducing the new concept of "optimistic legal realism" and by analysing recent shifts in discourse on equality and trans rights in Scotland. Cowan's contribution is not a study of either law or identity as such, but of trans individuals' narratives about equality and discrimination in their lives. It also highlights how people negotiate "inside" and "outside" the trans and cisgender communities around them. In light of the particular attention currently being given in the UK to whether gender identity and expression should be regulated, and the policing of gendered spaces, Cowan argues that we must pay attention to trans people's narratives; their intersectional experiences of equality and life generally in Scotland—and elsewhere—require nuanced and sensitive consideration.

In the concluding chapter, we (Senthorun Raj and Peter Dunne) bring together key themes and questions evoked by the seven substantive contributions to this collection. Framing our analysis through the lenses of four case studies, we reflect upon both the potential advantages, but also the necessary compromises, of coming within the law, and we ask what queers in the UK might gain from continuing to "play"[39] outside law's formal boundaries. Our focus in this analysis is on four areas of recent, ongoing and future domestic law reform: (1) proposed reforms to the Gender Recognition Act 2004; (2) the Government Equalities Office "Call for Information" on the lived experience of intersex populations; (3) the hostile environment created within national immigration rules; and (4) the introduction of LGBT-inclusive Relationships and Sex Education in English schools. Our reflections on each of these case studies not only consider how a queer reading of law, and the insights offered by our seven contributions, can encourage a more responsive, meaningful engagement with LGBTIQ lives; rather, they also point to processes for respecting, validating and enhancing queer well-being which are removed from (and are not contingent upon) institutionalised structures of law.

[39]Davina Cooper, *Feeling Like a State: Desire, Denial, and the Recasting of Authority* (Durham: Duke University Press, 2019), 24–25.

References

Adler, Libby. *Gay Priori: A Queer Critical Legal Studies Approach to Law Reform.* Durham: Duke University Press, 2018.

Ahmed, Sara. *Willful Subjects.* Durham: Duke University Press, 2014.

Andrini, Simona. "Max Weber's Sociology of Law as a Turning Point of His Methodological Approach", *International Review of Sociology* 14(2) (2004): 143–150.

Barnard, Ian. *Queer Race: Cultural Interventions in the Racial Politics of Queer Theory.* New York: Peter Lang, 2004.

Bell, David and Jon Binnie,. *The Sexual Citizen: Queer Politics and Beyond.* Cambridge: Polity, 2000.

Berlant, Lauren. "Starved." In *In After Sex? On Writing since Queer Theory*, edited by Janet Halley and Andrew Parker, 79–90. Durham: Duke University Press, 2011.

Boyd White, James. "Law as Language: Reading Law and Reading Literature", *Texas Law Review* 60 (1981-1982): 415–446.

Butler, Judith. *Gender Trouble: Feminism and the Subversion of Identity.* New York: Routledge, 1990.

Collier, Richard. "Straight Families, Queer Lives? Heterosexual(izing) Family Law." In *Sexuality in the Legal Arena*, edited by Carl Stychin and Didi Herman, 164–178. London: The Athlone Press, 2000.

Cooper, Davina. *Feeling Like a State: Desire, Denial, and the Recasting of Authority.* Durham: Duke University Press, 2019.

Cooper, Jonathan, et al. "Brexit: The LGBT Impact Assessment", *Gay Star News*, April 2018. https://research-information.bris.ac.uk/files/154151661/PETER_DUNNE_PURE_VERSION.pdf.

Crenshaw, Kimberlé. "Mapping the Margins: Intersectionality, Identity Politics, and Violence against Women of Color", *Stanford Law Review* 43 (1991): 1241–1300.

Danisi, Carmello, Moria Dustin and Nuno Ferreira. "Queering Brexit: What's in Brexit for Sexual and Gender Minorities?" In *Gender and Queer Perspectives on Brexit,* edited by Moira Dustin, Nuno Ferreira and Susan Millns, 239–272. Palgrave Macmillan, 2019.

Edelman, Lee. "Ever After." In *After Sex? On Writing since Queer Theory*, edited by Janet Halley and Andrew Parker, 110–119. Durham: Duke University Press, 2011.

Eng, David. *The Feeling of Kinship: Queer Liberalism and the Racialization of Intimacy.* Durham: Duke University Press, 2010.

Foucault, Michel. *The History of Sexuality (Volume 1): The Will to Knowledge.* New York: Random House, 1978.

Gonzalez-Salzberg, Damian. *Sexuality and Transsexuality Under the European Convention on Human Rights: A Queer Reading of Human Rights Law.* Oxford: Hart, 2019.

Grabham, Emily. *Brewing Legal Times: Things, Form and the Enactment of Law.* Toronto: University of Toronto Press, 2016.

Halberstam, Jack. *The Queer Art of Failure.* Durham: Duke University Press, 2011.
Hammer, Leonard. *A Foucauldian Approach to International Law: Descriptive Thoughts for Normative Issues.* Aldershot: Ashgate, 2007.
Haritaworn, Jin, Adi Kuntsman and Sylvia Posocco. "Introduction." In *Queer Necropolitics,* edited by Jin Haritaworn, Adi Kuntsman and Sylvia Posocco, 1–27. Abingdon: Routledge, 2014.
Hart, HLA. *The Concept of Law,* 2nd Edition. Oxford: Oxford University: Press, 1994.
Johns, Fleur. *Non-Legality in International Law: Unruly Law.* Cambridge: Cambridge University Press, 2013.
Leckey, Robert. "Introduction: After Legal Equality." In *After Legal Equality: Family, Sex, Kinship,* edited by Robert Leckey, 1–22. Abingdon: Routledge, 2015.
Love, Heather. *Feeling Backward: Loss and the Politics of Queer History.* Cambridge: Harvard University Press, 2009.
Moran, Leslie. "What Kind of Field Is 'Law, Gender and Sexuality'? Achievements, Concerns and Possible Futures", *Feminist Legal Studies* 17 (2009): 309–313.
Otto, Diane. "Introduction: Embracing Queer Curiosities." In *Queering International Law: Possibilities, Alliances, Complicities, Risks,* edited by Dianne Otto, 1–11. Abingdon: Routledge, 2017.
Raj, Senthorun Sunil. *Feeling Queer Jurisprudence: Injury, Intimacy, Identity.* Abingdon: Routledge, 2020.
Sedgwick, Eve. *Tendencies.* Durham: Duke University Press, 1993.
Sharpe, Alex. *Sexual Intimacy and Gender Identity 'Fraud': Reframing the Legal and Ethical Debate.* Abingdon: Routledge, 2018.
Spade, Dean. *Normal Life: Administrative Violence, Critical Trans Politics & The Limits of Law.* Brooklyn: South End Press, 2011.
Stychin, Carl. *A Nation by Rights: National Cultures, Sexual Identity Politics, and the Discourse of Rights.* Philadelphia: Temple University Press, 1998.
Stychin, Carl. *Governing Sexuality: The Changing Politics of Citizenship and Law Reform.* Oxford: Hart, 2003.
Stychin, Carl. "Same-Sex Sexualities and the Globalization of Human Rights Discourse", *McGill Law Journal* 49 (2004): 951–968.
Thoreson, Ryan. *Transnational LGBT Activism: Working for Sexual Rights Worldwide.* Minneapolis: University of Minnesota Press, 2014.
Valverde, Marianna. *Chronotopes of Law: Jurisdiction, Scale and Governance.* Abingdon: Routledge, 2015.
Weber, Cynthia. *Queer International Relations.* Oxford: Oxford University Press, 2016.
Wiegman, Robyn, and Elizabeth Wilson. "Introduction: Antinormativity's Queer Conventions", *Differences* 26(1) (2015): 1–25.
Wiegman, Robyn. "Sex and Negativity; or What Queer Theory Has for You", *Cultural Critique* 95 (2017): 219–243.

Colonising, Protecting, and Punishing Queer Outsiders in Law

Queer Legacies of Colonialism

Kay Lalor

1 Introduction

The ongoing effects of the British Empire's criminalisation of sodomy in its colonies have received considerable legal, political and public attention.[1] Less well attended however, is the related issue of the queer legacy of colonialism *in UK law*. It is this legacy that this chapter addresses. The chapter argues that the approach of British political and legal actors to the UK's colonial history is inherently paradoxical. Most notably, while there is some acknowledgement of the colonial past, there is a refusal to fully account for the ongoing effects of this past in the present, or for how geopolitical relations that maintain dynamics of "here" and "there" or "inside" and "outside" reduce the possibility of meaningful action. In contrast, a queer approach to this colonial legacy is one that confronts these paradoxes and in so doing, prepares for the possibility of radical and overarching structural change.

[1] Pippa Crerar, "Theresa May Says She Deeply Regrets Britain's Legacy of Anti-Gay Laws," *The Guardian*, April 17, 2018; Alok Gupta, "This Alien Legacy the Origins of "Sodomy" Laws in British Colonialism," ed. Human Rights Watch (2008); Michael Kirby, "The Sodomy Offence: England's Least Lovely Criminal Law Export?" in *Human Rights, Sexual Orientation and Gender Identity in the Commonwealth: Struggles for Decriminalisation and Change*, edited by Corinne Lennox and Matthew Waites (Institute of Commonwealth Studies, 2013).

K. Lalor (✉)
Manchester Metropolitan University, Manchester, UK
e-mail: k.lalor@mmu.ac.uk

S. Raj and P. Dunne (eds.), *The Queer Outside in Law*, Palgrave Socio-Legal Studies,
https://doi.org/10.1007/978-3-030-48830-7_2

To trace the queer legacy of colonialism in UK law, it is important to distinguish between the colonial era, as an historical period marked by European territorial acquisition[2]; imperialism, as the operation of power beyond state borders that may or may not involve territorial conquest[3]; and coloniality as the ongoing effects of colonial history, or the "continuity of colonial forms of domination after the end of colonial administrations".[4] Equally important is the positioning of queerness in relation to colonialism, coloniality and imperialism. "Queer" here is not a catch all term for the LGBTQIAA+[5] community, nor is it simply a designation of non-normative identities or behaviours. Instead, following Colebrook, conditions of the queer are those which expose how "the normal is achieved, produced, effected and also, therefore exposed as contingent, constituted and open to change".[6] Queerness is not simply about disrupting norms or categories of identity. It requires the repetition of previously unquestioned categories, norms, "doxa" and assumptions, in new forms that challenge the "laziness of common sense"[7] and explore the unacknowledged potentialities contained within. Thus, the queer, postcolonial and spatio-temporal analysis in this chapter seeks to expose how colonially produced hierarchies and inequalities exist in the present and limit possibilities for future action. This approach views "inside" and "outside" in space, time and law as unfixed, but structurally interdependent, and seeks to think how these structurally interdependent relations could configure new possibilities for action.

The chapter first considers how the queer legacy of colonialism must necessarily contend with coloniality—or its denial—and the legal implications of this. It then traces one instance of how this manifests through a close analysis of a 2017 House of Commons backbench debate on "Global LGBT Rights".[8] Spatio-temporal irregularities within the debate are used to identify the presence of paradox at the heart of UK approaches to LGBT rights. The final section of the chapter uses Deleuzian scholarship of paradox to analyse how dichotomies of space, time, identity and law, that developed from the colonial encounter continue to structure and limit UK approaches to LGBT rights.

[2]Antony Anghie, *Imperialism, Sovereignty and the Making of International Law* (Cambridge: Cambridge University Press, 2007), 11.

[3]Ibid.

[4]Ramón Grosfoguel, "The Epistemic Decolonial Turn," *Cultural Studies* 21, nos. 2–3 (2007): 219.

[5]A variety of abbreviations—LGBT, LGBTI and LGBTQI, among others—are used in the literature. In this chapter, I use the formulation that is most appropriate to the point under discussion.

[6]Claire Colebrook, "On the Very Possibility of Queer Theory," in *Deleuze and Queer Theory*, edited by Chrysanthi Nigianni and Merl Storr (Edinburgh: Edinburgh University Press, 2009), 21.

[7]Claire Colebrook "Queer Vitalism," *New Formations* 68 (2010).

[8]HC Deb 26 October 2017, vol 630, col 515.

For Deleuze, paradoxes are simultaneously moments of impasse and moments when our assumptions and axioms are revealed as limited and lacking. This revelation demands a re-working of those assumptions, opening up creative and radical moments of change. As such, Deleuzian paradox aligns closely with Colebrook's approach to queerness. The key impasse with which this chapter engages is the refusal, or inability, to fully acknowledge the ongoing effects of coloniality within British law and politics. This refusal results in the repetition of well-meaning expressions of support for SOGI (sexual orientation and gender identity) communities but limits the field of possibilities for meaningful or radical action. Indeed, a full engagement with the paradox of the queer legacy of colonialism in UK law would demand radical, structural changes that would go far beyond the current parameters of "Global LGBT Rights".

2 Temporalities of Coloniality and Law

Attentiveness to coloniality reveals how "habits of imperial engagement surround us"[9] far beyond the end of the colonial era as an historical period. This is the case both for former colonies and for former colonial powers whose material, political and legal realities are shaped by the ongoing presence of coloniality.

A full accounting of the effects of all aspects of British colonialism is beyond the scope of this chapter, but it is important to note the extent to which the colonial "civilizing mission", based on dichotomies of cultural difference, underpinned and justified imperial violence,[10] the transfer of resources and wealth from colonies to colonisers,[11] and the destruction of the philosophies and ontologies of those who were colonised.[12] Law played a central role in British colonial expansion and the ongoing legacy of British legal re-ordering can be found in contemporary domestic and international legal orders.[13] With regards SOGI, in 2018, Prime Minister Theresa May

[9]Lauren Benton and Lisa Ford, *Rage for Order the British Empire and the Origins of International Law, 1800–1850* (Cambridge, MA: Harvard University Press, 2016), 192.

[10]Anghie, *Imperialism, Sovereignty and the Making of International Law*, 3.

[11]Aditya Mukherjee, "Empire: How Colonial India Made Modern Britain," *Economic and Political Weekly* 45, no. 50 (2010).

[12]Raewyn Connell, *Southern Theory* (Cambridge: Polity, 2007).

[13]Benton and Ford, *Rage for Order*; Anghie, *Imperialism, Sovereignty and the Making of International Law.*

expressed "deep regret" for the British imperial role in perpetuating homophobic legislation.[14] Criminalisation of "offences against the order of nature" was developed in legal instruments such as Macaulay's Penal Code in India and the Griffiths Penal Code in Queensland.[15] These became templates for legal frameworks elsewhere in the empire.[16]

A number of different elements of the ongoing effects of empire are significant to the analysis undertaken in this chapter. First is the underlying logics of coloniality: the ontological divide between the European self and the racialized, colonial other.[17] Second are the forms of knowledge, knowledge production, action and law that grew from this foundational split—the structural violence of coloniality grounded in identities of civilised/uncivilised, self/other, centre/periphery that persist in the present.[18] Related to this is the extent to which modern, racialized, middle-class identity and domestic practices were produced through colonial logics.[19] Finally, as TWAIL (Third World Approaches to International Law) scholars have demonstrated, key legal structures—including modern statehood and sovereignty—emerged from the colonial encounter.[20]

Even with the persistence of imperial legal forms and the ongoing debates about the effect of colonialism and de-colonialism on British society and

[14]Crerar, "Theresa May Says She Deeply Regrets Britain's Legacy of Anti-Gay Laws". It is important not to flatten out the specifics of how colonial forms of violence and control manifested in different locations. The existence of the same law in different states does not mean that the law was equally enforced either during the colonial era or currently. Nor does it mean that all precolonial societies were equally tolerant or (intolerant) of behaviours or identities beyond a heterosexual matrix.

[15]Kirby, "The Sodomy Offence"

[16]Ibid.

[17]Grosfoguel, "The Epistemic Decolonial Turn"; Walter D. Mignolo, "Decoloniality and Phenomenology: The Geopolitics of Knowing and Epistemic/Ontological Colonial Differences," *The Journal of Speculative Philosophy* 32, no. 3 (2018).

[18]Anghie, *Imperialism, Sovereignty and the Making of International Law*; Raewyn Connell, *Southern Theory*; Walter D. Mignolo, "Global Coloniality and the World Disorder: Decoloniality After Decolonization and Dewesternization After the Cold War," World Public Forum "Dialogue of Civilizations," 2016.

[19]Anne McClintock, *Imperial Leather: Race, Gender and Sexuality in the Colonial Contest* (London: Routledge, 1995), 5.

[20]Anghie, *Imperialism, Sovereignty and the Making of International Law*; Ikechi Mgbeoji, "The Civilised Self and the Barbaric Other: Imperial Delusions of Order and the Challenges of Human Security," *Third World Quarterly* 27, no. 5 (2006).

culture,[21] there remains a relative "lightness" to the "weight of empire"[22] for the UK. British history is shaped by empire but it has a relative degree of control over how it acknowledges, represents and addresses its imperial past.[23] Empire is carefully positioned in British legal imaginaries, which means that the racialized hierarchies that persist in the postcolonial era, the peripheralization of (racialized) groups and nations,[24] the axiomisation of certain forms of political and legal organisation are not a factor in sanitised "regret" for imperial laws.

Ironically, the persistence of imperial legal structures does not mean that they are particularly stable. Both TWAIL and transnational legal literatures have emphasised the precarity of current international legal orderings.[25] Whether it be through "legal fragmentation" and the coexistence of a multiplicity of legal orders,[26] the failure of traditional legal orders to fully grasp the complexity of transnational developments[27] or through the operation of legal power by non or quasi-legal bodies,[28] the role of the state as a legal actor is in a situation of transformation and flux.[29] While the weight of empire and coloniality may be relatively "light" in the UK, current conditions mean that structures of international law and power (many of which are products of the colonial era) are somewhat precarious. One effect of this is a loss of certainty, or as Zumbansen notes, "institutional structures that we expect to provide

[21]Stephen Howe, "Internal Decolonization? British Politics Since Thatcher as Post-Colonial Trauma," *Twentieth Century British History* 14, no. 3 (2003); Richard Price, "One Big Thing: Britain, Its Empire, and Their Imperial Culture," *Journal of British Studies* 45, no. 3 (2006); Bernard Porter, "Further Thoughts on Imperial Absent-Mindedness," *The Journal of Imperial and Commonwealth History* 36, no. 1 (2008); Stuart Ward, ed. *British Culture and the End of Empire* (Manchester: Manchester University Press, 2001).

[22]Alia Al-Saji, "SPEP Co-Director's Address: Hesitation as Philosophical Method—Travel Bans, Colonial Durations, and the Affective Weight of the Past," *The Journal of Speculative Philosophy* 32, no. 3 (2018); Frantz Fanon, *Black Skin, White Masks* (London: Pluto, 1986).

[23]Al-Saji, "Hesitation as Philosophical Method"; Priyamvada Gopal, "Redressing Anti-Imperial Amnesia," *Race & Class* 57, no. 3 (2016).

[24]Grosfoguel, "The Epistemic Decolonial Turn".

[25]See particularly Balakrishnan Rajagopal, "Counter-Hegemonic International Law: Rethinking Human Rights and Development as a Third World Strategy," *Third World Quarterly* 27, no. 5 (2006).

[26]Dana Burchardt, "Intertwinement of Legal Spaces in the Transnational Legal Sphere," *Leiden Journal of International Law* 30, no. 2 (2017).

[27]Luis Eslava, "Istanbul Vignettes: Observing the Everyday Operation of International Law," *London Review of International Law* 2, no. 1 (2014); Aihwa Ong, "(Re)Articulations of Citizenship," *PS: Political Science and Politics* 38, no. 4 (2005).

[28]Mark James and Guy Osborn, "The Olympics, Transnational Law and Legal Transplants: The International Olympic Committee, Ambush Marketing and Ticket Touting," *Legal Studies* 36, no. 1 (2016).

[29]Ralf Michaels, "Globalisation and Law: Law Beyond the State" in *Law and Social Theory*, edited by Reza Banakar and Max Travers (Oxford: Hart, 2013).

guidance with regard to who has and who can effectively assume political responsibility and agency today become ever more volatile".[30] This volatility is experienced as loss: "loss of being able to adequately depict, express and capture the complexity of the developments which engulf us".[31]

It is important to note that the precarity of colonially produced frameworks of international law and state sovereignty manifests differentially—not all states are equally vulnerable to international legal and political changes,[32] nor are states necessarily singular entities—they fulfil a multiplicity of positions and roles.[33] For the purposes of this chapter however, the tensions here outlined call into question state power and capacity to manage dichotomies of inside/outside. Contained within this is a challenge to strict, structural separations between transnational, international and domestic jurisdictions.[34] This demonstrates the extent to which the forms that state power takes are historically produced and thus changeable or even vulnerable. Inside and outside of state borders, law or even culturally differentiated identities of self/other are not fixed positions; they are changing and changeable polarities that are formulated, enunciated and represented with varying degrees of success in different spatio-temporal locations.

This means that in the context of the queer legacy of colonialism in UK law, there is a fundamental instability at play: a simultaneous turning away from the "unaddressed and unredressed imperial past",[35] even while products of that past inform norms of sovereignty, statehood national identity and authority. This occurs even as those norms are rapidly undermined by the increasing complexity of the international sphere within which the UK now exists. The legacy of empire therefore encompasses a complex temporality in which the past is reproduced, represented and denied, even as it remains a key

---

[30]Peer Zumbansen, "How, Where and for Whom? Interrogating Law's Forms, Locations and Purposes," in *Legal Studies Research Paper Series*, ed. Dayan Farias Picon (London: Dickson Poon School of Law, Kings College London, 2016), 6.

[31]Ibid. While it beyond the scope of this chapter to deal with all manifestations of this sense of loss, there has been considerable analysis of the relationship between empire and Brexit. See Nadine El-Enany "Things Fall Apart: From Empire to Brexit Britain," *IPR Blog*, May 2, 2017, http://blogs.bath.ac.uk/iprblog/2017/05/02/things-fall-apart-from-empire-to-brexit-britain/.

[32]Luis Eslava, *Local Space, Global Life: The Everyday Operation of International Law and Development* (Cambridge: Cambridge University Press, 2015).

[33]Paisley Currah, "The State," *TSQ: Transgender Studies Quarterly* 1, nos. 1–2 (2014).

[34]Eslava, *Local Space, Global Life*; Carol J. Greenhouse, "Nationalizing the Local: Comparative Notes on the Recent Restructuring of Political Space," in *Human Rights in the 'War on Terror'*, edited by Richard Ashby Wilson (Cambridge: Cambridge University Press, 2005); Aihwa Ong, "(Re)Articulations of Citizenship," *PS: Political Science and Politics* 38, no. 4 (Oct 2005) (2005); Zumbansen, "How, Where and for Whom? Interrogating Law's Forms, Locations and Purposes".

[35]El-Enany, "Things Fall Apart".

source of legal and political authority in the face of a fragmenting international order. This temporality is paradoxical, and in this sense, it foreshadows the paradoxes that develop in the House of Commons debate analysed below.

3 The House of Commons and Global LGBT Rights: Spatio-Temporal Legacies of Empire

That the queer legacy of colonialism must consider temporalities of empire and coloniality is unsurprising. However, as Valverde insists, temporality is also spatial, and in this respect, the way in which legal actors imagine space and power becomes an important vector of analysis.[36] In analysing how modern British political/legal actors imagine space, time and power in the context of SOGI, I analyse a single House of Commons debate on "Global LGBT Rights" from 2017.[37]

The debate was organised by the All-Party Parliamentary Group (APPG) on Global LGBT Rights. The APPG was established in 2015 to "advance LGBT rights around the world" by providing "a forum for parliamentarians and organisations across the public, private and third sectors to work together to champion LGBT rights and push back against abuse and discrimination".[38] The APPG's work thus centres on awareness raising, diplomacy and networking. Its power to legislate—even in the House of Commons—is negligible and it can instead only seek to influence current discourse.

In 2018, the APPG was involved in attempts to place LGBT rights on the agenda at the Commonwealth Heads of Government Meeting (CHOGM), hosted by the UK.[39] This lobbying around LGBT at CHOGM reflects a growing perspective among some political actors, that the UK can and should use its influence within the Commonwealth to secure LGBT rights protections.[40] As a result, the APPG's backbench debate acts as a microcosm of legal and policy issues relevant to the UK's approach to LGBT issues both at home and elsewhere. By unpicking legal and epistemological structures of the debate, it is possible to centre the way in which outside and inside remain relative and changeable positions within UK law. More simply, inside/outside

[36] Mariana Valverde, *Chronotopes of Law: Jurisdiction, Scale and Governance* (Abingdon: Routledge, 2015).

[37] "Global LGBT Rights" HC Deb 26 October 2017, vol 630, col 515.

[38] Kay Lalor and Katherine Browne, "Here versus There: Creating British Sexual Politics Elsewhere," *Feminist Legal Studies* 26, no 2 (2018).

[39] APPG on LGBT Rights, "Meeting with Foreign Office Minister," *APPG*, December 19, 2017.

[40] APPG on LGBT Rights, "Parliamentary Group on Global LGBT Rights Launches Major New Inquiry," *APPG*, July 23, 2015.

are not fixed binary identities but positions on a co-constituting continuum. "Outside" as the space of "elsewhere", violence or otherness, only exists in relation to the "inside" as a UK space of safety and tolerance. Exploring these dynamics allows the tracing of how the queer outside exists *within* UK law.

The backbench debate begins with an explicitly spatial metaphor of a "Tale of Two Worlds":

> This is a tale of two worlds. In one, as we saw in this House, we have seen the near completion of rights for LGBT people, full recognition in law—with some exceptions, of course, throughout the UK—culminating, four years ago, in the passing of same-sex marriage legislation by overwhelming majorities in this House and the other place. In a 16-year period, 25 countries around the world have passed same-sex marriage legislation, while others have passed legislation recognising civil partnerships.
>
> …
>
> There is another world, too. I am talking about a world in which 75 countries criminalise same-sex activity between consenting adults. That covers 2.9 billion people. Some 40% of the world's population live in these jurisdictions, which means that more than 400 million people live under laws that punish same-sex activity and punish it with the death penalty.[41]

The instinct behind the "Tale of Two Worlds" is not malicious and does not completely obscure ongoing problems in the UK, but it does unthinkingly reproduce a colonial logic. The previous section highlighted the extent to which the fundamental binary encounter of the coloniser/colonised has shaped legal and political modernity.[42] This encounter rests on and facilitates a spatial dichotomy of "here and there" (or inside and outside), a culturalisation of difference and a civilising mission in which those elsewhere must be "enlightened". Weber highlights how in Victorian colonial discourse, figurations of the "savage", "primitive", "colonized" and "underdeveloped" manifested as sexualized, racialized and perverse.[43] These figurations persist in modernity and facilitate a paradigm in which the dangerous, feared and other is projected "elsewhere": a realm that is necessarily anarchic and uncontrolled. Under empire, imperial man required a dangerous, racialized, sexualised savage subject to justify imperial rule. In the current era, this binary persists, but the racialized other is homophobic rather than sexually

[41] HC Deb 26 October 2017, vol 630, col 515.

[42] Anghie, *Imperialism, Sovereignty and the Making of International Law*.

[43] Cynthia Weber, *Queer International Relations: Sovereignty, Sexuality and the Will to Knowledge* (Oxford: Oxford University Press, 2016), 21; Jasbir K. Puar, *Terrorist Assemblages: Homonationalism in Queer Times* (Durham: Duke University Press, 2007), 75.

licentious.[44] These dynamics are—unintentionally—present in the "Tale of Two Worlds" and support a binary configuration of sexuality, statehood and sovereignty. As such, the structures of the colonial past are present within the space of the debate, but their ongoing effects are "unattended".[45]

This unacknowledged colonial legacy of cultural differentiation sits alongside a more explicit discomfort with the discussion of empire:

> [Lloyd Russell-Moyle]
>
> It was the imperial law—combined with our imposition of the imperial Christian religion at the time and expressed by an imperial English language—that enforced the homophobia that still exists in so many of our Commonwealth countries. It was often enforced against the practices and will of the local historical narrative in those countries…
>
> [Luke Graham]
>
> "The hon. Gentleman is raising a lot of historical points, which is fine, but does he agree that now is the opportunity to use some of our long-standing relationships with these countries to improve those LGBT rights and follow our good example?"
>
> [Lloyd Russell-Moyle]
>
> That is exactly what I am coming to. I am trying to say that it is our duty to speak up because we were the ones that historically imposed some of these laws.[46]

The exchange above is a forceful illustration of how coloniality structures systems of law and policy, even while the ongoing effects of colonialism are denied.[47] This is a scalar movement that depoliticises the histories of the Commonwealth's origins, but also the broader history of the emergence of international law from the colonial encounter. It invests authority in certain legal and political bodies and invests in these bodies the capacity to determine the "right" way to move forward.[48] Moreover, this de-politicisation permits

[44]Although this homophobic "other" can also be cast as sexually perverse. See Puar, *Terrorist Assemblages*.

[45]Al-Saji, "Hesitation as Philosophical Method".

[46]HC Deb 26 October 2017, vol 630, col 539.

[47]Anghie, *Imperialism, Sovereignty and the Making of International Law*, 220.

[48]Mariana Valverde, "Jurisdiction and Scale: Legal 'Technicalities' as Resources for Theory," *Social & Legal Studies* 18, no. 2 (2009); Valverde, *Chronotopes of Law*.

a kind of necessary forgetting that allows the past misdeeds of empire to be carefully and completely confined to history. In this relocation of violence, there is a paradox at play: be it the violence of SOGI oppression that is exported overseas, or the horrors of imperial control that is safely confined by the past, the rhetorical structure of the debate allows a distancing that ensures that violence remains in another time and place, even while MPs participate in calling for its end.

4 Progress and Paradoxes of the Tale of Two Worlds

The passages discussed in the section above contain an implicit progress narrative typical of LGBTI progress narratives more generally.[49] In particular, the debate deploys a multiplicity of temporalities that maintain particular boundaries of inside/outside. "Elsewhere" or the outside is "backward" because it has not yet progressed along a teleologically defined path; thus, these backward "others" remain on the "wrong side of history". Yet the progressive "inside" distinguishes itself through a set of ahistorical manoeuvres thorough which the colonial histories, the tools of progress (the law) and the structures through which the categories of inside and outside, are depoliticised and presented as axiomatic, neutral and timeless.[50]

Within the debate the binary separation between the Global North and the Global South is accompanied by an underpinning teleological assumption that those nations who have not yet progressed, must "catch up" or, as one MP noted, that it "is up to progressive countries like ours to lead the way in global LGBT rights".[51] This particular comment should not be decontextualised or overplayed—it sits within a larger speech that highlights that the UK needs to "get its house in order"[52] and address ongoing exclusion, marginalisation and bullying of LGBTQI individuals. What is significant however, is the extent to which such comments emphasise the idea of linear progress towards LGBT rights "justice".

[49]See particularly Weber, *Queer International Relations*, 104–142.
[50]Ibid.
[51]HC Deb 26 October 2017, vol 630, col 527.
[52]Ibid.

The problematic aspects of linear progress have been scrutinised with reference to human rights law generally,[53] and LGBT rights specifically.[54] Not only do these narratives maintain already existing hierarchies and modes of legal and political organisation, they also reinforce the power and authority of those who are already deemed to have progressed. In so doing, they often legitimise the—usually legal—tools through which progress has been achieved. This flattens out the specificity of local and national action, universalises (and dematerialises) the material experiences of queer legal realities and presents the (legal) tools of progress as axiomatic, rather than as one possible route towards justice.

Scholarship of law and time has emphasised law's role in producing temporal rhythms, organising time, facilitating linearities, "emphasizing, erasing, and recasting historical events".[55] Even the reliance on frameworks of "Global LGBT Rights" are an enactment of a kind of legal temporality which calls upon the double function of rights as universal and timeless, while also materially embedded and progressively able to realise change. It is striking how much this framework is reflected in the debate:

> …we are still on a journey in this country even though we have legislated in many areas, and we have to understand that other countries will also take a long time to get to where we want them to get—they cannot just legislate. We have to use all the tools that are at our disposal, and colleagues on both sides of the House have mentioned some of them. We have soft power that we can exert due to our historical relationships with many countries, and I hope that we put such issues on the agenda for the upcoming Commonwealth Heads of Government meeting.[56]

The "necessary forgetting" of empire discussed above is clear in the lack of acknowledgement of the imperial dynamics of the "historical relationships" in this passage. Here, the journey along the path of (or towards) LGBT rights protections carries with it a duty to use soft power and historical relationships to promote the protection of LGBT rights. A debate that opens by celebrating *legal* progress thus makes clear the powerlessness of the UK to legislate anywhere outside UK territory, even to repeal laws that were originally written by British colonial administrators. The tools that MPs have

[53]Kathryn McNeilly, "Are Rights Out of Time? International Human Rights Law, Temporality, and Radical Social Change," *Social & Legal Studies* (2018).

[54]Weber, *Queer International Relations*.

[55]Renisa Mawani, "The Times of Law," *Law and Social Inquiry* 40, no. 1 (2015): 261.

[56]HC Deb 26 October 2017, vol 630, col 530.

available are soft law: diplomacy, "historical relationships" and other forms of non-legal pressure.

This means that while the power of law is venerated as the marker of civilisation and progress in the "Tale of Two Worlds", UK MPs have few legal tools at their disposal to secure global LGBT rights and the "rational power of law" is ultimately revealed as limited. There is a deeper parallel here with British colonial faith in law reform in its colonies, which nonetheless proceeded "chaotically and unevenly"[57] through a series of experiments that reflected a "complex and fluid world order with many makers".[58] In the context of colonial criminalisation of sodomy for example, very similar iterations of criminal penalties can be found in a multiplicity of different legal codes, some of which persist into modernity. But these penalties were externally imposed without reference to different indigenous values or customary law.[59] Moreover, colonial criminalisation also marks a failure of the rational power of law in Britain itself. During the colonial era, jurists and legal reformers sought to draft and impose a modern, simplified, codified criminal law.[60] This ultimately failed in Britain, but was imposed—unevenly—in Britain's colonies. Current attempts to bring about decriminalisation—as has occurred *within* British law—are marked by a failure to reach "inside" those jurisdictions that retain (or sustain) such laws, even while the structural (and imperially informed) relationship of the "Tale of Two Worlds" is maintained.

In this regard, there is a collapse—and a paradox—of the relationship between legal/non-legal and inside/outside. Transnational developments in LGBTI rights may use the language of rights, but are never purely legal, but rather assemblages of law, politics and diplomacy, that cannot be divorced from hierarchies of current and historical power relationships. The "rational power" of law alone will not secure SOGI justice, nor is it the primary tool of UK MPs seeking global LGBT rights, even as they draw upon the UK's own legal progress to justify their engagement with these issues. Moreover, as the section below argues, even as the structure of the debate relies on a framework of inside/outside, MPs own engagement with and imagination of how insider and outsiders are positioned calls this binary framework into question.

[57] Benton and Ford, *Rage for Order*, p. 6.
[58] Ibid.
[59] Gupta, "This Alien Legacy".
[60] Kirby, "The Sodomy Offence".

5 Queer Production of Camaraderie and Kinship

A key element of the debate is its spatial and temporal expulsion of violence "elsewhere". Ironically, the very location of the debate—in the Global North—contributes to the ease within which this expulsion can proceed. Or, as Al-Saji notes when discussing the "affective weight" of empire:

> Haunting the interstices of the present and structuring its joints, this past is *differentially* remembered, cognized, and felt by differently positioned subjects. This maps an epistemology of ignorance...by means of which imperial formations and racial imaginaries hide their workings.[61] (emphasis in the original)

In the context of the debate, the past is carefully positioned and selectively recalled. Ongoing structures of coloniality and modernity—the "colonial matrix of power"[62] are disregarded even as they provide the basis upon which the debate takes place. However, *simultaneously* with this act of spatio-temporal "forgetting" of colonial violence, MPs also work to emphasise their sense of kinship with LGBTQI communities around the world:

> [Lloyd Russell Moyle]
>
> Our role is to stand shoulder to shoulder with other LGBT activists—brothers and sisters—around the world and to support them.[63]
>
> [Hannah Bardell]
>
> As someone who took until I was 32 to come to terms with my own sexuality, I spent a lot of my early life hiding from myself, my feelings and my emotions, and from the truth of who I am and who I love. But I never, ever had to hide from the state or the police, or out of fear of being persecuted or killed.[64]
>
> [Crispin Blunt]
>
> When I say "we", I am thinking of the role that we can play as parliamentarians. We should not underestimate the huge challenge that faces our

[61] Al-Saji, "Hesitation as Philosophical Method," 337.

[62] Mignolo, "Decoloniality and Phenomenology"; Mignolo, "Global Coloniality and the World Disorder".

[63] HC Deb 26 October 2017, vol 630, col 540.

[64] Ibid. col 534.

> parliamentary colleagues in other countries that, because of religious beliefs and the influence of religion in those societies, are in the same state as the United Kingdom in the 1950s when it comes to attitudes to LGBT people.[65]
>
> [Nigel Evans]
>
> Growing up in Swansea, I wondered whether it was braver of me to come out as a Conservative or gay. I have tried both and it does not seem to have done me any harm.[66]

Thus, legal and political cleavages that re-inscribe dynamics of Global North/Global South, civilised/uncivilised are undercut by claimed personal connections with LGBTQI individuals elsewhere.

The point here is not to dismiss genuinely felt connections with LGBTQI people elsewhere in the world, or to suggest that a shared sense of kinship cannot exist. But it is significant that even while violence is expelled "elsewhere", a sense of kinship and connection is maintained. The debate only makes sense if the suffering queer is both "here and there", "inside and outside", within the framework of the debate. Through these rhetorical moves, Global South SOGI subjects—both real and imagined—are compelled to represent both the closeness of shared identity and the distance of structural violence, in a manoeuvre, which both upsets and maintains logics of inside and outside.

The simultaneous closeness and distance also reveals the jurisdictional struggle over Global South LGBTQI individuals, and the lack of power these individuals often have in responding to this struggle.[67] Such individuals are metaphorically and legally "stretched" across different locations, as they are claimed as subjects by multiple legal and regulatory systems—domestic, foreign, international and transnational. The tensions of this position are myriad, spatio-temporally specific and sometimes dangerous.[68] This positioning across multiple legal fields creates possibilities for strategies that draw attention to, challenge and upend accepted structural binaries and thus

[65]Ibid. col 526.

[66]Ibid. col 521.

[67]See Valverde, *Chronotopes of Law* for a discussion of how these struggles are often depoliticised.

[68]See Adrian Jjuuko and Fridah Mutesi, "The Multifaceted Struggle against the Anti-Homosexuality Act in Uganda," in *Envisioning Global LGBT Human Rights: (Neo)Colonialism, Neoliberalism, Resistance and Hope*, edited by Nancy Nicol, et al. (London Institute of Commonwealth Studies, 2018) and Adrian Jjuuko, "International Solidarity and Its Role in the Fight Against Uganda's Anti-Homosexuality Bill," in *Gender, Sexuality and Social Justice: What's Law Got to Do with It?* edited by Kay Lalor, et al. (Institute of Development Studies, 2016) for a discussion of these tensions in Uganda.

"undermine the dichotomy between colonizer and colonized, self and other on which the civilizing mission is based".[69] Yet the reality is often that the vast diversity and contingency of sexual and gender identity and experience is reified, flattened and dominated by those who are most visible and powerful, or most able to engage with Western power brokers.[70] The MPs at the debate were clearly aware of this problematic dynamic, but this awareness does not negate the fact that to become visible in the debate, queer subjects had to become part of British MPs' stories.

The central role of the politics of affect and of visibility in the debate is not surprising.[71] What is striking however, is the deployment of emotion and visibility in the production of unanimity and consensus. The MPs quoted above come from different political parties and have generally adopted wildly different policy positions. Yet within this particular debate, the normally antagonistic House of Commons was remarkably collegiate:

> It is right that across the House, on an entirely non-partisan basis…We have sent a signal today—and I am grateful that both Her Majesty's Opposition and the Government have reinforced that signal—that abuses of LGBT rights cannot be tolerated.[72]

The camaraderie of the debate, and the forms of kinship that it imagines, reproduces in microcosm the "Tale of Two Worlds". Unanimity is made possible through its binary relationship with the violent other. There is broad agreement on the deeper structural and epistemological questions that are brought into play (but not named) in the course of the debate: law facilitates progress, progress is relatively linear, those who have progressed have a duty to assist elsewhere, and empire is firmly confined to the past. The situation in the

[69]Anghie, *Imperialism, Sovereignty and the Making of International Law*, 319. Ugandan activists did this in the case of *Sexual Minorities Uganda v Scott Lively* Civil Action 3:12-CV-30051 (MAP) (US District Court for the District of Massachusetts). See Kay Lalor, "Encountering the Past: Grand Narratives, Fragmented Histories and LGBTI Rights 'Progress'," *Law and Critique* 30, no. 1 (2019).

[70]Phillip M. Ayoub and David Paternotte, eds., *LGBT Activism and the Making of Europe: A Rainbow Europe?* (Basingstoke: Palgrave MacMillan, 2014), 15.

[71]Emotion/affect and visibility have played an important role in queer politics. On queer affect see Sally R. Munt, *Queer Attachments: The Cultural Politics of Shame* (Aldershot: Ashgate, 2007); Senthorun Raj, "A/Effective Adjudications: Queer Refugees and the Law," *Journal of Intercultural Studies* 38, no. 4 (2017). On queer visibility see e.g. Ashley Currier, "Behind the Mask: Developing LGBTI Visibility in Africa," in *Development, Sexual Rights and Global Governance*, edited by Amy Lind (London: Routledge, 2010); Eve Kosofsky Sedgwick, *The Epistemology of the Closet* (Hemel Hempstead: Harvester Wheatsheaf, 1991); Andrew Gorman-Murray and Catherine J. Nash, "LGBT Communities, Identities and the Politics of Mobility: Moving from Visibility to Recognition in Contemporary Urban Landscapes," in *The Routledge Research Companion to Geographies of Sex and Sexuality*, edited Gavin Brown and Kath Browne (London: Routledge, 2016).

[72]HC Deb 26 October 2017, vol 630, col 548.

UK may not be perfect, but it is progressing in the right direction, and problems are a matter of individual violence rather than overarching structural or "cultural" factors.

This is why one of the few interventions that challenged these narratives was so striking. Rather than drawing on her personal experiences, Joanna Cherry contacted a campaigning organisation to ask for guidance on which issues to raise during the debate. The outcome highlighted the UK's treatment of LGBT asylum seekers:

> If we in the United Kingdom want to promote ourselves as supportive of LGBT+ rights and if we want to stand here and criticise other countries that are not, we must, across the parties, tackle the disgraceful treatment that some LGBTI+ asylum seekers and refugees receive in the United Kingdom.[73]

Cherry makes visible those LGBTI+ bodies that disrupt and challenge comfortable assumptions that, despite individual instances of violence, the UK is on the right path—especially with respect to its law. She emphasises a structural failure in UK law that traps SOGI asylum seekers figuratively within bureaucratic mazes and literally within detention centres. Implicit here is a demand to acknowledge that, if queer people are indeed kin, then we have failed them, not just in the safely distant days of empire, but in the immediate present.

Cherry's intervention is notable in that it demands concrete and achievable action within the UK, but in so doing, it must necessarily maintain a binary of inside/outside. The call for asylum protections for those coming to the UK from elsewhere holds to the narrative of the legally regulated inside and dangerous outside. The disruption that she presents is to the effectiveness of UK law in offering protection to those "others" who seek sanctuary here.[74] The challenge is to go beyond this intervention to face the underpinning paradoxes within which the queer legacy of colonialism starts to emerge. It is to this challenge that the final section of this chapter turns.

[73] Ibid. col 542–543.

[74] Thank you to Kath Browne and Sen Raj for helpful comments on this point.

6 Exposing Queer Paradoxes Within Legal Institutions

The aim of this chapter is not to dismiss or ridicule the clearly deeply felt desire to improve the situations of LGBTQI individuals and groups worldwide. There is value, however, in considering "how we come to understand ourselves as subjects of various legal regimes, how certain things come to be governed, how certain disciplinary and regulatory knowledges and practices congeal into institutional forms".[75] The sections above considered how practices of coloniality congeal in institutional and paradoxical forms within British law and government. To take these paradoxes seriously is to view them not as contradictions that can be easily resolved, but as a framework that can be used to expose queer legacies of colonialism in UK law and how the unacknowledged presence of coloniality within UK legal processes inhibit the possibility of more far-reaching action to secure SOGI justice.

In this context, Deleuzian scholarship of paradox is particularly useful:

> ...paradoxes have a two-fold function...On the one hand, they have a critical function demonstrating the limits of given claims and positions, most often those based on common sense and on hidden presuppositions about identities. On the other hand, paradoxes have a generative function, that is, the paradox generates a problem which itself leads to a series of speculative partial solutions, where partial means the problem recurs but is transformed.[76]

The first form of paradox is present in the debate—there is much discussion of violence suffered by LGBTQI individuals overseas—but the solutions offered are limited and contradictory. Temporally, spatially and legally, the UK remains trapped. In facing violence "elsewhere", UK politicians either turn to past relations and forms of power, or project onto the spaces of "elsewhere" the legal solutions through which the UK has "progressed". They engage in the "ritual application of human rights principles" in a way that universalises, dematerialises and abstracts specific situations and problems.[77] As such, the debate begins with an already established solution to a

[75] Dean Spade, "Laws as Tactics," *Columbia Journal of Gender and the Law* 21, no. 2 (2012): 41.

[76] James Williams, *Gilles Deleuze's Philosophy of Time: A Critical Introduction and Guide* (Edinburgh: Edinburgh University Press, 2011), 52; See also Gilles Deleuze, *The Logic of Sense*, ed. Constantin V. Boundas, trans. M. Lester and C. Stivale (London: Continuum, 2004), p. 3.

[77] Gilles Deleuze, "On Human Rights" L'Abécédaire de Gilles Deleuze, avec Claire Parnet. Video edited Montparnasse, 1996, accessed March 27, 2020, http://www.generation-online.org/p/fpdeleuze10.htm.

perceived problem[78]—the "Tale of Two Worlds" emphasises LGBT rights, legal progress and legislative solutions to LGBTQI suffering. This means that problems experienced by LGBTQI individuals must always be understood in such a way as to fit with these already established, rights-based solutions.

In this sense, the legal solutions offered and the conceptual foundations upon which they rest are insufficient to the task of responding to questions of SOGI injustice. Moreover, while within the House of Commons, the UK's leadership and national identity as enlightened and progressive may be celebrated, elsewhere in the world, where the weight of empire is heavier, this dynamic operates very differently. Public interventions by UK authorities into the treatment of LGBTQI subjects in former colonies have been met with considerable backlash in recent years.[79] Moreover, in some recent cases in which colonial era laws have been challenged or overturned, there is a sense of an elision of decriminalisation with decolonisation. In this regard, the recent Indian Supreme Court judgement *Navtej Johar v Union of India* is worth quoting at length:

> A hundred and fifty eight years ago, a colonial legislature made it criminal, even for consenting adults of the same gender, to find fulfilment in love. The law deprived them of the simple right as human beings to live, love and partner as nature made them. The human instinct to love was caged by constraining the physical manifestation of their sexuality. Gays and lesbians were made subordinate to the authority of a coercive state. A charter of morality made their relationships hateful. The criminal law became a willing instrument of repression. To engage in 'carnal intercourse' against 'the order of nature' risked being tucked away for ten years in a jail. The offence would be investigated by searching the most intimate of spaces to find tell-tale signs of intercourse. Civilisation has been brutal.[80]

Here, the Indian Supreme Court creates a "Tale of Two Worlds" where the UK represents a cruel colonial past from which India must depart.

The debate around SOGI in India is not just one of decoloniality—it confronts sexuality, gender, decriminalisation, patriarchy, class and caste, among others.[81] The point in presenting this small legal snapshot, however,

---

[78] Gilles Deleuze, *Bergsonism*, trans. Hugh Tomlinson and Barbara Habberjam (New York: Zone Books, 1991), 16; Gilles Deleuze, *Difference and Repetition*, trans. P Patton (London: Continuum, 2011), 201.

[79] BBC News, "Uganda fury at David Cameron Aid Threat Over Gay Rights," *BBC News*, October 31, 2011, https://www.bbc.co.uk/news/world-africa-15524013.

[80] Writ Petition (Criminal) No.76/2016 at 2.

[81] Siddharth Mohansingh Akali, "Learning from Suresh Kumar Koushal V. Naz Foundation Through Introspection, Inclusion, and Intersectionality: Suggestions from within Indian Queer Justice

is to question whether the UK can offer anything to this Indian debate, other than to be a representative of a colonial past that continues to structure dynamics of oppression in the present. *Navtej Johar* could be taken as an example of the kind of legal progress celebrated in the House of Commons, but the UK debate cannot or will not engage fully with the present reality of coloniality. As such, the solutions that it offers in the form of the progressive advancement of legal inclusion of LGBTQI subjects is rendered less powerful by its refusal to acknowledge the extent to which "civilization has been brutal".

It is important not to overstate the UK's powerlessness: India is just one example of how a Commonwealth state has responded to British anti-sodomy laws in recent years. And beyond pure legal paradigms, the UK has been able to offer aid—be it through quiet diplomatic support, training or financing projects that have helped LGBTQI groups.[82] Some UK groups have been able to offer legal support in certain circumstances.[83] It is noticeable however that these actions are often ad hoc, acts of quiet diplomacy, or undertaken in response to requests from groups in the Global South. The UK *can* act to support LGBTQI rights, but in a way that is fractured, reactive and multi-directional.

There is, therefore, a structural contradiction at the heart of the House of Commons debate. The paradoxes here are not minor impasses or easily resolvable misunderstandings, but products of an inherently flawed system. As Bruce-Jones (who also contributes to this collection) argues, there is a certain comfort in ignoring the flaws of the system within which we work as it "allows us to focus on the 'positive'... to defer to the current system, as it unarguably saves lives while politically viable alternatives are curtailed".[84] Something similar is present in the House of Commons debate and within UK approaches to global LGBT rights more generally. There is comfort to be found in using the tools that we have—however limited—to try to respond to violence and injustice. The queer legacy of colonialism in UK law, however, is

Movements," *Berkeley Journal of Gender, Law and Justice* 31, no. 1 (2016); Aniruddha Dutta, "Contradictory Tendencies: The Supreme Court's Nalsa Judgment on Transgender Recognition and Rights," *Journal of Indian Law and Society* 5 (2014); Vikram Raghavan, "Navigating the Noteworthy and Nebulous in Naz," in *Law Like Love*, edited by Arvind Narrain and Alok Gupta (New Delhi: Yoda Press, 2011).; Semmalar, Imaan, "Gender Outlawed: The Supreme Court Judgment on Third Gender and Its Implications", *Round Table India*, April 19, 2014, accessed March 27, 2020, http://roundtableindia.co.in/index.php?option=com_content&view=article&id=7377:because-we-have-a-voice-too-the-supreme-court-judgment-on-third-gender-and-its-implications&catid=120:gender&Itemid=133.

[82]Foreign and Commonwealth Office, *An FCO Programme for Promoting the Human Rights of LGBT People*, London. 2010; Government Equalities Office, *Policy Paper: LGBT Action Plan 2018: Improving the Lives of Lesbian, Gay, Bisexual and Transgender People*, London. 2018.

[83]Jjuuko and Mutesi, "The Multifaceted Struggle Against the Anti-Homosexuality Act in Uganda".

[84]See his chapter in this collection.

that paradox breaks through, whether it is acknowledged or not. The linear, "common sense", progressive arguments of the debate are interrupted by the un-thought or unsaid presence of coloniality—the "excess" without which the debate would collapse into incoherence.[85]

This is why an approach that uses queerness to expose how the "normal" is "contingent, constituted and open to change"[86] is necessary. This approach involves acknowledging the second aspect of Deleuze's paradox–as generative of new and creative solutions to problems. Yet, by acknowledging the paradoxes at the heart of the debate, we must also then acknowledge that these paradoxes support a number of other associated truisms that are then called into question.[87] To do this would be to challenge all that has been achieved so far, because it asks the question of what a queer justice would look like outside the framework of colonial binaries, civilising missions, the legal production of justice and stable sexual and gendered identities. It would open up the blind spots in the UK narrative of progress in a way that goes far beyond Cherry's intervention on LGBT asylum, and instead call into question the conceptual and structural foundations of our political and legal orderings.

What would be required here is a process that replays or re-works our assumptions in a way that calls those assumptions into question. To do this is to fully feel the weight of the colonial past and to challenge the imperial structures that animate our present. A queer approach in this case would require attentiveness to temporality in a way that challenged spatial paradigms of inside and outside. It is one that would acknowledge the fluidity of the "Tale of Two Worlds" and the extent to which stable binaries of cultural or legal difference are ultimately restrictive and limited. It would strengthen our awareness of interconnection with others not just as a duty to help individuals elsewhere to "catch up", but as a responsibility to participate in dismantling global hierarchies.[88] Such a practice is compelled to face the way that violence exists within those spaces that are deemed safe and thus renders irrelevant the spatial binary of the two worlds.[89] Similarly, it challenges what El-Enany terms "legal idolatry"—a belief in the power of rights to bring justice, that does not recognise the administrative and biopolitical dimension of rights for managing disenfranchised populations.[90] It would also be open to the

[85]Rosi Braidotti, *Transpositions* (Cambridge: Polity, 2006), 174; Deleuze, *The Logic of Sense*, 78.

[86]Colebrook, "On the Very Possibility of Queer Theory," 21.

[87]Thanks to Mark James for this formulation.

[88]Rosi Braidotti, "On Putting the Active Back into Activism," *New Formations* 68 (2009).

[89]See Bruce-Jones' chapter in this collection.

[90]Nadine El-Enany, "On Pragmatism and Legal Idolatry: Fortress Europe and the Desertion of the Refugee Special Issue: Critical Approaches to Migration Law," *International Journal on Minority and Group Rights* 22, no. 1 (2015).

precarity of the way in which "the transnational legal sphere is characterized by the coexistence of multiple legal orders and regimes",[91] and to the limitations of an international system that has not escaped its foundations in the colonial encounter.

There is a vulnerability to this position—it involves acknowledgement that the future may be significantly different from the past and that expected trajectories of progress cannot be relied upon. It requires that the weight of empire be felt more fully. The irony, however, is that these questions and challenges are not inserted into UK law from elsewhere. The queer legacy of colonialism in UK law is that there is no "queer outside"—queerness sits within UK law as a Deleuzian paradox or "aleatory point" that brings connection and meaning amidst disjunction or even nonsense.[92] Queerness here is an exposure of limitations, and a challenge to re-work those limitations into new solutions. To do this means revisiting the painful legacy of colonialism and coloniality in UK law and addressing that legacy, not as a self-contained past, but as an ongoing present.

7 Conclusion

While this chapter has focused on a debate on global LGBT rights, it offers a perspective on queer legacies of colonialism that goes far beyond questions of gender and sexuality. The legacy of colonialism in UK law is present in our legal orderings, our relations with and perceptions of the rest of the world, and in our construction of our national identity. In the queer Deleuzian reading advanced in the final part of this chapter, a queer legacy of colonialism is one that demands that we re-work these orderings, identities and relationships in a way that challenges that which is taken as axiomatic and more fully acknowledges the weight of the past. In the simplest terms, this was never a tale of two worlds, and the ongoing attachment to this framing and its associated spatio-temporal assumptions, obscures the more complex paradoxes at play, and thus the possibility of more far-reaching change.

Thus, an analysis of the APPG's approach to "Global LGBT Rights" in its backbench debate suggests that it is inherently paradoxical, but an engagement with these paradoxes can be productive. In this respect, there is no queer outside to our colonial legacy in UK law: queerness sits within, unacknowledged and sometimes un-thought, but a necessary presence that gives sense to contradictory positions. To confront that queer paradox is to give up our

[91] Burchardt, "Intertwinement of Legal Spaces in the Transnational Legal Sphere," 305.
[92] Deleuze, *The Logic of Sense.*

sense of legal certainty, knowledge and progress, and to think beyond the framework of the state, identity and law. This is not necessarily something that members of the APPG on LGBT Rights would be comfortable doing, but to ignore the queer, paradoxical heart of the debate does not make it disappear—it remains, as a contradiction. It offers insight into how we might proceed but makes no secret of the scope of the task. As such, the fact that a House of Commons debate on global LGBT rights is necessarily paradoxical is no surprise. Whether we can face this paradox remains as an unspoken challenge.

References

Akali, Siddharth Mohansingh. "Learning from Suresh Kumar Koushal V. Naz Foundation Through Introspection, Inclusion, and Intersectionality: Suggestions from Within Indian Queer Justice Movements." *Berkeley Journal of Gender, Law and Justice* 31, no. 1 (2016): 121–82.

Al-Saji, Alia. "SPEP Co-Director's Address: Hesitation as Philosophical Method—Travel Bans, Colonial Durations, and the Affective Weight of the Past." *The Journal of Speculative Philosophy* 32, no. 3 (2018): 331–59.

Anghie, Antony. *Imperialism, Sovereignty and the Making of International Law.* Cambridge: Cambridge University Press, 2007.

APPG on LGBT Rights. "Parliamentary Group on Global LGBT Rights Launches Major New Inquiry." *APPG*, July 23, 2015.

———. "Meeting with Foreign Office Minister." *APPG*, December 19, 2017.

Ayoub, Phillip M., and David Paternotte, eds. *LGBT Activism and the Making of Europe: A Rainbow Europe?* Basingstoke: Palgrave Macmillan, 2014.

BBC News. "Uganda Fury at David Cameron Aid Threat Over Gay Rights." *BBC News*, October 31, 2011. https://www.bbc.co.uk/news/world-africa-15524013.

Benton, Lauren, and Lisa Ford. *Rage for Order the British Empire and the Origins of International Law, 1800–1850.* Cambridge, MA: Harvard University Press, 2016.

Braidotti, Rosi. *Transpositions.* Cambridge: Polity, 2006.

———. "On Putting the Active Back into Activism." *New Formations* 68 (2009).

Bruce-Jones, Eddie. "Death Zones, Comfort Zones: Queering the Refugee Question." *International Journal of Minority and Group Rights* 22, no. 1 (2015): 101.

Burchardt, Dana. "Intertwinement of Legal Spaces in the Transnational Legal Sphere." *Leiden Journal of International Law* 30, no. 2 (2017): 305–26.

Colebrook, Claire. "On the Very Possibility of Queer Theory." In *Deleuze and Queer Theory*, edited by Chrysanthi Nigianni and Merl Storr. Edinburgh: Edinburgh University Press, 2009.

———. "Queer Vitalism." *New Formations* 68 (2010).

Connell, Raewyn. *Southern Theory.* Cambridge: Polity, 2007.

Crerar, Pippa. "Theresa May Says She Deeply Regrets Britain's Legacy of Anti-Gay Laws." *The Guardian*, April 17, 2018.
Currah, Paisley. "The State." *TSQ: Transgender Studies Quarterly* 1, no. 1–2 (2014): 197–200.
Currier, Ashley. "Behind the Mask: Developing LGBTI Visibility in Africa." In *Development, Sexual Rights and Global Governance*, edited by Amy Lind. London: Routledge, 2010.
Deleuze, Gilles. *Bergsonism*. Translated by Hugh Tomlinson and Barbara Habberjam. New York: Zone Books, 1991.
———. "On Human Rights." L'Abécédaire de Gilles Deleuze, avec Claire Parnet. Video edited Montparnasse, 1996. http://www.generation-online.org/p/fpdeleuze10.htm.
———. *The Logic of Sense*. Translated by M. Lester and C. Stivale, Edited by Constantin V. Boundas London: Continuum, 2004. 1969.
———. *Difference and Repetition*. Translated by P Patton. London: Continuum, 2011. 1968.
Dutta, Aniruddha. "Contradictory Tendencies: The Supreme Court's NALSA Judgment on Transgender Recognition and Rights." *Journal of Indian Law and Society* 5 (2014): 225–36.
El-Enany, Nadine. "On Pragmatism and Legal Idolatry: Fortress Europe and the Desertion of the Refugee Special Issue: Critical Approaches to Migration Law." *International Journal on Minority and Group Rights* 22, no. 1 (2015): 7–38.
———. "Things Fall Apart: From Empire to Brexit Britain." *IPR Blog*, May 2, 2017. http://blogs.bath.ac.uk/iprblog/2017/05/02/things-fall-apart-from-empire-to-brexit-britain/.
Eslava, Luis. "Istanbul Vignettes: Observing the Everyday Operation of International Law." *London Review of International Law* 2, no. 1 (2014): 3–47.
———. *Local Space, Global Life: The Everyday Operation of International Law and Development*. Cambridge: Cambridge University Press, 2015.
Fanon, Frantz. *Black Skin, White Masks*. London: Pluto, 1986. 1952.
Gopal, Priyamvada. "Redressing Anti-Imperial Amnesia." *Race & Class* 57, no. 3 (2016): 18–30.
Gorman-Murray, Andrew, and Catherine J. Nash. "LGBT Communities, Identities and the Politics of Mobility: Moving from Visibility to Recognition in Contemporary Urban Landscapes." In *The Routledge Research Companion to Geographies of Sex and Sexuality*, edited by Gavin Brown and Kath Browne. London: Routledge, 2016.
Greenhouse, Carol J. "Nationalizing the Local: Comparative Notes on the Recent Restructuring of Political Space." In *Human Rights in the 'War on Terror'*, edited by Richard Ashby Wilson. Cambridge: Cambridge University Press, 2005.
Grosfoguel, Ramón. "The Epistemic Decolonial Turn." *Cultural Studies* 21, nos. 2–3 (2007): 211–23.
Gupta, Alok. "This Alien Legacy the Origins of "Sodomy" Laws in British Colonialism." *Human Rights Watch*, 2008.

Howe, Stephen. "Internal Decolonization? British Politics Since Thatcher as Post-Colonial Trauma." *Twentieth Century British History* 14, no. 3 (2003): 286–304.

James, Mark, and Guy Osborn. "The Olympics, Transnational Law and Legal Transplants: The International Olympic Committee, Ambush Marketing and Ticket Touting." *Legal Studies* 36, no. 1 (2016): 93–110.

Jjuuko, Adrian. "International Solidarity and Its Role in the Fight Against Uganda's Anti-Homosexuality Bill." In *Gender, Sexuality and Social Justice: What's Law Got to Do with It?* edited by Kay Lalor, Elizabeth Mills, Arturo Sánchez García, and Polly Haste. Institute of Development Studies, 2016.

Jjuuko, Adrian, and Fridah Mutesi. "The Multifaceted Struggle Against the Anti-Homosexuality Act in Uganda." In *Envisioning Global LGBT Human Rights: (Neo)Colonialism, Neoliberalism, Resistance and Hope*, edited by Nancy Nicol, Adrian Jjuuko, Richard Lusimbo, and Nick J. Mulé. London: Institute of Commonwealth Studies, 2018.

Kirby, Michael. "The Sodomy Offence: England's Least Lovely Criminal Law Export?" In *Human Rights, Sexual Orientation and Gender Identity in the Commonwealth: Struggles for Decriminalisation and Change*, edited by Corinne Lennox, and Matthew Waites. London: Institute of Commonwealth Studies, 2013.

Kneen, B. *The Tyranny of Rights*. Ottowa: The Ram's Horn, 2009.

Lalor, Kay. "Encountering the Past: Grand Narratives, Fragmented Histories and LGBTI Rights 'Progress'." *Law and Critique* 30, no. 1 (April 1, 2019): 21–40.

Lalor, Kay, and Katherine Browne. 2018 "Here Versus There: Creating British Sexual Politics Elswhere." *Feminist Legal Studies* 26, no. 2: 205–13.

Mawani, Renisa. "The Times of Law." *Law and Social Inquiry* 40, no. 1 (2015): 253–63.

McClintock, Anne. *Imperial Leather: Race, Gender and Sexuality in the Colonial Contest*. London: Routledge, 1995.

McNeilly, Kathryn. "Are Rights Out of Time? International Human Rights Law, Temporality, and Radical Social Change." *Social & Legal Studies* 28, no 6 (2019): 817–38.

Mgbeoji, Ikechi. "The Civilised Self and the Barbaric Other: Imperial Delusions of Order and the Challenges of Human Security." *Third World Quarterly* 27, no. 5 (2006): 855–69.

Michaels, Ralf. "Globalisation and Law: Law Beyond the State." In *Law and Social Theory*, edited by Reza Banakar and Max Travers. Oxford: Hart, 2013.

Mignolo, Walter D. "Global Coloniality and the World Disorder: Decoloniality After Decolonization and Dewesternization After the Cold War." *World Public Forum "Dialogue of Civilizations"*, 2016.

———. "Decoloniality and Phenomenology: The Geopolitics of Knowing and Epistemic/Ontological Colonial Differences." *The Journal of Speculative Philosophy* 32, no. 3 (2018): 360–87.

Mukherjee, Aditya. "Empire: How Colonial India Made Modern Britain." *Economic and Political Weekly* 45, no. 50 (2010): 73–82.

Munt, Sally R. *Queer Attachments: The Cultural Politics of Shame*. Aldershot: Ashgate, 2007.

Ong, Aihwa. "(Re)Articulations of Citizenship." *PS: Political Science and Politics* 38, no. 4 (2005): 697–99.

Porter, Bernard. "Further Thoughts on Imperial Absent-Mindedness." *The Journal of Imperial and Commonwealth History* 36, no. 1 (2008): 101–17.

Price, Richard. "One Big Thing: Britain, Its Empire, and Their Imperial Culture." *Journal of British Studies* 45, no. 3 (2006): 602–27.

Puar, Jasbir K. *Terrorist Assemblages: Homonationalism in Queer Times*. Durham: Duke University Press, 2007.

Raghavan, Vikram. "Navigating the Noteworthy and Nebulous in Naz." In *Law Like Love*, edited by Arvind Narrain and Alok Gupta. New Delhi: Yoda Press, 2011.

Raj, Senthorun. "A/Effective Adjudications: Queer Refugees and the Law." *Journal of Intercultural Studies* 38, no. 4 (2017): 453–68.

Rajagopal, Balakrishnan. "Counter-Hegemonic International Law: Rethinking Human Rights and Development as a Third World Strategy." *Third World Quarterly* 27, no. 5 (2006): 767–83.

Sedgwick, Eve Kosofsky. *The Epistemology of the Closet*. Hemel Hempstead: Harvester Wheatsheaf, 1991.

Semmalar, Imaan. "Gender Outlawed: The Supreme Court Judgment on Third Gender and Its Implications." *Round Table India*, April 19, 2014. http://roundtableindia.co.in/index.php?option=com_content&view=article&id=7377:because-we-have-a-voice-too-the-supreme-court-judgment-on-third-gender-and-its-implications&catid=120:gender&Itemid=133.

Spade, Dean. "Laws as Tactics." *Columbia Journal of Gender and the Law* 21, no. 2 (2012): 40–71.

Valverde, Mariana. "Jurisdiction and Scale: Legal 'Technicalities' as Resources for Theory." *Social & Legal Studies* 18, no. 2 (2009): 139–57.

———. *Chronotopes of Law: Jurisdiction, Scale and Governance*. Abingdon: Routledge, 2015.

Ward, Stuart, ed. *British Culture and the End of Empire*. Manchester: Manchester University Press, 2001.

Weber, Cynthia. *Queer International Relations: Sovereignty, Sexuality and the Will to Knowledge*. Oxford: Oxford University Press, 2016.

Williams, James. *Gilles Deleuze's Philosophy of Time: A Critical Introduction and Guide*. Edinburgh: Edinburgh University Press, 2011.

Zumbansen, Peer. "How, Where and for Whom? Interrogating Law's Forms, Locations and Purposes." In *Legal Studies Research Paper Series*, edited by Dayan Farias Picon. London: Dickson Poon School of Law, Kings College London, 2016.

Death Zones, Comfort Zones: Queering the Refugee Question

Eddie Bruce-Jones

1 Introduction

> In the context of contemporary projects of security and state violence, lesbian and gay rights discourse occupies a recuperative role for institutions and practices long contested by anti-racist, anti-colonial, feminist and queer intellectual traditions and social movements.[1]

Ten years ago, in 2010, the UK Supreme Court rendered a watershed decision in HT & HJ v. Secretary of State for the Home Office, eliminating what has been described as the "discretion test"[2] for gay and lesbian refugees and calling attention to the challenges that had been faced by claimants applying

[1]Dean Spade, "Under the Cover of Gay Rights", 37 *New York University Review of Law and Social Change* (2013) 97.

[2]This refers to the guiding principle in UK asylum law jurisprudence, overturned by *HT & HJ*, that would require the deportation of applicants claiming persecution on the basis of sexuality if it was shown that they could be discreet about their sexuality upon return, so as to avoid persecution. See *HJ (Iran) and HT (Cameroon)* v. *Secretary of State for the Home Department* [2010] UKSC 31.

A version of this chapter originally appeared in the *International Journal on Minority and Group Rights* 22 (2015) pp. 101–127, published by Brill Nijhoff.

E. Bruce-Jones (✉)
Birkbeck College, University of London, London, UK
e-mail: e.bruce-jones@bbk.ac.uk

S. Raj and P. Dunne (eds.), *The Queer Outside in Law*, Palgrave Socio-Legal Studies,
https://doi.org/10.1007/978-3-030-48830-7_3

for sexuality-based asylum in the UK. Alongside this decision, and for years prior to it, scholars and practitioners had been documenting and theorising some of the particular challenges facing gay and lesbian asylum seekers in Europe, Commonwealth countries and elsewhere.[3]

In the intervening years, there have been important judgments on sexual-orientation-based asylum handed down at the European level, including the Joined Cases of X, Y and Z[4] and A, B and C[5] at the Court of Justice of the European Union and the case of ME v. Sweden at the European Court of Human Rights in Strasbourg.[6] Discussing sexual rights among international lawyers, migration lawyers and activists, by virtue of the material necessity to provide and rely on country reports and context-based evidence from claimants' countries of origin, has shuttled between sexual rights and refugee rights, and in the years since the HT and HJ judgment, this tension has been teased out before a wide and attentive public. The liberal or leftist approach has been mainly to view expansion of the scope of protection of gay and lesbian refugees as a step in the right direction, towards protection of basic human rights and, in the case of HT and HJ, a more appropriate way to conceive of persecution on the basis of sexuality than the so-called "discretion" test had been. The decision effectively offers protection not only to those who lived openly as gay, lesbian or bisexual in their countries of origin, but also to those who concealed this part of their public lives for fear of persecution. In LC (Albania) v SSHD,[7] the UN High Commissioner for Refugees submitted that the HT and HJ decision should imply a legal presumption

[3]See e.g., Jenni Millbank, "'The Ring of Truth': A Case Study of Credibility Assessment in Particular Social Group Refugee Determinations", *International Journal of Refugee Law* 21, no 1 (2009): 1–33.

[4]*Joined Cases C-199/12, C-200/12 and C-201/12 (X, Y and Z) v. Minister voor Immigratie en Asiel* [2014] 2 CMLR 16 (ruling that the existence of criminal laws "which specifically target homosexuals supports the finding that those persons must be regarded as forming a particular social group", that criminal laws per se do no constitute persecution, and that applicants cannot be expected to be discreet about their sexuality in their respective countries of origin). For a detailed analysis of the judgment and its implications, see *X, Y and Z: A Glass Half Full for "Rainbow Refugees?"* June 3, 2014, International Commission of Jurists, Briefing.

[5]*Joined Cases C-148/13, C149/13 and C-150/13 (A, B and C)* [2015] 2 CMLR 5.

[6]*M.E.* v. *Sweden* (ECtHR, 26 June 2014). In this judgment, the Court accepted that the Libyan asylum applicant was in a relationship with N (a transsexual woman), but did not accept that he would face a risk of persecution if returned to Libya to make his family reunification application (required by Swedish law) because the level of violence was not seen as credible and he had presented N as a woman to his family over skype, which ostensibly indicated that he was choosing to live discreetly. Setting the credibility issue aside, this judgment relies to a large extent on the notion that LGBTIQ people should be required to be discreet in certain situations, without questioning whether the discretion is for fear of persecution. *Cf. HT and HJ* case, *supra* note 2.

[7]*LC (Albania) v. Secretary of State for the Home Department and the United Nations High Commissioner for Refugees* [2017] ECWA Civ 351.

that those LGBTQ people living in countries where they would face persecution if they were to live openly, conceal their sexual identities at least partially in fear of persecution.[8]

However, while the HT and HJ judgment has been regarded as mainly a positive advancement for protecting individuals fleeing sexuality-based persecution, aspects of such asylum claims reveal ways in which these advancements serve to reinforce and discipline not only sex, sexuality and gender norms, but also cultural stereotypes, as well as our core assumptions about the goals and limitations of the refugee law system. Such advancements are shifts in the legal regulation of refugee status that, just below the surface, re-instantiate professional and disciplinary expectations not to address certain issues that are critical to understanding sexuality both in the context of defining persecution as well as in articulating the global justice aims of the international refugee law system. The HT and HJ moment, then, marks an appropriate time to ask what it would mean to "queer" refugee law.

By "queer", I am referring partly to what James Hathaway and Jason Pobjoy discuss in their important article on HT and HJ, "Queer Cases Make Bad Law", wherein the term "queer" recalls an "overtly political challenge" to the assimilationist politics inherent in expectations of refugee claimants' narratives of sexual selfhood and gender identity.[9] I agree with Hathaway and Pobjoy that cases such as HT and HJ, while they seem to protect asylum applicants more completely, force applicants to couch their claims in conventional culturally specific western terminology (e.g., through use of the terms "homosexual" and "gay" to describe sexuality) and do not challenge normative conceptions of sexuality.[10] However, on a more fundamental level, I depart from Hathaway and Pobjoy and contend that cases like HT and HJ are not "queer" cases with regard to critically conceptualising refugee law. Such cases reproduce language and legal ideologies that engender a strict Western view not only of sexuality and gender, but also of culture, race, history and the geopolitics of violence. While Hathaway and Pobjoy do not set out to

---

[8]UN High Commissioner for Refugees (UNHCR), *L.C. (Albania) v. Secretary of State for the Home Department: Case for the Intervener*, 22 March 2017, C5/2014/2641, available at https://www.refworld.org/docid/58de68dd4.html [accessed 26 June 2020], The UNHCR, as intervener, poses the rhetorical question "in what circumstances may it be said that the concealment will be entirely unrelated to the objective reality that if their protected identity became known, the individual would be persecuted?" The UK Lesbian and Gay Immigration Group, which supports LGBTI asylum applicants and advocates for policy and legal reform of asylum processes, supports the paradigm of protection that the UNHCR suggests. See UKLGIG Briefing: Applying HJ (Iran) and HT (Cameroon) to asylum claims based on sexual orientation (June 2018) 16. Available online at https://uklgig.org.uk/wp-content/uploads/2019/11/UKLGIG-on-HJ-Iran.pdf [Last accessed 26 June 2020].

[9]James Hathaway and Jason Pobjoy, "Queer Cases Make Bad Law", *New York University Journal of International Law and Politics* 44, no 2 (2012): 315–389.

[10]Ibid.

engage with the term "queer" in their article in this way, I would like to take up the analytic lens that the deployment of such a term can provide.

The other aspect of "queer" that I am referring to is what Jack Halberstam proposes with the idea of a queer methodology. Halberstam notes:

> A queer methodology, in a way, is a scavenger methodology that uses different methods to collect and produce information on subjects who have been deliberately or accidentally excluded from traditional studies of human behavior. The queer methodology attempts to combine methods that are often cast as being at odds with each other, and it refuses the academic compulsion toward disciplinary coherence.[11]

While Halberstam deploys the idea of a queer methodology as it relates to the study of human behaviour, I apply it in considering refugee law, both in theory and in practice. As theoreticians, we are disciplined to regard refugee law as the best solution for those fleeing persecution. Given the current geopolitical order, it represents the best of many evils, or, given the near impossibility of the devolution of borders and states, the possible among impossibilities. As practitioners we realise that, whatever critiques of the refugee law system we may advance outside of court, when before a tribunal and navigating the straight-laced gauntlet of legal techniques necessary to achieve a positive refugee status determination for a client, it is at best impractical to mention the critical perspective one might otherwise have towards refugee law. It would be disorienting and, some will certainly argue, unrealistic to reject disciplinary coherence, particularly in the case of legal advocacy—one will not win a case if one blatantly ignores the mechanics of the legal claim. The present analysis is meant as a provocation to reassess the desired outcome of refugee law by unsettling some of its core assumptions.

This chapter builds upon my earlier work to examine why the UK serves as a suitable point of departure to unsettle core assumptions of refugee law both within its doctrinal underpinnings and from outside the scope of its application. This chapter is meant to be self-reflective, considering both activist and academic entry into the issue of refugee law and its relationship to activism around decriminalisation of same-sex sexual activity. The UK plays a central role in global discussions on decriminalisation, given its prominence as the administrative and political head of the Commonwealth. In the particular context of repression of sexual diversity, the UK has, as Kay Lalor makes clear in the previous chapter, left behind a trail of criminal legal provisions,

[11] Jack Halberstam, *Female Masculinity* (Durham: Duke University Press, 1998) 13.

outlawing same-sex sexual activity in former colonial territories. These provisions are still in play, existing as valid law or being litigated actively in courts by way of local initiative. Section 377 of the Indian Penal Code was, after decades of litigation, declared unconstitutional by the Indian Supreme Court as recently as 2018,[12] and a ruling in Trinidad and Tobago has declared the relevant criminal provision unconstitutional.[13] Meanwhile similar provisions have been expanded into harsher ones by the parliament of Uganda.[14] Additionally, due to the publicity of recent UK case law regarding sexuality and gender-based refugee claims, most notably the HT and HJ decision,[15] the UK has become a locus for discussing LGBTIQ[16] refugee issues in Europe and beyond.

2 Sexuality-Based Asylum and Decriminalisation of Same-Sex Activity

While refugee law is concerned essentially with helping individuals gain residency rights in a foreign territory in order to escape state-sponsored or state-complicit persecution,[17] the international promotion of human rights law is primarily concerned with securing constitutional human rights protection within individual nation-states. In the case of the rights of LGBTIQ claimants, refugee protection and international efforts to increase human rights-based protection in national constitutional settings are carried out with largely different processes, but share a common set of discourses, challenges and dangers.[18] It is important to reflect upon the two strands of work with a common frame of reference in order to best understand the contingencies that undergird them both.

[12] *Navtej Singh Johar & Others v. Union of India*, Supreme Court of India, 6 September 2018.

[13] "Trinidad and Tobago Judge Rules Homophobic Laws Unconstitutional", *The Guardian*, April 13, 2018, accessed July 29, 2019, https://www.theguardian.com/world/2018/apr/13/trinidad-and-tobago-sexual-offences-act-ruled-unconstitutional.

[14] Amy Fallon and Owen Bowcott, "Uganda Politicians Celebrate Passing of Anti-Gay Laws", *The Guardian*, February 24, 2014, accessed March 17, 2020, www.theguardian.com/world/2014/feb/24/uganda-president-signs-anti-gay-laws.

[15] *HT and HJ* case, *supra* note 2.

[16] Lesbian, gay, bisexual, trans, intersex and queer.

[17] 1951 Convention Relating to the Status of Refugees' (United Nations, 1951); 1967 Protocol Relating to the Status of Refugees (United Nations, 1967).

[18] It is important to note here that the abbreviation LGBTIQ is perhaps not as deeply entrenched in the particular approach to and understanding of sexual politics that LGBT is. However, neither term is necessarily applicable to all contexts. They both suffer from some of the same shortcomings as the language of universality with regards to human rights, notably the difficulty in coordinating local meaning with such global vernacular.

Asylum lawyers in immigration tribunals are primarily concerned with securing refugee status for individual applicants in receiving countries, rather than with attempting to change the conditions in applicants' countries of origin, although the persecution is often immediately related to these conditions. The most direct reason for this is that refugee cases, like other cases, are scripted for answering certain legal questions to the exclusion of other potentially related questions. The presumption is that, within the set of human rights-based remedies available to refugees, determining the official refugee status of an applicant is largely independent of related social change activism that seeks to alter the conditions that make protection necessary in the first place—or at least such discussions are not thought to be appropriate in the courtroom.

The concern of the refugee lawyers advocating for increased protections for LGBTIQ refugees is to prove that claimants are being persecuted on the basis of sexuality, as defined and understood by applicable case law or, alternatively, to change the way the case law is interpreted to the same effect. Meanwhile, queer theorists and those concerned with the limited sense in which sexuality is discussed in both these contexts remind us that sexuality, in many people's lived experience, is not limited to binary self-identification in terms of sex, gender and sexuality.[19] Numerous advocates and academics are active in both international decriminalisation of same-sex sexual activity and LGBTIQ refugee claims advocacy, though perhaps in different capacities and fora.

There is a professional expectation that these two strands of advocacy be kept separate. A refugee status determination hearing or immigration tribunal is not a receptive venue for debating the limits of geopolitics as a conceptual framework for considering violence, as this lies outside of the framework categories familiar to the judiciary. The framework used in refugee claims is, as discussed, firmly rooted in the logic of politically defined borders, jurisdictions and corresponding cultural and social attitudes. However, the discourses related to decriminalisation and refugee protection share common terms,

[19]This discussion is not only limited to academia. For example, the UK Lesbian and Gay Immigration Group published a 2018 report assessing Home Office decision making on LGBTI claims, which identifies the persistent expectation by Home Office agents that LGBT people would have a particular type of coming out experience. See UKLGIG, *Still Falling Short: The Standard of Home Office Decision-Making in Asylum Claims Based on Sexual Orientation and Gender Identity*, 2018, accessed July 22, 2019, https://uklgig.org.uk/wp-content/uploads/2018/07/Still-Falling-Short.pdf. The report claims that "[i]n many cases this expectation of sophistication is erroneous as it relies on stereotypes of LGBTQI + people, which in addition to being sexual stereotypes are culturally misaligned. Not everyone will have gone through introspective soul-searching and retrospective interpretation of their experiences, so as to be able to offer a narrative identifying their own emotions as central to their identity. or containing milestones which might be recognisable in some Western contexts" (p. 23).

including "culture", "human rights" and "safety", as well as various ideological renderings of Europe as a benevolent safe haven for new (non-European)[20] migrants. Paying careful attention to the global dynamics of "racism" in the sense to which Ramon Grosfoguel[21] refers (particularly in respect of those in the zones of non-being) and conditions that echo colonial and other divides (beyond simply the North–South divide or the West–Rest divide) will enable one to view the connections between racism and migration and to be wary of the types of interventions that exacerbate the conditions in these spaces of precariousness rather than catalyse an empowering set of tools, logics and frameworks.

There are also challenges that accompany the specialised nature of advocacy and rights-based social change activism. The activist working on decriminalisation may lobby national government, liaise with NGOs where same-sex sexual activity is criminalised, lend financial support, initiate educational campaigns and demonstrate solidarity with local groups and individual activists. The legal practitioner (also an activist—the distinction is arbitrary to some degree, but it is important to note that different discursive and professional expectations govern different types of practice) may, among other things, create legal historiography, lend specialised assistance to local organisations and even strategically litigate through constitutional challenge, in partnership with local organisations. None of these are straightforward strategies and they each approach social change in different, sometimes competing ways. Regardless of strategy, it remains that human rights law reform considers the law in a broad context, while refugee law considers local laws and their contexts to a relatively limited extent.

3 Comfort Zones and Death Zones

There is a dual aesthetic that shapes both the study and practice of refugee law which can be summarised as a self-reinforcing polarity of comfort and death. This polarity refers mainly to how we regard the ideological and material substance of refugee claims, but it also describes how we view ourselves in

[20]An exception to this is the relatively recent case of Russia having implemented harsh laws against sexual minorities, which has increased the number of LGBTIQ refugees fleeing from Russia to other parts of Europe.

[21]I am referring here to Grosfoguel's elaboration of zones of being and non-being in his lecture series on Decoloniality in Berlin as well as a recorded lecture he gave at the Islamic Human Rights Commission in the UK on December 11, 2012 called "Is Islamophobia Racism?" Grosfoguel traces the intellectual history of "racism" in broad terms to mean the exclusion of certain groups from the "zones of being" and relegation into the "zones of non-being" wherein their lives are much more precarious and characterised by violence.

light of the total predicament of the refugee system, including the conditions that necessitate such a system. I will begin with a reflection on the concept of "comfort".

The type of comfort that I mean is two-fold. First, there is the comfort that many advocates and scholars have in the assumption that legal logics adequately describe social realities. For example, there is comfort with human rights discourse that arranges the world into geopolitical realms of safety and danger. In the case of the rights of LGBTIQ individuals this cartography is, at its most overt, expressed with the evolution narrative that extends from criminalisation of gay sex to recognition of same-sex marriage, entrenching a linear rights model within the familiar civilising discourse of social "progress". Beyond the problematic use of an evolutionary schema, what is presumed to be the furthest point of progression in the schema is recognition of same-sex marriage, which can also be critiqued as an unimaginative, violent institution, advocacy for which has relegated other issues affecting a broad range of queer people and people of colour to the political margins.[22] This advances a flat, impoverished picture of society—using the parameters of rights and rights-granting national jurisdictions, rather than a lived reality full of contingencies and power relations that shape not only experiences of sexuality, but experiences of location at the junctions of law, politics, gender, sexuality, race, class, etc. Comfort with this language of rights also allows what Nadine El-Enany has referred to as "legal idolatry"[23] or the belief that where rights exist, justice is bound to follow, rather than viewing a myriad of other exclusionary administrative measures that exist alongside rights as technologies for curtailing material or substantive benefits for disenfranchised people on the other end.

The other type of comfort that I mean is the comfort that accompanies adherence to disciplinary or professional discourses by practitioners and advocates. The advocate for LGBTIQ refugees in this scenario, whether lawyer, activist or policy champion, attempts to widen the scope of protection for LGBTIQ refugees by identifying gaps in coverage, or advocating for one particular person to gain asylum, while generally maintaining the legitimacy of the refugee system.[24] While practitioners in the courtroom advocate for

[22]For examples of such critiques, see Jeffrey Redding, "Dignity, Legal Pluralism and Same-Sex Marriage", *Brooklyn Law Review* 75, no 3 (2010) 791; Dean Spade, "Under the Cover of Gay Rights", *N.Y.U. Review of Law and Social Change* 37, no 1 (2013): 79.

[23]Nadine El-Enany, "On Pragmatism and Legal Idolatry: 'Fortress Europe' and the Desertion of the Refugee", *International Journal of Minority and Group Rights* 22, no 1 (2015): 7–38.

[24]See Guglielmo Verdirame, "A Friendly Act of Socio-Cultural Contestation: Asylum and the Big Cultural Divide", *International Law and Politics* 44 (2012): 559–572. It is important to note that refugee claims advance human rights discourse in prominent ways, though filtered through the propositions regarding torture and contextual assumptions regarding persecution as per the Geneva Convention rather than the transposition of international norms to national constitutions.

singular clients, some cases, such as HT and HJ, can result in significant shifts in jurisprudence.[25] However, the situations that prompted the persecution are met with the decriminalisation strategy taken by other lawyers and activists, many of whom know one another, are active in the same circles, or occasionally also do refugee work. Even in the context of this strategy, refugee law is regarded as better than nothing, though essentially a superficial quick-fix solution that can and should be made obsolete by a more sustainable transformation of the conditions that enable persecution. However, does thinking of a unique local source already oversimplify the contingencies of structural violence faced by people owing to their sexuality, gender or any other grounds? Does thinking in accordance with the professional disciplinary expectations of refugee law or constitutional revision regarding sexual activity or identity commit us to the tunnel vision of single-issue provincialism and risk compounding problems in other areas of social life? There is comfort in not answering or, better, not asking these questions. This comfort allows us to focus on the "positive"—the refugee system allows those privileged enough to cross a border, and often the sea, to ask for protection and get it.[26] It allows us as academics, activists and practitioners, to defer to the current system, as it unarguably saves lives while broad alternatives are curtailed by a deeply entrenched global infrastructure for policing movement. It is with the discomfort posed by these questions that I shift to discuss the concept of death.

If the promise of comfort is central to the refugee law system, then the spectre of death is the other atrium of the system's discordant heart. The title of this chapter is borrowed from Etienne Balibar's idea of "death zones".[27] With this concept, Balibar reminds us that spaces defined by extreme violence exist within Europe, not only outside of it. This is to be seen as a corollary to the assumption that Europe is a zone of safety and that refugees abroad will flee persecution over there to enjoy a haven right here. In "Outlines of a Topography of Cruelty", Balibar inverts the typical narrative of Europe as the place synonymous with human rights and safety by pointing to the extreme violence that occurs within Europe against those without European

[25] *HT and HJ* case, *supra* note 2. The decision rejected what had been commonly known as the "discretion test" for lesbian and gay asylum applicants, with the effect that claimants are no longer expected to return to their countries of origin to live discreetly if they would only do so for fear of persecution were they to live as openly gay or lesbian.

[26] I am referring mainly to the regime set out by the 1951 UN Convention on the Status of Refugees (the "Geneva Convention").

[27] Etienne Balibar, "Outlines of a Topography of Cruelty: Citizenship and Civility in the Era of Global Violence", *Constellations* 8, no 1 (2001): 15–29.

citizenship and, thus, without the full protection of a European state.[28] In describing these zones, he argues:

> In the end it would be my suggestion that the 'g[l]obalization' of various kinds of extreme violence has produced a tendential division of the 'globalized' world into life-zones and death zones. Between these zones (which indeed are intricate, frequently reproduced within the boundaries of single country or city), there exists a decisive and fragile superborder, which raises fears and concerns about the unity and division of mankind – something like a global and local 'enmity line,' like the 'amity line' which existed in the beginning of the modern European seizure of the world. It is this superborder, this enmity line, that becomes at the same time an object of permanent show and a hot place for intervention. But also for nonintervention.[29]

Here, Balibar describes "extreme violence" as "without borders or beyond borders" rather than "violence of the border". This is important, as it suggests that locating the violence of refugee law at the border (and we are familiar with the trope of border violence that frames a great deal of refugee work in Europe—illustrative phrases like "the guarded gate", "the treacherous sea", "Fortress Europe" easily come to mind) limits more thorough consideration of violence as it obscures the widespread violence within the borders and beyond the borderline. The superborder framework for identifying violence considers extreme violence to be something that is not shaped solely by the policing of the political boundaries of the state, but also inter-subjective and inter-institutional domains that can exist within the nation and even within cities and localities.[30]

Public discourse with regard to threateningly large refugee "flows" into Europe and the parallel vernacular of "saving" the refugees regularly deployed in media discourse does not mirror the lived reality of many refugees and asylum seekers. For those without European citizenship, the obstacles to accessing a better life in Europe can be another hell with different wallpaper. We know from the experiences shared by many refugees of the perils in Europe, from drowning on the high seas[31] to suffering abuse by private

[28] Ibid.

[29] Ibid., p. 24.

[30] Ibid.

[31] Consider the case of a ship of Eritrean and Sudanese refugees capsizing off the coast of the Italian island of Lampedusa in October 2013, in which an estimated 300 people drowned. Such tragedies are considered, by some, to represent structural policy failures which do not assist refugees in their journeys across the treacherous sea. See e.g., Hans Jurgen Schlamp, "Europe's Failure: Bad Policies Caused the Lampedusa Tragedy" *Der Spiegel Online,* October 4, 2013, accessed November 2, 2014, www.spiegel.de/international/europe/lampedusa-tragedy-is-proof-of-failed-european-refugee-policy-a-926081.html; Anna Dolidze, "Lampeduza and Beyond: Recognition, Implementation and

enforcement agents,[32] to living in destitution if one's claim is rejected.[33] Both the journey and the destination are zones of danger for the precarious condition of entering Europe as a refugee.[34] The lived reality of these death zones exist within the shadows of the refugee law Leitmotif of rescue that, in my account, constitutes the comfort zone in which we imagine ourselves, as advocates working from within the United Kingdom and elsewhere. In the context of refugee law, the concept of the "death zone" requires us to look critically at the supposed "location" of human rights, the violence from within Europe, but also the violence of citizenship in general, and specifically, the violence done in the name of policing access to European citizenship.[35]

What might be gained from reorienting our framing of refugee law with a queer perspective, rejecting for a moment the "compulsion towards disciplinary coherence"?[36] What creative potential might we unlock by thinking about this cartography of safety and danger, using Balibar's notion of the "death zone"[37] and reflecting on the concepts of "zones of being and non-being", as articulated by Fanon[38] and interpreted by Ramón Grosfoguel and others? It may help us to identify shortcomings of refugee law, as well as

---

Justiciability of Stateless Persons' Rights Under International Law", *Interdisciplinary Journal of Human Rights Law* 6 (2011–2012): 123. For an overview of documented refugee deaths at European borders over the last two decades, see *List of 17306 Documented Refugee Deaths through Fortress Europe*, 1 November 2012, UNITED for Intercultural Action, accessed November 2, 2014, www.unitedagainstracism.org/pdfs/listofdeaths.pdf.

[32]Consider, for example, the death of asylum applicant Jimmy Mubenga during his forced removal from the UK by the privately contracted security service G4S. See Matthew Taylor and Robert Booth, "Jimmy Mubenga Death: G4s Guards Will Not Face Charges", *The Guardian,* July 17, 2012, accessed November 2, 2014, www.theguardian.com/uk/2012/jul/17/jimmy-mubenga-guards-no-charges.

[33]*Between a Rock and a Hard Place: The Dilemma Facing Refused Asylum Seekers*, *The Refugee Council*, December 1, 2012, accessed November 2, 2014, www.refugeecouncil.org.uk/assets/0000/1368/Refugee Council Between_a_Rock_and_a_Hard_Place_10.12.12.pdf.

[34]Nina Perkowski, "A Normative Assessment of the Aims and Practices of the European Border Management Agency Frontex", *Working Paper Series No. 81* (Refugee Studies Centre, Oxford, 2012). See also Judith Sunderland, "Europe Failing to Tackle Boat Tragedies in Mediterranean", Human Rights Watch, 12 September 2012, accessed November 2, 2014, www.hrw.org/news/2012/09/12/europe-failing-tackle-boat-tragedies-mediterranean.

[35]For example, the European Union agreement with Libya on the interception of refugees at sea has been cited as knowingly placing refugees in peril. See Charles Heller, Lorenzo Pezzani, Itamar Mann, Violeta Moreno-Lax and Eyal Weizman, "Opinion: 'It's an Act of Murder': How Europe Outsources Suffering as Migrants Drown", *New York Times*, December 26, 2018, accessed June 1, 2019, https://www.nytimes.com/interactive/2018/12/26/opinion/europe-migrant-crisis-mediterranean-libya.html.

[36]Halberstam, *supra* note 11, p. 13.

[37]Balibar, *supra* note 27, p. 24.

[38]Frantz Fanon, *The Wretched of the Earth*, translated by C. Farrington (London: Penguin Books, 1963).

dangers of a silo-approach to sexuality rights as a form of "homonationalism"[39] in the context of refugee law.

Jasbir Puar, in Terrorist Assemblages, introduces the concept of homonationalism as the "imbrications of American exceptionalism [...] increasingly marked through or aided by certain homosexual bodies".[40] This concept has been applied outside of the context of American exceptionalism to other contexts in which states have bolstered their own particular forms of exceptionalism through the instrumentalisation of gay rights.[41] I would like to suggest that the refugee context provides fertile ground for examining this concept as it relates to the maintenance of a commitment to geographical organisation of spaces of violence and salvation. The refugee context also provides a window for viewing the appropriation of refugee stories in an effort to instrumentalise a narrative that "violence that occurs over there" as a politics of renewed and legitimated violence against countries imputed to be persecutory.

4 First Rupture: The Problem with Mapping

Both efforts to globally decriminalise same-sex sexual activity, as well as refugee law advocacy, attempt to know the subject and to locate the subject in a schema of relative violence or safety, comfort or death. This "knowing" involves a process of mapping, both in terms of a corporeal and psychological mapping of the refugee subject as well as a global geopolitical mapping of culture and society.

4.1 Anti-Queer Knowing

The structure of rights-based remedies, whether constitutional reform or refugee protection, force us as advocates to reckon with the "paradox of rights" as discussed by Wendy Brown, by which she refers to our frustration with rights-based approaches as we observe and criticise the systems of structural power in which rights are articulated and executed.[42] In describing

---

[39] Jasbir Puar, *Terrorist Assemblages. Homonationalism in Queer Times* (Durham: Duke University Press, 2007) 335. While Puar examines the concept of homonationalism in the context of the "war on terror", I apply it here to human rights strategies that place certain interests into hierarchies of importance.

[40] Ibid., p. 4.

[41] Ibid.; Spade, *supra* note 22.

[42] Wendy Brown and Janet Halley (eds.), *Left Legalism/Left Critique* (Durham: Duke University Press, 2002).

one aspect of the "paradox of rights", in relation to contemplating remedies to gender violence, Brown argues:

> Rights function to articulate a need, a condition of lack or injury, that cannot be fully redressed or transformed by rights, yet within existing political discourse can be signified in no other way. Thus rights for the systematically subordinated tend to rewrite injuries, inequalities, and impediments to freedom that are consequent to social stratification as matters of individual violations and rarely articulate the conditions producing or fomenting that violation. Yet the absence of rights in these domains leaves fully intact these same conditions.[43]

Brown describes the basic dilemma of rights for people in positions of relative disempowerment as both freeing from and constitutive of systematic gender oppression. One aspect of this is that rights, as a framework for identifying remedies, define injuries (and, by extension, allow what is beyond the scope of such definition to fall outside of the coverage of the right). Rights are also constructed in relation to a predetermined beneficiary. In her example of women's rights, Brown considers various constructions of "woman" that are produced in order to secure certain rights, but notes that relying on women's equality to men may further entrench the subordination of women by relying on a fictional subject position (women, who are granted the "rights of men") and by fragmenting women, as a group, along the lines that divide their lives in other ways, including "racial, class, sexual and gendered power".[44]

This type of rights dilemma or "paradox" also describes the situation of LGBTIQ people claiming refugee status, in Europe, for example. Protection of trans and gender non-binary applicants does not typically feature as such in the judgments on claims brought by LGB applicants, due to the differences in how they are expected to establish their membership in a particular social group (PSG), though many applicants may be affected by common modes or tactics of oppression. In order to gain asylum as an LGB claimant, one must convince a judge that one is being persecuted on the basis of her sexuality, which may mean articulating one's story in a way that conforms to the expectations of the judge, including what the judge understands by sexuality. This may express itself by way of an essentialised understanding of how a lesbian, gay man or bisexual person is "supposed" to act, speak or behave.[45]

---

[43]Ibid., p. 432.

[44]Ibid., pp. 430–431. *See also* Kimberlé Crenshaw, "Mapping the Margins: Intersectionality, Identity Politics and Violence Against Women of Color", *Stanford Law Review* 43, 6 (1991): 1241–1299.

[45]Millbank, *supra* note 3.

This essentialising produces a stereotype that erases potentially decisive differences among those from different contexts who might be applying for asylum. For example, the fact of having had sex with a person of the opposite sex or having been involved in a heterosexual relationship neither precludes being gay or lesbian (or bisexual or otherwise not exclusively heterosexual), nor does it necessarily safeguard an applicant from being perceived as gay or lesbian.[46] However, such an assumption that heteronormative gender roles and same-sex sexual desire are somehow mutually exclusive still exists among adjudicators.

The applicant's body is inspected in visceral ways in the course of mapping out sexuality. In some of the more extreme cases in Europe, "evidence" of sexual desire has been procured by way of plethysmography (an attempt to scientifically measure sexual arousal through visual stimuli and attaching electrodes to the genitals).[47] More routinely, at least in the UK until relatively recently, asylum applicants have felt pressured to prove their sexuality according to sex-act-based criteria, sometimes submitting videos and photographs into evidence to prove their identities through sex acts.[48] Some indications show that there have been positive improvements in Home Office interrogation procedures to reduce this pressure.[49] Other applicants have felt compelled to render verbal accounts of their sexual encounters or participation in same-sex relationships. One cannot help but to imagine these various forms of bodily inspection as a part of the economy of morality and sexual politics that shapes other aspects of the allocation of human rights—it is one that assigns value to a certain type of subject, a certain form of story, particular forms of evidence and a certain narrative of (the body's relation to) danger. Of course, this is not peculiar to the LGBTIQ refugee, though

[46]*See* Joseph Landau, "'Soft Immutability' and 'Imputed Gay Identity': Recent Developments in Transgender and Sexual-Orientation-Based Asylum Law", *Fordham Urban Law Journal* 32, 2 (2004).

[47]*Testing Sexual Orientation: A Scientific and Legal Analysis of Plethysmography in Asylum and Refugee Status Proceedings*, February 2011, Organisation for Refuge Asylum And Migration, accessed November 2, 2014, http://www.oraminternational.org/images/stories/PDFs/testing%20sexual%20orientation%20feb%202011%20download.pdf.

[48]Videos and photographs are used in certain asylum status determination hearings; *See* Dan Hodges, "Getting Gay Asylum Seekers to Prove Their Sexuality Is Perverse—But How Do You 'Codify' Love?", *The Telegraph,* February 27, 2013, blogs.telegraph.co.uk/news/danhodges/100204483/getting-gay-asylum-seekers-to-prove-their-sexuality-is-perverse-but-how-do-you-codify-love/. See also a US account of having to shape sexuality to fit a certain stereotypical expectation, Dan Bilefsky, "For Gays Seeking Asylum in U.S. Encounter a New Hurdle", *New York Times,* January 11, 2011, accessed March 17, 2020, www.nytimes.com/2011/01/29/nyregion/29asylum.html?pagewanted=all&_r=0. The use of photographic and video evidence was also addressed in a recent Advisory Opinion of the Court of Justice of the European Union. AG Sharpston, *supra* note 6.

[49]See *Still Falling Short*, supra note 19.

in the LGBTIQ narrative, the body and its sexual potentialities take on an undeniable centrality.

In reading the body in this way, through the mechanics of refugee rights provision, for its sexual potentiality, its relationship to a legible narrative and to an imagined space, the body is positioned not only sexually but racially, culturally and politically. The act of reading and assessing the body, aside from reconstructing a colonial scene where resources and bodies are carefully balanced in an economy of labour, fear and desire, also constructs the world and power through the lens of empire. In other words, the gaze of knowing cast upon the body is a colonial gaze, invested in policing the body as much as policing resources and geopolitical integrity.[50]

4.2 Failures of Geopolitical Logics

Global efforts to repeal various countries' national laws criminalising same-sex sexual activity are often invested in a related mapping project around human rights—one that slices the world into domains of protection and violence. "Decriminalisation" as a global co-ordination of political and legal reform efforts is also, like any other such project, a discursive one. Focus on criminal laws, then, as a central mode of social change starts down a path with a particular ideological trajectory and scope. This can be posited as a naming-and-shaming project, or as a legal tool for mapping the current state of the law in every country.[51] While maps emphasise a way of thinking about legal and political battles regarding repressive laws as fought along the borders of states, which can itself be problematic in the ways that Balibar suggests with the idea of the superborder, it is not only the graphic representation that creates the danger of retrenchment of organising violence around geopolitical borders.[52] One danger of thinking of violence as a function of state assemblage rather than in accordance with what Fanon refers to as "zones of being" and "zones of non-being"[53] is that it reproduces a public civilising discourse, one that uses states' laws as a proxy for the composite repression within the state. Of course, repressive laws have a violent effect, and one should not ignore these

[50]For an analysis of the racialised transformation of gender in the context of colonialism, which speaks to this type of corporeal scrutiny, see Steven Pierce and Anupama Rao, *Discipline and the Other Body: Correction, Corporeality, Colonialism* (Durham: Duke University Press, 2006) 11–14.

[51]See e.g., Lucas Paoli Itaborahy and Jingshu Zhu, "2013 State-Sponsored Homophobia Report" (International Lesbian, Gay, Bisexual, Trans- and Intersex Association, 2013).

[52]Balibar, *supra* note 27, p. 24.

[53]Frantz Fanon, *Black Skin, White Masks*, translated by C. L. Markmann (New York: Grove Press, 1967) 8.

laws as instruments of social repression. Also, it is useful for refugee practitioners to understand what countries will, at least partly by virtue of their laws, serve as willing recipient countries for refugees. However, one should be critical of using law as a proxy for the possibility of violence for a few reasons.

First, and very practically, focusing on the laws as a proxy for violence highlights the violence done by the State and risks trivialising other forms of violence. This is especially true in the context of the decriminalisation project. For example, violence against women is legally prohibited in South Africa, but it is nonetheless commonplace.[54] As it happened, certain refugee cases in the UK had relied on a map published by ILGA in order to either affirm or negate the likelihood that persecution was taking place in particular countries based on whether the state had criminalised same-sex sexual activity or provided protections for LGBTIQ people.[55] Although it is currently being discussed, criminalisation of same-sex sexual activity has not often been interpreted to constitute per se persecution. Conversely, a lack of criminal prohibition of gay sex does not negate the presence of persecution, not least of all because persecution can be perpetrated by non-state actors.[56] This is an important distinction, and although any refugee law practitioner should know this, it can be taken advantage of in the battle to persuade the presiding judge of the likelihood of state complicity or inability to protect. For this reason, ILGA included a section addressed to refugee practitioners in

[54]David Smith, "Teenage Lesbian Is Latest Victim of 'Corrective Rape' in South Africa", *The Guardian,* May 9, 2011, accessed March 17, 2020, www.theguardian.com/world/2011/may/09/lesbian-corrective-rape-south-africa. See also E. P. Motswapong, "Surviving Behind the Mask: Lesbians and Gays in Botswana", in *Queering Paradigms,* edited by B. Scherer (New York: Peter Lang, 2010) 350.

[55]This was reported to ILGA by a UK-based advocate who had witnessed such reliance.

[56]See S. Chelvan, "From Sodomy to Safety? The Case for Defining Persecution to Include Unenforced Criminalisation of Same-Sex Conduct" *VU University Amsterdam, Fleeing Homophobia Conference,* 5–6 September 2011; Laurynas Biekša, "The Refugee Qualification Problems in LGBT Asylum Cases", *Jurisprudence* 18, no 4 (2011): 1559. Chelvan points to Italian practice and cites the Fleeing Homophobia report that states "Criminalisation reinforces a general climate of homophobia (presumably accompanied by transphobia), which enables State agents as well as non-State agents to persecute or harm LGBTIQs with impunity. In short, criminalization makes LGBs into outlaws, at risk of persecution or serious harm at any time". He and the report cite Italy and Austria as having best practice. Italy, for example, sees the laws as persecutory per se because they prevent the realisation of a basic human right. One must go through the process of proving credibility, however, which is where the claims seem to fail. He also notes that art. 9 of the 2004 Qualification Directive provides that persecution under the Geneva Convention must be sufficiently serious by nature or repetition as to constitute a violation of Human Rights as per ECHR or be an accumulation of various measures, and can take the form of "legal, administrative, police and/or judicial measures, which are in themselves discriminatory or which are implemented in a discriminatory manner", 2004 Qualification Directive, European Council (European Community, 2004). See also Jenni Millbank, "The Right of Lesbians and Gay Men to Live Freely, Openly and on Equal Terms Is Not Bad Law: A Reply to Hathaway and Pobjoy", *International Law and Politics* 44 (2012): 496–527. Millbank notes that the UK in particular has been reluctant to view criminal laws as persecutory per se.

the forward of the most recent reports on State-Sponsored Homophobia to make this distinction clear.[57]

The second problem of using the law as a proxy for the existence of anti-gay and anti-trans violence is when this lens is used to view Europe, where various far-reaching protections exist in many countries. Here, it is not that the violence in Europe therefore goes unaddressed when it occurs, but rather that violence elsewhere is depicted on the map and in the imagination as a socio-cultural problem that others have but that Europe does not. This re-instantiates fears that fuel stereotypes about Africa and Islam. It also orients ways of being in one's sexuality in a Eurocentric way, drawing quite a flat picture of sexuality.[58] In the process of essentialising postcolonial societies, mapping along political borders can also oversimplify and misrepresent other patterns of violence, for example, regional or localised violence owing to regional instability that leads to what migration scholars refer to as internal displacement.[59]

The cartography of spaces and taxonomies of people and culture in the spirit of knowing for the purpose of disseminating rights in a moral, political and material economy is anti-queer. It reifies Eurocentric ideas of sexuality and culture and supports the saviour narrative of human rights, subtly re-inscribing borders and the legitimacy of brutal restrictions on movement. It also masks systems of power responsible for violence within and beyond the borders.

5 Second Rupture: The Problem with Human Rights

Frantz Fanon dislocates violence from geopolitics and instead describes zones of "being and non-being", which can be present anywhere and are contingent on power relations beyond state repression.[60] Fanon is explicit in his description of this zone of nonbeing as a type of hell, a space for the non-human.[61]

[57]See *ILGA 2012 State-Sponsored Homophobia Report*, May 2012, ILGA, L. Itaborahy.

[58]Rahul Rao, "On 'Gay Conditionality', Imperial Power and Queer Liberation", *Kafila*, January 1, 2012.

[59]See Patricia Tuitt, "The Territorialization of Violence", in *Critical Beings: Law, Nation, and the Global Subject*, edited by Peter Fitzpatrick and Patricia Tuitt (Farnham: Ashgate, 2004) 226.

[60]Fanon, Black Skin, White Masks, *supra* note 52, p. 8.

[61]Ibid. He notes here: "the black man is not a man". On the same page he continues, "The black is a black man; that is, as the result of a series of aberrations of affect, he is rooted at the core of a universe from which he must be extricated. The problem is important. I propose nothing short of the liberation of the man of color from himself. We shall go very slowly, for there are two camps; the white and the black". Fanon, in *Black Skin, White Masks*, looks at colonialism, and settler colonialism

Though in "Black Skin, White Masks" Fanon limits his observations to the French Antilles,[62] he makes observations about the structural continuities among colonial societies and extends those observations in "The Wretched of the Earth". In this volume, Fanon notes that the violence of colonialism is violence that continues to regulate the actions and resistance of colonized people, and he insists that this persists even after geopolitical colonialism has ended. He notes that "[t]o break up the colonial world does not mean that after the frontiers have been abolished lines of communication will be set up between the two zones". He also notes that there are some colonized elites who politically purchase their ways into positions of power between settler colonials and natives, in the case of settler colonialism in Africa.[63]

The intent focus on political power, coloniality and racism inherent in Fanon's framing of violence in "zones of being and nonbeing" provides a way to look at refugee law that goes in a different direction from the national-cultural framework typically used to assess country situations for refugees.[64] Verdirame rightly argues that refugee law is an area of immense political contestation because "implicit in any grant of asylum is a censure of the country of origin of the refugee".[65] He notes the slippage that is apparent in the process of granting asylum, from offering a "place of refuge" to advancing values that are, in the tradition of human rights, steeped in the language of "culture", and as a function of nation-state thinking, reliant on a basic geopolitics of cultural or social morality.

The latter point, along with its allusion to a more profound critique of sovereignty (not addressed in this chapter) sets the backdrop for a more careful approach to viewing oppression and repression. First, those in political power should not be seen as representative of culture in such a way that allows nation to be conflated with culture, nor culture to be conflated with violence. It is enough that culture is a word that is virtually impossible to define and depends on its context for meaning, certainly when it sits in conjunction

in particular, to trace the line between the two camps. This line may be what Balibar might describe an "enmity line". However, Fanon also applies the framework of being and non-being to other forms of slavery, epidermal schema of oppression, etc., as implicit in his term "man of color".

[62]Ibid., p. 14.

[63]Fanon, *The Wretched of the Earth*, *supra* note 38, pp. 34–35.

[64]*See* Ramon Grosfoguel, "The Epistemic Decolonial Turn", *Cultural Studies* 21, nos 2–3 (2007): 220. Grosfoguel refers not only to "classical" colonialism, but also to what he calls "colonial situation" including "the cultural, political, sexual, spiritual, epistemic and economic oppression/exploitation of subordinate racialized/ethnic groups by dominant racialized/ethnic groups with or without the existence of colonial administrations".

[65]Verdirame, *supra* note 24.

with legal logics.[66] Madhavi Sunder suggests that, in certain legal contests, "culture" is a system of power that produces content articulated by those in political power on behalf of the greater "culture". She uses various case examples from the US context to illustrate tension created within the structure of legal argument when one occupies the voice of cultural representative while being at the margins of power with respect to perceived cultural authenticity and representational legitimacy.[67] This tends to further marginalise those disenfranchised subsets of potentially already disenfranchised groups.

Balibar's "death zones" concept, as well as Fanon's "zones of being" and "non-being", help us to reorient ourselves in relation to the assumptions of spaces of safety and violence with respect to refugee law in two ways. The concepts help us to reconfigure spatial violence into violence that follows particular people and subject positions from one place to another, which in turn draws our attention to shortcomings built into the refugee law system. Secondly, the concepts launch a more fundamental critique of refugee law in general, pointing to historical contingencies that call into question the moral basis for restrictions on free movement, particularly given the fact that refugee law is only available to a select and privileged few—those with the necessary material or political resources.[68]

5.1 The Recurring Problem of "Culture"

As the state-centred apparatuses of refugee law, international human rights and domestic constitutional reform are all contingent upon a rights framework of some sort, it is important to also critically assess the role of rights-based approaches in dealing with sex-, sexuality- and gender-based violence. Until refugees are given official asylum status or other similar residency allowance, they do not have the rights of citizens and, even then, they may need to wait some years before acquiring full political rights. This negates the drawing of full rights and protections along national borders and supports Balibar's idea of the enmity line—there are people living in the same space under very different conditions. Extreme forms of violence are found within most states and are organised around relations of power, including race, gender, citizenship status, religion and other separations between the "zones of being and non-being".

66See Peter Fitzpatrick, "The Damned Word: Culture and Its (in)Compatibility with Law", *Law, Culture and the Humanities* 1, no 1 (2005): 2–13.

67Madhaver Sunder, "Cultural Dissent", *Stanford Law Review* 54 (2001): 495–567.

68See Satvinder Juss, *International Migration and Global Justice* (Hampshire: Ashgate, 2007); Balibar, *supra* note 27.

In a certain way, refugee law can be seen as bringing human rights imperialism full circle. The project of strengthening human rights standards through constitutional reform is concerned with a slightly but crucially different set of discursive practices than refugee protection. This difference compounds the paradox of rights. The logic of refugee protection is that the state is unable or unwilling to protect its citizen within its political borders, which sets into motion the narrative of saving the citizen-subject from her state of origin. This narrative locates human rights as existing within the receiving state, enabling and empowering logics of providing refuge to a defector at a cost. The refugee is often described as having escaped from a dangerous culture or condition into a better one. For many, this is the central function of refugee law,[69] regulated of course by strict political and economic interests in the receiving countries.[70,71]

The logic of global decriminalisation of same-sex sexual activity is, in general, seen as a struggle for equality on the basis of sexual orientation and gender identity. This struggle is pitched mainly as one in favour of universal human rights, with the underlying logic that rights protection in countries outside of Europe will mean fewer refugees will need to cross borders to gain protection within Europe. This logic predominates despite the relatively small number of refugees that enter Europe each year, given the global migration of refugees. However, the focus on inequality tends to take specific form and the type of equality that is prioritised is quite specific—both specific to the type of rights that should be afforded as well as the lesser prioritisation of other interests. This approach is marked by a familiar discourse within LGBTIQ activist groups, one that suggests that countries can be envisioned to exist along a continuum of rights protections for LGBTIQ people, from criminal sanctions to marriage.

[69] *Cf.* Ibid., p. 201. Juss critically assesses the narrowness of refugee law by positing that refugee law today constitutes "an attempt by the international community to reconcile two irreconcilables: humanitarian need on the one hand and sovereign state control on the other". Such critique seeks to address a need greater than the scope permitted by the mechanisms of refugee law. A politics of recognising this mismatch is the difference between Juss' critique and conventional legitimations of the scope of refugee law and policy.

[70] This includes for example persecution, which is a specific type of violence, that must be extreme, involve state action or unwillingness or inability to act, and be proven rigorously. See Matthew E Price, *Rethinking Asylum: History, Purpose, and Limits* (Cambridge: Cambridge University Press, 2009) 279.

[71] One politically contentious and often-used phrase for describing migration policy is the "opening of the floodgates". This language is meant to emphasise the sheer volume of people crossing the border into Europe, for example, drowning its citizens. This image is completed with another phrase, "swamping", which is meant to describe cultural depletion through immigration. For examples, see Sajid Qureshi, "Opening the Floodgates?: Eligibility for Asylum in the USA and the UK", *Anglo-American Law Review* 17 (1988): 83–107.

Critiques of this evolutionary continuum model, which posits LGBTIQ rights as a discrete issue by which one can assess the relative social sophistication of a given country, are numerous. One significant critique is that it is at best disingenuous and likely impossible to disentangle the politics of sexuality from other forms of oppression, and similarly impossible to distinguish between local forms of oppression from transnational and historically contingent ones. Indeed, Fanon would likely argue that racial power relations in colonial societies create zones regulated by violence, which exacerbates other forms of oppression within those zones.

The use of rights remedies for sexuality and gender identity-related discrimination and violence evokes discussion regarding the role of the international community, particularly as regards the contested role of colonialism for many countries, including members of the Commonwealth. LGBTIQ people from within different local contexts are not necessarily approaching the issues in the same ways as certain human rights advocates from outside of those contexts for various reasons. One reason may be a question of strategy. For example, in the autumn of 2011, the United States of America and the United Kingdom indicated that treatment of local gay and lesbian people would be taken into account when determining future allocation of foreign aid to Malawi. This approach was criticised by a significant number of African-based NGOs, which argued that sexual minorities would experience violent backlash in the country as a result. This type of aid-conditioning measure was also subsequently warned against in the case of Uganda, where a Ugandan based human rights organisation implored Western activists not to call for aid-conditionality.[72]

Another key difference in approach from local actors when confronted with a global agenda for a particular type of right for sexual and gender minorities is that some local movements are rooted in a different understanding of sexuality and gender norms, and actors within those movements may find it difficult to articulate the local politics of sexuality through the framework of "LGBTIQ rights" as such.[73] The types of dissent from

[72]Rao, *supra* note 58; G. Ogwaro, "Press Release: Guidelines for Supporting the Ugandan LGBTI Effort to Advocate against the Anti-Homosexuality Bill", in *Civil Society Coalition on Human Rights & Constitutional Law* (Refugee Law Project, Makerere University School of Law, 2012). See also Hakan Seckinelgin, "Same-sex Lives Between the Language of International LGBT Rights, International Aid and Anti-Homosexuality", *Global Social Policy* 2 (2018).

[73]For examples, see Stephen Murray and Will Roscoe, *Boy-Wives and Female Husbands: Studies in African Homosexualities* (New York: St. Martin's Press, 1998); Brinda Bose and Subhabrata Bhattacharyya, *The Phobic and the Erotic: The Politics of Sexualities in Contemporary India* (Calcutta and New York: Seagull Books, 2007); Sylvia Tamale, *African Sexualities: A Reader* (Oxford: Pambazuka Press, 2011); Brian Whitaker, *Unspeakable Love: Gay and Lesbian Life in the Middle East* (Berkeley: University of California Press, 2006).

within different cultural systems are differently contingent. This relates to the different local sexual and gender politics, and attempting to alter the relative position of those in a given local setting by pressing hard for universal human rights irrespective of the complex entanglement of sexuality with other issues is potentially to enact more violence upon not only sexual minorities, but all of those in the "zones of non-being".

5.2 The Spectre of Colonialism

At both academic and activist conferences on LGBTIQ refugees, country conditions are inevitably discussed, and while in the courtroom there is no space for deep discussion about local historical and political contingencies, colonialism features centrally in discussions among activists, advocates and academics outside of court. Former Justice of the High Court of Australia and member of the Commonwealth's Eminent Persons Group, Michael Kirby, views the legal criminalisation of gay sex through the historical lens of British colonial expansion.[74] He notes that the relevant section of the Indian Penal Code recently declared unconstitutional, written by Lord Thomas Macaulay, was the most copied code. Article 377 on Unnatural Offences had been copied in many British territories including Zambia, Malaysia, Singapore and Fiji.[75] Consensual same-sex sexual activity is, in these contexts, "linked and equated to the conduct of violent sexual criminal offences".[76] The Griffith Penal Code written for Queensland was used in a great deal of Australia but copied in Papua New Guinea, Nigeria, Kenya, Uganda and Tanzania, among other places.[77] As we know, similar laws exist in Botswana, Cameroon, The Gambia, Ghana, Mauritius, Jamaica and other territories.[78]

Verdirame warns us not to view western export or colonial imposition of criminal sanctions against lesbians and gay men as the sole reason that homophobia exists in colonized areas.[79] I agree with this when, as Verdirame suggests, the issue is one of blame or support for the proposition of pre-colonial societies being sexual utopias. While these laws developed in locally

[74]This figure is from the human rights organisation, Erasing 76 Crimes, which is an information and campaigning platform to repeal anti-gay laws. See *Erasing 76 Crimes website,* accessed August 30, 2019, https://76crimes.com/39-commonwealth-nations-still-have-anti-lgbti-laws/.

[75]Ibid, p. 67.

[76]Ibid.

[77]Ibid.

[78]Ibid., p. 76.

[79]Verdirame, *supra* note 24.

specific ways out of a common set of principles connected to colonial practices, to change the framing of "exportation of homophobia" to more of a synthesis of a common legal framework across over forty countries over a few centuries is surely more concrete and more accurate. Perhaps one can speak instead of the colonial transfer of particular forms or expressions of anti-queer bigotry. This suggests that one should not envision pre-colonial societies as free from sexual and gender oppression, but it acknowledges that we continue today to grapple with the mechanisms of pernicious colonial laws, and this fact tends to complicate the discussion around specific forms of oppression faced by those in colonial societies.

6 Conclusion: The Refugee Project Reconsidered

So, what does a queer and decolonial analysis have to do with refugee claims? Perhaps these lenses have less to do with individual refugee claims and more to do with rethinking refugee law generally, and with it, freedom of movement, conceptions of extreme violence and nation-state thinking. If the conventional understanding of refugee law's purpose is to help victims of persecution to escape violence in one state by admitting them into another state, albeit through a very rigorous set of bureaucratic barriers and a potentially treacherous journey to new shores, we need to seriously consider in what ways this conception of violence artificially circumscribes, prioritises and describes certain notions of extreme violence (that which is construed as persecution) and not others.

The enactors of the two strategies, increased protection of LGBTIQ refugees and decriminalisation via domestic legal reform, are involved in a common discussion and, many times, are the same people. This means that a core group of advocates has two sets of strategies in mind at the same time. Such duality is nothing new to advocates and theorists who both see the limits of rights-based approaches while understanding the traction that rights can have in the context of larger social movements.[80] As advocates for refugee protection, we should be wary of the argument that the proliferation of universal human rights (e.g., sexuality-based rights as a global discourse) can or should have the "positive benefit" of curtailing refugee migration

[80]For more on this dilemma, see Wendy Brown, "Suffering the Paradoxes of Rights", in Brown and Halley, *supra* note 41. See also Dean Spade, "Their Laws Will Never Make Us Safer: An Introduction", in *Against Equality: Prisons Will Not Protect You*, edited by Ryan Conrad (Oakland: AK Press, 2012).

into Europe. This argument demonises immigration generally, and once this sentiment is mobilised as fear, the foreseeable result is an increase of repressive measures limiting immigration, including administrative and economic measures that make migrating to Europe more difficult, not to mention the process of acquiring refugee status. In the UK in recent years, the Hostile Environment Policy and the Brexit Referendum have demonstrated the reactionary link between fostering negative images of refugees with promoting more restrictive migration policies.[81] This may also mean that we, as advocates, need to resist the rhetoric of the "bogus applicant" and the heightened scrutiny around credibility by painting a realistic picture of conditions in the countries of origin. Unmitigated by a strong sense of free movement and a much broader concept of the conditions of extreme violence (not merely violence that legally qualifies as persecutory) and its multiple contingencies, we may remain stuck in the quagmire of reifying geopolitically dependent understandings of extreme violence and thinking of zones of danger along predominantly national or cultural lines.

We must also note that the reification of states as containers for violence and corresponding rights allows a bio-geo-political worldview to be instrumentalised to the misfortune of those groups who are disenfranchised or who do not inhabit positions of power within states. The concept of homonationalism in the context of refugee law makes a straightforward and crucial intervention in this regard. In a nutshell, focus on LGBTIQ violence as a cultural or geopolitical condition mutes the violence of colonialism and the "zones of being and nonbeing" that Fanon asserts organise violence in the world, and renders invisible the "superborders" or "enmity lines" that separate those who experience extreme violence from those who do not. This reinforces both perceptions of profound "cultural" difference between what is colloquially termed "the West" and "the Rest", without consideration of the richness of historical contingency and the extreme forms of violence that persist as a result. Conversely, heralding LGBTIQ rights as the pinnacle of social sophistication, as seen through the lens of human rights, may privilege certain forms of violence over others—Western homophobia over non-Western homophobia, sexual violence over racial violence, sexual liberation struggles at any cost "over there" over fighting racial, gender-based and status-based oppression "right here" in Europe. Puar's interpretation of

[81]This is most clearly evidenced by the 2012 Hostile Environment Policy (subsequently renamed the Compliant Environment Policy), which seeks to make life in the UK administratively difficult for those without proper paperwork, but in effect, it makes it difficult to migrate to the UK in general and fosters the racialized surveillance of certain groups. See e.g., UN General Assembly, *Report of the Special Rapporteur on contemporary forms of racism, racial discrimination, xenophobia and related intolerance*, 41st Session, 24 June–12 July 2019.

sexuality being taken up to reinforce American national exceptionalism fits well with Balibar's understanding of European citizenship as an exceptional and profoundly violent institution that serves to bolster European cultural and political privilege.

Moving forward from the reflections advanced here, we might ask in what format and amidst what constellation of praxis a queering of refugee law might be most transformative. Will thinking through a lens of radical disavowal of disciplinary rules help academics and legal practitioners reconfigure the sexual subject of migration law, and perhaps with it the legal subject in general? From within what matrix of race, migration, colonial subjectivity, sexuality, sex, religion or other situated identity might we envision a form of regulation beyond refugee law, which would do less violence upon the subject of the law while ensuring material safety? Is it possible to adhere to the spirit of the Geneva Convention without a critical focus on power, coloniality and the violence done to refugees in the receiving state?

Given the interventions discussed, the first question that occurs is—where does this leave activists doing this work? This question is both a general question of how to do the work as well as a literal question of place—where might such work be done?

One example of a variety of coalition politics and trans-political activism is the activism of the "Stansted 15". In March 2017, a group of fifteen human rights activists prevented the deportation of sixty people to West Africa by chaining themselves to the plane.[82] Some of the activists are from the group Lesbians and Gays support the Migrants, a collective with the mission of fighting against racism and anti-migrant policies as queer (LGBTIQA +) people.[83] The fifteen activists successfully prevented the deportation of the plane, which they argued was important, given the Home Office's "deport now, appeal later" approach, coupled with the real danger that many people face when forcibly removed to countries from which they fled.[84] The activists were subsequently found guilty under terrorism laws involving "endangering safety at an aerodrome"—laws drafted largely to respond to the Lockerbie

[82]Beth Perkin and Charlotte England, "Stansted 15: Activists Who Stopped Deportation Charter Flight Convicted Of Terrorism Charge," *Novara Media*, December 10, 2018, accessed July 29, 2019, https://novaramedia.com/2018/12/10/stansted-15-activists-who-stopped-deportation-charter-flight-convicted-of-terrorism-charge/.

[83]Lesbian and Gays Support the Migrants, accessed February 4, 2019 https://lgsmigrantsbristol.wordpress.com/about-us/. According to the collective's website, although the name of the organisation, "lesbians and gays", has not been changed since the 1980s, the group "is inclusive of all sexualities and gender identities."

[84]George Steer, "The UK's Prosecution of Peaceful Protesters Is Raising Fears About Anti-Terror Laws," *Time Magazine*, February 8, 2019, accessed July 29, 2019, https://time.com/5506750/stansted-15-britain-protest-court-immigration/.

Bombing of 1988. This seems to be a dubious overreach applied to this form of protest—particularly as the plane was not even moving when the activists chained themselves to it.[85] The importance of understanding anti-racist and migrant rights struggles as central to the political activism that we engage in as queer activists is that it demonstrates quite a different model of engagement queer politics than a mainstream LGBT + rights approach might suggest.

One needs to challenge the basic assumptions upon which human rights are articulated, including our understanding of where violence is located and what constitutes violence, including epistemological violence. Accordingly, one needs to examine the nature of certain rights-based solutions to violence. Using refugee law as an example, we need to ask what violence refugee law is meant to preclude, whether refugee law works, at what cost, and whether it should be radically rethought over the long term.

If we rely on human rights protections and the current refugee law regime, we could choose to do so in a way that, at the very least, acknowledges the death zones that Balibar refers to in describing violence against non-European citizens in Europe. This could potentially be done by granting full citizenship protections to those who are in the process of applying for refugee status. While this is a cosmetic fix, it does some work towards alleviating some of the state violence committed against refugees once they have landed in Europe. For example, having the right to work, full freedom of movement within the receiving state, and easy access to basic legal and medical services would be important to any person potentially fleeing persecution.

In the case of LGBTIQ people, very careful treatment of the credibility assessment around the applicant's narrative of sexuality is essential and critical thinking about not only sexuality, but intersectional identity, global geopolitical power relations and the history of colonialism should be considered. While taking one at her word may not be the most politically viable suggestion for a test of credibility, one must certainly avoid the types of exclusionary practices that some LGBTIQ people have reported encountering, from intimidating or insensitive border guards, the lack of privacy when stating their reasons for seeking asylum, and judges who are incredulous of their claims because they either have children or had been in heterosexual relationships. That said, taking claimants' stories at their word would perhaps be considered more transformative, perhaps even queer, in refusing to re-inscribe systems of power that stagnate other forms of systemic violence and colonial relations.

---

[85] The activists were, however, spared jail time, being given suspended sentences and community service orders.

When "the right to live freely and openly" relies on an outwardly subjective assessment of an applicant's credibility, is there not an obligation on the part of recipient states to be profoundly deferential to the stories of those claiming persecution? In the case of LGBTIQ people, could this suggest that states should consider not requiring corroborating evidence for the establishment of gay or trans identity? Or, from a different angle, does the British role in disseminating criminal laws in any way help to tip the balance in favour of viewing these laws as persecutory per se?[86] From within the comfort zone of legal rules and the traditional development of policy implementing those rules, it would be impossible and perhaps taboo to acknowledge the link on an individual basis. But should there nonetheless be a general policy of viewing these leftover laws as persecutory, given the recent history of empire and the continued existence of the Commonwealth? Could queering refugee law be one way to help us rethink migration or, at least, help externalize the costs of colonialism?

References

Balibar, Etienne. "Outlines of a Topography of Cruelty: Citizenship and Civility in the Era of Global Violence", 8:1 *Constellations* (2001).

Biekša, Laurynas. "The Refugee Qualification Problems in LGBT Asylum Cases", 18:4 *Jurisprudence* (2011).

Bilefsky, Dan. "For Gays Seeking Asylum in U.S. Encounter a New Hurdle", *New York Times*, 11 January 2011. www.nytimes.com/2011/01/29/nyregion/29asylum.html?pagewanted=all&_r=0.

Bose, Brinda, and Subhabrata Bhattacharyya. *The Phobic and the Erotic: The Politics of Sexualities in Contemporary India* (Calcutta and New York: Seagull Books, 2007).

Brown, Wendy and Janet Halley (eds.). *Left Legalism/Left Critique* (Durham: Duke University Press, 2002).

Crenshaw, Kimberle. "Mapping the Margins: Intersectionality, Identity Politics and Violence against Women of Color", 43:6 *Stanford Law Review* (1991).

Dolidze, Anna. "Lampeduza and Beyond: Recognition, Implementation and Justiciability of Stateless Persons' Rights Under International Law", 6 *Interdisciplinary Journal of Human Rights Law* (2011–2012).

El-Enany, Nadine. "On Pragmatism and Legal Idolatry: 'Fortress Europe' and the Desertion of the Refugee", 22:1 *International Journal of Minority and Group Rights* (2015).

[86]For a discussion of the prospects of recognising per se persecution on the level of the European Union, see S. Chelvan, *supra* note 56.

Fallon, Amy, and Owen Bowcott. "Uganda Politicians Celebrate Passing of Anti-Gay Laws", *The Guardian*, 24 February 2014. www.theguardian.com/world/2014/feb/24/uganda-president-signs-anti-gay-laws.

Fanon, Frantz. The *Wretched of the Earth*, translated by C. Farrington (London: Penguin Books, 1963).

Fanon, Frantz. *Black Skin, White Masks*, translated by C. L. Markmann (New York: Grove Press, 1967).

Fitzpatrick, Peter, "The Damned Word: Culture and Its (In)Compatibility with Law", 1:1 *Law, Culture and the Humanities* (2005).

Grosfoguel, Ramon. "The Epistemic Decolonial Turn", 21:2–3 *Cultural Studies* (2007).

Halberstam, Jack. *Female Masculinity* (Durham: Duke University Press, 1998).

Hathaway, James and Jason Pobjoy. "Queer Cases Make Bad Law", 44:2 *New York University Journal of International Law and Politics* (2012).

Heller, Charles et. al. "Opinion: 'It's an Act of Murder': How Europe Outsources Suffering as Migrants Drown", *New York Times*, 26 December 2018. https://www.nytimes.com/interactive/2018/12/26/opinion/europe-migrant-crisis-mediterranean-libya.html.

Hodges, Dan. "Getting Gay Asylum Seekers to Prove Their Sexuality Is Perverse—But How Do You 'Codify' Love?", *The Telegraph*, 27 February 2013. blogs.telegraph.co.uk/news/danhodges/100204483/getting-gay-asylum-seekers-to-prove-their-sexuality-is-perverse-but-how-do-you-codify-love/.

Juss, Satvinder. *International Migration and Global Justice* (Hampshire: Ashgate, 2007).

Landau, Joseph. "'Soft Immutability' and 'Imputed Gay Identity': Recent Developments in Transgender and Sexual-Orientation-Based Asylum Law", 32:2 *Fordham Urban Law Journal* (2004).

Millbank, Jenni. "'The Ring of Truth': A Case Study of Credibility Assessment in Particular Social Group Refugee Determinations", 21:1 *International Journal of Refugee Law* (2009).

Millbank, Jenni. "The Right of Lesbians and Gay Men to Live Freely, Openly and on Equal Terms Is Not Bad Law: A Reply to Hathaway and Pobjoy", 44 *International Law and Politics* (2012).

Motswapong, E. P. "Surviving Behind the Mask: Lesbians and Gays in Botswana", in B. Scherer, *Queering Paradigms* (New York: Peter Lang, 2010).

Murray, Stephen and Will Roscoe. *Boy-Wives and Female Husbands: Studies in African Homosexualities* (New York: St. Martin's Press, 1998).

Ogwaro, G. "Press Release: Guidelines for Supporting the Ugandan LGBTI Effort to Advocate Against the Anti-Homosexuality Bill", in *Civil Society Coalition on Human Rights & Constitutional Law* (Refugee Law Project, Makerere University School of Law, 2012).

Perkin, Beth, and Charlotte England. "Stansted 15: Activists Who Stopped Deportation Charter Flight Convicted Of Terrorism Charge," *Novara Media*,

10 December 2018. https://novaramedia.com/2018/12/10/stansted-15-activists-who-stopped-deportation-charter-flight-convicted-of-terrorism-charge/.

Perkowski, Nina. "A Normative Assessment of the Aims and Practices of the European Border Management Agency Frontex", Working Paper Series No. 81 (Refugee Studies Centre, Oxford, 2012).

Pierce, Steven, and Anupama Rao. *Discipline and the Other Body: Correction, Corporeality, Colonialism* (Durham: Duke University Press, 2006).

Price, Matthew E. *Rethinking Asylum: History, Purpose, and Limits* (Cambridge: Cambridge University Press, 2009).

Puar, Jasbir. *Terrorist Assemblages. Homonationalism in Queer Times* (Durham: Duke University Press, 2007).

Qureshi, Sajid. "Opening the Floodgates?: Eligibility for Asylum in the USA and the UK", 17 *Anglo-American Law Review* (1988).

Rao, Rahul. "On 'Gay Conditionality', Imperial Power and Queer Liberation", *Kafila*, 1 January 2012. www.kafila.org/2012/01/01/on-gay-conditionality-imperial-power-and-queer-liberation-rahul-rao/.

Redding, Jeffrey. "Dignity, Legal Pluralism and Same-Sex Marriage", 75:3 *Brooklyn Law Review* (2010).

Schlamp, Hans Jurgen. "Europe's Failure: Bad Policies Caused the Lampedusa Tragedy", *Der Spiegel Online*, 4 October 2013. www.spiegel.de/international/europe/lampedusa-tragedy-is-proof-of-failed-european-refugee-policy-a-926081.html.

Seckinelgin, Hakan. "Same-Sex Lives Between the Language of International LGBT Rights, International Aid and Anti-Homosexuality", 2 *Global Social Policy* (2018).

Smith, David. "Teenage Lesbian Is Latest Victim of 'Corrective Rape' in South Africa", *The Guardian*, 9 May 2011. www.theguardian.com/world/2011/may/09/lesbian-corrective-rape-south-africa.

Spade, Dean. "Their Laws Will Never Make Us Safer: An Introduction", in Ryan Conrad (ed.), *Against Equality: Prisons Will Not Protect You* (Oakland: AK Press, 2012).

Spade, Dean. "Under the Cover of Gay Rights", 37 *New York University Review of Law and Social Change* (2013).

Steer, George. "The UK's Prosecution of Peaceful Protesters Is Raising Fears About Anti-Terror Laws", *Time Magazine*, 8 February 2019. https://time.com/5506750/stansted-15-britain-protest-court-immigration/.

Sunder, Madhaver. "Cultural Dissent", 54 *Stanford Law Review* (2001).

Sunderland, Judith, "Europe Failing to Tackle Boat Tragedies in Mediterranean", *Human Rights Watch*, 12 September 2012. www.hrw.org/news/2012/09/12/europe-failing-tackle-boat-tragedies-mediterranean.

Taylor, Matthew, and Robert Booth. "Jimmy Mubenga Death: G4s Guards Will Not Face Charges", *The Guardian*, 17 July 2012. www.theguardian.com/uk/2012/jul/17/jimmy-mubenga-guards-no-charges.

Tuitt, Patricia. "The Territorialization of Violence", in Peter Fitzpatrick and Patricia Tuitt (eds.), *Critical Beings: Law, Nation, and the Global Subject* (Farnham: Ashgate, 2004).

UKLGIG. *Still Falling Short: The Standard of Home Office Decision-Making in Asylum Claims Based on Sexual Orientation and Gender Identity*, 2018. Available online at https://uklgig.org.uk/wp-content/uploads/2018/07/Still-Falling-Short.pdf.

Verdirame, Guglielmo. "A Friendly Act of Socio-Cultural Contestation: Asylum and the Big Cultural Divide", 44 *International Law and Politics* (2012).

Whitaker, Brian. *Unspeakable Love: Gay and Lesbian Life in the Middle East* (Berkeley: University of California Press, 2006).

The DSSH Model and the Voice of the Silenced: Aderonke Apata—The Queer Refugee: "I Am a Lesbian"

S. Chelvan

1 Introduction

This chapter addresses the experiences of the Queer Refugee—a "person seeking asylum"[1] due to their non-heteronormative sexual conduct—within the United Kingdom's immigration system. Drawing upon the high-profile case study of Aderonke Apata, a Nigerian-born queer woman, who spent 13 years navigating the UK's asylum processes, the chapter reveals the myriad, significant ways in which refugee frameworks in this country have been (and, in many ways, continue to be) incapable of understanding non-heterosexual and non-cisgender experiences of sexual orientation and gender identity. Drawing upon the author's extensive practice and academic research in the

[1] See also "We Are Human—Manchester Declaration—We Are Human (June 21, 2017)," African Rainbow Family: LGBTI Equality, Last modified April 23, 2018, accessed March 21, 2020, https://africanrainbowfamily.org/2018/04/23/we-are-human-manchester-declaration/.

Ethics approval granted by King's College London in November 2017 as part of PhD in Law. There is no anonymity order in place.
Apata, Statement in support of fresh asylum and human rights claim, August 1, 2016 [1] ('08/16 FCS').

S. Chelvan (✉)
33 Bedford Row Chambers, London, UK
e-mail: s.chelvan@33bedfordrow.co.uk

S. Raj and P. Dunne (eds.), *The Queer Outside in Law*, Palgrave Socio-Legal Studies,
https://doi.org/10.1007/978-3-030-48830-7_4

field, the chapter advocates a new departure, which moves beyond stereotypes and assumptions. Rather, the UK asylum system must centre the voice and lived reality of the Queer Refugee, creating space to acknowledge and process difference, stigma, shame and harm. It was only by showing greater openness to the complexity of personal history—a trait shared by many queer individuals—that the UK immigration structures finally understood and validated the claims of Aderonke Apata. This chapter explores what can be learned from the Apata case study and, while accepting the de facto reality of national borders and immigration rules, asks what reforms can be implemented to achieve a more responsive, queer asylum framework.

There are currently two major obstacles to obtaining a positive status determination in relation to sexual orientation in the UK: flawed credibility assessments and the residue of so-called "discretion" tests, both parasitic factors following the landmark UK Supreme Court judgment in 2010, *HJ (Iran) and HT (Cameroon) v Secretary of State for the Home Department*[2] (*HJ(Iran)*). Since *HJ (Iran)*, it has not been possible for asylum decision-makers in this jurisdiction to issue an adverse ruling solely because, if returned to a country of origin, a gay, lesbian or bisexual (LGB) individual might be able to hide their sexual orientation in circumstances where, if open, that person would have a well-founded fear of persecution.[3]

In the wake of *HJ (Iran)*, the Home Office did start to improve first-instance decision-making and, for a time at least, appeared committed to implementing the Supreme Court's guidance on sexual orientation claims.[4] However, this new approach turned out to be merely temporary; it was soon replaced with a wave of refusal decisions, which focussed on the first limb of *HJ (Iran)*[5]: the need to establish that an individual is gay or will be perceived to be gay on return. This mirrored the stance of the Australian authorities following their High Court judgment addressing discretion in 2003 in *Appellant S395*[6]—summarised by Millbank as moving "from discretion

[2] *HJ (Iran) and HT (Cameroon) v Secretary of State for the Home Department* [2010] UKSC 31.

[3] Laura Milliken Gray, *Failing the Grade* (London: UK Lesbian and Gay Immigration Group, 2010), accessed March 27, 2020, https://uklgig.org.uk/wp-content/uploads/2014/04/Failing-the-Grade.pdf. 98–99% of the 50 LGB asylum decisions analysed.

[4] UK Lesbian and Gay Immigration Group, *Missing the Mark: Decision Making on Lesbian Gay (Bisexual, Trans and Intersex) Asylum Claims* (London: UK Lesbian and Gay Immigration Group, September 2013), 4 and 6, accessed March 27, 2020, https://uklgig.org.uk/wp-content/uploads/2014/02/Missing-the-Mark.pdf.

[5] *HJ (Iran)* (n 4), [82] 596, 647E–F (Lord Rodger).

[6] *Appellant S395/2002 and anor v Minister for Immigration and Multicultural Affairs; Appellant S* [2004] INLR 233.

to disbelief."[7] The inability of the Home Office and applicants in understanding "How to prove gay?" led to negative asylum decisions based solely on credibility grounds.[8] It has entrenched a culture of disbelief, which drives applicants to extreme lengths to "prove their sexual orientation or gender identity to the satisfaction of the Home Office and immigration judges."[9]

There currently exists a gap in the academic literature, where there are ad hoc pieces on asylum claims based on sexual orientation and/or sexual identity based on the dominant mood of celebration of human rights saving refugee law. But these assertions are abstract, providing no appreciation of how these claims manifest and how these principles play out through litigation. As a Barrister, I have applied my experiences to identify, firstly, what the answer should be, and then to "write the formula" to be able to litigate on behalf of LGB people seeking asylum in the UK.[10] This pathway has led to a unique insight into the evolution of the corresponding law, policy and practice over the past two decades. In this chapter, I draw upon legal source material from litigation in the Apata case, not usually in the possession of the academic commentator, in order to analyse, critique and support both the legal and academic propositions relating to the Queer Refugee.[11]

2 The DSSH Model

When she, he or they[12] arrive in the UK, the Queer Refugee is faced with various government and judicial officials, ranging from not only the Immigration Officer, the Home Office interviewing officer, or the Immigration Judge, but also new found friends, lovers, or fellow detainees and (if able to access

[7]Jenni Millbank, "From Discretion to Disbelief: Recent Trends in Refugee Determination on the Basis of Sexual Orientation in Australia and the United Kingdom," *The International Journal of Human Rights* 13, no. 2 (2009): 391.

[8] *UKLGIG* (2013) (n 6).

[9]Calogero Giametta, *The Sexual Politics of Asylum* (Abingdon: Routledge, 2017), 84.

[10]See for example, S. Chelvan, "Put Your Hands Up If You Feel Love," *Journal of Immigration, Asylum and Nationality Law* 25, no. 1 (2011): 55; Mark Harper and others, *Same Sex Marriage and Civil Partnerships: The New Law* (Jordans, 2014).

[11] *R (Aderonke Adejumoke Apata) v Secretary of State of the Home Department* [2016] EWCA Civ. 802. I obtained, in November 2017, ethics approval from the Ethics Committee at King's College London for use of this material. In the case of other material including e-mails, they have been part of open correspondence, or found in the public domain and/or are not subject to legal privilege.

[12]Reference to those who self-identify as gender-fluid or non-binary with respect to gender identity, or expression.

one) a lawyer, who additionally requires them to "Prove Gay"—in circumstances where they overwhelmingly have spent their past lives hiding in the temporary refuge of the shadows.

This chapter provides one possible route to positively determining sexual identity refugee claims—the "Difference, Stigma, Shame and Harm (DSSH) Model"[13] as a positive, and not (negatively) determinative tool, to establish sexual orientation in a humane manner, with the voice of the person seeking asylum being the only non-corroborated source necessary to "prove" actual or imputed identity. This model seeks to address the gap in decision-making on claims based on sexual identity, making clear if the model does not apply, then the DSSH model is not to be used as a determinative model to refuse a claim for asylum.

The DSSH Model was endorsed by the United Nations High Commission for Refugees (UNHCR) in 2012,[14] and since 2015, the UK's Home Office[15] joined other national authorities and NGOs in applying the model to interviews and decision-making relating to protection claims relating to sexual or gender identity and expression. The model provides trigger questions, rather than a questionnaire, to prompt the investigation of the narrative of a person seeking asylum, using the broad categories and subcategories within them of "Difference" (identifying both subjectively and objectively), "Stigma" (recognition of the negative external recognition of difference by those agents surrounding the individual [family, neighbours, society]), "Shame" (the impact of stigma on the individual) and "Harm" (fear of harm to be directed to the individual due to this difference) to establish a liner narrative to the protection claim.

The DSSH Model is not based on "the presence or absence of certain stereotypical behaviours or appearance" to conclude, or disprove, a claim,[16]

---

[13] S. Chelvan and Gábor Gyualai, "Chapter XI: Asylum Claims Based on Sexual Orientation or Gender Identity," in *Credibility Assessment in Asylum Procedures: A Multidisciplinary Training Manual Volume 2*, edited by Gábor Gyulai (Budapest: Hungarian Helsinki Committee, 2015), 59–91. See also S. Chelvan. 'Migrant Law Clinic: Episode Two: LGBT+ Asylum: The Emotional Journey and the DSSH Model.' No5 Barristers' Chambers, broadcast September 15, 2020. Accessed 25 September 2020, http://www.youtube.com/watch?y=R5lhliw1djg&t=931s.

[14] United Nations High Commissioner for Refugees, *International Protection Guidelines No. 9 Claims to Refugee Status Based on Sexual Orientation and/or Gender Identity Within the Context of Article 1A (2) of the 1951 Refugee Convention and 1967 Protocol* (Geneva, UNHCR, October 23, 2012), 15 [62].

[15] UK Home Office, *The Home Office Response to the Independent Chief Inspector's Report: 'An Investigation into the Home Office's Handling of Asylum Claims Made on the Grounds of Sexual Orientation' March–June 2014* (London: Home Office, 23 October 2014), accessed March 27, 2020, https://assets.publishing.service.gov.uk/government/uploads/system/uploads/attachment_data/file/365654/ResponseAsylumClaimsBasisSexualOrientation.pdf.

[16] UNHCR, *Beyond Proof: Credibility Assessment in EU Asylum Systems* (Geneva: UNHCR, May 2013), 71–72, 71, accessed March 27, 2020, http://www.unhcr.org/51a8a08a9.pdf.

but is designed to address broad themes in order for the applicant to "tell their narrative in a full and respective way, and make the credibility assessments as they would for any other evidence."[17] The model is based on an emotional journey of the Queer Refugee, who is here in the UK claiming asylum, due to the essential human emotion—"fear"—in this case "fear of persecution." By this linear exploration of these four broad categories, the decision-maker, and more importantly the Queer Refugee, is able to hang the individual emotional journey leading to the refugee claim. Decision-makers who reject the presence of emotional journeys are those who ignore the basic building blocks of what it means to be human—to experience emotions through life. The DSSH Model acts as a prism in order to be recognised as a refugee, by moving away from external stereotypes and providing a suggested narrative framework to better reflect those who are "different," thereby ending discretion analysis, by going through imputation of sexual identity (by being "not straight-enough") and getting back to the original wording of the Refugee Convention and the reason for claiming asylum, one of difference and not sameness.

This chapter proposes an approach within the context of the law in order for the "narrative" to be spoken. The published academic commentaries do not focus on the role of the legal representative *prior* to when a claim for asylum has been made with the Home Office, or the appeal is litigated in the arena of the courtroom,[18] in order to overcome the institutional barriers to gain refugee status in the UK. This "safe space" must be created by the lawyer, who may have only met an individual for the first time to draft a statement in support of the claim for asylum. This space, a room, must be an environment where the person seeking asylum is not disturbed, is informed they will not be at risk from the lawyer who is assisting them in drafting their statement, or be interrupted by the authorities who would seek to remove them from this space in order to detain them prior to removal or deportation. The creation of the space may involve the following example, which I use in my own practice, having already completed basic introductions[19]: "No-one is going to harm you, or detain you, or take you away from this place and send you back. You are in a safe space. It is your turn to speak, and my turn to listen." The response to this simple declaration is almost immediate, the

[17]Nicole LaViolette, e-mail message to author, June 11, 2012.

[18]For a detailed critique of the processes before the UK tribunals, see John R. Campbell in *Bureaucracy, Law & Dystopia in the UK Asylum System*, edited by Satvinder S. Juss (London: Routledge, 2017). Campbell in Chapters 3 and 4 of his book addresses case preparation (bar detailed analysis of statement preparation) and in Chapter 5, the work of Immigration Judges. Campbell does not address claims based on sexual identity within the *HJ (Iran)* framework.

[19]Example drawn from author's practice since 2001 (emphasis stressed when saying these words).

audible sigh, or the non-verbal signals including visible relaxation seen by the lowering of the shoulders and sitting into the chair.

If a language interpreter is required, then there must have been established a relationship of professional trust between the lawyer and the interpreter, to ensure there is no transference of negative cultural, religious or social norms through verbal and non-verbal signals, thereby limiting full disclosure. The interpreter must be from the chosen gender of the person seeking asylum and should not be from the same country of origin, in case there is a fear of disclosure, or risk to family members. In adopting this model, this will involve a substantial period of time in drafting and preparing the protection claim, in some cases, up to three months.[20]

The person seeking asylum, if they have not applied at port, would in any event be burdened with a statutory adverse credibility finding for "failure by the claimant to take advantage of a reasonable opportunity to make an asylum claim or human rights claim."[21] Little weight is attached to an adverse finding connected to delay, as credibility is to be assessed "in the round."[22]

On this basis, it is highly advisable that the Queer Refugee does not claim asylum until the statement has been fully prepared, as the individual not only needs the physical space, but additionally the temporal space, in order to collect their thoughts, process their emotions and draft "their story." This will involve numerous client conferences where the story is told in waves of disclosure, both exhibiting pain and joy, following the establishment of a relationship of trust with the lawyer. The central evidence, where the model has so far been applied, is that there is very likely to be a detailed statement, in the tens of pages, rather than the few pages common in pre-asylum interview submissions, constrained only by time and funding constraints.[23]

The existing academic analysis has been centrally (with respect to the conveyance of the person seeking asylum of their "story") within the theatre

[20]Tim Heap, "Attitude Pride Awards: The Human Rights Lawyer Defending LGBT Asylum Seekers From Deportation," *Attitude magazine*, July 7, 2018, accessed August 18, 2018, https://www.attitude.co.uk/article/attitude-pride-awards-the-human-rights-lawyer-defending-lgbt-asylum-seekers-from-deportation/18411/. Danila Stepin's story, "He was introduced by a friend to Chelvan, who then spent three months putting together a case to secure his asylum claim."

[21]Section 8 of the Asylum and Immigration (Treatment of Claimants, etc.) Act 2004.

[22]*JT (Cameroon) v Secretary of State for the Home Department* [2008] EWCA Civ. 878, [2009] 1 WLR 1411.

[23]Public funding is available for those seeking asylum as long as they meet the funding and merits tests. Nevertheless, this funding is extremely limited, and the number of legal aid lawyers is limited. This approach relies on the good will of legal aid lawyers to work for no pay in order to fully prepare an application and/or appeal. Contrary to what is recorded by Campbell (2017), lawyers do work over and above the constraints of legal aid (Controlled Legal Representation) and will meet appellants prior to the day of the hearing in order to address matters arising in the appeal, thereby avoiding meeting for the first time on the day of the hearing. See *Campbell* (2017) (n 20), Chapters 3 and 4.

of a court room, with various players ascribed roles and deficiencies, with the interplay between law and emotions.[24] What comes to the forefront is the inability of the litigant to be able to speak, and the creation of a "closet" based on the "unspeakability"[25] of the subject matter, which silences the refugee from disclosure thereby disengages them in such a way as to establish the platform for adverse credibility and the rejection of the claim. The need to be found credible by the administrative or judicial decision-maker limits the scope of establishing the "ring of truth" does not invade this space, as this arena is not a judicial one, but a space which provides temporal refuge from the outside world, in order to tell their story. This provides a platform for the Queer Refugee, a category encompassing all non-straight people seeking asylum, rather than the "non-normative" refugee who "chooses" to fit into a Western narrative.[26]

The rest of the chapter evidences how the use of the DSSH model to "prove gay" for some applicants works, by situating the "queerness" of the person seeking asylum in UK law and discussing the case of Aderonke Apata.

3 The Queer Refugee (Queer Outside Law) and the Queer Refugee (Queer Inside Law)

The term "Queer Refugee" is used here to encompass all non-straight (heterosexual), self-identifying, and identified people seeking asylum, as a single unit of legal personality to catch all non-straight, non-gender conforming claims for international surrogate protection made pursuant to the Refugee Convention[27] and corresponding domestic guidance (both statute and case law). Where references are to positive status and identity, the direction this chapter seeks to travel, then capital letters are applied within the text ("Queer Refugee") i.e. the Queer Inside Law. Where this same category of

---

[24]Senthorun Raj, "A/Effective Adjudications: Queer Refugees and the Law," *Journal of Intercultural Studies* 38, no. 4 (2017): 453.

[25]Toni A.M. Johnson, "On Silence, Sexuality and Skeletons: Reconceptualizing Narrative in Asylum Hearings," *Social & Legal Studies* 20 (2011): 57, 66–69.

[26]Jordan Keene and Aydan Greatrick, *Improving Service Provision for Non-Normative Refugees and Asylum Seekers in the UK: Recommendations for Policy and Practice* (London: Centre for Transnational Development and Collaboration, November 2017), accessed August 19, 2018, http://ctdc.org/wp-content/uploads/2017/11/LGBT-Asylum-Seekers-Policy-Brief.pdf, (6)2 "[a]ny individual whose sexual practice or gender performance challenges or subverts social norms ... [who] may not be able to or want to identify with identity categories such as LGBT." See also Aydan Greatrick, *Queer (Im)mobilities and the 'Refugee Crisis': Examining Stakeholder Responses to Sexual Minority Refugees in Turkey* (UCL Migration Research Unit Working Papers No. 2017/1, London, 2017).

[27]*The 1951 Refugee Convention and 1967 Protocol.*

people seeking asylum is a reference to negative status category, for example, proscribed as a result of law (arising from discretion) or other negative usage, capitals are deliberately not used ("queer refugee")—i.e. the Queer Outside Law.

Both the queer refugee and the Queer Refugee fears persecution; this includes prosecution, "curative" rape, or murder, due to their inability to successfully "prove" they are "straight enough" to the potential persecutor, due to their non-conformity, their "difference." This difference is both perceived and/or actual, noting the risk of persecution emanates from the potential persecutor's perception of difference, thereby identifying the individual to be subjected to persecution. It aims to provide a direct challenge to the current legal understanding on asylum claims based on (sexual or gender) identity and/or expression in the UK, who face a demand to label themselves "within" the current contemporary categories of lesbian, gay, bisexual, trans, intersex, questioning, etc.—LGBTIQ+ by the aforementioned actors—"the system." Where the additionally largely Global North terms include the individual sub-categories of LGBT+, sexual orientation, sexual identity, they also include the words of discrimination, hate and violence—including "homosexual," "sodomite," "battyman" and are words used where cited in the original source material. These words of hate and harm provide the historical, social and/or legal context to understand the queer refugee.

This chapter uses the history of one person seeking-asylum, Aderonke Adejumoke Apata ("Apata"), as an example of how the DSSH model was successfully used to enable a positive grant of asylum, following a thirteen-year journey to seek sanctuary in the UK.[28] As her lead Counsel from April 2015 until her positive grant of asylum on 1 August 2017, I have access to source material, not usually in the possession of the academic commentator, bringing her narrative and claim within the zone and cradle of legal protection, making decision-makers engage with queerness in a positive way to grant protection. Apata's thirteen-year human roller-coaster, through countless applications, deceptions, criminal offending, solitary confinement and litigation, culminated on 1 August 2017, with the Home Office granting her asylum; accepting her claim to refugee protection as a lesbian. Apata's case symbolises one of the strongest contemporary examples of a legal process

[28]Apata originally intended to seek refuge in Canada. 'It was my intention to go to Toronto in Canada. Sincerely I did not want to come here. I had to pick up my luggage here otherwise I would not be here' ([2.21] May 11, 2004—Screening Form level 2—claim for asylum).

systematically failing, and then eventually succeeding in affording protection by making space to consider the Queer Refugee In Law.[29]

The use of the DSSH Model in gaining positive refugee status determination, brings Apata and all those who have succeeded in gaining refugee status, from "the Queer Outside Law" into "the Queer Inside Law." As Apata, for the first time, said in June 2017, when recording her Attitude Magazine Pride Award 2017 video, linking her narrative to "Difference," thereby evidencing the underlying force of the DSSH Model[30]:

> I knew when I was in Nigeria that I was *different* and that was when I was aged 10. But I didn't know what it was? Why I was *different*? What it was all about until I was 16 years old when I had my first kiss. (emphasis added)

In the next section, I cite from Apata's primary source documentation, including the administrative and judicial decisions in order not to dilute and misinterpret, but to reflect the muddle queer differences pose in law and to suggest how the Queer Refugee can untangle the highly complex immigration cases they inhabit.

4 The History of the *Apata* Case

Apata sought to prevent deportation by making an asylum application in February 2012 on her sexual identity as a lesbian. In October 2012, the First-Tier Tribunal dismissed her claim. Without any legal representation, Apata

[29]See media reporting of Aderonke's success (e.g.) Diane Thompson, "Nigerian Gay Rights Activist Wins UK Asylum After 13 Year Battle," *The Guardian*, August 14, 2017, accessed February 5, 2018, https://www.theguardian.com/world/2017/aug/14/nigerian-gay-rights-activist-aderonke-apata-wins-uk-asylum-claim-13-year-battle; Jack Ashton, "Nigerian Gay Rights Activist Who Judge Accused of 'Faking' Her Sexuality Wins 13-Year Legal Battle for Asylum in the UK," *The Independent*, August 11, 2017, accessed February 5, 2018, http://www.independent.co.uk/news/uk/home-news/nigeria-gay-rights-activist-aderonke-apata-uk-asylum-granted-high-court-fake-sexulaity-lesbian-lgbt-a7888931.html; Meka Beresford, "Nigerian LGBT Activist Wins 13 Year Legal Battle to Be Granted UK Asylum," *Pink News*, August 12, 2017, accessed February 5, 2018, http://www.pinknews.co.uk/2017/08/12/nigerian-lgbt-activist-wins-13-year-legal-battle-to-be-granted-uk-asylum/; Roxy Bourdillon, "Aderonke Apata: 'I Felt Dehumanised When the Home Office Said I Was Pretending to Be a Lesbian'," *Diva magazine*, August 15, 2017; and "Attitude Pride Winner Wins Asylum Bid to Stay in the UK," *Attitude Magazine*, August 10, 2017, accessed February 5, 2018, https://attitude.co.uk/article/15599/attitude-pride-award-winner-wins-asylum-bid-to-stay-in-the-uk/ (no longer on-line).

[30]Attitude Pride Awards 2017—Aderonke Apata (Attitude magazine: Youtube, Published July 24, 2017), accessed February 6, 2018, https://www.youtube.com/watch?v=tTu49PxAfMg: "After fleeing horrific abuse in Nigeria and seeking sanctuary in Britain, one asylum seeker hit the headlines when she was accused of lying about being a lesbian and had her application rejected. Now she is a vocal critic of the system and helps other queer applicants."

drafted and submitted her own application for judicial review against the removal directions. In April 2014, she submitted a DVD and photographs of herself and her girlfriend "H" having sex, to "prove" that she was a lesbian. In her hearing before the High Court, the Home Office barrister claimed Apata was fabricating her claim, noting that she has had children and that she had altered her dress and demeanour deliberately. The High Court dismissed her claim but, while the Court of Appeal did not allow her appeal, it granted Apata the ability to make a fresh claim based on the new evidence presented. On 1 August 2017, Apata was informed of the Home Office's decision to grant her asylum, ending her thirteen-year journey for freedom.

From May 2004 to July 2016, Apata remained a Queer Refugee Outside law. She was subjected to the heteronormative confines of law through the overlapping episodes of the 2004 false asylum claim, the false marriage applications, the criminal convictions, the 2012 deportation proceedings and the 2013–2016 judicial review proceedings. It was only from August 2016 that Apata redefined herself as a queer person within the terms of UK law, through the prism of the DSSH Model, leading to the UK Home Office's grant of refugee status on 1 August 2017.

5 The Queer Outside Law

The early history of Apata's experience of being queer to the UK refugee system needs to be placed within the context of the UK government's approach of sexual identity claims from November 2004, and the concept of voluntary discretion to refuse asylum. This notion of discretion highlighted the norm that the majority of queer people would be voluntarily "discreet" rather than face persecution directly by being open (flight rather than fight). First introduced through Home Office legal submissions and adopted by the Court of Appeal in November 2004 in the case of *Z*,[31] the "discretion test" allowed decision-makers to refuse asylum to people who could return home and be "discreet" to avoid persecution caused by "religious, social and cultural mores."[32]

In July 2010, the UK Supreme Court struck down this test, as the underlying rationale of the Convention was to allow people to live freely and openly without fear of persecution. Lord Rodger provided the binding guidance for fact-finding Tribunals. First, the individual had to "prove" they were gay, or

[31] *Z v Secretary of State for the Home Department* [2004] EWCA Civ. 1578, [2005] Imm AR 75.
[32] *HJ (Iran) and HT (Cameroon) v Secretary of State for the Home Department* [2009] EWCA Civ 172, [2009] Imm AR 600.

would be perceived as gay, on return to their country of origin. Second, the country background evidence had to demonstrate "openly" gay people had a well-founded fear of persecution. The Tribunal would then assess whether the individual would be open on return. If they would be, as the majority would be, "voluntarily discreet," then they would not be granted refugee status if this was a reason wholly unconnected with a fear of persecution. If, however, a "material reason" for this voluntary discretion was due to a fear of persecution they would succeed in their protection claim. This "test" continued to leave a lacuna of claimants who would be returned to countries where it had been accepted, if discovered, they would be persecuted, but as they would "successfully adopt" discretion based on reasons unconnected with fear of persecution (the basis of the claim for asylum) they should be returned.

Prior to her May 2004 arrival, the UK's Asylum and Immigration Tribunal had only the previous year in 2003 started to promulgate country guidance cases, none of which related to sexual identity. The Home Office's 2004 position on Nigeria, soon to be enhanced with discretion reasoning, was that it would be safe to relocate to the Christian south, and be "discreet," noting such discretion would be reasonably tolerable. During her substantive asylum interview on 15 May 2004, four days after her discovery in the UK, Apata said the following:

> 'Question 30: What was your reason for leaving Nigeria?'
>
> There are many reasons. My inlaws accused me of being involved in witchcraft to convert their son to become a Christian. They wanted us to reconvert to Muslim this we refuses [sic]. Now so they go [sic] support of other local Muslims to bring us to the mosque by force and were threatening to kill us and they fulfills [sic] that promise by killing my two brothers who are living with me and they accuses [sic] me of adultery and I am to be tried by Sharia court and they kill one of my sons.

Importantly, this accusation of adultery has a ring of truth, but the omission would haunt Apata's encounters with the UK authorities. In answer to Question 89 of the May 2004 substantive asylum interview, evidencing the stigma, shame and harm she feared as a result of events in Nigeria, in a single sentence, Apata said the following:

> 'Question 89: Do you experience any other difficulties in Nigeria that you have not already mentioned in this interview?'
>
> I have no other problems but being ostracised and badly labelled and my life in danger.

Lesbians and bisexual women in Nigeria are labelled as being under the spell of witchcraft with corresponding witch-hunts of gay people accepted by the Home Office, as reflected in the published policy in 2018 up to April 2019.[33]

Apata, through her fear of deportation following disclosure, did not disclose that the risk arose from her sexual identity as a lesbian and she did not link this fear to the series of acts leading to her past-persecution and risk on return. These acts included the marriage to a Muslim man (in order to disguise her actual sexual identity) who converted to Christianity to marry her, which resulted in her being perceived as being involved with witchcraft to "convert" others. Her subsequent adultery, the subsequent murder of her son from an angry mob, the torture she endured resulting in her summoning before a Sharia Court[34] were presented in the claim without linking the accusation of adultery and witchcraft to having been outed by her husband's family with respect to her same-sex relationship with her girlfriend "K."[35] This omission made Apata queer outside law, as she had not disclosed her actual basis of claim and therefore failed to "prove" that she was a refugee. As Apata stated in her 1 August 2016 fresh claim statement, her reasons for non-disclosure were multi-layered[36]:

> …I didn't want to report one authority to another as I wasn't sure of the consequences of such actions. I had been in the closet all my life prior to entering the UK in 2004. …so I didn't know how to speak to anyone about my sexuality. I wasn't sure what the environment in the UK was for people like me and also didn't know that sexual orientation was a basis of claim.

Following her failed asylum application, Apata then went underground and disappeared within the Nigerian and African diaspora, reinforcing her position outside both legal structures of recognition and social communities that did not make space for her sexuality. She had to hide her sexual identity from both in order to survive.

[33]UK Home Office, *Country Information and Guidance: Nigeria: Sexual Orientation and Gender Identity* (London: Home Office) [2.2.5] and [2.2.7], accessed February 3, 2018, https://www.gov.uk/government/uploads/system/uploads/attachment_data/file/566196/NGA_CIG_SOGI.pdf now replaced by April 2019 where witchcraft is no longer cited, *Country Policy and Information Note: Nigeria: Sexual orientation and gender identity or expression.*

[34]Before the Tribunal (September 24, 2012), there was evidence relied on by Apata regarding further proceedings before the Sharia Court (p. 8) (IA/15464/2012) (promulgated on October 10, 2012): January 2012 letter from her former girlfriend [K] in Nigeria.

[35][8.2] (October 4, 2004 determination: Appeal Number: AS/1088/2004): "Aderonke Junoke Apata (aka Tina Ronke Apata) Appeal Heard: 1 September 2004 before Mr R Battersby, Adjudicator (Immigration Appellant Authority: Manchester) (Promulgated 4 October 2004)."

[36]*08/16 FCS'*, [69].

> [74] I started living in the shadows after I had left the NASS [National Asylum Support Services] accommodation. I became homeless and slept rough. The only way I could survive was by living on the down low in the Nigerian community which meant hiding my sexual identity for fear of being attacked. This was the only option I had to enable me to get by. However it was becoming an awkward situation for me in the Nigeria community without a male relationship and based on my applications for leave to remain on this as I knew of no other way to avoid being returned to Nigeria...

As Dugan makes clear from speaking to Apata in 2015:

> '... pressure from the Nigerian church she was attending to get married and renounce her sexuality. The basic truth is that whatever country you come from, when you're here in the UK you end up in community from you own country that are still the same as they are back home' she says.[37]

This lived experience of "passing" and having to "prove straight" in diaspora communities in the UK was imposed on Apata due to her lack of any legal status and her need to be able to survive, both economically and without harm. Chikwendu draws from Queer/LGBT+ Nigerian women living within the diaspora in the US to note the use of the "closet" to hide queer identity[38]:

> [How t]hey relate to being Nigerian is informed by the way they relate to being queer, which is in turn informed by the ways they are marked as Black, ... circular consciousness ...in our understandings of power and agency, and consciousness as the catalyst for strategies for daily survival.
>
> Living in-between ... is not freely chosen but is a positionality that is thrust upon them. They struggle with how to be Nigerian and something else, ... acknowledging shared connections and histories, while also maintaining that something else ... this need to be something else is a catalyst for change.

As Apata stated in her fresh claim statement in August 2016 with respect to her decision to disassociate with the Nigerian diaspora in the UK[39]:

---

[37] Emily Dugan, *Finding Home: Real Stories of Migrant Britain* (London: Icon Books, 2015), 231, 239 'Chapter 9: Aderonke'. The narrative recorded by Dugan does not fully accord chronologically or factually with the narrative disclosed to her legal team, including referring in the same page to a 2011 marriage to a Nigerian man, an issue raised in the 2010 FTT determination, but rejected due to confusion of Apata at the hearing, but raised with respect to a marriage with a different man, this time with British nationality in March 2011.

[38] Meremu Chikwendu, "Circular Consciousness in the Lived Experiences of Intersectionality: Queer/LGBT Nigerian Diasporic Women in the USA," *Journal of International Women's Studies* 14, no. 4 (2013): 34, 44.

[39] *08/16 FCS*, [76].

> I have disassociated myself from the Nigerian community here in the UK because of the constant pain and agony of being seen differently by them and the torture that brings to me. I feel so happy and free following that bold decision to remove myself from living amongst the Nigerian community.

This forced deception continues even after flight, especially where the applicant finds themselves forced to exist within the diaspora—one stringently enforcing conservative traditional historical customary notions of (heterosexual) society from the country of origin, providing a necessary re-engagement in order to survive. It is through the existence of having to live within the Nigerian diaspora in the UK that Apata's experience of the double-bind of gender and sexual identity should be read.

This makes the investigation of the notion of "Difference" within the DSSH Model a significant positive tool, as it provides a platform, which describes in detail the juxtaposition of the Queer Refugee Outside Law (the queer refugee) to be replaced by disclosure of the true lived experiences as the Queer Refugee in order to obtain positive status determination and be a Queer Inside Law.

Seeking employment without any lawful leave, in order to survive, led to two criminal convictions. Following the second conviction, the Home Office served a Notice of Intention to Make a Deportation Order to Apata. On 7 February 2012, Apata signed an Assistant Voluntary Return to Nigeria. This all changed on 9 February 2012[40]: "Leading up to the 2012 hearing, I was informed by [J][41] that I would be at risk of persecution due to my sexual identity if I returned to Nigeria's [sic] the Same Sex Bill was about to be signed into law in Nigeria." This led Apata in her Screening interview on 13 February 2012 to state the following to the authorities (for the first time since her 11 May 2004 arrival):

> '4.2. Can you BRIEFLY explain why you cannot return to your home country?'
>
> I CANNOT RETURN TO NIGERIA BECAUSE OF MY SEXUALITY AS A LESBIAN.[42]

The substantive asylum interview following this disclosure resulted in a case officer asking (impermissible) questions[43] on sexual activities to establish her

[40] *08/16 FCS*, [78].

[41] Friend of Apata who knew her and of her relationship with her girlfriend 'K' in Nigeria.

[42] Capital letters, and occasional underlining, used to ask and answer questions in this form.

[43] *Joined Cases C-148/13, C149/13 and C-150/13 (A, B and C)* [2015] 2 CMLR 5.

sexual identity,[44] rather than questions relating to Apata's recognition of her "difference", or emotions and feelings associated with her sexual identity as a lesbian. This evidences why the DSSH Model works, as even prior to the use of the model in Apata's case in 2016, her answers to Question 30 and Question 89 in her 15 May 2004 asylum interview, cited earlier in this chapter, aligned to three of the four triggers of the DSSH Model: Stigma, Shame and Harm. By the time of her 2012 interview, where she disclosed her actual sexual identity as a lesbian, the Home Office took an impermissible approach asking questions relating solely to sexual activity, rather than investigating her identity and lived experience.[45] These questions, asked by the (female)[46] Home Office interviewing officer, included[47]:

> 'Question 66: When did you find out that your sexual orientated [sic]'
>
> When I was in my teenage years at school.
>
> 'Question 67: Did you have any sexual activities with other girls in school'
>
> Yes I did. Mainly after school. We had to hide in case we were caught.

Apata recounted her feelings after separation from her girlfriend evidencing her feelings and emotions towards her lover:

> 'Question 79: When did things change between you.'
>
> She went and got married. It was an arranged marriage. She never wanted to be in that relationship.
>
> 'Question 80: What did you do and how did you feel.'
>
> I felt terrible. I was losing the only person that I could express my feeling sexual behaviours to. I tried to convince her not to marry but she couldn't.
>
> 'Question 81: What arrangements did you make between you.'

[44]No question-marks are found in the transcript at the end of each question, providing the inference in the author's view that these were not questions to be asked and answered, but trigger statements used to support the rejection of the claim.

[45]Question 2: Who did you live with in Nigeria: I lived with my late husband; Question 3: What happened to him: He was killed; Question 4: By whom was he killed [sic]: By the Muslim community where we lived and by his own family; Question 5: What was his cause of death. I was informed he was stabbed in heart after being caught by a gang of Muslims ... Question 7: What year did the incident take place: 2006; ... Question 10: Why was your husband killed: It was an "Honour" Killing because he had converted from Muslim to Christianity.

[46]Gender of the interviewing officer is recorded to avoid a stereotypical assumption that this was a straight man fixated with the sexual activities of lesbians.

[47]No question-marks are found in the transcript at the end of each question, providing the inference by me that these were not questions to be asked and answered, but trigger statements used to support the rejection of the claim.

We agreed to continue seeing each other when we could and continue keeping our relationship a secret.'

...

'Question 84: Do you still feel the same way about her even though she is married.'

Yes, I do, strongly.

Apata connected her fear of return directly to her sexual identity:

'Question 89: What would happen to you if you returned to Nigeria?'

My life is still in danger. I still have that death sentence hovering over my head. I cannot live as a Christian amongst the Muslim community and also because of my sexuality I fear persecution from government and the Sharia Law in the area. It is a criminal offence in Nigeria to be homosexual. The sentence is a harsh one and leads to death.

Her 2012 asylum interview was the first time Apata linked the stabbing of her son and fleeing Nigeria with her sexual identity as a lesbian—nearly eight years after her arrival in the UK on 11 May 2004. This was also the first time Apata referred to the murder of her former husband in Nigeria in 2006 by the mob, leading to her daughter E's fleeing Nigeria for the UK.

However, the one missing part of the narrative not explored by the Home Office interviewer and, therefore, not disclosed by Apata was with respect to her experiences of and emotions connected with her recognition of her "Difference", by her and by those who would harm her. Instead, there existed a fixation with sexual activities as establishing identity at paragraph 50 of the 12 June 2012 negative decision on the asylum claim, one replicated from the same erroneous approach rued unlawful by the Court of Appeal in 2009 in *NR (Jamaica)*[48]:

The only credence which can be given to your sexual orientation claim is in relation to any sexual activities you may have undertaken since you have been detained which have been same sex ones, the only possible option given the conditions of your incarceration. You have not lived openly as a lesbian in

[48] *NR (Jamaica) v Secretary of State for the Home Department* [2009] EWCA Civ. 856, [2010] INLR 159 [22] (Goldring LJ) citing the factual findings of the 2008 Upper Tribunal (DIJ Shaerf): "We find that as a healthy, energetic and engaged young woman in such institutions she had and took the opportunity to continue her experimentations with her sexual identity: indeed, there was no alternative except celibacy." The author was Counsel for the appellant at all stages including the remitted appeal, where it was held that she was "exclusively a lesbian" (Resident Immigration Judge Pinkerton).

> either Nigeria or the UK. ... It is concluded that you are not a lesbian as you claim although you may have had sexual relationships with women during your recent periods of detention.

Additionally, such an approach is unlawful as a matter of EU law, as it is contrary to art. 4 of the 2004 Minimum Standards Qualification Directive[49] and art. 7 (privacy) of the Charter of Fundamental Rights of the European Union[50] constituting an impermissible approach to the investigation of sexual activities as a method of investigation, following the December 2014 judgment of the Court of Justice of the European Union in the *A, B, and C* case.[51] This position is recorded by the Home Office since February 2015[52] in their Asylum Policy Instructions on sexual identity claims—investigation of sexual activities must not occur.

Where Apata does provide corroborative evidence of her sexual identity, it comes from her former girlfriend [K] in Nigeria, whom she had been caught having the adulterous relationship with, leading to Apata fleeing Nigeria for Canada. The evidence of K is addressed at paragraph 44 of the June 2012 reasons for refusal letter:

> You also submitted email correspondence from the woman you allege to have had a 20 year relationship with when you lived in Nigeria, [K]. [K] confirms a long term relationship with you from 1984 until you left Nigeria. She refers to your masculine appearance and it was this appearance which attracted her

[49]Council Directive (2004/83/EC) on 29 April 2004 on minimum standards for the qualification and status of third country nationals and status of persons as refugees or persons who otherwise need international protection and the content of the protection guaranteed. Since January 31, 2020, the domestic The Refugee or Person in Need of International Protection Regulations 2006 (SI. 2006, no. 2525) apply the provisions of the Directive as retained law (see Section 2 of the EU [Withdrawal] Act 2018). Regulation 2 of the 2006 Regulations, providing the definition of a refugee in line with the Refugee Convention is found within paragraph 334 of the Immigration Rules, in force as of 11 February 2020: (ii) they are a refugee, as defined in regulation 2 of The Refugee or Person in Need of International Protection (Qualification) Regulations 2006.

[50]Charter of Fundamental Rights of the European Union, *Official Journal L 83, 30.3.2010, P. 0389 – 0403.*

[51]*ABC* (2015), [64]. cf with the Upper Tribunal's continuing (unlawful) reliance on *SD (military service -sexual identity) Turkey CG* [2013] UKUT 00,612 (IAC) where it seeks investigation on whether an individual is, or will be perceived as "passive" and thereby at risk of persecution during military service in Turkey (promulgated 5 December 2013), accessed August 24, 2018, https://tribunalsdecisions.service.gov.uk/utiac/2013-ukut-612.

[52]UK Home Office, *Asylum Policy Instruction on Sexual Orientation Issues in the Asylum Claim (Version 6)* (London: Home Office, 3 August 2016), page 29 of 41, accessed March 27, 2020, https://www.gov.uk/government/uploads/system/uploads/attachment_data/file/543882/Sexual-orientation-in-asylum-claims-v6.pdf "Communicating *sexually explicit policy to claimants* ... When such narratives are offered (excepting allegations of sexual attack or rape), the interviewer should make the following declaration" (*emphasis added*) [preventing further disclosure or filing of prohibited material].

> to you in the first instance (witness statement paragraph 4) and that your masculine appearance and demeanour would have a bearing on the persecution you would suffer if returned to Nigeria (witness statements paragraph 16). However, in your asylum account, you failed to indicate that you suffered any persecution while in Nigeria as a result of your appearance or sexual orientation given that [K] claims you were of manly appearance when she knew you. It is noted that in your application for a certificate of approval to marry Mr [A] dated 30 August 2008 you submitted photographs to support your claim. In these you are distinctly feminine in appearance as you are in the photographs of you at [S's] wedding of 29 January 2011, all of which are on file. The genuineness of [K]'s statement cannot be relied upon.

The photographs on the Home Office file relating to the 2008 (false) marriage application are read as "feminine." Here, the need to fix sexual identity and/or expression resulted in a rejection of a person's sexual identity, when it has a gender expression, is directly linked to straight norms (i.e. feminine equals straight). Apata is queer refugee (Outside Law) to the terms of legal protection because the decision-maker fixates on stereotypes of gender expression that are used to establish credibility. This approach can be contrasted with the written evidence of K, Apata's former girlfriend from Nigeria, who conveyed how Apata expressed her gender, and conceptualised her gender identity:

> [4] I was attracted to Aderonke in the first instance by her masculine appearance – soft manly voice and look.
>
> [5] Aderonke never wore female clothing throughout our four year (1984-88) study term at the University. Even after we left the University.
>
> [6] I believe that Aderonke was born lesbian/gay. Aderonke never had feelings for men whilst we were together as partners. I recall her telling me of how she hated male relationship and cannot imagine two men in a relationship if she went for any. I was bisexual and had no problem with opposite sex relationship.
>
> [7] Aderonke used to tell me how she would love to transform to male in the future.
>
> [8] On several occasions, people would make comments towards Aderonke's behaviour, dressing and appearance that she looks like a man.
>
> [9] I was Aderonke's girlfriend right through from University and beyond until she fled for the United Kingdom in 2004 as a result of the religious persecution she experienced from her late husband [...] family and the Muslim community.
>
> ...
>
> [14] We always feel a strong sense of shame and stigma about our sexual orientation and feel that we would be persecuted for our identity. It was never

possible for an LGB person to alert the authorities to our need for protection. This is because protection will not be forthcoming. We also come from cultures where we have never openly discussed our sexual orientation.

In rejecting Apata's claim for protection, the Home Office noted:

> When you were refused asylum in 2004, your claim was considered so improbable that the immigration judge stated: 'I find the appellant's account is a fabrication designed to gain her entry to and residence in the United Kingdom' (paragraph 11.3). Your actions described above, including the nature of the offences you committed, show that you have continued to use deception for your own ends since 2004.

This reflects a position adopted unliterally by the Home Office in assessing subsequent claims, where the findings on credibility by the fact-finding Tribunal with respect to the original claim, coupled with criminal offending, are not merely treated as a starting point for credibility assessment in accordance with the guidance in *Devaseelan*,[53] but act as a straight-jacket suffocating and providing no room for deviating from an assessment devoid of positive "belief." This produces the queer refugee (Queer Outside Law) as the process of investigation and credibility assessment fails to engage with the reality of the lived experiences of the non-conforming Queer Refugee (Queer Inside Law).

6 The Queer Inside UK Law—The Fresh Claim and the DSSH Model

The central fallacy arising from the current discretion test in *HJ (Iran)* is unless the applicant "successfully" adopts a heterosexual narrative, then they will be at risk of harm. Apata's marriage contracted in Nigeria with her former husband was based not on free choice, let alone love—it was a mechanism to evade detection while she continued (unsuccessfully) to conduct her same-sex love affair with her girlfriend K, detracting in the short-term unwarranted attention of her family and community. Therefore, the heterosexual narrative was not part of her path to discovery of her sexual identity as a lesbian, but a veil to evade detection, as she had already identified to herself and her lover her actual identity as a lesbian.

[53] *Justin Surendran Devaseelan v Secretary of State for the Home Department* (HR/3442/01) [2003] Imm A.R. 1 cf *AA (Somalia) and AH (Afghanistan) v. Secretary of State for the Home Department* [2007] EWCA Civ. 1040 [2008] Imm. A.R. 241 [15] "[n]ot to be read restrictively" (Hooper LJ).

The July 2016 Court of Appeal judgment[54] held the findings of the Judge below were merely obiter dicta, i.e. non-binding.[55] As Dugan states[56]:

> For lesbian and bisexual asylum seekers, the suggestion that credible same-sex attracted asylum seeker will not have led a 'heterosexual' narrative is especially damaging. For example, in a 2014 [sic] UK case involving a Nigerian lesbian who had twice been married and had children, a Home Office barrister stated that, while the government conceded that she had 'indulged in same sex activity' it denied her claim in part because '[y]ou can't be heterosexual one day and a lesbian the next day. Just as you can't change your race.'

The citation in Dugan's text is drawn from Counsel for the Secretary of State's submissions to the Deputy High Court Judge in Apata's judicial review hearing before the High Court in March 2015,[57] as reported in *The Independent* newspaper in May 2015.[58] It is important to highlight that this report is taken from proceedings prior to Apata being given a "safe space" to tell her story with the assistance of the DSSH Model.

Apata's engagement with her need to adopt a heteronormative narrative in order to evade harm by marrying her Muslim husband in Nigeria, and then attempting to enter marriages in the UK, illustrates the steps taken by Queer Refugees in order to evade identification and subsequent persecution—a veil so transparent and flimsy, it will eventually slip as the false narrative has to be maintained not for one day, or one week, but for the rest of their lives. This is why "voluntary discretion" only for personal choice or social reasons as a basis to refuse refugee status via the portal of Lord Rodger's binding guidance at paragraph 82 of *HJ (Iran)*, ignores the fact this is not due to an act of "discretion" and silence, but one of positively having to "prove straight."

---

[54] *Apata* (2016, CA) (n 13).

[55] Ibid., [28] (*as per* Burnett LJ).

[56] Dugan (2015) (n 39), 313–314 (fn. 147).

[57] *R (Apata) v. Secretary of State for the Home Department* [2015] EWHC 888 (Admin) [35] (*as per* Deputy high Court Judge John Bowers QC) "It was submitted by Mr Baird that the Claimant could not be a member of the particular social group of lesbians because she had had children or heterosexual relationships. I do not accept this. … This Claimant says in her appeal from the FTT that 'it took me several years to identify with my sexuality as a gay woman.' I accept that she has had some same sex relationships but I do not accept that this in itself renders her a member of a particular social group."

[58] Emily Dugan, "Home Office Says Nigerian Asylum-Seeker Can't Be a Lesbian as She's Got Children," *The Independent*, May 27, 2015, accessed August 8, 2018, https://www.independent.co.uk/news/uk/home-news/home-office-says-nigerian-asylum-seeker-can-t-be-a-lesbian-as-she-s-got-children-10083385.html. See also for quotes from the Home Office Barrister cited in the last sentence: Aubrey Allegretti, "Nigerian Lesbian Aderonke Apata Pleads for UK Judge to Save Her Life," *Huffington Post*, March 5, 2015, accessed February 5, 2017, http://www.huffingtonpost.co.uk/2015/03/03/asylum-apata-lesbian-court_n_6793376.html.

At no time prior to August 2016 had Apata been asked to address "when did you first realise you were Different?,"[59] or address other broad category triggers connected to Stigma, Shame and Harm, components of the DSSH Model[60]:

> [4] I have never previously been asked questions about my feelings and emotions about my sexual identity and my life as a lesbian. This is the first time I have ever been asked about these type of questions (about the way I felt different, the stigma and shame and the harm it caused).

This lightbulb moment for the applicant, led to disclosure of a detailed narrative over many hours,[61] enabled Apata to signpost in her own life, one which is unconnected entirely with attraction and is connected with non-conformity with expected gender role. The paragraphs below are a selection from the twenty-six paragraphs in her statement citing her evidence in response to the DSSH Model triggers, illustrating the level of detail Apata is able to provide to support her emotional journey[62]—her narrative of Difference, Stigma, Shame and Harm as a Queer Refugee.

6.1 Difference

> [5] I recall from when I was 10-11 years old, I knew I was not like any other girls. I used to wear boys clothes. ... deep within me I knew I was different, unique, but I never knew what I was. Even when it came to playing with and having age appropriate activities generally identifies [sic] with boys. I would play football and boxing with boys. These made me comfortable and happy.
>
> ...

[59]See *CREDO2* for examples of trigger questions. Cf Jasmine Dawson and Paula Gerber, "Assessing the Refugee Claims of LGBTI People: Is the DSSH Model Useful for Determining Claims by Women for Asylum Based on Sexual Orientation?" *International Journal of Refugee Law* 29, no. 2 (2017): 292. Both Dawson and Gerber's analysis of the DSSH model is fundamentally flawed, as all case examples cited by them, including Apata's pre-August 2016 proceedings, had no evidence of the DSSH model being applied to construct the narratives of the queer refugees. The DSSH model was first used to draft Apata's statement for the Fresh Claim in August 2016.

[60]*08/16 FCS*, [4].

[61]Ibid., drafted by Apata with the assistance of her solicitor and colleague at his firm.

[62]Cynthia Orchard, *Sexual Border: Does the UK Adequately Protect People Seeking Asylum Based on Risk of Persecution Relating to Sexual or Gender Identity or Expression?* (London: Asylum Aid, February 2018), accessed 9 August 2018, https://www.asylumaid.org.uk/wp-content/uploads/2018/02/Policy-briefing-Sexual-Borders-Feb-2018.pdf; UK Lesbian and Gay Immigration Group, *Still Falling Short* (London: UK Lesbian and Gay Immigration Group, July 2018), accessed August 9, 2018, https://uklgig.org.uk/wp-content/uploads/2018/07/Still-Falling-Short.pdf.

> [7] My mother allowed me to wear boys' clothes and dress like a boy because I was happier and comfortable in them. .... My fellow school children used to call me a boy. This name calling was upsetting for me. I remember my mum used to say to anyone who made such comments about me that I didn't create myself and that they should let me be. I recognised this 'difference' in my pre-sexual awakening that I did not fit in with how other girls acted or were supposed to behave.

In describing her sexual awakening in her teenage years, Apata recounted the following, highlighting conduct linked directly with her emotions and affections[63]:

> [8] When I was 15-16 years old, I had a relationship with one of my female school friends called [X]. She brought a (lesbian) porn magazine to the classroom for me to look through with her. She was an outcast. I recall when I kissed [X], that moment was unique in that it started with a mixed feeling of uncertainty about whether to go along, a gut feeling to just do it, and nervousness stemming from the fact that my rational conscience, which normally yells out to me what's right and what's not, was dead silent. I was at the edge of a cliff one moment and the very next moment my gut feeling pushed me off and I experienced perhaps my first leap of faith.
>
> ...
>
> [10] It's funny to think that a moment could be big enough to engulf my entire universe. It was a like a moment of Nirvana now that I think of it. I didn't even realize when I had closed my eyes. ...When I finally broke away from the kiss I could see her ... And that's when I became my old self again and it finally sunk in that life just became more beautiful.

To reflect her sense of membership of the group, Apata makes the clear connection with other outcasts, i.e. her recognition of non-conformity:

> [13] As very difficult as it was to talk about sexual feelings, homosexuality etc. then, I could recognise the 'others' as they were always alone and never were with too many people around them – just like I was.

6.2 Stigma

In recounting stigma, Apata identified her knowledge of how the church was used as a vessel to target those who are different—people who are not in

[63] *08/16 FCS*, [8], as per the *Yogyakarta Principles* (2007) definition of sexual orientation, accessed August 20, 2018, https://yogyakartaprinciples.org/introduction/.

relationships with different sex partners. That this provided the basis of establishing the "particular social group" to which Apata belonged was imputed by the norms of acceptable expression of sexual identity (including gender-sex norms) held by the potential persecutor of those who are "not straight enough":

> [14] When I was about 15 years old, preachings from my church (which were not different from other churches) about how society condemns people who are not in relationship with opposite sex partners – calling them devils, witches and wizards, sinners, animals and all sorts of derogative [sic] names made me really sad – knowing that I was one of these people but unable to stand up and challenge such discriminatory utterances and treatment.
>
> [15] .... Amongst the list of sinful things they would mention were witchcraft, being possessed by evil spirits and engaging in same sex activities. .... I remember saying to them that I am equally a Christian which I am anyway; that I believe in God and read the Bible. This was in a way me trying to identify as 'normal' and not one of the 'others'. I was always felling depressed and ashamed of myself for being me.

6.3 Shame

With respect to shame, Apata recounted the following narrative of her feelings of marginalisation, becoming 'a shadow' due to her difference:

> [20] The recognition of the stigma attached to being a lesbian in my country made my soul bleed. My heart bitterly cried, for I was torn between both worlds listening to how homosexuals were being stigmatised and knowing that I was one of them; yet unable to challenge it.
>
> [21] A once smart and brilliant child became a shadow. I had no-one to talk to about what I was feeling and no place to go and identify with others like me. I was trapped and hidden in my own world. Darkness was my only companion for the only rays of light were school and my faith. But abuse and stigma also emanated from them too.

6.4 Harm

Recounting the harm she has suffered in the past and the harm she feared on return, Apata linked to recognition of her identity by the potential persecutor:

> [28] If I were returned to Nigeria, I would have to hide who I am (an open and proud lesbian as I previously [sic] living in the UK) as I fear persecution. This is because, should I try to continue to live openly as a lesbian, I would be at risk of being killed by vigilantes and/or imprisoned by the Nigerian Government as it is against the law to be a lesbian in Nigeria. In prison, I will experience torture and violence of all kinds including bullying, teasing, harassment, physical assault…
>
> [29] I am afraid for my safety in Nigeria. I have pursued my case for refugee status in the High Court and because I am afraid for my safety if I am returned to Nigeria.

Apata was granted asylum on 1 August 2017. Speaking in December 2017 about her reaction to the news at the time of notification of the grant of asylum, Apata stated[64] that she was "crying on the phone with my solicitor when he broke the news to me." Now, while she is relieved to be safe, the trauma of her previous uncertainty is still with her.

> I have constant nightmares and flashbacks…I'm very grateful to whoever it was in the Home Office who finally decided to grant me leave to remain, but I'll never get those 13 years I lost back. They should have been the best years of my life.

7 Where Next for the Queer Refugee?

Apata's case illustrates that there is a clear reliance on stereotypes in relation to gender norms and expression that lead to negative decisions by both the Home Office and the UK courts and tribunals. In Apata's case, the Home Office's earlier rejection included the assertion that there was a lack to the genuineness of K's 2012 statement based purely on relying on Apata's expression of her gender in 2008 and 2011, rather than on an account of the expression of Apata's gender from 1984 to 2004 while in Nigeria, prior to facing persecution. But this evidence points to the value of the DSSH Model to support Queer non-conforming ("not straight enough") Refugees who seek protection from the Refugee Convention in order to become Queer Inside Law.

The voluminous material pre-dating the 2012 determination would concern any lawyer dissecting the determination to discern any arguable

[64]Diane Thompson, "'I Have Nightmares': People Threatened with Deportation Reveal What Happened Next," *The Guardian*, 1 January 2018, accessed 5 February 2018, https://www.theguardian.com/uk-news/2018/jan/01/i-have-nightmares-people-threatened-with-deportation-reveal-what-happened-next.

grounds of appeal. Nevertheless, the manner in which the 2012 Tribunal readily accepted any shred of Apata's claim to be in straight relationships but rejected in its entirety any evidence supporting her claim to her sexual identity as a lesbian is troubling. This rendered Apata to be a Queer Outside Law.

Having received the negative determination, Apata recounts the steps that she took in contacting her then solicitors and other legal practitioners, stating in 2016[65]:

> When the Tribunal's judgment was handed down, I contacted my solicitor...and asked when they were going to put in an application for an appeal against the judgment. I was informed that the Barrister could not find any error of law in the judgment so there was no basis for an appeal. I contacted another firm...to see if they could assist in lodging the appeal. I was asked if I had a solicitor and I replied that my solicitor had informed me that there was no error of law in the judgment. [These solicitors] said that if [my solicitors] couldn't find any error in the judgment then they could not assist me in an application to appeal....I was forced to draft the grounds of appeal by myself.

This exchange shows why there is an urgent need for expertise in this field of law and how the agents for exclusion of the Queer Refugee not only include Judge and the Home Office, but also lawyers who are constrained by lack of expert engagement in these claims. Nevertheless, since the adoption and application of the DSSH model, the Queer Refugee increasingly has space Inside UK law.

References

Allegretti, Aubrey. "Nigerian Lesbian Aderonke Apata Pleads for UK Judge to Save Her Life," *Huffington Post*, March 5, 2015. http://www.huffingtonpost.co.uk/2015/03/03/asylum-apata-lesbian-court_n_6793376.html.

Ashton, Jack. "Nigerian Gay Rights Activist Who Judge Accused of 'Faking' Her Sexuality Wins 13-Year Legal Battle for Asylum in the UK," *The Independent*, August 11, 2017. http://www.independent.co.uk/news/uk/home-news/nigeria-gay-rights-activist-aderonke-apata-uk-asylum-granted-high-court-fake-sexulaity-lesbian-lgbt-a7888931.html.

Beresford, Meka. "Nigerian LGBT Activist Wins 13 Year Legal Battle to Be Granted UK Asylum," *Pink News*, August 12, 2017. http://www.pinknews.co.uk/2017/08/12/nigerian-lgbt-activist-wins-13-year-legal-battle-to-be-granted-uk-asylum/.

[65] *08/16 FCS*, [81].

Bourdillon, Roxy. "Aderonke Apata: 'I Felt Dehumanised When the Home Office Said I Was Pretending to Be a Lesbian'," *Diva Magazine*, August 15, 2017.

Campbell, John R., in *Bureaucracy, Law & Dystopia in the UK Asylum System*, ed. Satvinder S. Juss (London: Routledge, 2017).

Chelvan, S. "Put Your Hands Up If You Feel Love," *Journal of Immigration, Asylum and Nationality Law* 25, no. 1 (2011): 55.

Chelvan, S., and Gábor Gyualai. "Chapter XI: Asylum Claims Based on Sexual Orientation or Gender Identity," in Gábor Gyulai, eds. *Credibility Assessment in Asylum Procedures: A Multidisciplinary Training Manual Volume 2* (Budapest: Hungarian Helsinki Committee, Budapest, 2015).

Chikwendu, Meremu. "Circular Consciousness in the Lived Experiences of Intersectionality: Queer/LGBT Nigerian Diasporic Women in the USA," *Journal of International Women's Studies* 14, no. 4 (2013): 34.

Dugan, Emily. *Finding Home: Real Stories of Migrant Britain* (London: Icon Books, 2015).

Dugan, Emily. "Home Office Says Nigerian Asylum-Seeker Can't Be a Lesbian as She's Got Children," *The Independent*, May 27, 2015. https://www.independent.co.uk/news/uk/home-news/home-office-says-nigerian-asylum-seeker-can-t-be-a-lesbian-as-she-s-got-children-10083385.html.

Giametta, Calogero. *The Sexual Politics of Asylum* (Abingdon: Routledge, 2017).

Greatrick, Aydan. *Queer (Im)mobilities and the 'Refugee Crisis': Examining Stakeholder Responses to Sexual Minority Refugees in Turkey* (UCL Migration Research Unit Working Papers No. 2017/1, London, 2017).

Harper, Mark, et al. *Same Sex Marriage and Civil Partnerships: The New Law* (Jordans, 2014).

Heap, Tim. "Attitude Pride Awards: The Human Rights Lawyer Defending LGBT Asylum Seekers From Deportation," *Attitude magazine*, July 7, 2018. https://www.attitude.co.uk/article/attitude-pride-awards-the-human-rights-lawyer-defending-lgbt-asylum-seekers-from-deportation/18411/.

Johnson, Toni A.M. "On Silence, Sexuality and Skeletons: Reconceptualizing Narrative in Asylum Hearings," *Social & Legal Studies* 20 (2011): 57.

Keene, Jordan, and Greatrick, Aydan. *Improving Service Provision for Non-normative Refugees and Asylum Seekers in the UK: Recommendations for Policy and Practice* (London: Centre for Transnational Development and Collaboration, November 2017). Accessed August 19, 2018, http://ctdc.org/wp-content/uploads/2017/11/LGBT-Asylum-Seekers-Policy-Brief.pdf.

Millbank, Jenni. "From Discretion to Disbelief: Recent Trends in Refugee Determination on the Basis of Sexual Orientation in Australia and the United Kingdom," *The International Journal of Human Rights* 13, no. 2 (2009): 391.

Milliken Gray, Laura. *Failing the Grade* (London: UK Lesbian and Gay Immigration Group, 2010). Accessed March 27, 2020, https://uklgig.org.uk/wp-content/uploads/2014/04/Failing-the-Grade.pdf.

Orchard, Cynthia. *Sexual Border: Does the UK Adequately Protect People Seeking Asylum based on Risk of Persecution relating to Sexual or Gender*

Identity or Expression? (London: Asylum Aid, 2018). Accessed August 9, 2018, https://www.asylumaid.org.uk/wp-content/uploads/2018/02/Policy-briefing-Sexual-Borders-Feb-2018.pdf.

Raj, Senthorun. "A/Effective Adjudications: Queer Refugees and the Law," *Journal of Intercultural Studies* 38, no. 4 (2017): 453.

Thompson, Diane. "Nigerian Gay Rights Activist Wins UK Asylum After 13 Year Battle," *The Guardian*, August 14, 2017. https://www.theguardian.com/world/2017/aug/14/nigerian-gay-rights-activist-aderonke-apata-wins-uk-asylum-claim-13-year-battle.

Thompson, Diane. "'I Have Nightmares': People Threatened with Deportation Reveal What Happened Next," *The Guardian*, January 1, 2018. https://www.theguardian.com/uk-news/2018/jan/01/i-have-nightmares-people-threatened-with-deportation-reveal-what-happened-next.

UK Home Office. *The Home Office Response to the Independent Chief Inspector's Report: 'An Investigation into the Home Office's Handling of Asylum Claims Made on the Grounds of Sexual Orientation' March-June 2014* (London: Home Office, October 23, 2014). Accessed March 27, 2020, https://assets.publishing.service.gov.uk/government/uploads/system/uploads/attachment_data/file/365654/ResponseAsylumClaimsBasisSexualOrientation.pdf.

UK Home Office. *Asylum Policy Instruction on Sexual Orientation Issues in the Asylum Claim (Version 6)* (London: Home Office, August 3, 2016), page 29 of 41. Accessed February 11, 2020, https://www.gov.uk/government/uploads/system/uploads/attachment_data/file/543882/Sexual-orientation-in-asylum-claims-v6.pdf.

UK Home Office. *Country Information and Guidance: Nigeria: Sexual Orientation and Gender Identity* (London: Home Office). Accessed February 3, 2018, https://www.gov.uk/government/uploads/system/uploads/attachment_data/file/566196/NGA_CIG_SOGI.pdf.

UK Lesbian and Gay Immigration Group. *Missing the Mark: Decision Making on Lesbian Gay (Bisexual, Trans and Intersex) Asylum Claims* (London: UK Lesbian and Gay Immigration Group, September 2013). Accessed March 27, 2020, https://uklgig.org.uk/wp-content/uploads/2014/02/Missing-the-Mark.pdf.

UK Lesbian and Gay Immigration Group. *Still Falling Short* (London: UK Lesbian and Gay Immigration Group, July 2018). Accessed August 9, 2018, https://uklgig.org.uk/wp-content/uploads/2018/07/Still-Falling-Short.pdf.

Mapping the Manifestations of Exclusion: Challenging the Incarceration of Queer People

Felicity Adams and Fabienne Emmerich

1 Introduction

Prisons are sites of coercion, harm, pain, and violence.[1] They function to sustain and strengthen the capitalist system through their failure to rehabilitate and reintegrate prisoners into society.[2] Prisons are central to promoting neoliberal rationalities that exclude those who are deemed unempowerable and unenterprising; such as people of colour, the working class, and other vulnerable groups. In effect, the prison functions to safeguard those who

[1]Nils Christie, "Prisons in Society, or Society as Prison—A Conceptual Analysis," in *Prisons Past and Future*, ed. J.C. Freeman (London: Heinemann, 1978) 179–188.

[2]Jeffrey Reiman and Paul Leighton, *The Rich Get Richer and the Poor Get Prison: A Reader* (Boston, MA: Allyn & Bacon, 2010).

[3]Sarah Lamble, "Sexual Citizenship, Social Movements and the Expanding Carceral State," in *Queer Necropolitics*, edited by Jin Haritaworn, Adin Kuntsman and Sylvia Posocco (Oxford: Routledge, 2014) 151–171, 152. Through their privatization, predominantly in the UK and US, prisons have also become key sites that drive neoliberal economies as part of the prison industrial complex. The development of the prison industrial complex is facilitated through the creation of labour, the function of which is driven by socio-economically disadvantaged groups; see e.g. Ruth Wilson Gilmore, *Golden Gulag: Prisons, Surplus, Crisis and Opposition in Globalising California* (Berkeley: University of California Press, 2007).

F. Adams (✉) · F. Emmerich
Keele University, Keele, UK
e-mail: f.e.adams@keele.ac.uk

F. Emmerich
e-mail: f.emmerich@keele.ac.uk

S. Raj and P. Dunne (eds.), *The Queer Outside in Law*, Palgrave Socio-Legal Studies,
https://doi.org/10.1007/978-3-030-48830-7_5

profit from the neoliberal order, from the Other(s) who are perceived to endanger the continuation of these capitalist systems.[3]

Prisons are deeply gendered institutions that enforce a gender binary and perpetuate heteronormative gender performativity.[4] Queer people challenge gender-normative and heteronormative power relations that the prison's binary structure produces. They experience magnified forms of violence within the prison including physical and sexual violence, verbal abuse, isolation and the denial of healthcare.[5] There have been attempts at providing tailored, inclusive responses to imprisonment. These efforts are various; ranging from policies aimed at "managing" the specific needs of transgender prisoners within existing prison sites to expanding the prison system through the creation of prisons for non-binary people.[6] This is intended as part of a broader initiative to best accommodate queer prisoners within the prison environment and on the outside following the completion of their sentence.[7]

While many commend the various attempts to assuage the exclusion of queer prisoners, these reformist approaches fail to address the structural violence generated by the coercive and binary nature of the prison system. As Dean Spade reinforces, they merely "reify the racialized-gendered control of prisons".[8] This is because they overlook the prison as a site that forces queer prisoners to "inhabit identities that [they] had rejected as part of their sense of selfhood".[9] Simultaneously, they neglect that homophobia and transphobia are intrinsic to the existence and functioning of the criminal justice system.[10]

We argue that these confinement spaces produce varieties of exclusion for queer people in prison who challenge the gendered binaries inherent in the material construction of imprisonment. They are deemed both vulnerable

---

[4]Eamonn Carrabine and Brian Longhurst, "Gender and Prison Organisation: Some Comments on Masculinities and Prison Management," *The Howard Journal* 37, no. 2 (1998): 161–176; Judith Butler, *Gender Trouble* (New York and Abingdon: Routledge, [1990] 2007).

[5]Bent Bars Project, "Prison Abolition Is a Queer Issue," *Bent Bars Project* (2011) 1322.

[6]See the case of Tara Hudson, who was incorrectly housed within a designated unit for individuals with significant mental health and physical needs in the men's prison estate because of her gender identity. See Anon, "First UK Transgender Prison Unit to Open," *BBC News*, March 3, 2019, accessed 20 March 2020, https://www.bbc.co.uk/news/uk-47434730; Anon, "New Non-Binary Prison in Scotland?" *Corporate Watch*, Jan 17, 2018, accessed March 27, 2020, https://corporatewatch.org/new-non-binary-prison-in-scotland/.

[7]"The Care and Management of Individuals Who Are Transgender," HM Prisons and Probation Service, 31 October 2019.

[8]Dean Spade, "The Only Way to End Racialized Gender Violence in Prisons Is to End Prisons: A Response to Russell Robinson's 'Masculinity as Prison'," *The Circuit*, Paper 4, (2012), 184–195, 191.

[9]Julia C. Oparah, "Feminism and the (Trans)gender Entrapment of Gender Nonconforming Prisoners," *UCLA Women's L.J.* 18 (2012): 239–271, 241.

[10]Eric A. Stanley and Dean Spade, "Queer (In)Justice, 'Queering Prison Abolition, Now?'" *American Quarterly* (2012): 115–127, 122.

and threatening.[11] In short, they are considered difficult prisoners.[12] As a consequence they face multiple manifestations of exclusion.

The purpose of this chapter is to explore how the law on prisoners' rights legitimises and reinforces these normative relations of power with a focus on three areas: (a) gender recognition: the systemic exclusions of transgender identities; (b) isolation of visible and vulnerable queer prisoners and (c) the heightened surveillance of long-term relationships. Before we move on to the analysis of multiple exclusions of queer prisoners that is reproduced in particular prisoners' rights cases, the subsequent section sets out the theoretical framework. This is centred on heteronormative and gender-normative power relations in prison that produce queer prisoners in an irreconcilable paradox as both vulnerable and threatening.

2 Queer Prisoners: Vulnerable and Threatening

We take a Foucauldian perspective of power. Michel Foucault, in his seminal work "Discipline and Punish", questioned the centrality of the prison in contemporary punitive regimes, as well as the broader question of how power functions.[13] For Foucault, the prison functions in many ways similar to other institutions in industrialised societies, such as the factory and the school, to produce docile bodies through disciplinary power.[14] In his later work, on governmentality and biopower, he found that liberalism/neoliberalism produced a particular form of power, power as government.[15] Liberalism/neoliberalism as rationalities of power in combination with technologies of power aims at creatively and reflexively shaping people's conduct to enhance the wellbeing of the population as a whole (biopower).[16] Through governance and self-governance, the aim is to secure the wellbeing of the population—through e.g. sanitation, health and safety regulations, public

[11]Robyn Emerton, "Transgender Prisoners: Law, Prison Administration, and the Emerging Tension Between Human Rights and Risk" (PhD dissertation, Keele University, 2018).

[12]Mary Corcoran, *Out of Order: The Political Imprisonment of Women in Northern Ireland 1972–1998* (Cullompton: Willan Publishing, 2006).

[13]Michel Foucault, *Discipline and Punish* (London: Penguin Books, [1977] 1991).

[14]Foucault, *Discipline and Punish.*

[15]Mitchell Dean, *Governmentality: Power and Rule in Modern Society*, 2nd edn. (Los Angeles: Sage, 2010), 18. See also Michel Foucault, *The Birth of Biopolitics: Lectures at the Collège de France, 1978–1979* (Basingstoke: Palgrave Macmillan, 2008).

[16]Dean, *Governmentality*, 18; Rose and Miller cited in Eamonn Carrabine, *Power, Discourse and Resistance: A Genealogy of the Strangeways Prison Riot* (Dartmouth: Ashgate, 2004).

health insurance—to support the capitalist economy through enterprising labour.[17] Crucially, Foucault argued that governmentality reconfigured and co-opted other forms of power, such as disciplinary power and sovereignty.[18] Under liberalism/neoliberalism, sovereignty is democratised and is, therefore, understood through a human rights discourse; the utility produced through disciplinary power shifts towards a general utility through regulation; and power as government becomes processes directed at the wellbeing and labour of the population in which "the subject is revealed in its social, biological and economic form".[19] For Foucault then, power is relational; it requires a subject who can resist[20]; and power is productive or persuasive as well as coercive.[21]

Applying this approach to incarceration, gendered power relations produce homogenised conceptions of men and women prisoners and reinforce hierarchical gender relations. Both the works of Kelly Hannah-Moffat and Eamonn Carrabine separately have shown that power in prison is diffused through mundane practices, routines and local decision-making.[22] Power in prison functions in a way to creatively and reflexively shape prisoners' conduct through productive and repressive forms of power. The neoliberal strategies, empowerment and responsibilization, to shape prisoners' conduct so that they can be integrated into society, are aimed at governance at a distance through self-regulation and self-monitoring. They nevertheless depend on coercive, disciplinary governing strategies directed at those who are perceived as resistant or are deemed unempowerable, namely those who are not capable nor willing to self-govern pursuant to neoliberal strategies.[23] These governing strategies can be understood as producing prisoners as governable subjects.[24]

Prisons, then, are deeply gendered institutions that enforce a gender binary and perpetuate heteronormative gender performativity.[25] Judith Butler highlights that gender is a performative rather than an expressive act.[26] It is

[17] Dean, *Governmentality*, 30.

[18] Michel Foucault, "Governmentality," in *The Foucault Effect: Studies in Governmentality: With Two Lectures by and an Interview with Michel Foucault*, ed. Graham Burchell, Colin Gordon and Peter Miller (Chicago: University of Chicago Press, 1991) 87–104.

[19] Dean, *Governmentality*, 122.

[20] Michel Foucault, *Society Must Be Defended* (London: Penguin Books, 2004) 29.

[21] Dean, *Governmentality*, 58.

[22] Kelly Hannah-Moffat, *Punishment in Disguise: Penal Governance and Federal Imprisonment of Women in Canada* (Toronto: University of Toronto Press, 2001). Carrabine, *Power, Discourse and Resistance*.

[23] Hannah-Moffat, *Punishment in Disguise*.

[24] Thomas Ugelvik, *Power and Resistance in Prison: Doing Time, Doing Freedom*, Palgrave Studies in Prisons and Penology (Basingstoke, UK: Palgrave Macmillan, 2014).

[25] Carrabine and Longhurst, *Gender and Prison Organisation.*

[26] Judith Butler, *Gender Trouble.*

continuously produced through repetition/variation of the gendered self within the constraints of discursive practices that produce binary dominant gender ideals and, at the same time, obscure their derivative origin.[27] Prisons reflect "a hyper expression of traditional gender roles".[28] Men's prisons are characterised by a hypermasculine environment in which a degree of violence and aggression is deemed acceptable or an unavoidable part of prison culture for men.[29] This in turn facilitates violence against prisoners by officers—and also violence between prisoners for transgressions from the hypermasculine performance.[30] Gender-normative masculinity in prison perpetuates a heterosexist environment in which homophobia, transphobia and misogyny are amplified.

Women's imprisonment, in contrast, is characterised by numerous contradictory discourses that require women to be both "in control" (e.g. coping and caring) and "out of control" (e.g. in need of protection).[31] Women's prisons are constructed as spaces of "feminine" passivity, dependence and emotion, with gender non-conformity among women seen as evidence of their delinquency.[32] Consequently, women and/or gender non-conforming prisoners are considered to violate normative femininity and, therefore, prisons function to "Discipline, Infantalize, Feminize, Medicalize and Domesticize".[33] Whereas governance strategies—namely control, rehabilitation or normalisation—for men who conform to the dominant ideals of masculinity are centred on their offending behaviour, the risk that they pose to society and the institution. These gendered governing strategies produce binary prisoner identities: the normal man versus the dangerous, disruptive, violent and foreign man.[34] These are still within the scope of possible identities within the hypermasculine imaginary of gender performance. More

[27]Judith Butler, *Gender Trouble*.

[28]Lori Girshick "Out of Compliance: Masculine-Identified People in Women's Prisons," in *Captive Genders: Trans Embodiment and the Prison Industrial Complex*, edited by Eric A. Stanley and Nat Smith (Edinburgh, UK and Oakland, CA: AK Press, 2011) 215–234, 217.

[29]Joe Sim, "Tougher Than the Rest? Men in Prison," in *Just Boys Doing Business? Men, Masculinities and Crime*, ed. Tim Newburn and Elizabeth A. Stanko (London: Routledge, 1994) 100–117.

[30]Lori Girshick, "Out of Compliance," 217.

[31]P. Carlen, *Sledgehammer: Women's Imprisonment at the* Millennium (London: Macmillan Press, 1998) 67–68.

[32]Lori Girshick, "Out of Compliance," 217.

[33]Pat Carlen and Chris Tchaikovsky, "Women in Prison," in *Criminal Women: Autobiographical Accounts*, edited by Pat Carlen, Jenny Hicks, Josie O'Dwyer, Diana Christina and Chris Tchaikovsky (Cambridge: Polity Press, 1985) 182.

[34]This reflects the racialized dimension at the core of incarceration that has already been highlighted.

significantly for our analysis is the binary normal man versus the "difficult" Other, who is considered dangerous/risky as well as vulnerable.[35]

LGBTIQ+ people in prison are othered to a degree through homogenization in two groups, sexual orientation and gender identity.[36] Moreover, the process involves the stripping away of intersected identities, such as race, class, age, ability.[37] Trans women/men who present in their lived gender and genderfluid/non-binary people are extremely visible and subject to transphobia as well as enhanced governing strategies,[38] whereas queer people may feel unsafe to be open about their sexuality. In all cases, the prison's protective regimes operate on a spectrum of isolation from solitary confinement to Vulnerable Prisoner Units.[39] All of these involve restrictions of access to exercise, association, work and education. Julia Oparah, in her analysis that disrupts the fixed category of woman through an "anti-racist" gender queer framework, writes that the prison's rigid gender binary forces trans/gender non-conforming people to "inhabit a gender identity that [they] had rejected as a fundamental part of their sense of selfhood".[40] Through her nuanced framework she draws out the intersectional experiences of race, class and gender non-conformity of incarceration in a rigid binary system.[41]

The prison represents a site of coercion in particular for people with fluid gender identities and sexualities, who experience violent and coercive hostility. Gail Mason, in her study on homophobic violence writes that homophobic-related violence is distinct from gendered violence.[42] It can be understood as violence that not only affects queer people's everyday practices

---

[35]Corcoran, *Out of Order*.

[36]This is evidenced in ways in which official statistics are collected, namely the percentage of LGB or other prisoners and the number of trans prisoners in a year. For 2017/18, 2.7% of prisoners who declared were LGB or other and 139 trans prisoners out of 83,263 incarcerated people. A breakdown to age, gender and ethnicity is only produced for trans prisoners, e.g. 9% BAME (27% BAME in overall prison population). Ministry of Justice, NOMS Annual Offender Equalities Report 2016/17, Ministry of Justice Statistics Bulletin, November 30, 2017, https://assets.publishing.service.gov.uk/government/uploads/system/uploads/attachment_data/file/760093/hmpps-offender-equalities-2017-18.pdf. NOMS only really started collecting some data on LGB and trans people in prison from 2015/2016 Offender Equalities Report. The first report was published in 2013.

[37]Eric Stanley, "Introduction: Fugitive Flesh: Gender Self-Determination, Queer Abolition and Trans Resistance," in *Captive Genders: Trans Embodiment and the Prison Industrial Complex*, edited by Eric Stanley and Nat Smith (Edinburgh, Oakland and Baltimore: AK Press, 2011) 7–20.

[38]See subsection Gender Recognition.

[39]See subsection Isolation.

[40]Julia C. Oparah, "Feminism and the (Trans)gender Entrapment of Gender Nonconforming Prisoners," *UCLA Women's L.J.* 18 (2012): 239–271, 241.

[41]Oparah, "(Trans)gender Entrapment," 270.

[42]Gail Mason, *The Spectacle of Violence: Homophobia, Gender and Knowledge* (London and New York: Routledge, 2002).

for avoiding harm, but also "knowledge systems through which we construct and recognise sexual identities".[43] In her analysis of the interrelationship of power and violence, she finds that power relations that produce exclusionary regimes centred on gender, sexuality, race (and gender identity) are constitutive of violence.[44] Queer and gender fluid people challenge these binary gendered governing strategies and the biological determinism implicit in the structure of imprisonment.

It is important to note that prisoners' subjectivity is contested in prison. People in prison negotiate power relations within the institution through a sense of self that is formed outside and reflects wider social constructions of gender, race, class, sexuality, gender identity, ability and age.[45] Exposed to asymmetric power relations, they nevertheless engage in everyday struggles with other prisoners and staff over food, exercise, visits and association to retain a degree of choice and autonomy.[46] Queer prisoners engage in hidden resistance practices that challenge the heteronormative prisoner subject to create better alternative subject positions.[47] Within the context of penal governing strategies, this resistant subjectivity is conceived as a paradox, both vulnerable and threatening. This paradox in turn produces varieties of exclusion for queer prisoners that will be explored in the following section.

3 Varieties of Exclusion

Queer prisoners are doubly excluded in prison. Due to the forced gender binary together with high prevalence of homophobia and transphobia, predominantly in men's prisons but not exclusively, many queer prisoners are faced with either keeping their identities hidden or being exposed to ridicule, bullying and harassment.[48] This has been highlighted as a "cycle of invisibility" that exposes them to further risks and harms.[49]

---

[43] Mason, *Spectacle of Violence*, 3.

[44] Mason, *Spectacle of Violence*, 135.

[45] Mary Bosworth, *Engendering Resistance: Agency, and Power in Women's Prisons* (Aldershot, UK: Dartmouth Publishing Company, 1999); Stanley, "Fugitive Flesh."

[46] Mary Bosworth and Eamonn Carrabine, "Reassessing Resistance: Race, Gender and Sexuality in Prison," *Punishment and Society* 3, no. 4 (2001): 501–515.

[47] Ugelvik, *Doing Time*.

[48] Nicola Carr, S. Siobhán McAlister and Tanya Serisier, "Out on the Inside: The Rights, Needs, and Experiences of LGBT People in Prison," Irish Penal Reform Trust, 2016; Mia Harris, "British Prisons Must Now Recognise Gender Fluid and Non-binary Inmates," *The Conversation*, November 16, 2016, accessed March 27, 2020, https://theconversation.com/profiles/mia-harris-288195.

[49] Peter Dunn, "Slipping Off the Equalities Agenda: Work with LGBT Prisoners," *Prison Service Journal* 206 (2013): 3–10, 6.

In this part of the chapter we explore how the law on prisoners' rights reinforces gender-normative and heteronormative conceptions through the multiple manifestations of exclusion of queer prisoners: gender recognition—the systemic exclusions of transgender identities; isolation of visible and vulnerable queer prisoners; heightened surveillance of long-term relationships.

3.1 Gender Recognition: The Systemic Exclusions of Transgender Identities

Concerted efforts have been made to advance the inclusion of transgender and more fluid identities within society. However, existing legal approaches continue to ostracise these identities in various ways. For example, transgender and gender non-conforming identities are consistently excluded from entering freely into some conventional societal practices that are often pursued nonchalantly by their cis counterparts, such as sexual-based intimacy and family life.[50] This is driven by the common law's appropriation of biology and anatomy as the standard by which to privilege those identities it deems worthy of inclusion. Simultaneously, the common law eschews those identities deemed less worthy of inclusion to the periphery of the legal conscience.[51]

The law's failure to accommodate the needs of transgender people within wider society is amplified in the context of the prison, due to the hypervisibility of transgender prisoners and, consequently, their heightened vulnerability within the prison environment.[52] Transgender prisoners are exposed to heightened levels of vulnerability within the prison because their gender expression digresses from the heteronormative prison environment.[53] As a site, the prison has legitimised the exposure of transgender prisoners to an increased hybrid visibility-vulnerability, because it places restrictions upon such items supporting inmates' gender expression.[54] Although prison guidelines state that "[a]ll individuals in our care must be supported to express the gender with which they identify", Emerton identifies the significant barriers

[50] *McNally* [2013] EWCA Crim 1051, *J v B and The Children* [2017] EWFC 4.

[51] *Corbett v Corbett* [1970] 2 ALL ER 33, *McNally [2013]*.

[52] Stephen Whittle, Lewis Turner, and Maryam Al-Alami, *Engendered Penalties: Transgender and Transsexual People's Experiences of Inequality and Discrimination* (London and Manchester: Press for Change and Manchester Metropolitan University, 2007) 21.

[53] Valerie Jenness and Sarah Fernstermaker, "Agnes Goes to Prison: Gender Authenticity, Transgender Inmates in Prisons for Men, and Pursuit of 'The Real Deal'," *Gender and Society* (2013): 5–31, 12.

[54] *R (on the application of Green) v Secretary of State for Justice* [2013] EWHC 3491 (Admin).

hindering access to specific healthcare for transgender prisoners.[55] Thus, in providing only formal access to these essential services, prisons can be said to increase the visibility of transgender prisoners and, thus, exacerbate their pre-existing vulnerabilities, because "they do not conform to the dictates of an extremely heteronormative and masculinist environment".[56]

The exclusionary jurisprudential approach towards criminalised transgender people and those with more fluid gender identities can be traced back to the common law prior to the enforcement of the Human Rights Act 1998.[57] The Court of Appeal decision in *Regina v Frederick William Harris* illustrates the judiciary's historically cisnormative and exclusionary approach towards LGBTQI+ people and imprisonment.[58] Harris concerned a transgender appellant who appealed their sentence for various fraudulent-related offences.[59] Initially, Justice Goddard accorded weight to the appellant's distress and fear of potential violence should their gender history become common knowledge among their peers within the prison.[60] In considering this, Justice Goddard allowed the defendant's appeal and proposed that all prison sentences should run concurrently.[61]

While the judgment in *Harris* may appear to reflect an enlightened and progressive perspective, in merely providing a concurrent sentence, Justice Goddard failed to give full consideration to the prison as enforcing the "hyper expression of traditional gender roles".[62] As such, the judge can be said to have failed to properly reflect on the well-documented nature of the prison as a site endorsing violence and exclusion specifically for transgender people. In failing to critically reflect upon the suitability of the prison for the appellant in terms of their gender identity, the judgment simply privileged the "niceties of [law's] internal structure and the beauty of its logical processes".[63] Thus, the judicial approach adopted in *Harris* suggests that the law prioritises the prison system's regulation of gender in the binary sense above supporting the

---

[55]See Emerton, "Transgender Prisoners: Law, Prison Administration," 269. See also the previous policy: PSI 17/2016, Transsexual Prisoners. [4.2].

[56]Jenness and Fernstermaker, "Gender Authenticity," 10.

[57]The Human Rights Act 1998 came into force in 2000.

[58]*R v Frederick William Harris [2000]* WL 1027092.

The term 'cisnormative' describes the approach that "assum[es] people experience harmony between their gender identity and their anatomy, and privileges those who do"; Alex Sharpe, *Sexual Intimacy and Gender Identity 'Fraud': Reframing the Legal and Ethical Debate* (Abingdon: Routledge, 2018).

[59]*Harris* [2000], [2].

[60]*Harris* [2000] [9]–[10].

[61]*Harris* [2000] [11].

[62]Stanley and Smith, *Captive Genders*, 217.

[63]Roscoe Pound, "Mechanical Jurisprudence," *Columbia Law Review* (1908).

autonomy and welfare of transgender prisoners.[64] In short, the judge gives precedence to the legal status quo above ensuring that the prison system can suitably accommodate the appellant.

Further, the court diminishes the autonomy and welfare of transgender prisoners by emphasising the appellant's gender identity as hindering the decision-making process.[65] The judge problematized the gender identity of the appellant above troubling the innate transphobia and homophobia of the prison environment.[66] In preserving the use of imprisonment in this instance, the judge consciously exposed the appellant to multiple forms of exclusion and oppression within the prison, such as; prejudice, discrimination and violence.[67]

Although the judge was informed about the defendant's legitimate fears of a possible attack within the prison in light of transphobic attitudes, she refrained from imposing a suspended prison sentence. The reluctance to provide the defendant with a suspended sentence arose despite the judge's ability to access the doctrine of judicial notice.[68] Although the ambit of judicial notice is unclear, Alex Sharpe suggests that this rule could allow for judges to refer to the "well-documented pattern of discrimination and violence experienced by transgender and other gender non-conforming people" within judgments.[69] Thus, in theory such an approach could ensure that the law protects people with more fluid gender identities from the well-evidenced violence of imprisonment by addressing their transgression of the law from within society rather than from within the confines of the prison.

Instead, the judge in *Harris* reified existing cisnormative approaches towards criminal justice. This is because the judge "bar[red] open inquiry [to] the normative desirability of alternative judicial decisions, and thus naturaliz[ed] contingent doctrinal choices".[70] Therefore, the failure to challenge

[64]Stanley and Spade, "Queering Prison Abolition," 120.

[65]*Harris* [2000] [9].

[66]Rebecca Mann, "The Treatment of Transgender Prisoners, Not Just an American Problem—A Comparative Analysis of American, Australian, and Canadian Prison Policies Concerning the Treatment of Transgender Prisoners and a 'Universal'Recommendation to Improve Treatment," *Law and Sexuality Review, Lesbian Gay Bisexual and Legal Issues* 15 (2006): 91–134, 6.
Harris [2000] [9].

[67]*Harris* [2000] [11].

[68]Alex Sharpe, "Queering Judgment: The Case of Gender Identity Fraud," *Journal of Criminal Law* (2017): 417–435.

[69]Sharpe, "Queering Judgment," 6. Sharpe highlights that in accessing judicial notice the information highlighted must be "so notorious, or clearly established, or susceptible to demonstration by reference to a readily obtainable and authoritative source, that evidence of their existence is unnecessary."

[70]Hanoch Dagan, "The Realist Conception of Law," *The University of Toronto Law Journal* (2007): 607–660, 618.

the use of custodial sentences for queer prisoners resulted in the double-exclusion of the appellant from mainstream society and within the prison. Fundamentally, the decision in *Harris* represents a missed opportunity to contest gender-normative approaches to incarceration and criminal justice.[71]

3.1.1 Permitting Prison Transfer: Lighting the Touch Paper for Inclusive Reform?

More recent jurisprudence indicates the desire to better accommodate transgender people within the prison estate. In *R (on the application of B) v Secretary of State for Justice (AB)*, the High Court heard an application to challenge the decision denying the transfer of a transgender woman to the women's prison estate.[72] The applicant was a transgender woman, who had not undertaken a gender affirmation operation as part of her transition, and who was granted a Gender Recognition Certificate (GRC) in 2006 in line with the Gender Recognition Act (GRA) 2004.[73] Despite legal recognition of her gender status, her requests to be placed within a prison correlating with her gender status were denied. The applicant's transfer to the women's prison estate was crucial in accessing a physical gender reassignment to support her gender transition. The Gender Identity Clinic would not approve gender reassignment surgery until the claimant could demonstrate that she had lived as a woman in a woman's prison for two years.[74] However, the prison authorities deemed it inappropriate to transfer the claimant to a women's prison and they continued to hold her within the Vulnerable Prisoners Unit.[75] As part of the judgment, the court recognised that this denied the claimant even the prospect of accessing physical gender affirmation surgery.[76]

Encouragingly, the judge held that the refusal to transfer the claimant was unjustified and, in doing so, the prison service had disproportionately interfered with the claimant's personal autonomy in violation of art. 8 of

[71] See Sharpe, "Queering Judgment" for an alternative approach to judgment writing as a means of reconfiguring historic juristic constructions of gender; while also remaining faithful to the constraints and conventions imposed by traditional judicial method. Exploring the potential of establishing gender-fluid approaches to judicial decision-making within a criminal law context would be a valuable avenue of further research.

[72] *R (on the application of B) v Secretary of State for Justice* [2009] EWHC 2220.

[73] *AB* [2009]. Under Section 9(1) of the GRA 2004, the individual in receipt of the certificate must be recognised within their acquired gender and sex upon its issue.

[74] *AB* [2009] [7].

[75] *AB* [2009] [4].

[76] *AB* [2009] [7] and [49].

the European Convention on Human Rights (ECHR).[77] Although the judge recognised imprisonment as involving the restriction of personal autonomy to some extent, he characterised the failure to transfer the claimant to the women's prison estate as "going beyond that which imprisonment is intended to do".[78] In summary, the judge declared:

> When issues so close to the identity of a prisoner as here, so intimately concerned with her personal autonomy, the deployment of resources as a justification for the infringement of rights must be clear and weighty in order to be proportionate. Here they are neither.[79]

In outlining the high standard required to justify an infringement on individuals' personal autonomy and identity, the judgment underlines the law's commitment to safeguarding the fundamental needs of those with more fluid gender identities. In doing so, the passage also highlights the tension between the legal recognition of transgender prisoners' gender identity and the punitive institutional norms that seek to deny this recognition. Ultimately, in safeguarding the claimant's right to autonomy and privacy, the law indicates its increased commitment to including transgender prisoners more effectively into the prison estate. Again, however, this judgment does little to challenge the culture of transphobia at the very root of the prison.

3.1.2 Prison Service Policies: A Transformative Approach Towards Transgender Prisoners?

In the past, official guidelines have legitimised the partial inclusion of transgender prisoners and the absolute exclusion of prisoners with more fluid gender identities.[80] The National Offenders Management Service (NOMS) Instructions on managing transgender prisoners (PSI-07/2011) was enacted in response to the shortcomings identified in the *AB* case. The purpose of PSI-07/2011 was to outline the duties of prison service professionals in managing the rights and specific needs of incarcerated transgender people.[81] These duties included ensuring the fair treatment of transgender people, providing an equivalent quality of care to transgender prisoners who have been diagnosed with gender dysphoria as they would expect to receive from

[77] *AB* [2009] [49].
[78] *AB* [2009] [49].
[79] *AB* [2009] [77].
[80] *Green* [2013].
[81] *AB* [2009] [18].

the NHS, and allowing them to wear clothes that support their gender identity.[82]

Outwardly, the PSI 07/2011 appears to have provided incarcerated transgender people with a plethora of assurances that their gender identity would be effectively supported and safeguarded. However, the wording of the policy was inclusive only of those who proposed to live "permanently [in] the gender opposite to the one assigned at birth".[83] As a result, the policy excluded a multiplicity of individuals whose gender expressions deviate from their gender in the heteronormative sense. Thus, the policy compelled individuals to either convey their gender in a rigid manner reflecting the policy in order to have their needs met, or to risk having their needs overlooked by authentically portraying their gender identity.

The policy also extended a high degree of discretion to prison professionals to make important decisions about the lives of transgender people. Prison officers who possess limited knowledge and training opportunities to address sensitive matters like gender identity were given considerable discretion in implementing this policy.[84] Similarly, they were extended considerable discretion in crucial decisions including in the placement of transgender inmates within the prison most suitably aligning with the prisoner's gender identity.[85] Given the combined lack of expertise and considerable scope in which to implement the policy, Lamble highlights that the policy provided a platform to foster archaic attitudes towards gender identity. Similarly, Mia Harris and Robyn Emerton argue that the policy limited and denied transgender prisoners their basic needs to express and have their gender identity recognised.[86] In sum, although the PSI 07/2011 appears progressive in recognising the specific needs and rights of some transgender prisoners, the policy also limited its protection to those performing gender in the binary sense.

The alienation of individuals who are perceived as falling outside the remit of the policy is evident in *R (on the application of Green) v Secretary of State for Justice*.[87] The case challenged the decision made by the prison governor to prohibit supportive gender items on security grounds, including a wig and tights to an incarcerated transgender person.[88] *Green* argued that the decision

---

[82]PSI 07/2011, Transsexual Prisoners. 1.5, 2.2, 3.3.

[83]PSI 07/2011, Transsexual Prisoners. 1.1, 3.2.

[84]Sarah Lamble, "Rethinking Gendered Prison Policies: Impacts on Transgender Prisoners," *ECAN Bulletin* 10 (2012).

[85]Lamble, Gendered prison policies.

[86]Lamble, Gendered prison policies.

[87]*Green* [2013].

[88]A detailed list of the items requested can be found at paragraph 35 of the judgment.

contravened PSI 07/2011, as well as violating her rights enshrined under the Equality Act 2010.[89]

Initially, the judge acknowledged the complexity of the prison environment for transgender people and for those with more fluid gender identities.[90] Similarly, he recognised that the hostility and ignorance towards transgender people within the prison environment increased the exposure of transgender prisoners to potential instances of sexual and physical violence.[91] Encouragingly, he accorded weight to the "profound" importance of recognising an individual's gender identity and gender transition.[92] However, the judge ruled that the prohibition of the items represented a legitimate and necessary security and discipline measure.[93] Rather than addressing the culture of transphobia within the prison environment, the judge problematized *Green*'s gender identity as an issue that is "likely to materially affect the good order of the other wings".[94] This mirrors more historic jurisprudence established by *Harris*, as once again the judge missed the opportunity to address the foundation of transphobia within the prison. In failing to trouble these embedded attitudes within the prison estate, the court perpetuates the very discrimination that the law purports to protect society against.[95]

Perhaps, more concerning is the judge's refusal to recognise and accommodate the identity of the transgender claimant properly within the judgment. Towards the end of the judgment, he makes inferences to the claimant's biological and anatomical makeup and physical appearance in a manner which casts doubt on the authenticity of her gender status.[96] The judge states:

> The claimant is a man seeking to become a woman – but he is still of the male gender and a male prisoner. He is in a male prison and until there is a Gender Recognition Certificate, he remains male. A woman prisoner cannot conceivably be the comparator as the woman prisoner has (either by birth or election) achieved what the claimant wishes. Male to female transsexuals are not automatically entitled to the same treatment as women – until they become women.[97]

[89] Section 13 (1) *Equality Act 2010*; *Green* [2013] [31]–[32], [34], and [65].
[90] *Green* [2013] [2], [28], and [46].
[91] *Green* [2013] [2], [28], and [46].
[92] *Green* [2013] [2].
[93] *Green* [2013] [37] and [71].
[94] *Green* [2013] [46].
[95] Dunn, "Slipping Off," 14.
[96] *Green* [2013] [10]–[11].
[97] *Green* [2013] [68].

In narrowly conceptualising the claimant's gender identity in essentialist terms, the judge merely reifies archaic jurisprudence.[98] Further, the judge perpetuates the false premise that transgender people must undergo a physical gender transition in order to be perceived as living authentically in their true gender. Thus, he can also be said to contravene the Equality Act 2010, as he fails to accord the same respect to transgender prisoners, such as Green, who are "proposing to undergo" or who are "undergoing" a "process (or part of a process) for the purpose of reassigning the person's sex".[99] Ultimately, it is clear that the essentialist legacy of *Corbett v Corbett (Otherwise Ashley) (No 1)* remains despite the enactment of the Equality Act 2010, which was heralded as a "new beginning" in terms of equality for some of the most vulnerable members of our society.[100]

Following the self-inflicted deaths of transgender women prisoners—Vikki Thompson, Joanne Latham and Jenny Swift—after they were incorrectly placed in the men's prison estate, the Government was compelled to revise the former rigid and essentialist PSI-2011.[101] A new policy PSI-17/2016 came into effect in January 2017 with the promise of extending a "more flexible approach to location" and protection of those transgender prisoners who express their gender in binary terms, but also to those with more fluid gender identities and non-binary prisoners.[102] Harris and Emerton commend the largely progressive stance provided by the revised PSI embracing the swifter and more transparent process of location supported by the convening of "Transgender Case Boards".[103] Despite the more progressive stance of PSI-17/2016, Robyn Emerton highlights that media outlets consistently problematize the inclusion of transgender people within the prison environment.[104] This concern has since been amplified more recently by

---

[98] *Corbett* [1970] represented the authority on determining sex and gender until the enactment of the Gender Recognition Act 2004. The case concerned the applicant, Arthur Corbett, who issued legal proceedings to annul the marriage with his spouse, April Ashley, on the grounds that she was male. Upon the construction of invasive and chromosomal, gonadal and genital tests to determine the sex of April Ashley, Lord Justice Ormerod ruled that sex was fixed at birth and unalterable, meaning that Ashley would only be recognised as male for the purposes of marriage law in England and Wales. In permitting the annulment of the marriage between the couple on the basis of rigid and biological conceptions of sex, Omerod J refused to recognise Ashley's gender identity as a woman.

[99] Section 7 (1) *Equality Act 2010.*

[100] Bob Hepple, "The New Single Equality Act in Britain," *The Equality Rights Review* (2010): 11–24, 22.

[101] Anon, "Transgender Prison Deaths: Watchdog Calls for Action," *BBC News*, January 10, 2017, accessed March 27, 2020, https://www.bbc.co.uk/news/uk-38562714.

[102] PSI 07/2016, Transgender Prisoners 1.3, 2.3, 2.4, 2.5.

[103] Mia Harris and Robyn Emerton, "New Policy on Transgender Prisoners: Progressive But Can Prisons Keep Pace?" *Inherently Human*, November 21, 2016. Accessed November, 17 2020, https://inherentlyhuman.wordpress.com/2016/11/21/new-policy-on-transgender-prisoners-progressive-but-can-prisons-keep-pace/.

[104] Robyn Emerton, "Transgender Prisoners," 4

gender-critical feminists following the transfer of Karen White to the women's prison estate.[105]

While PSI-17/2016 extend protection to a diverse range of genders, the policy reinforces the need to demonstrate "consistent evidence" of living in an authentic gender.[106] Thus, while the policy takes steps to include a range of transgender prisoners who experience their gender in binary terms, Harris and Emerton highlight that non-binary prisoners will continue to be placed within either the men's or women's prison estate depending on their legal gender.[107] Thus, arguably, PSI-17/2016 decreases the vulnerability of some transgender prisoners by offering limited opportunities to lessen their visibility within the prison. This is the reverse for non-binary prisoners, who are left increasingly vulnerable within the prison because they are rendered invisible by inadequate institutional policies. Therefore, while some gender identities are granted more substantive, but nonetheless limited, inclusion, others receive only formal protection and thereby remain on the periphery of the legal conscience.

At the time of writing, the Government has once again sought to implement a new policy, the Transgender Policy Framework (2020) for the care and management of individuals who are transgender.[108] The new framework "The Care and Management of Individuals who are Transgender" is a detailed risk management strategy that is designed to strike a "balance" between maintaining the wellbeing and safety of "transgender" people and others occupying the prison estate. It makes several key amendments to the former PSI-17/2016 including, an extension to the period in which to convene the Initial Local Transgender Case Board and the mandatory completion of an "Advance Disclosure" form prior to each Local and Complex Transgender Case Board.[109] Unlike the previous PSI-17/2016, the new framework explicitly centres the "balance[ing] of risks and the promot[ion] of the safety of all"; suggesting that the policy was heavily influenced by the case concerning Karen White and subsequent pressure groups.[110] Further in-depth research must be undertaken to explore the specific impacts of this recent policy change on transgender people, intersex, non-binary, gender fluid people and cross-dressers who are also encompassed under this policy.

---

[105]For a nuanced analysis of the Karen White case see Alex Sharpe, "Foxes in the Henhouse: Putting the Trans Women Prison Debate in Perspective," *Inherently Human*, September 11, 2018, accessed March 27, 2020, https://inherentlyhuman.wordpress.com/2018/09/11/foxes-in-the-henhouse-putting-the-trans-women-prison-debate-in-perspective/.

[106]PSI 17/2016, Transgender Prisoners. 2.4.

[107]Harris and Emerton, "New Policy."

[108]"The Care and Management of Individuals Who Are Transgender," HM Prisons and Probation Service, 31 October 2019.

[109]The Care and Management of Individuals who are Transgender, 2019.

[110]The Care and Management of Individuals who are Transgender, 2019, 1.6.

3.2 Isolation of Visible and Vulnerable Queer Prisoners

Queer prisoners who become visible or trans prisoners who are hyper-visible and who raise incidents of bullying, harassment or abuse and ask for protection are often isolated and placed in conditions amounting to (or near to) solitary confinement.[111] In 2013, two judgments were delivered on the issue of gay men placed in solitary confinement after they asked for protection: in the first case, *X v Turkey*, the European Court of Human Rights (ECtHR) questioned the protective nature of solitary confinement to protect prisoners from a homophobic environment and raised particular concerns about the conditions and the duration of the isolation.[112] Similar questions were also raised in an Irish case, *Connolly v Governor of Wheatfield Prison.*[113]

In *X v Turkey*, the ECtHR found both a violation of art. 3 ECHR, relating to inhuman and degrading treatment, along with a violation of art. 14, which related to discrimination on grounds of sexual orientation. The claimant, a gay man was kept in solitary confinement for eight months and 18 days with no contact to other prisoners and no exercise. In effect, he could only leave his cell when he received visits. In addition, his cell was badly lit, dirty and rat-infested. The authorities justified this form of isolation as protective custody.

In European human rights jurisprudence, solitary confinement itself does not violate art. 3 ECHR. Over time, the courts have maintained that complete sensory and social isolation would invariably meet that threshold.[114] Since then, the test has been revised to include an assessment of:

> the particular conditions, the stringency of the measure, its duration, the objective pursued and its effects on the person concerned (see *Rohde v. Denmark*, no. 69332/01, § 93, 21 July 2005).[115]

The success in X's case is partly due to the extreme conditions to which he was subject. The European Court of Human Rights noted that the claimant's conditions were worse than those of prisoners on whole-life sentences or

---

[111] Interim report of the Special Rapporteur on Torture to the UN General Assembly, 5 August 2011, A/66/268, p. 19 cit. in Penal Reform International and APT, LGBTI persons deprived of their liberty: framework for preventive monitoring, 2nd ed. 2015, https://cdn.penalreform.org/wp-content/uploads/2016/01/lgbti-framework-2nd-ed-v7-web.pdf, p. 11.

[112] *X v Turkey*, App. No. 24626/09 (ECtHR, 27 May 2013).

[113] *Connolly v Governor of Wheatfield* Prison [2013] IEHC 334.

[114] *Kröcher and Möller v Switzerland*, App. No. 8463/78 (ECmHR, 1978).

[115] *X v Turkey* [2003] [40].

those who posed a specific security risk, even though he was in protective custody.[116] The complete social isolation, as well as the unsanitary conditions, combined with the supposedly protective purpose met the extremely high threshold under art. 3 ECHR. They found that "the conditions of detention in solitary confinement were capable of causing him both mental and physical suffering and a feeling of profound violation of his human dignity".[117] Crucially, it seems that the judges clearly questioned the extent to which solitary confinement can have a protective function.

Significantly, the ECtHR maintained that the isolation of queer prisoners on protective grounds needed to be justified with a clear, legitimate aim as well as a proportionate response. In this case, they found that the isolation was solely discriminatory, namely based on his sexual orientation and this amounted to a violation of art. 14 ECHR. It is important to note that X's case was exceptional in terms of the deprivation that he suffered and the overt discrimination. Although the ruling challenges arbitrary decision-making, it fails to challenge the use of so-called protective isolation for vulnerable (in this case queer) prisoners. This is a theme that runs through the limited jurisprudence on the issue.

The Irish High Court, in *Connolly v Governor of Wheatfield Prison*, seems to have picked up the point that the isolation of queer prisoners for their protection needed to be based on a legitimate aim and needed to be a proportionate response in the circumstances.[118] Here, the Court's focus was on the legality of the solitary confinement, in particular the review process, the duration and any enhancements of the regime.

Mr. Connolly requested protection from the mainstream regime for fear of further violent, homophobic attacks.[119] Following a transfer to Wheatfield Prison in 2013, it was assessed that he was safe to be in the main regime. He objected and was then transferred to a segregation unit ("restricted regime"), where he was subject to 23-hour lock-up with one hour of exercise in the yard with other prisoners. He had access to items such as a television, books and magazines. However, he was excluded from education and other social activities. This decision was reviewed on a monthly basis.

[116]To put it in context, European human rights precedents that set out the test for the use of solitary confinement were cases in which prisoners were either in pre-trial detention for or convicted of very serious offences, such as drug trafficking/organized crime (*Rohde v Denmark* [69332/01] July 21, 2005), and terrorism (*Ramirez Sanchez* [59450/00] July 7, 2006).

[117]*X v Turkey* [2003] [45].

[118]*Connolly* [2013].

[119]Mainstream regime refers to prison wings that are not segregated spaces either for protection, punishment or containment.

The central question before the High Court was whether the solitary confinement of Connolly under the circumstances violated a provision in the Irish Constitution—to protect individuals from "unjust attack"—and whether this would justify his release. Mr. Justice Hogan found that Mr. Connolly's three months in solitary confinement for his protection was lawful. He maintained that solitary confinement is to be understood as an exceptional measure. Although he acknowledged the severely restrictive regime, he emphasised that the "voluntary" nature of the detention against the prison authorities' assessment, together with access to a television and reading material, as well as the medical support, went some way to mitigating the harm of solitary confinement. Moreover, the periodic review of the detention provided a mechanism to monitor Mr. Connolly's welfare. However, he added that the prison authorities were under a duty to monitor for signs of psychological distress. If the detention should be extended "indefinitely or for an extended period of months with no sign of variation" it may be considered unlawful.[120] He distinguished Mr. Connolly's case from an earlier judgment where the applicant had been subjected to complete sensory deprivation.[121]

Although Mr. Justice Hogan stressed the importance of duration, his ruling is clearly deferential. He maintained that the supervisory function of the court does not extend to setting prescriptive standards in relation to solitary confinement.[122] In this particular case, he repeatedly emphasised that Connolly was not being punished and that his conditions were ameliorated by some access to the social world. His refusal to leave segregation for fear of homophobic attacks seemed to have added legitimacy to the situation.

Judges are deferential in the prison context, in particular where there are security considerations. This also accounts for the high threshold under art. 3 ECHR, where segregation of prisoners needs to come close to complete sensory and social isolation.[123] The underlying assumption is that prisoners' rights are limited by the purposes of imprisonment. This was emphasised in the United Kingdom Supreme Court decision in *Bourgass*.[124] Lord Reed, in an unanimous judgment, maintained that prisoners had a right to "some

[120] *Connolly* [2013] [27].

[121] See *Kinsella* [2012] 1 I.R. 467. This mirrors the threshold set by the European Court of Human Rights mentioned above.

[122] This seems to be a broader problem in administrative rulings on prison standards, also in England and Wales. This is particularly the case relating to issues of security and order.

[123] See *Kröcher and Möller* (1978).

[124] *R (on the application of Bourgass and another)* SC [2015] UKSC 54.

degree of association"; however, the prison authorities have a wide discretion due to the complexities of managing that particular environment.[125] Prisoners had no "precisely defined entitlement to association as a matter of public law. The "amount of time which he is permitted to spend outside his cell, and the degree of association which he is in consequence permitted to have with other prisoners" was dependent on a number of factors.[126] This particular case concerned prisoners detained for violent and terrorist offences who were segregated for good order and discipline following various allegations of assault. Here, Lord Reed did not consider the implication for prisoners who are segregated for their own protection.

In the first instance, these spaces are designed and organised with security and surveillance in mind. Yet, segregation also doubles as a framework for protecting prisoners who are at risk in the main prison.[127] This means that prisoners are physically removed from the mainstream regime to either dedicated high security units designed to detain prisoners in solitary confinement or dedicated prison wings for vulnerable prisoners. As a consequence, they are not able to participate in the general activities (such as gym, library, education, work) at all (in the case of solitary confinement) or they may have reduced access (vulnerable prisoners). In England and Wales, there are different ways that prisoners can be segregated for protection: moved to designated segregation units, segregation in own cell or moved to a designated wing, so-called Vulnerable Prisoners Unit (VPUs). Prisoners who request protection may be moved to the prison's segregation unit, now Care and Separation Unit (CSU), temporarily until a space in a VPU becomes available.

In a comprehensive review of segregation units in England and Wales in 2015, "Deep Custody", Sharon Shalev and Edgar Kimmet found that six per cent of prisoners were segregated for their own protection.[128] This can include those who are at risk of self-harm, as well as prisoners who are at risk of harm from other prisoners. This "catch all" function is captured by a prison officer interviewed for the "Deep Custody" study. Segregation "can be for prisoners where basically there's nowhere else to place them. It's a case of needs must – there's nowhere else. It's protection for them and us (Officer)".[129]

[125] *R v Deputy Governor of Parkhurst Prison, Ex p Hague* [1992] 1 AC 58 cit. in *Bourgass* [2015] [122].

[126] *Ex p Hague* [1992] cited in *Bourgass* [2015], [122].

[127] Segregation of such prisoners is governed by Rule 45(1) of the Prison Rules 1999. Prisoners can be removed for the preservation of "good order or discipline" as well as "in his own interests".

[128] Sharon Shalev and Edgar Kimmet, *Deep Custody: Segregation Units and Close Supervision Centres in England and Wales*, Prison Reform Trust, 2015.

[129] Shalev and Kimmet, *Deep Custody*, 5.

For prisoners who are segregated, this means solitary confinement with little time spent outside their cell, mainly to have a shower or exercise in the yard. They are unlikely to have their personal belongings with them nor are they likely to have access to a television.[130] In "Deep Custody", they found that the conditions of confinement in segregation units or CSUs were not only restrictive but extremely deprived.

> Regimes … were impoverished, comprising little more than a short period of exercise, a shower, a phone call, and meals. In some units prisoners had to choose between having a shower and taking exercise or making a phone call in any one day. Most of the prisons we visited did not meet international standards in the provision of exercise.[131]

The severely harmful effects of solitary confinement to prisoners' mental and physical health are well-established.[132] They have been raised by international human rights bodies.[133] In the *Bourgass* case, the Minister and the prison authorities accepted that solitary confinement posed risks to prisoners' health and wellbeing. They emphasised that its use was restricted to a measure of "last resort where other means of addressing risk are considered insufficient".[134] Yet, there is still a significant lack of recognition from the prison authorities that solitary confinement or isolation are an inappropriate way to detain vulnerable prisoners.[135]

VPUs are dedicated spaces for prisoners in need of protection. While they resemble an ordinary wing, prisoners still face considerable restrictions. For instance, in a letter to "Inside Times" in 2012, a gay man wrote how following

---

[130]Prisons and Probation Ombudsman for England and Wales, *Learning Lessons Bulletin: Fatal Incident Investigations: Segregation* (June 2015), http://www.ppo.gov.uk/app/uploads/2015/06/Learning-Lessons-Bulletin-Segregation-final.pdf.

[131]Shalev and Kimmet, *Deep Custody*, 132.

[132]For a comprehensive review, see Peter Scharff Smith, "The Effects of Solitary Confinement on Prison Inmates: A Brief History and Review of the Literature," *Crime and Justice* 34, no. 1 (2006): 441–528.

[133]See the UN Special Rapporteur of the Human Rights Council on Torture and Other Cruel, Inhuman and Degrading Treatment or Punishment 2008 Istanbul Statement on the Use and Effects of Solitary Confinement cited *Bourgass* [2015] [38].

[134]*Bourgass* [2015] [40].

[135]Ariana Silvestri, "Prison Conditions in the United Kingdom," European Prison Observatory, 2013, https://www.crimeandjustice.org.uk/sites/crimeandjustice.org.uk/files/Prison%20conditions%20in%20the%20UK.pdf, p. 22. It is difficult to identify how this disproportionately affects LGBTIQ+ people as NOMS data on segregation does not include sexual orientation and gender identity. The most recent demographic data of numbers of prisoners segregated is listed in "Deep Custody," 148–149. They are split by ethnicity, age and gender. In the 2017/2018 Offender Equalities Annual Report, it is stated that number of segregation days among other data have been excluded due to poor quality of the data (see Ministry of Justice 2017/2018 Offender Equalities, 3).

abuse from other prisoners he was classified as a vulnerable prisoner and moved to the VPU.[136] His conditions of confinement changed considerably. He was mainly confined to his cell apart from one early session of basic education. In addition to this, he lost his job in the prison education block. He felt that this was unjustified and that he was treated unfairly as a gay man. Prisoners in varying degrees of social isolation are denied access to prison resources including education, recreation and work. Due to the homophobic and transphobic environment in the main prison regime, they may feel that it is risky for them to return.

Solitary confinement and other forms of segregation represent the essence of the prison's punitive capacity when all normalisation and rehabilitation measures are stripped away. It is widely recognised that prolonged social isolation is harmful. These isolation measures seem wholly unsuited as a means of protecting prisoners from systemic homophobia and transphobia. Not only are these spaces ill-suited for a protective function, the prison environment itself is incompatible for such a task. The "unempowerable" prisoners, which include those who are deemed in need of protection from the main regime, are essentially treated in the same way as the dangerous, risky and violent.

3.3 Separation and Relationship Recognition

In this final section, we critically engage with some more recent judgments on the way formalised relationships in prison challenge the heteronormative assumptions on prisoners' right to family life under art. 8 ECHR.[137] These are premised on the assumption that incarceration entails the separation of people in spousal relationships. Consequently, there is a recognition of the importance of relationships based on kinship to prisoners and, ultimately, their reintegration to society. The support of prisoners' family relationships is framed through the spatial and temporal separation with an emphasis on the facilitation of visits, correspondence and communication via technology. In this section, we explore how the courts have engaged with queer relationships in prison. The first issue has been the extension of inter-prison visits to queer couples. The second has been the separation of prisoners once relationships have been formalised.

[136]Erwin James, "Homophobia Is Still Rife in UK Prisons," *The Guardian*, September 25, 2012, accessed March 27, 2020, https://www.theguardian.com/society/2012/sep/25/homophobia-rife-uk-prisons.

[137]For a comprehensive overview of prisoners' rights under art. 8 ECHR, see Dirk Van Zyl Smit and Sonja Snacken, *Principles of European Prison Law and Policy: Penology and Human Rights* (Oxford: Oxford University Press, 2009).

3.3.1 Inter-prison Visits and the Quality of Family Life

In two consecutive applications, Charles O'Neill and William Lauchlan (O'Neill and Lauchlan), both serving life sentences with long tariffs, challenged the Scottish Prison Service's (SPS) decision to refuse inter-prison visits.[138] They claimed that, as a gay couple, the refusal amounted to a breach of their right to family life, art. 8 ECHR, and discrimination in breach of art. 14 ECHR.[139] In its second ruling, the Scottish Court considered two issues, first the legal validity of the Scottish inter-prison visit scheme and, secondly, whether the inter-prison visits extended to civil partnerships more broadly and to O'Neill and Lauchlan more specifically. The focus here will be on the latter.

In relation to the general question, the Court held that gay and lesbian couples were entitled to inter-prison visits.[140] In the particular circumstance of the case, Lord Stewart assessed the nature of the claimants' relationship. He held that the SPS did not fail to respect their right to family life nor did they discriminate against them. The question was whether the particular relationship amounted to "family life". According to Lord Stewart, family life:

> can refer to two different but overlapping things: it can refer to the type of relationship and it can refer to the quality of the relations between or among those concerned. There is no exhaustive definition of the relationships which attract the protection and support of Article 8 ECHR: ... Article 8 ECHR does not, for example, oblige the state to respect abusive, coercive and exploitative relationships ....[141]

The time and purpose of their togetherness was deemed central to establishing the quality of their relationship. In this case, the comparatively short periods together outside prison were dominated by their joint sexual violence

[138] *Charles O'Neill and William Lauchlan*, [2015] CSOH 93; [2015] CSOH 144 (*O'Neill and Lauchlan* [2015a] [2015b]). The Scottish Prison Service as well as its legal system are independent.

[139] The factual context of the decision is a bit strange in the sense that it changed in between the dates for the first (20–21 November 2014) and second hearing (12 May 2015). Following the first hearing, the Scottish Prison Service (SPS) changed its assessment of O'Neill and Lauchlan's relationship; it acknowledged that they had been in a same-sex relationship since before their detention in 2008. Furthermore, the SPS approved one inter-prison visit in that same period.

[140] *O'Neill and Lauchlan* (2015a) [10]. This is also the case in England and Wales, where inter-prison visits are governed by PSI 16/2011, Providing Visits and Services to Visitors [5.15]. See also *R (on the application of Bright) v Secretary of State for Justice, Bright v Governor of Whitemoor Prison CA (Civil Division)* [2014] EWCA Civ 1628; [2015] 1 W.L.R. 723; [2014] 12 WLUK 564 [14].

[141] *O'Neill and Lauchlan* (2015a) [15].

towards young boys.[142] Therefore, the judge found that the nature of their relationship did not come within the remit of art. 8 ECHR.

While the test of family life was applied restrictively in this case, there may be scope within this definition to broaden family life beyond heteronormative conceptions. Feminist critique centres on the privileging of heterosexual spousal relationships and correspondingly the "under-valuing of relationships of care, love and support".[143] Lord Stewart placed emphasis on "affection, confidence and dependence, that is financial, social and emotional dependence".[144] This could be interpreted as the extension of family life beyond the conjugal to other dependency models. Sue Westwood in her detailed analysis of the role of friendship relations to older, especially lesbian and gay, people and the ways in which law and social policy is adapting to the changing nature of relationships, summarises different models.[145] These include a reorientation away from spousal relationships to the centring of carer-dependent dyad[146]; an openness to valuing non-typical family configurations[147]; broadening next of kin and financial rights to alternative relationships[148]; application of contracts to formalise varied relationships[149]; as well as different registration schemes that could be opened up to non-spousal relationships.[150] In the conclusion, Westwood questions to what extent such alternative care and dependency relationships, including friendship, need to be or indeed should be formalised in law.

The formalisation of conjugal relationships in prison through civil partnerships or marriage challenges the heteronormative focus of the right to family life. Partners who live in the same space, be it the same prison wing or sharing a cell, openly subvert the forced separation of spouses inherent in incarceration. Arguably, they openly challenge the prison to its core. This is explored in the following section, which unpacks two recent judgments on whether the separation of prisoners from their partners should be considered a violation of the right to family life.

---

[142] This raises the question whether this family life test is equally applied to heterosexual couples in prison.

[143] Lynch cit. in Sue Westwood, "'My Friends Are My Family': An Argument About the Limitations of Contemporary Law's Recognition of Relationships in Later Life," *Journal of Social Welfare and Family Law* 35, no. 3 (2013): 347–363, 349.

[144] *O'Neill and Lauchlan* (2015a) [15].

[145] Westwood, "My Friends," 349.

[146] Fineman cited in Westwood, "My Friends," 349.

[147] Polikoff cited in Westwood, "My Friends," 349.

[148] Roseneil cited in Westwood, "My Friends," 349.

[149] Stychin cited in Westwood, "My Friends," 349.

[150] Barker cited in Westwood, "My Friends," 349.

3.3.2 Separating Prisoners from Their Partners

Two judgments have explored the legality of separating prisoners from their partners: *Bright and Keeley* and *Hopkins.*[151] *Bright and Keeley* [2014] involved combined applications: David Bright challenged the refusal to transfer his partner Beau Beale back onto the wing following allegations he had made against another prisoner, and to restrict further contact. Bright and Beale were planning to enter into a civil partnership. Andrew Keeley challenged the transfer of his partner John Doughty to another wing after the prison authorities had noticed them having sex. After the transfer, they entered into a civil partnership. Following further allegations of misconduct, they were also separated at work. Both Bright and Keeley argued that the decisions to separate them from their partners violated art. 8 of the ECHR.

The Court of Appeal granted permission to proceed and heard the case. Its decision was centred on three points: first, whether, under art. 8(2) ECHR, "in accordance with the law" requires a dedicated policy providing guidance for prisoners in long-term relationships to avoid separation; second whether the separation is proportionate; and third, whether prisoners are entitled to make representations before the decision is made.[152]

Lord Dyson agreed with the Secretary of State that it would be impracticable to devise a specific policy on allocation and separation of prisoners, due to the complex considerations beyond their sexuality and, in particular, security considerations. More specifically, he agreed that it would be unworkable to devise a policy on managing long-term relationships in prison. He maintained that, due to these complexities, art. 8(2) ECHR did allow for discretion. To avoid arbitrary decision-making, the discretion needed to be exercised for a proper purpose. The decision-maker should not discriminate against prisoners and was governed by the duty to act reasonably.[153] He summed up that the absence of such a policy did not fall foul of the art. 8(2) ECHR requirement that a restriction needed to be "in accordance with the law".[154] He also found that, in both cases, the decisions to separate the prisoners had been proportionate and that the prisoners had been able

---

[151] *R (on the application of Bright) v Secretary of State for Justice, Bright v Governor of Whitemoor Prison* CA (Civil Division) [2014] EWCA Civ 1628; [2015] 1 W.L.R. 723; [2014] 12 WLUK 564. *R (on the application of Hopkins) v Sodexo/HMP Bronzefield QB (Administrative Court)* [2016] EWHC 606 (Admin), 2016 A.C.D. 61.

[152] The applicants had been refused permission to apply for judicial review in the Administrative Court. On appeal, they received permission and the proceedings were retained in the Court of Appeal.

[153] *Bright and Keeley* [2014] para 33. Lord Dyson is referring to Wednesbury reasonableness: *Associated Provincial Picture Houses Ltd v Wednesbury Corporation* [1948] 1 KB 223.

[154] *Bright and Keeley* [2014] [35].

to participate in the decision-making process, if the complaint and appeal procedures are also taken into account. He did not agree that the procedural requirements under art. 8 ECHR placed a duty on the prison authorities to hear representations prior to separation.

The central problem with this judgment is the acceptance that a policy providing guidance on long-term relationships is unworkable. The applicants made a strong argument that there was a lack of certainty due to a failure to provide consistent guidance on whether long-term relationships should be supported, and whether public expressions of affection, tenderness as well as intimacy were deemed unacceptable in prison.[155] In fact, the decisions to separate were framed in internal policies that centred on the ban on sexual relations, indecency and insulting behaviour coupled with the "behavioural expectations" under the Incentives and Earned Privileges Scheme (IEP).[156] In evidence, a member of the National Offender Management Service (NOMS) explained that prisoners, who were found to have engaged in sexual relations, would no longer be able to share a cell. Whereas sexual behaviour in semi-public spaces would be considered indecent and insulting.

In a study on "Sex in Prison", published in the year after the judgment, the Howard League found that there seemed to be a lack of consistency of approach towards sex in prison, insufficient promotion of sexual health through access to condoms, and that staff were unsure how to react.[157] In general, consensual, hidden sex in prison was tolerated, as it is understood as a way to assert a sense of self. There seemed to be an assumption that prisoners showing signs of affection and tenderness were engaged in intimate relations. This could result in separation.[158] By accepting this framing, Lord Dyson reduced the issue of long-term relationships to sexual relationships. Moreover, he affirmed the prison authorities' views that questioned prisoners' capacity to enter into consensual sexual relationships, as well as the resource implications for establishing "true" consensual relationships.[159] Unsurprisingly, this is reflective of how queer sex/intimacy beyond the prison exists in the shadow of law and regulation.[160]

---

[155] *Bright and Keeley* [2014] [23].

[156] The IEP is a mechanism to promote compliance in prisoners through incentives and to punish prisoners with loss of "privileges" if they do not comply. For more information, see House of Commons Library, Research Briefings July 31, 2014, accessed May 20, 2019, https://researchbriefings.parliament.uk/ResearchBriefing/Summary/SN06942.

[157] Alisa Stevens, *Sex in Prison: Experiences of Former Prisoners. A Report for the Howard League's Commission on Sex in Prison*, The Howard League for Penal Reform, 2015, accessed May 25, 2019, https://howardleague.org/publications/sex-in-prison-experiences-of-former-prisoners/.

[158] Stevens, Sex in prison.

[159] *Bright and Keeley* [2014] [27].

[160] See Leslie J. Moran, *The Homosexual(ity) of Law* (London and New York: Routledge, 1996).

In turn, it is the mere possibility of sexual relations that are implicit in long-term relationships together with their visibility or formalisation that seem to be the deciding factors. Formally, pre-established long-term relationships give queer prisoners equal access to visits, as well as inter-prison visits. This is because these relationships seem to conform or are made to conform to gender-normative conceptions that enforce the separation of spousal relationships in prison. Their hypervisibility leads to a presumption towards separation.

This was the case in the second judgment, *Hopkins*, in which Michelle Hopkins challenged the decision to move her civil partner out of their shared cell into an adjacent cell after an initial three months in prison.[161] The decision was based on the "intimate relationship restriction", which banned women who were in a relationship from sharing a cell.

Among other issues, Justice Silber ruled on whether the separation violated arts. 3 and 8 ECHR. The applicant argued in both instances that, due to her disability, she needed the care and support of her civil partner. First, the separation from her civil partner had resulted in degrading treatment in accordance with art. 3 ECHR. Second, distinguishing her case from *Bright and Keeley*, she was entitled to receive the care and support that she needed from her civil partner. Justice Silber found that she had not suffered degradation to meet the threshold of art. 3 ECHR. And significantly, he concluded that both women were first and foremost prisoners and, therefore, that they had lost the right to choose "in whose company they can sleep because any custodial order inevitably curtails the right to enjoy many features of life outside prison".[162]

This starting point also influenced Justice Silber's approach to art. 8 ECHR. He held that art. 8 ECHR was not engaged, for their pre-existing relationship and rights to family life were framed by their incarceration like any other prisoner. The separation from your partner did not automatically engage art. 8 ECHR because this was a central aspect of imprisonment.[163] He added that, in case it was engaged, art. 8(2) ECHR would justify the authority's decision to prevent the women from sharing a cell, because the policy with its "intimate relationship restriction" was in accordance with the law and it promoted good order and discipline. Moreover, the decision was deemed proportionate because the women could apply to be located in the same wing.[164]

---

[161] *Hopkins* [2016].
[162] *Hopkins* [2016] [59]–[60].
[163] *Hopkins* [2016] [70].
[164] *Hopkins* [2016] [77].

Justice Silber reproduces the key heteronormative assumptions that came out of the *Bright and Keeley* judgment: first, that the prison involves separation from your family. This draws on the prisoners' rights jurisprudence around art. 8 ECHR that is deeply heteronormative and gender normative. At the centre is the assumption that prisoners, mostly men, are separated from their close family members—spouses, children, parents and siblings—by the prison walls. Prisons, then, have a positive duty to ensure prisoners maintain "effective contact" with family members, that is to facilitate visits, correspondence and communication.[165] For spouses or other family members who are both in prison, "maintaining effective contact" means that inter-prison visits can be facilitated on a three-monthly basis in addition to communication and correspondence.[166]

The second assumption is that queer relationships are deemed to threaten the fabric of the prison. The biggest threat to the prison's punitive capacity seems to be the perception that prison authorities were condoning sex in prison, which would invoke an exception to the blanket ban on sex in prison for long-term relationships.[167] Moreover, the ability to live in loving and caring relationships in prison is perceived as a threat to the fragile heteronormative institutional "equilibrium". For the supposedly more favourable treatment of queer couples would lead to "the likely unfavourable reaction of other prisoners who are not able to maintain their sexual relations".[168] This seems to be an inversion of formal equality where a supposed situational advantage for queer prisoners produced through the prison's gender binary needs to be rectified through the increased governance and closer surveillance of queer prisoners in open relationships. It is important to note how queer care

[165] *X v United Kingdom* (EComHR, 8 October 1982); *Messina v Italy (no 2)*, App. No. 25498/94 (ECtHR, 28 September 2000) [61]; *McCotter v UK*, App. No. 20479/92 (EComHR, 1992). And, correspondingly, family members of prisoners have a right to maintain relationships with their close relations in prison. For a comprehensive study: see Helen Codd, *In the Shadow of Prison: Families, Imprisonment and Criminal Justice* (Abingdon: Routledge, 2008).

[166] Inter-prison visits are governed by PSI 16/2011, Providing Visits and Services to Visitors, HM Prison and Probation Service, https://www.justice.gov.uk/offenders/psis/prison-service-instructions-2011 [5.15].

[167] *Hopkins* [2016] para 46.

[168] Lord Dyson in *Bright and Keeley* [27]. For the UK has a blanket ban on conjugal visits which has been upheld by the European Commission under the ECHR's margin of appreciation, see *ELH and PBH v UK* [1998] EHLR 231. Moreover, in an earlier judgment, the European Commission upheld a blanket ban on sex between married couples in prison, see *X and Y v Switzerland* (1978) 13 DR 241. In contrast, in 2011, the Supreme Court of Costa Rica ruled that conjugal visits needed to be extended to prisoners in same-sex relationships; see Acción de inconstitucionalidad contra el artículo 66 del Reglamento Técnico Penitenciario, Decreto Ejecutivo Número 33876-J, Exp: 08-002849-0007-CO, Res. No. 2011013800. cited in IPR and APR 2015.

emerges in response to a system that seeks to deny and punish (queer) intimacy. This moves the "queer outside" into the space of law (or prisons) and disrupts the (hetero)normativity it attempts to sustain.[169]

4 Conclusion

While there are increasing efforts to make prisons more hospitable and responsive to the unique experiences of queer prisoners, we argue that the inability to secure the universal and authentic inclusion of all sexualities and gender identities renders these attempts insufficient "reformist reforms".[170] Ultimately, many of these legal decisions and reforms are pursued with the intention of continuing the undisturbed production of capital by the prison under the pretence of instilling progressive and enlightened approaches towards criminal justice.

Our analysis of the jurisprudence reinforces the historical exposure of many queer prisoners to increased levels of violence and vulnerability through the reliance on the prison as a method of punishment. Some reconfigurations have been made recently to include some marginalised groups to an extent (e.g. non-binary people). However, these reforms overlook the reality that these marginalised groups are eternally excluded by the prison regardless of reform because they are in conflict with the underlying structure of the prison. Current protective regimes for queer prisoners that centre on isolation and exclusion seem wholly unsuited to challenging the systemic homophobia and transphobia within the prison system.[171] Within this environment, queer caring relationships are seen as a threat to the heteronormative order. The separation of queer couples in prison paradoxically is perceived as a way to achieve equality for the supposedly disadvantaged majority. However, the heightened surveillance that queer prisoners face, is neglected.

Following our examination of the jurisprudence, we refer back to Dean Spade's suggestion that the innate anti-queer, homophobic and transphobic nature of prisons means that the exclusion of queer prisoners will always remain an irreconcilable issue. Thus, rather than investing our collective efforts in the superficial "reformist reforms", which work within the confines of the existing exclusionary system, we align ourselves with fellow queer

[169] Thank you to Peter Dunne and Sen Raj for pointing this out.

[170] André Gorz, "Strategy for Labour," in *Theories of Labour Movement*, ed. Jon Dunlop (Detroit: Wayne State University Press, 1987), 100–117; Girshick, "Out of Compliance," 191.

[171] See Diane Taylor, "Officials Altered Records in Bisexual Prison Officer Case, Judge Says," *The Guardian*, May 28, 2019, accessed January 20, 2020, https://www.theguardian.com/world/2019/may/28/officials-altered-records-in-bisexual-prison-officer-case-judge-says.

abolitionist efforts to advocate for the abolition of the Prison Industrial Complex.[172] In this context, the abolition of the prison system requires a commitment to

> "addressing homophobia and transphobia in criminal punishment systems [and] rejects the quest for inclusion and recognition in violent legal and administrative apparatuses...and instead seeks the abolition of criminal punishment... It properly identifies the fruitlessness of seeking safety at the hands of the most significant perpetrators of racialized gendered violence".[173]

While it is important to engage in efforts to mitigate harm for queer prisoners who are already trapped in the PIC, fundamentally Stanley, Spade and Queer (In) Justice reinforce:

> We can't stop there – queer liberation and sexual and gender self-determination require that we reach toward abolition, not just of prisons, and for some of us, police, but of the systems that produce them, and which replicate systems of policing and punishment beyond prison walls.[174]

Acknowledgments We would like to thank Stella Coyle for research assistance and our friends and colleagues at Keele who provide such a collegiate research environment. We would also like to thank Peter Dunne and Sen Raj for their supportive and constructive comments. Felicity is grateful to Keele University School of Law for her doctoral scholarship. All errors remain our own.

References

Bent Bars Project. "Prison Abolition Is a Queer Issue." *Bent Bars Project* (2011).

Bosworth, Mary. *Engendering Resistance: Agency, and Power in Women's Prisons* (Aldershot: Dartmouth Publishing Company, 1999).

Bosworth, Mary and Eamonn Carrabine. "Reassessing Resistance: Race, Gender and Sexuality in Prison." *Punishment and Society* 3, no. 4 (2001): 501–515.

Butler, Judith. *Gender Trouble.* New York and Abingdon: Routledge, [1990] 2007.

---

[172] This is in no way intended to negate or to detract from the positive efforts many people make within the prison system and from the outside to challenge systemic harm and violence that differentiates on grounds of race, gender, sexuality and sexual identity.

[173] Spade, "Racialized Gender Violence," 195.

[174] Stanley, Spade, and Queer (In) Justice, "Queering Prison Abolition," 122.

Carlen, Pat. *Sledgehammer: Women's Imprisonment at the Millennium.* London: Macmillan Press, 1998.

Carlen, Pat and Chris Tchaikovsky. "Women in Prison." In *Criminal Women: Autobiographical Accounts,* edited by Pat Carlen et al., 182–186. Cambridge: Polity Press, 1985.

Carr, Nicola, Siobhán McAlister and Tanya Serisier. *Out on the Inside: The Rights, Needs, and Experiences of LGBT People on Prison* (Irish Penal Reform Trust, 2016).

Carrabine, Eamonn. *Power, Discourse and Resistance: A Genealogy of the Strangeways Prison Riot.* Dartmouth: Ashgate, 2004.

Carrabine, Eamonn and Brian Longhurst. "Gender and Prison Organisation: Some Comments on Masculinities and Prison Management." *The Howard Journal* 37, no. 2 (1998): 161–176.

Christie, Nils. "Prisons in Society, or Society as Prison—A Conceptual Analysis." In *Prisons Past and Future,* edited by J.C. Freeman, 179–188. London: Heinemann, 1978.

Codd, Helen. *In the Shadow of Prison: Families, Imprisonment and Criminal Justice.* Abingdon: Routledge, 2008.

Corcoran, Mary. *Out of Order: The Political Imprisonment of Women in Northern Ireland 1972–1998.* Cullompton: Willan Publishing, 2006.

Dagan, Hanoch. "The Realist Conception of Law." *The University of Toronto Law Journal* (2007): 607–660.

Dean, Mitchell. *Governmentality: Power and Rule in Modern Society,* 2nd ed. Los Angeles: Sage, 2010.

Dunn, Peter. "Slipping Off the Equalities Agenda: Work with LGBT Prisoners." *Prison Service Journal* 206 (2013): 3–10.

Emerton, Robyn, "Transgender Prisoners: Law, Prison Administration, and the Emerging Tension Between Human Rights and Risk" (PhD dissertation, Keele University, 2018).

"First UK Transgender Prison Unit to Open." *BBC News,* last modified March 3, 2019. Accessed March 27, 2020, https://www.bbc.co.uk/news/uk-47434730.

Foucault, Michel. *Discipline and Punish.* London: Penguin Books, [1977] 1991.

Foucault, Michel. "Governmentality" In *The Foucault Effect: Studies in Governmentality: With Two Lectures by and an Interview with Michel Foucault,* edited by Graham Burchell, Colin Gordon and Peter Miller, 87–104. Chicago: University of Chicago Press, 1991.

Foucault, Michel. *Society Must Be Defended.* London: Penguin Books, 2004.

Foucault, Michel. *The Birth of Biopolitics: Lectures at the Collège de France, 1978–1979.* Basingstoke: Palgrave Macmillan, 2008.

Gilmore, Ruth Wilson. *Golden Gulag: Prisons, Surplus, Crisis and Opposition in Globalising California* (Berkeley: University of California Press, 2007).

Girshick, Lori. "Out of Compliance: Masculine-Identified People in Women's Prisons." In *Captive Genders: Trans Embodiment and the Prison Industrial Complex,* edited by Eric A. Stanley and Nat Smith, 215–234. Edinburgh and Oakland: AK Press, 2011.

Gorz, Andre. "Strategy for Labour." In *Theories of the labour Movement*, edited by John Dunlop, Simeon Larson and Bruce Nissen, 100–117. Detroit: Wayne State University Press, 1987.

Hannah-Moffat, Kelly. *Punishment in Disguise: Penal Governance and Federal Imprisonment of Women in Canada.* Toronto: University of Toronto Press, 2001.

Harris, Mia. "British Prisons Must Now Recognise Gender Fluid and Non-binary Inmates." *The Conversation,* November 26, 2016. https://theconversation.com/profiles/mia-harris-288195.

Harris, Mia and Robyn Emerton. "New Policy on Transgender Prisoners: Progressive But Can Prisons Keep Pace?" *Inherently Human,* November 21, 2016. https://inherentlyhuman.wordpress.com/2016/11/21/new-policy-on-transgender-prisoners-progressive-but-can-prisons-keep-pace/.

Hepple, Bob, "The New Single Equality Act in Britain." *The Equality Rights Review* (2010): 11–24.

James, Erwin. "Homophobia Is Still Rife in UK Prisons." *The Guardian,* September 25, 2012. https://www.theguardian.com/society/2012/sep/25/homophobia-rife-uk-prisons.

Jenness, Valerie and Sarah Fernstermaker. "Agnes Goes to Prison: Gender Authenticity, Transgender Inmates in Prisons for Men, and Pursuit of 'The Real Deal'." *Gender and Society* (2013): 5–31.

Lamble, Sarah. "Rethinking Gendered Prison Policies: Impacts on Transgender Prisoners." *ECAN Bulletin* (2012): 7–12.

Lamble, Sarah. "Sexual Citizenship, Social Movements and the Expanding Carceral State." In *Queer Necropolitics,* edited by Jin Haritaworn, Adin Kuntsman and Sylvia Posocco, 151–171. Oxford: Routledge, 2014.

Mann, Rebecca. "The Treatment of Transgender Prisoners, Not Just an American Problem—A Comparative Analysis of American, Australian, and Canadian Prison Policies Concerning the Treatment of Transgender Prisoners and a "Universal" Recommendation to Improve Treatment." *Law and Sexuality Review, Lesbian Gay Bisexual and Legal Issues* 15 (2006): 91–134.

Mason, Gail. *The Spectacle of Violence: Homophobia, Gender and Knowledge.* London and New York: Routledge, 2002.

Ministry of Justice. *NOMS Annual Offender Equalities Report 2016/17, Ministry of Justice Statistics Bulletin,* November 29, 2018. Accessed March 27, 2020, https://assets.publishing.service.gov.uk/government/uploads/system/uploads/attachment_data/file/760093/hmpps-offender-equalities-2017-18.pdf.

Moran, Leslie J. *The Homosexual(ity) of Law.* London and New York: Routledge, 1996.

"New Non-Binary Prison in Scotland?" *Corporate Watch,* January 17, 2018. https://corporatewatch.org/new-non-binary-prison-in-scotland/.

Oparah, Julia. "Gender Nonconforming Prisoners." *UCLA Women's Law Journal* 18 (2012): 239–271.

Penal Reform International and APT. *LGBTI Persons Deprived of Their Liberty: A Framework for Preventive Monitoring,* 2nd ed. (2015). Accessed

March 27, 2020, https://cdn.penalreform.org/wp-content/uploads/2016/01/lgbti-framework-2nd-ed-v7-web.pdf.
Pound, Roscoe. "Mechanical Jurisprudence." *Columbia Law Review* (1908).
Prisons and Probation Ombudsman for England and Wales. *Learning Lessons Bulletin: Fatal Incident Investigations: Segregation* (June 2015). Accessed March 27, 2020, http://www.ppo.gov.uk/app/uploads/2015/06/Learning-Lessons-Bulletin-Segregation-final.pdf.
Reiman, Jeffrey and Paul Leighton. *The Rich Get Richer and the Poor Get Prison: A Reader.* Boston: Allyn & Bacon, 2010.
Scharff Smith, Peter. "The Effects of Solitary Confinement on Prison Inmates: A Brief History and Review of the Literature." *Crime and Justice* 34, no. 1 (2006): 441–528.
Silvestri, Ariana. *Prison Conditions in the United Kingdom* (European Prison Observatory, 2013). Accessed March 27, 2020, https://www.crimeandjustice.org.uk/sites/crimeandjustice.org.uk/files/Prison%20conditions%20in%20the%20UK.pdf.
Shalev, Sharon and Edgar Kimmet. *Deep Custody: Segregation Units and Close Supervision Centres in England and Wales* (Prison Reform Trust, 2015).
Sharpe, Alex. "Queering Judgment: The Case of Gender Identity Fraud." *Journal of Criminal Law* (2017): 417–435.
Sharpe, Alex. *Sexual Intimacy and Gender Identity 'Fraud': Reframing the Legal and Ethical Debate.* Abingdon: Routledge, 2018.
Sharpe, Alex. "Foxes in the Henhouse: Putting the Trans Women Prison Debate in Perspective." *Inherently Human*, September 11, 2018. https://inherentlyhuman.wordpress.com/2018/09/11/foxes-in-the-henhouse-putting-the-trans-women-prison-debate-in-perspective/.
Sim, Joe. "Tougher Than the Rest? Men in Prison." In *Just Boys Doing Business? Men, Masculinities and Crime*, edited by Tim Newburn and Elizabeth A. Stanko, 100–117. London: Routledge, 1994.
Spade, Dean. "The Only Way to End Racialized Gender Violence in Prisons is to End Prisons: A Response to Russell Robinson's 'Masculinity as Prison'." *The Circuit*. Paper 4, (2012): 184–195.
Stanley, Eric. "Introduction: Fugitive Flesh: Gender Self-Determination, Queer Abolition and Trans Resistance." In *Captive Genders: Trans Embodiment and the Prison Industrial Complex*, edited by Eric Stanley and Nat Smith, 7–20. Edinburgh, Oakland and Baltimore: AK Press, 2011.
Stanley, Eric A. and Dean Spade. "Queer (In)Justice, 'Queering Prison Abolition, Now?'." *American Quarterly* (2012): 115–127.
Stevens, Alisa. *Sex in Prison: Experiences of Former Prisoners: A Report for the Howard League's Commission on Sex in Prison* (The Howard League for Penal Reform, 2015). Accessed May 25, 2019, https://howardleague.org/publications/sex-in-prison-experiences-of-former-prisoners/.

Taylor, Diane. "Officials Altered Records in Bisexual Prison Officer Case, Judge Says." *The Guardian*. https://www.theguardian.com/world/2019/may/28/officials-altered-records-in-bisexual-prison-officer-case-judge-says.

"Transgender Prison Deaths: Watchdog Calls for Action." *BBC News*, January 10, 2017. https://www.bbc.co.uk/news/uk-38562714.

Ugelvik, Thomas. *Power and Resistance in Prison: Doing Time, Doing Freedom* (Basingstoke: Palgrave Macmillan, 2014).

van Zyl Smit, Dirk and Sonja Snacken. *Principles of European Prison Law and Policy: Penology and Human Rights*. Oxford: Oxford University Press. 2009.

Westwood, Sue. "'My Friends Are My Family': An Argument About the Limitations of Contemporary Law's Recognition of Relationships in Later Life." *Journal of Social Welfare and Family Law* 35, no. 3 (2013): 347–363.

Whittle, Steven, Lewis Turner and Maryam Al-Alami. *Engendered Penalties: Transgender and Transsexual People's Experiences of Inequality and Discrimination* (London and Manchester: Press for Change and Manchester Metropolitan University, 2007).

Queering the Outsides of Legal Gender and Sex

Genders that Don't Matter: Non-Binary People and the Gender Recognition Act 2004

Flora Renz

1 Introduction

Trans[1] and non-binary[2] people are increasingly becoming the focus of much research in, among other areas, sociology, medicine and law.[3] There is also a growing social and cultural awareness of diverse gender identities as evidenced by the still rare, but increasingly frequent, inclusion of trans characters in

[1] I am using "trans" rather than "transgender" or "transsexual" to accommodate a variety of identity categories that may not necessarily align with a binary understanding of sex and gender, encompassing identities such as genderqueer and agender more readily than the medically defined "transsexual". However, while some intersex people may identify as trans, intersex is generally used to describe a variety of bodily configurations that combine features that are normally considered solely "male" or "female". For a fuller exploration of the legal regulation of intersex experiences in the UK, see Garland and Travis (Chapter 7). I am using this here as a distinct term to reflect, in particular, the differential legal treatment for both groups of people.

[2] I am using non-binary to capture a variety of identities that do not align with a binary understanding of sex/gender.

[3] See e.g. Zowie Davy, *Recognizing Transsexuals: Personal, Political and Medicolegal Embodiment* (Burlington: Ashgate, 2012); Sally Hines, *Gender Diversity, Recognition and Citizenship: Towards a Politics of Difference* (London and New York: Palgrave Macmillan, 2013); Tam Sanger, *Trans People's Partnerships: Towards an Ethics of Intimacy* (Basingstoke: Palgrave Macmillan, 2010).

F. Renz (✉)
University of Kent, Canterbury, UK
e-mail: f.renz@kent.ac.uk

S. Raj and P. Dunne (eds.), *The Queer Outside in Law*, Palgrave Socio-Legal Studies,
https://doi.org/10.1007/978-3-030-48830-7_6

mainstream television programmes.[4] The American magazine, *Time*, argued in 2014 that society has reached the "Transgender Tipping Point" with trans rights becoming the new civil rights frontier.[5] However, in most of these contexts trans and non-binary people, and the social/legal issues affecting this group disproportionately, such as the legal regulation of sex/gender,[6] are still treated as marginal or outliers in terms of their specific concerns regarding legal recognition and protection.

At the same time while there is increasing public awareness of people who do not identify with a binary understanding of gender, this is only slowly being translated into legal and policy debates, although several states[7] have recently begun to offer legal recognition beyond the traditional female and male categories.[8] However, it should be noted that, at present, legal recognition varies hugely by jurisdiction with some countries, like Germany and Austria, restricting this to intersex people, while other states, such as Malta and New Zealand, explicitly including non-binary people within their legal framework.[9]

In the United Kingdom, until the Gender Recognition Act 2004 (GRA) came into force, trans people were unable to legally change their birth certificates to accurately reflect the way they experienced their gender identity. Previous case law from the courts in England and Wales had defined sex and gender in primarily biological and absolutely binary terms,

[4]Sarah Hughes, "Transparent Season One Is Free for a Day—Here's Why You Should Watch It" *The Guardian*, January 23, 2015, accessed April 20, 2015, http://www.theguardian.com/tv-and-radio/2015/jan/23/transparent-season-one-free-on-amazon-for-a-day.

[5]Katy Steinmetz, "The Transgender Tipping Point" *Time Magazine*, May 29, 2014, accessed May 1 2018, http://time.com/135480/transgender-tipping-point/.

[6]While sex and gender are commonly understood as distinct concepts, with sex referring primarily to biological factors and gender being used to describe the social and cultural interpretation of these factors, in the context of legal regulation these two concepts are often either conflated (see e.g. *R [on the application of Christie Elan-Cane] and Secretary of State for the Home Department* [2018] EWHC 1530 [Admin] para. 96) or, because of linguistic and cultural reasons, do not exist with the same level of distinction in other jurisdictions. Therefore, I will be using sex/gender as an umbrella term to capture this ambiguity.

[7]See, e.g. Niraj Chokshi, "Canada Introduces 'X' as a Third Sex Category for Passport Holders", August 25, 2017, accessed December 1, https://www.nytimes.com/2017/08/25/world/americas/rkans-passport-x.html. Curtis M Wong, "Arkansas Has Been Offering a Nonbinary Gender Option on State IDs for Years" *HUFFINGTON POST*, October 17, 2018, accessed December 1, 2018, https://www.huffingtonpost.com/en-try/rkansas-gender-neutral-state-id-option_us_5bc79f75e4b0d38b5874a669; Australian Government, Australian Government Guidelines on the Recognition of Sex and Gender. Commonwealth of Australia, July 2013. Bundesministerium des Innern, für Bau und Heimat. 2018. Entwurf eines Gesetzes zur Änderung der in das Geburtenregister einzutragenden Angaben. Berlin.

[8]See also Jessica Calrke, "They, Them and Theirs" *Harvard Law Review* 132, no 3 (2019): 894.

[9]Lena Holzer, *Non-Binary Gender Registration Models in Europe: Report on Third Gender Marker or No Gender Marker Options* (ILGA Europe, 2018).

and that case law had made several highly problematic assumptions about trans people.[10] For example, the English courts assumed that trans people were intentionally deceiving either potential partners, or indeed the State, by wanting to access marriage rights, while being in same-sex relationships.[11]

The GRA has supposedly revolutionised gender rights in the UK by moving away from a biological understanding of sex/gender and by making it possible for trans people to amend the sex marker on their birth certificates, gain access to legal rights, and as a result enjoy protection against discrimination.[12] However, this legal framework is now more than 15 years old and has changed very little in this time. For instance, the GRA currently makes no accommodations for people who do not identify with a binary understanding of gender. This is somewhat unsurprising when considering case law, such as *Corbett v Corbett*, of which it emerged—a case that codified an explicitly biological and binary understanding of both sex and gender in law.[13] Although the European Court of Human Rights in *Goodwin v UK*[14] forced the UK to move away from this biological model to some extent, the GRA is not free from this earlier influence and retains the purely binary understanding of sex and gender expressed in earlier case law.[15]

In this chapter, I will first consider some of the current legal reform proposals under discussion in England and Wales[16] (as well as in Scotland), before considering alternative approaches from other jurisdictions, specifically using the examples of Australia and Germany. While certain countries, such as Malta and Canada,[17] may provide more definite examples of non-binary

[10]See, e.g. *Corbett v Corbett* [1971] p. 83; *Bellinger v Bellinger* [2003] 2 AC 467.

[11]See, e.g. Alex Sharpe, "Endless Sex: The Gender Recognition Act 2004 and the Persistence of a Legal Category" *Feminist Legal Studies* 15, no 1 (2007):57–84; Stephen Whittle, "The Opposite of Sex Is Politics—The UK Gender Recognition Act and Why It Is Not Perfect, Just Like You and Me: FORUM" *Journal of Gender Studies* 15, no 3 (2006): 267–271.

[12]See, e.g. Alex Sharpe, "Gender Recognition in the UK: A Great Leap Forward" *Social & Legal Studies* 18, no 2 (2009):241–245. Under s. 7 of the Equality Act 2010, an individual can benefit from the "gender reassignment" protected characteristics irrespective of whether they have obtained a Gender Recognition Certificate.

[13]*Corbett v Corbett (Otherwise Ashley) (No 1)* [1971] 2 All ER 33.

[14]*Goodwin v United Kingdom* (28957/95) [2002] Fam. Law 738.

[15]See, e.g. Sharon Cowan, "'That Woman Is a Woman!' The Case of Bellinger v. Bellinger and the Mysterious (Dis) Appearance of Sex: Bellinger v. Bellinger [2003] 2 All ER 593; [2003] FCR 1; [2003] 2 WLR 1174; [2003] UKHL 21", *Feminist Legal Studies* 12, no 1 (2004): 79–92; Flora Renz, "The Gender Recognition Act 2004 and Transgender People's Legal Consciousness" (Ph.D., Kent Law School, University of Kent, 2017).

[16]On 22 April 2020, the Minister for Women and Equalities, Liz Truss MP, advised the Commons Select Committee on Women and Equalities that she would be setting out the government's proposals for reforming the GRA in the summer 2020. On 22 September 2020, Truss announced that the Government would not recommend substantive changes to the requirements for obtaining a Gender Recognition Certificate.

[17]See also, Sharon Cowan (Chapter 8 in this edited collection).

recognition, the jurisdictions chosen here provide some of the most detailed outlines of legal and judicial decision-making in considering the question of whether law can move beyond a binary legal framework. I will finally consider the limitations of both the current reform proposals and existing legal frameworks and in particular to what extent they can be read as queer "inside" and "outside" the legal sphere.

2 Reforming the Gender Recognition Act 2004

To situate the issue of reforming the GRA, it is crucial to first understand the existing framework of the legislation. It should be noted that, at its inception, the GRA covered sex/gender markers on a variety of identification documents, such as passports and driving licenses. However, in the intervening years these documents have become "easier" to change and no longer require a person to go through the process set out in the GRA.[18]

At present, in all parts of the UK, anybody who wants to obtain a Gender Recognition Certificate (GRC) to legally change their sex on their birth certificate has to meet four specific conditions. Applicants must be 18 years or over, they have to be diagnosed as having or as having had gender dysphoria, they need to prove that they have lived in the "acquired" gender[19] for two years prior to the application and, lastly, they need to swear that they will remain in that gender for the rest of their lives.[20]

The most important part of the GRC application process is contained in ss. 5–7 of the application form.[21] These sections implement the evidentiary requirements set out in s.3 of the GRA. Specifically, this part of the application form asks applicants to provide evidence to prove that they have lived in their gender for the last two years prior to applying for a GRC. The application form here explicitly refers to the applicant's "new" gender.[22] Although this term may be used simply for linguistic ease and to avoid confusion, it

[18]While it was possible to change some ID documents prior to the introduction of the GRA, in practice the availability of this option was often inconsistent and reliant on the discretion of officials.

[19]Although this is the language of the GRA, I will not use it in this chapter as it does not align with the self-understanding of most trans people regarding their sex/gender.

[20]Sections 3–4 Gender Recognition Act 2004. On the difficulties of enforcing the permanence requirement, see Emily Grabham, "Governing Permanence: Trans Subjects, Time, and the Gender Recognition Act", *Social & Legal Studies* 19, no 1 (2010): 107–126.

[21]HM Courts & Tribunal Service. (November 2016) T450—Application for a Gender Recognition Certificate.

[22]Ibid., p. 6.

nevertheless implies two underlying rationalities. Firstly, that the applicant has not always been that gender, which is a type of reasoning that contradicts the lived experience of many trans people who would argue that they have in fact always been that gender, but have not been recognised as such by society at large. This means that there is an inherent tension within the GRA between its stated aim of providing "recognition" while at the same time referring to a person's gender as something that is only newly "acquired". Secondly, that there is a specific point at which one changes from one gender to another with no acknowledgement that there may be an in-between position or a more gradual change or even a context-dependent move back and forth between these categories.

As such, from the outset, the GRA is underpinned by an understanding of sex/gender, which is a binary dichotomy. Within the language of the GRA there are clearly only two options and a person has to be able to show evidence of their life as one or the other to successfully navigate this process. Overall, both the language and the requirements of the GRA mean that the recognition process privileges certain narratives—those that support a stable, fixed and, most importantly, binary model of sex/gender identity, over others that are effectively deemed unworthy of recognition. As such, individuals who do not identify as solely either male or female are not able to obtain legal recognition of their gender identity under the present system and although other types of identification documents are no longer governed by the GRA, they nevertheless follow the same binary paradigm. This clearly relegates those who do not fit within the current framework to an "outsider" status as their identities simply cannot fit within a purely binary legal system.

Some potential reforms for the existing legal framework were set out by the Transgender Equality report published in January 2016 by the House of Commons Select Committee on Women and Equalities.[23] Crucially, the report notes the complete lack of legal provision for non-binary people.[24] At the same time, it is strongly critical of the medicalised approach of the GRA, particularly in regard to the evidentiary requirements contained therein, which are inherently exclusionary to those not willing or able to undergo specific types of gender confirmation surgery and at the same time serve to pathologise non-cisgender identities.[25] Implicitly, the medical aspect of the GRA also further serves to exclude people who do not identify with a binary understanding of gender, as they are less likely to undergo the full

[23]House of Commons Women and Equalities Committee. 2016. Transgender Equality. House of Commons London: The Stationery Office Limited.

[24]Ibid., p. 79.

[25]Ibid., pp. 79–80.

range of procedures commonly referred to as "gender confirmation surgery" and are also likely to have more difficulty accessing appropriate medical care in the first place.[26] In its recommendations, the report suggests that the GRA should urgently be updated to reflect both of these concerns. In many ways, the report was ground-breaking in the sense that it officially acknowledged the existence and concerns of non-binary identified people; a category that did not even rate a mention in previous official debates about the GRA in 2003 and 2013.[27]

The key recommendation of the report in regard to provisions for non-binary people is that the government should "look into the need to create a legal category for those people with a gender identity outside that which is binary and the full implications of this".[28] However, there is no mention of the wider legal impact such a change could potentially have. For instance, if gender identity in a legal context were going to include three categories, would this also impact other gender-based legislation, such as the Equality Act 2010 with regards to sex-based discrimination? Although the law in England and Wales, and in the two other UK jurisdiction to which the GRA applies, is now largely gender-neutral, there are nevertheless some remaining areas where a person's legal gender can affect their treatment in law. Those areas would undoubtedly be affected by any move towards a third gender category. For example, in the context of assisted reproduction the Human Fertilisation and Embryology Act 2008 includes a definition of both "motherhood" and "fatherhood"—and both would need to be significantly amended to deal with a third legal category.[29]

At the same time, the report also suggests moving towards a "non-gendered" approach for recording official information.[30] This latter recommendation would appear to be one of the most interesting recommendations both for binary and non-binary identified individuals, but it is sadly not

[26]see e.g. Titia F. Beek et al., "Partial Treatment Requests and Underlying Motives of Applicants for Gender Affirming Interventions" *The Journal of Sexual Medicine* 12, (11) (2015): 2201–2205; Arlene Istar Lev, "Gender Dysphoria: Two Steps Forward, One Step Back" *Clinical Social Work Journal* 41, no. 3 (2013): 288–296; Ben Vincent and Ana Manzanzo. "History and Cultural Diversity". In *Genderqueer and Non-Binary Genders*, edited by Christina Richards, Walter Pierre Bouman and Meg-John Barker (London: Palgrave, 2017).

[27]House of Lords. January 29, 2004. "Gender Recognition Bill". 656 (31); House of Lords. June 24, 2013. "Marriage (Same Sex Couples) Bill—Committee (3rd Day)". 746 (22).

[28]House of Commons Women and Equalities Committee. 2015. Transgender Equality. House of Commons London: The Stationery Office Limited, p. 11.

[29]Section 33 and sections 35–39 Human Fertilisation and Embryology Act 2008. See also *TT, R (On the Application Of) v The Registrar General for England and Wales* [2019] EWHC 2384 (Fam) (25 September 2019).

[30]House of Commons Women and Equalities Committee. 2016. Transgender Equality. House of Commons London: The Stationery Office Limited, p. 9.

developed further other than the suggestion that gender should only be recorded "where it is a relevant piece of information".[31] In general, the introduction of an additional category for non-binary people, while perhaps beneficial to some people, is likely to raise similar concerns to those related to the existing binary gender categories. Even if this category was purely based on a "self-declaration" approach, in line with the wider proposal of the report, it would be likely to still remain exclusionary towards some people—such as those who do not identify with any gender at all, those who do not wish to go through an official process to "confirm" their gender or those who are unable to access the application process due to economic and other reasons.[32]

In some ways the abandonment or removal of legal gender status may be considered a more queer approach to dealing with the question of how non-binary people should be included in law, as it provides an alternative to a mere proliferation of categories, which will likely impose further normative limits and definitions of different types of genders. Potentially the removal of legal status could remove the distinction between those "inside" the law, by virtue of having access to legal recognition of their gender and those in the "outside" due to the exclusionary effects of the current binary system. However, it would be difficult to argue that the removal of legal gender status will inherently lead to a better or more inclusive legal framework as it runs the risk of merely covering up prevailing discrimination and exclusion by essentially taking a formal equality type approach to non-binary inclusion without addressing structural conditions that privilege some genders over others.[33]

Although this report is not legally binding, the government, in its response to the report, committed to reviewing the GRA with the intent to "streamline and de-medicalise the gender recognition process".[34] In line with its response to the Transgender Equality report, in Autumn 2017, the government launched a consultation regarding the GRA without making any commitments towards accommodations for non-binary people.[35] At the same time the Scottish government proposed to remove the need for medical evidence and evidence regarding the applicants' gender over the

---

[31]Ibid., p. 86.

[32]See also Flora Renz, "The Gender Recognition Act 2004 and Transgender People's Legal Consciousness" (Ph.D., Kent Law School, University of Kent, 2017).

[33]On this point see also Davina Cooper, "A Very Binary Drama: The Conceptual Struggle for Gender's Future" *feminists@law* 9, no 1 (2019): 1–36; Davina Cooper and Flora Renz, "If the State Decertified Gender, What Might Happen to its Meaning and Value?" *Journal of Law & Society* 43, no 4 (2016): 483–505.

[34]Government Equalities Office. July 2016. Government Response to the Women and Equalities Committee Report on Transgender Equality, pp. 10–11.

[35]Government Equalities Office, "New Action to Promote LGBT Equality" (2017), accessed October 2, 2017, https://www.gov.uk/government/news/new-action-to-promote-lgbt-equality.

two years prior to the application (under the current Gender Recognition Reform (Scotland) Bill, individuals would have to have lived in their acquired gender for a period of three years prior to their application).[36] Unlike the English consultation, the Scottish consultation considered potential options for including non-binary identities within a legal regulatory framework. The results suggested that more than 60% of respondents thought that the government should take action to recognise non-binary people—although non-binary options have not now been included within the Gender Recognition Reform (Scotland) Bill.[37]

While the exact scope, if any, of future parliamentary efforts at including non-binary people is currently unclear, the High Court simultaneously considered a case for judicial review of the current gender marker system for UK passports. In *R (on the application of Christie Elan-Cane) and Secretary of State for the Home Department [2018] EWHC 1530 (Admin)*, the High Court was asked to determine whether it is lawful not to have an alternative gender option, specifically an "X" designation, for those who do not identify as either male or female. The claimant in this case identified as "non-gendered" and was trying to obtain a passport that reflected this fact, as an "X" gender marker is a pre-existing option that the International Civil Aviation Organisation uses as a shorthand to indicate that gender is "unspecified". It should be noted that, in the UK, a change of one's gender marker in a passport does not amount to a change of one's legal gender status as this remains governed by the GRA framework. Interestingly, if Elan-Cane's claim had been successful this would have led to a scenario where there could have been not just a mismatch between one's gender marker on passports versus birth certificate, which is already possible, but more generally between the types of gender markers available on different legal documents. Although this was never raised as a concern in the case itself, this in some ways would have contributed to a queerer legal understanding of gender where there is a possibility of a person possessing a proliferation of different genders that are recognised as equally legally valid, due to the different frameworks governing amendments to different documents, while at the same time contradicting each other.

Despite ultimately not succeeding in terms of gaining recognition for non-binary identities (a decision which was upheld on appeal[38]), this case

[36]Scottish Government, "Review of the Gender Recognition Act 2004 [Consultation]" November 9, 2017, accessed May 5, 2018, http://www.gov.scot/Publications/2017/11/5459. See also Scottish Government, "Gender Recognition Reform (Scotland) Bill: Consultation". December 17, 2019, accessed March 17, 2020. https://www.gov.scot/publications/gender-recognition-reform-scotland-bill-consultation-scottish-government/pages/6/.

[37]The Scottish Government. November 2018. Review of the Gender Recognition Act 2004: Analysis of Responses to the Public Consultation Exercise—Report. Edinburgh, p. 81.

[38]*R (On the Application of Elan-Cane) v Secretary of State for the Home Department* [2020] EWCA Civ 363. On 10 November 2020, the United Kingdom Supreme Court granted leave to appeal [*R*

is nevertheless instructive in how such claims become construed in a legal context. When summing up the facts of the case, Mr Justice Jeremy Baker describes Elan-Cane's identity primarily defined through medical treatment while also noting the "importance" on a personal level of official recognition.[39] Although the wider negative consequences of identifying outside the binary and of not having legal recognition are highlighted,[40] gender here becomes primarily constructed as an individual matter or an individual rights claim. However, more broadly the judgment highlights that gender is an important part of a person's "personal and social identity", which suggests that gender here is understood as at least to some extent relational (i.e. that being a specific gender or no gender at all is derived from relations and interactions with others).[41] Nevertheless, in relying on art. 8 of the European Convention on Human Rights, Elan-Cane's claim ultimately becomes framed in the language of the right to a private life and as something that is ultimately determined through and vital to personal identity.[42] As such, gender here is primarily conceptualised as something that is and should be recognised as doing otherwise, as argued for instance by Judith Butler, leads to the impossibility of "persist[ing] (in my being) without norms of recognition that support my persistence".[43] In some ways, this approach, despite potentially justifying a fundamental rewriting of existing legal categories, does little to unsettle existing conventional understanding of what it means to be a "man" or a "woman" in law, but simply considers the introduction of a separate third category while leaving the others untouched. As mentioned above this may highlight the limitations of legal attempts at inclusion that rely on the introduction of a third category. While potentially bringing some who are currently outside law's legal gender regime within its boundaries, such approaches nevertheless are also underpinned by the same normalising tendencies as other forms of legal gender recognition.

The High Court's judgment ultimately acknowledges that "the claimant has a justifiably strong personal interest in gaining full legal recognition as

---

(on the application of Elan-Cane) (Appellant) v Secretary of State for the Home Department (Respondent), UKSC 2020/0081].

[39] *R (on the application of Christie Elan-Cane) and Secretary of State for the Home Department* [2018] EWHC 1530 (Admin), para 2–4.

[40] Ibid., para 65–67.

[41] Ibid., para. 102 cf. Sarah Fenstermaker and Candace West, *Doing Gender, Doing Difference: Inequality, Power, and Institutional Change* (New York: Routledge, 2013).

[42] Ibid., para. 103–108; it is likely that this strategy was chosen as previous cases on gender recognition have focused on and succeeded on this basis.

[43] Judith Butler, *Precarious Life: The Powers of Mourning and Violence* (London and New York: Verso, 2004), p. 32.

being a non-gendered individual", but suggests that this is a separate issue from the challenge to the current passport policy.[44] Part of the basis for the rejection of the claimant's arguments seems to be the fact that this case focuses on passports rather than birth certificates, the latter of which are argued to be "of fundamental importance in recording and establishing the applicant's gender identity", while passports apparently are not despite being the far more commonly used form of identification.[45] Although this is an accurate distinction in legal terms, as only birth certificates formally certify a person's legal gender, this may also highlight a fundamental disconnect between those documents the law recognizes as important and those that hold importance for individuals in their day-to-day life. It also creates a strange double bind where gender markers on passports are seemingly not fundamental enough to require government action but gender markers on birth certificates are so fundamental that they remain outside the scope of this legal challenge and are solely subject to the government's ongoing consultation. As a result of this and the fact that the government's review of potential reforms has not been concluded, the court ultimately ruled that art. 8 of the European Convention of Human Rights did not impose a positive obligation on the government to accommodate people who do not identify as either male or female. However, the judgment strongly suggests that this could be reconsidered if the government does not sufficiently consider accommodations for non-binary people in their consultation.

3 Moving Beyond Two Categories in Other Jurisdictions

As the legal framework for gender recognition in the UK is currently under review and legal challenges have so far been unsuccessful, it seems fruitful to consider how other jurisdictions have attempted to engage with rights claims beyond binary gender categories. Specifically, in this part, I will consider the approaches taken in Australia and Germany in providing legal recognition of genders beyond the female/male binary.

[44] *R (on the application of Christie Elan-Cane) and Secretary of State for the Home Department* [2018] EWHC 1530 (Admin), para. 113.

[45] Ibid., para. 116.

3.1 Australia

One obvious comparator for considering legal inclusion of non-binary people, which was also raised in *R (on the application of Christie Elan-Cane) and Secretary of State for the Home Department [2018] EWHC 1530 (Admin)* is Australia. Australia is, in many ways, representative of a number of jurisdictions—including parts of Canada,[46] parts of the USA[47] and New Zealand[48]—that permit the use of an "X" gender marker on various ID documents. American states offer the most limited version of non-binary recognition because—as a result of federal rules—such efforts are generally restricted to state ID cards, driving licenses and, in some cases, insurance cards. In Canada, due to a similar federal system, the possibilities for non-binary recognition also vary depending on the individual rules of each province or territory, however, in contrast to the USA, some Canadian jurisdictions also allow for the amendment of birth certificates with an "X" marker. In contrast, New Zealand now also permits the recording of an "X" marker on passports. In all three countries, these changes seem to be primarily aimed at non-binary, rather than intersex people, and therefore do not restrict this option solely to intersex people.

Australia was one of the earliest adopters of the "X" gender marker and, since 2013, has permitted any adult who wishes to do so, to use "X" as a gender marker for all federal documents including passports.[49] The government guidance specifies that "X" signifies "any person who does not exclusively identify as either male or female" and therefore, in principle, opens this category up to encompass a variety of different gender identities. This model is also in line with the one proposed by Elan-Cane in the judicial review case discussed in the previous section.

Arguably an "X" marker could potentially accommodate a variety of different identities and effectively serve as a catch-all for everyone not identifying as solely male or female. However, the Australian government reserves the right to demand various types of evidence to "confirm" a person's gender

[46]W. Strong, "Transgender N.W.T. Residents Can Now Change Birth Certificates to Reflect Gender" *CBC News,* July 15, 2017, accessed March 27, 2020, https://www.cbc.ca/news/canada/north/nwt-transgender-legislation-changes-1.4206782.

[47]Sam Levin, "'Huge Validation': Oregon Becomes First State to Allow Official Third Gender Option" *The Guardian,* June 15, 2017, accessed October 1, 2017, https://www.theguardian.com/us-news/2017/jun/15/oregon-third-gender-option-identity-law.

[48]Te Tari Taiwhenua/Internal Affairs, "Information about Changing Sex/Gender Identity", February 15, 2018, accessed March 27, 2020, https://www.passports.govt.nz/what-you-need-to-renew-or-apply-for-a-passport/information/.

[49]Australian Government, Australian Government Guidelines on the Recognition of Sex and Gender. Commonwealth of Australia (July 2013).

identity.[50] Additionally, the "X" marker is at least on an official level intended to only be available for trans and intersex people, or "sex and gender diverse" people as per the government materials. As such, it does not seem to be intended, for instance, for someone simply wishing to not disclose their gender identity.

Parallel to the change in Australian policy that allowed for the use of "X" gender markers, the Australian High Court also considered a case brought against the New South Wales Registry of Births, Deaths and Marriages by Norrie[51] based on the Registry's refusal to permit the use of a "non-specific" sex marker.[52] Norrie, who was assigned male at birth, had undergone gender affirmation surgery but considered this to "not resolve her sexual ambiguity" and therefore applied in 2009 to have her sex registered as "non-specific".[53]

The High Court judgment starts by recognising that "not all human beings can be classified by sex as either male or female".[54] However, again, similarly to the Elan-Cane case, Norrie's identity is primarily defined in terms of medical treatment and procedures. Norrie herself argued that the recording of her sex marker was a matter of recording the "truth" and avoiding "misinformation".[55] Unlike the framing of arguments in the *Elan-Cane* case, the recognition of a new sex/gender marker in *Norrie* is not solely requested on the basis of avoiding harm caused by a lack of recognition, but instead is based on an appeal to factual accuracy. This is taken up in the judgment, which describes the task of the registrar as being to "[record] the facts supplied".[56] Sex/gender here is understood as a matter of fact that can be determined through medical evidence as well as the "good faith declaration" by the respondent in this case. Again, this primarily conceptualises sex/gender as an individualistic or personal matter. This may be partially due to the nature of legal disputes, which favour rights-based arguments made by individuals, but it nevertheless also ignores other competing understandings of gender that would centre its social, relational or even oppressive dimensions. Due to its specific focus the judgment leaves other sex/gender categories unchallenged

[50]Australian Government: Department of Foreign Affairs and Trade. N.D, "Sex and Gender Diverse Passport Applicants", accessed May 15, 2018, https://www.passports.gov.au/passports-explained/how-apply/eligibility-citizenship-and-identity/sex-and-gender-diverse-passport.

[51]Norrie is referred to by female pronouns in her submission to the High Court and the judgment notes that she wished to be referred to with female pronouns. As such, this chapter will follow this approach.

[52]*NSW Registrar of Births, Deaths and Marriages v. Norrie* [2014] Case S273/2013.

[53]Ibid., para. 9–11.

[54]Ibid., para. 1.

[55]Ibid, para. 30.

[56]Ibid., para. 36.

in favour of allowing the use of an alternative sex/gender marker for Norrie and others in New South Wales.

While Norrie clearly does not identify with a binary understanding of sex, the decision is supported by a medicalised understanding of sex and gender. Although the court does not go so far as to say this would be a requirement for other applications, Norrie's specific case relies in part on the fact that she underwent gender affirmation surgery, which at the time would have only been available to those explicitly defining their gender in binary terms. Although in the intervening years the medical system has become more open to the inclusion of non-binary individuals, not all non-binary people can or would want to access some type of gender affirmation surgery. Therefore, the inclusion of medical details in this present case raises the question to what extent this legal option will ultimately be available to those whose bodies do not easily fit within a binary system or who may even explicitly seek to exist outside this binary.

3.2 Germany

Although "X" is perhaps the most common alternative category to the traditional M/F binary, the German Constitutional Court (BVerfG) recently ruled in favour of a different option in its decision on German birth registers (*1 BvR 2019/16 (2017)*).[57] This decision was in response to a complaint brought by an intersex person against the existing law requiring gender registration on the basis of a binary female/male system. Germany's personal status law had been amended in 2013 in order to allow parents of intersex children to avoid or delay registering a gender marker on the child's birth certificate that may be, or may become, inaccurate.[58] The complainant, represented by the campaign group Die dritte Option (the third option), argued that this constituted a "negative" recognition of non-binary individuals, as the gender marker was left blank, and was therefore a form of gender-based discrimination.[59]

[57]The BVerfG, likewise, had already acknowledged in previous decisions the right to determine one's own gender identity within the context of existing (binary) gender options. More recently, the Court has made this right explicit. In a 2008 decision (*1 BvL 10/05 (2008)*), the Court recognised the existence of a constitutional "right to recognition of one's self-determined gender identity" (*Recht auf Anerkennung der selbstbestimmten geschlechtlichen Identität*). See, further, Peter Dunne and Jule Mulder, "Beyond the Binary: Towards a Third Sex Category in Germany?" *German Law Journal* 19, no 3 (2018): 627–648.

[58]Die dritte Option, "Verfassungsbeschwerde", September 2, 2016, accessed May 2, 2018, http://dritte-option.de/wp-content/uploads/2013/06/Dritte-Option_Anonymisierte-Verfassungsbeschwerde-2016.pdf.

[59]The group reasoned that it was necessary to seek a positive, third, non-binary registration option (and not the abolition of gender registration) in order to obtain a ruling that would take the

In its 2017 decision, the BVerfG agreed with the complainant and argued that the current birth/gender registration system violated the right to the free development of a person's identity as encompassed in art. 2 of Germany's Basic Law. Having one's gender identity accurately recognised in law is therefore a fundamental right that the government needs to accommodate. More specifically, the BVerfG ruled that the government needed to provide either a "positive" third gender option (likely to be either "inter" or "divers"), that acknowledges non-binary identities in a positive way rather than erasing them from documents entirely or abandon the recording of gender on birth certificates entirely. Although the case itself was brought by an intersex person, the text of the judgment suggests that this decision could, at least in principle, apply to anyone.[60] This case raises parallels to both *Elan-Cane* and *Norrie*, as the BVerfG focuses both on the need for "accuracy" or "truth" regarding a person's sex/gender, as well as the idea that sex/gender is a fundamentally constitutive part of a person's identity and personality and therefore needs to be legally recognised.

Although it is currently unclear to what extent the UK government will recognise non-binary identities, it seems likely that an equivalent to Australia's "X" marker will be introduced in the medium term (despite the omission from the Gender Recognition Reform (Scotland) Bill).[61] This would be in line with the arguments advanced in the *Elan-Cane* judicial review case and would likely be the easiest administrative option as "X" is already a recognised passport marker unlike any potential alternative option. However, this option would potentially be subject to the same critique advanced by the BVerfG in its most recent case. Although the BVerfG specifically criticised the option of simply leaving the gender marker blank, using an "X" for unspecified as per the original aviation authority guidance arguably follows the same spirit by classing those who use it as inherently other.

In rejecting such a negative designation, the BVerfG relied on its interpretation of gender as an inherent if not constitutive part of one's personality—one that has "outstanding significance" both to the individual and others.[62] As the right to free development of one's personality is a constitutional right

place of the existing option to not register a newborn child, with its accompanying administrative protocols that were viewed as creating a pressure for medical/surgical intervention in order to secure a registration rather than a non-registration (see Chapter 7, Garland and Travis, in this collection for a more in-depth discussion of this topic).

[60]On this potential ambiguity of the scope of the judgment, see also, Peter Dunne and. Jule Mulder, "Beyond the Binary: Towards a Third Sex Category in Germany?" *German Law Journal* 19, no 3 (2018): 627–648, p. 642.

[61]The Scottish Government. November 2018. Review of the Gender Recognition Act 2004: Analysis of Responses to the Public Consultation Exercise—Report. Edinburgh.

[62]1 BvR 2019/16, para. 38–39.

under German law, the government therefore has a positive obligation to ensure that people can fully express their gender identity and are protected in doing so. A negative gender marker that only applies to a specific group of people is an inherent violation of this principle and serves to other those who use it. Using this type of argument specific to the German law, but also prevalent in other trans jurisprudence, which increasingly focuses on gender as primarily a private aspect of one's identity, rather than the art. 8 ECHR claim advanced by *Elan-Cane*, allowed the court to construct all gender identities as of worthy of protection, development and recognition. However, it may also be worth thinking about to what extent a negative marker may provide a "queerer" form of recognition. In some sense the absent marker provides a greater freedom to avoid categorisation for those perceived as existing outside the gender binary while at the same time providing some legal recognition of this fact, due to it being explicitly reflected on birth certificates. At the same time, it is also evident how this can be perceived as exclusionary and stigmatising if this is the only form of recognition available and may even be applied against a person's self-understanding, as might be the case when applications are made by parents on behalf of children.

Nevertheless, the BVerfG leaves a number of key issues unaddressed. Specifically, German law and language are both strongly intertwined with a binary understanding of sex/gender. For instance, two German cases that were decided parallel to the BVerfG decision challenged the current legal system of registering the parents of a newborn child. Under German law, a change of a person's first name is only permissible under exceptional circumstances, including in cases of a change of sex/gender as codified in the *Transsexuellengesetz* (Transsexual Law) and treated as effectively equivalent to a change of a person's legal sex/gender status. Therefore, in both cases, the question for the court was not only to consider the specific parental role (mother/father) that should be assigned to the respective parents on the birth certificate, but also which first name should be used for the parent due to the gender specificity of German naming regulations.[63] Both claimants had legally changed their sex and name prior to having their children but the courts refused both claimants applications to be listed in a parental role that matched their changed legal sex and further ruled that the claimants had to be registered under their previous first name in order to avoid a mismatch between parental status and the gender indicated by their names. Due to the lack of gender-neutral terminology in both German society and jurisprudence,[64]

[63] *Az. XII ZB 660/14* (2017) and *Az. XII ZB 459/16* (2017).

[64] For instance, in *Az. XII ZB 660/14* (2017) the judgment highlights that the legal status of motherhood is solely defined through the capacity to give birth to the child in question. See *OH and GH v Germany*, App. Nos. 53568/18 and 54941/18 (European Court of Human Rights).

introducing a third gender category that is more than purely symbolic is likely to require significant further legal amendments.

The German government in December 2018 implemented the BVerfG decision by adding a new paragraph, § 45b, to the *Personenstandsgesetz* (Personal Status Law). This amendment allows the change of a person's legal sex/gender status to "divers" as a third option or the removal of this status marker, but is limited to intersex people who can provide medical evidence that attests to "a variant of sex development" (translated from German).[65] With this, the government has seemingly chosen the most narrow interpretation of the BVerfG decision, but nevertheless fails to address what the effect of this will be on the remaining legal provisions that currently depend on a binary model. In some ways, the government's approach makes explicit the biological link that was only hinted at in *Norrie*. Here, the legal recognition of genders beyond the binary becomes legally linked to biological "facts", while other reasons for a person to exist outside the binary are not deemed suitable for legal recognition. It also problematically equates intersex variations with gender diversity.

While some intersex people may wish to be recognised outside the female/male dichotomy (e.g. the claimant in the BVerfG decision), Garland and Travis' contribution to this collection clearly illustrates that many individuals do not. This means that, overall, this new provision serves to maintain the outsider status of non-binary people, while only bringing some intersex people inside the ambit of legal recognition.

Beyond the specific criticism advanced by the German constitutional court against negative gender markers, and the criticisms made against the restrictive interpretation of the German government of the BVerfG decision,[66] there is further theoretical criticism of extending the existing legal gender recognition framework to include a "third" option. Having access to legal recognition and legal protection of one's identity status is undoubtedly beneficial, even if only in symbolic terms.[67] While the introduction of a third gender category or gender marker would rectify the explicit exclusion of non-binary people from the existing legal recognition process, the introduction of such a

[65]Bundesministerium des Innern, für Bau und Heimat. 2018. Entwurf eines Gesetzes zur Änderung der in das Geburtenregister einzutragenden Angaben. Berlin.

[66]Die dritte Option, "Statement zur beschlossenen PStG-Reform: Ein Schritt nach vorn, aber noch kein verfassungskonformes Gesetz", December 13, 2018, accessed December 20, 2018, http://dritte-option.de/statement-zur-beschlossenen-pstg-reform-ein-schritt-nach-vorn-aber-noch-kein-verfassungskonformes-gesetz/.

[67]See e.g. the issue of third gender recognition in Nepal: Michael Bochenek and Kyle Knight, "Establishing a Third Gender Category in Nepal: Process and Prognosis" *Emory Int'l L. Rev.* 26 (2012): 11–41.

third category can also be read as the introduction of a new normative category for the purpose of assimilation of currently non-normative genders.[68] As Jasbir Puar suggests, a rights-based approach to trans and other gender non-conforming bodies is to some extent always an attempt at normalisation and generally exclusionary to those who are unable to meet specific official standards or requirements: "This trans(homo)nationalism is therefore capacitated, even driven, not only by the abjection of bodies unable to meet proprietary racial and gendered mandates of bodily comportment, but also by the concomitant marking of those abjected bodies as debilitated".[69] Particularly in light of the decision of the German government to link the new gender marker to intersex "conditions", this suggests that the only legally "valid" reason for moving beyond the gender binary is a biological one. Hence, while in this instance one specific group may have moved from the outside to the inside of this legal framework, this also involves a new process of redrawing and shoring up the boundaries of what it means to be recognised by law as validly gendered and what kind of people or bodies can be recognised as such.

Hence, the current legal trend towards adding additional legal categories to an existing system of legal gender recognition to accommodate non-binary identities may suggest that, following Judith Butler, new genders are becoming or are made intelligible through legal recognition.[70] As this is a developing area, at the moment it is difficult to assess whether the introduction of a third gender category can challenge a binary, categorical understanding of gender or whether it instead simply reifies a tripartite system of gender categories to replace the existing binary system. Introducing a third gender marker for official legal documents also does little to challenge the pervasive gendering of both public and private spaces, which routinely serves to impose gendered norms on those entering these spaces.[71] While passports and birth certificates may provide some of the most explicit markers of which identities are valid within legal spaces, they often have little or no impact on the way in which policies and quasi-legal rules continue to delineate who is

---

[68]See also the critique of this, e.g. Surya Munro, "Transmuting Gender Binaries: The Theoretical Challenge" *Sociological Research Online* 17, no 1(2007): 90–104.

[69]Jasbir Puar, *The Right To Maim: Debility, Capacity, Disability* (Durham and London: Duke University Press, 2017), p. 35.

[70]Judith Butler, *Gender Trouble: Feminism and the Subversion of Identity* (London and New York: Routledge, 1999), pp. 1, 22.

[71]Petra L. Doan, "The Tyranny of Gendered Spaces—Reflections from Beyond the Gender Dichotomy" *Gender, Place & Culture* 17, no 5 (2010): 635–654.

permitted to access spaces or services as can be seen in recent debates around women-only spaces in particular.[72]

In this process of providing a stable and legally intelligible and recognisable category, there also seems to be a concurrent process of implicitly stabilising and reifying the other two sex/gender categories. It is notable that the new German category "divers" seems to suggest that while this new third option may contain a multitude of different identities, the other two are conversely limited to two clear identities with no room for diversity of genders. Similarly, the more common "X" marker has been defined by the Australian government as applying to "sex and gender diverse" people, again implicitly suggesting that the other two categories do not cover such diversity. This is of course not to suggest that having access to a third gender marker is not both practically and symbolically meaningful to people, but it nevertheless raises the question of whether this third category mainly serves to channel gender non-conformity away from the two pre-existing categories rather than offering a wider challenge to the legal categorisation of sex/gender as a whole.[73]

4 Conclusion

The introduction of these new categories also raises the question as to who will choose these new gender markers. Official discussions in various jurisdictions, such as the UK and Germany, suggest that the campaigns for a third gender marker are primarily advanced by a very small group of trans, non-binary and intersex people, seemingly an even smaller minority than those interested in a change of legal gender more generally. For instance, in *R (on the application of Christie Elan-Cane) and Secretary of State for the Home Department [2018] EWHC 1530 (Admin)*, the evidence cited in the judgment suggests that only about 7000 people in the UK identify as non-binary, with an even smaller subset wishing to use a third gender marker. Similarly, the German BVerfG assumed that the new gender marker was primarily desired by intersex people who do not identify with the gender binary, a likely even smaller group. As such the official understanding of a "third" or non-binary gender option is still that this is an exception granted to a minority group, with the default, or "normal", gender options remaining

[72]Davina Cooper, "A Very Binary Drama: The Conceptual Struggle for Gender's Future" *feminists@law* 9, no 1 (2019): 1–36.

[73]See also Davina Cooper and Flora Renz, "If the State Decertified Gender, What Might Happen to its Meaning and Value?" *Journal of Law & Society* 43, no 4 (2016): 483–505.

as male and female. However, in principle these new options could be taken up by a much wider range of people. For instance, although the exact scope of the new German law is currently limited, the BVerfG has previously ruled that various medical requirements for a change of one's gender marker were unconstitutional. It therefore seems possible that further legal challenges will be brought to remove some of the restrictions on the new third gender option going forward.

Considering that the number of people identifying as non-binary seems to be increasing,[74] is it possible to imagine a future legal landscape in which a third gender option becomes the default or "normal" option? And if so, is this then merely a step towards ultimately removing legal gender entirely? Although this might at first glance seem to be a fanciful option, it has now been repeatedly mentioned as a possibility both by courts and by legislators. This seems to be in part because the relevance of gender for legal purposes is steadily decreasing, with gender-neutral legislation increasingly becoming the norm and gender's relevance as an identifying marker being supplanted by more sophisticated methods like DNA or facial recognition. If gender markers beyond the current dominant binary system become more prevalent, this would likely raise questions about the administrative value of retaining the current system of legally certifying gender at all. This is not to suggest that the law *should* move in this direction but rather to highlight that, while two decades ago the mere act of moving from one gender category to another seemed legally almost impossible, the wholesale removal of such categories seems to gradually be becoming a more imaginable option. At the same time the removal of gender markers, rather than the introduction of a third one, may hold greater potential for moving beyond law's tendency to constantly (re)create new insider/outsider distinctions in its efforts to maintain intelligible legal categories.

References

Australian Government. *Australian Government Guidelines on the Recognition of Sex and Gender*. Commonwealth of Australia (July 2013).

Beek, Titia F. et al. "Partial Treatment Requests and Underlying Motives of Applicants for Gender Affirming Interventions" *The Journal of Sexual Medicine* 12, no 11 (2015): 2201–2205.

[74]Jack Harrison, Jaime Grant, and Jody L. Herman, "A Gender Not Listed Here: Genderqueers, Gender Rebels, and Otherwise in the National Transgender Discrimination Survey," *LGBTQA Policy Journal at the Harvard Kennedy School* 2 (2012): 13–24.

Bochenek, Michael, and Kyle Knight. "Establishing a Third Gender Category in Nepal: Process and Prognosis" *Emory Int'l L. Rev.* 26 (2012): 11–41.

Bundesministerium des Innern, für Bau und Heimat, Entwurf eines Gesetzes zur Änderung der in das Geburtenregister einzutragenden Angaben. Berlin (2018).

Butler, Judith. *Gender Trouble: Feminism and the Subversion of Identity* (London and New York: Routledge, 1999).

Butler, Judith, *Precarious Life: The Powers of Mourning and Violence* (London and New York: Verso, 2004).

Chokshi, Niraj. "Canada Introduces 'X' as a Third Sex Category for Passport Holders" *New York Times,* August 25, 2017. Accessed March 27, 2020. https://www.nytimes.com/2017/08/25/world/americas/canada-passport-x.html.

Clarke, Jessica. "They, Them and Theirs" *Harvard Law Review* 132, no 3 (2019): 894.

Cooper, Davina. "A Very Binary Drama: The Conceptual Struggle for Gender's Future" *feminists@law* 9, no 1 (2019): 1–36.

Cooper, Davina, and Flora Renz. "If the State Decertified Gender, What Might Happen to its Meaning and Value?" *Journal of Law & Society* 43, no 4 (2016): 483–505.

Cowan, Sharon. "'That Woman Is a Woman!' The Case of Bellinger v. Bellinger and the Mysterious (Dis) Appearance of Sex: Bellinger v. Bellinger [2003] 2 All ER 593;[2003] FCR 1;[2003] 2 WLR 1174;[2003] UKHL 21" *Feminist Legal Studies* 12, no 1 (2004): 79–92.

Davy, Zowie. *Recognizing Transsexuals: Personal, Political and Medicolegal Embodiment* (Burlington: Ashgate, 2012).

Die dritte Option. "Verfassungsbeschwerde", September 2, 2016. Accessed 2018. http://dritte-option.de/wp-content/uploads/2013/06/Dritte-Option_Anonymisierte-Verfassungsbeschwerde-2016.pdf.

Die dritte Option. "Statement zur beschlossenen PStG-Reform: Ein Schritt nach vorn, aber noch kein verfassungskonformes Gesetz", December 13, 2018. Accessed December 20, 2018. http://dritte-option.de/statement-zur-beschlossenen-pstg-reform-ein-schritt-nach-vorn-aber-noch-kein-verfassungskonformes-gesetz/.

Doan, Petra L. "The Tyranny of Gendered Spaces—Reflections from Beyond the Gender Dichotomy" *Gender, Place & Culture* 17, no 5 (2010): 635–654.

Dunne, Peter, and Jule Mulder. "Beyond the Binary: Towards a Third Sex Category in Germany?" *German Law Journal* 19, no 3 (2018): 627–648.

Fenstermaker, Sarah, and Candace West. *Doing Gender, Doing Difference: Inequality, Power, and Institutional Change* (Abingdon: Routledge, 2013).

Government Equalities Office. "New Action to Promote LGBT Equality", July 23, 2017. Accessed March 27, 2020. https://www.gov.uk/government/news/new-action-to-promote-lgbt-equality.

Harrison, Jack, Jaime Grant, and Jody L. Herman. "A Gender Not Listed Here: Genderqueers, Gender Rebels, and Otherwise in the National Transgender

Discrimination Survey" *Lgbtq Policy Journal at the Harvard Kennedy School* 2 (2012): 13–24.

Hines, Sally. *Gender Diversity, Recognition and Citizenship: Towards a Politics of Difference* (London and New York: Palgrave Macmillan, 2013).

Holzer, Lena. *Non-Binary Gender Registration Models in Europe: Report on Third Gender Marker or No Gender Marker Options* (ILGA Europe, 2018).

House of Commons Select Committee on Women and Equalities. *Transgender Equality* (London: House of Commons, The Stationery Office Limited, 2016).

House of Lords. "Marriage (Same Sex Couples) Bill—Committee (3rd Day)", 24 June 2013, 746 (22).

House of Lords. "Gender Recognition Bill", January 29, 2004, 657 (31).

Hughes, Sarah. "Transparent Season One Is Free for a Day—Here's Why You Should Watch It" *The Guardian*, January 23, 2015. http://www.theguardian.com/tv-and-radio/2015/jan/23/transparent-season-one-free-on-amazon-for-a-day.

Killelly, Daniel. "Exclusive: Hollyoaks Writer Jonathan Larkin Talks Blessing Transgender Story", May 15, 2014, *Digital Spy*.

Lev, Arlene Istar. "Gender Dysphoria: Two Steps Forward, One Step Back" *Clinical Social Work Journal* 41, no 3 (2013): 288–296.

Levin, Sam. "'Huge Validation': Oregon Becomes First State to Allow Official Third Gender Option" *The Guardian*, June 15, 2017. https://www.theguardian.com/us-news/2017/jun/15/oregon-third-gender-option-identity-law.

Lyons, Izzy. "Transgender Man in Fight to Be Recognised as Father of His Child" *The Telegraph*, February 12, 2019, https://www.telegraph.co.uk/news/2019/02/12/transgender-mans-fight-child-motherless-opposed-government/.

Monro, Surya. "Transmuting Gender Binaries: The Theoretical Challenge" *Sociological Research Online* 17, no 1 (2007).

Puar, Jasbir. *The Right To Maim: Debility, Capacity, Disability* (Durham and London: Duke University Press, 2017).

Renz, Flora. "The Gender Recognition Act 2004 and Transgender People's Legal Consciousness" (Ph.D., Kent Law School, University of Kent, 2017).

Sanger, Tam. *Trans People's Partnerships: Towards an Ethics of Intimacy* (Basingstoke: Palgrave Macmillan, 2010).

The Scottish Government. "Review of the Gender Recognition Act 2004 [Consultation]", November 9, 2017. Accessed March 27, 2020. http://www.gov.scot/Publications/2017/11/5459.

The Scottish Government. *Review of the Gender Recognition Act 2004: Analysis of Responses to the Public Consultation Exercise—Report* (Edinburgh: November 9, 2017).

Sharpe, Alex. "Endless Sex: The Gender Recognition Act 2004 and the Persistence of a Legal Category" *Feminist Legal Studies* 15, no 1 (2007): 57–84.

Sharpe, Alex. "Gender Recognition in the UK: A Great Leap Forward" *Social & Legal Studies* 18, no 2 (2009): 241–245.

Steinmetz, Katy. "The Transgender Tipping Point" *Time Magazine*, May 29, 2014. Accessed March 27, 2020. https://time.com/135480/transgender-tipping-point/.

Strong, W. "Transgender N.W.T., Residents Can Now Change Birth Certificates to Reflect Gender" *CBC News*, July 15, 2017. http://www.cbc.ca/news/canada/north/nwt-transgender-legislation-changes-1.4206782.

Te Tari Taiwhenua/Internal Affairs. "Information About Changing Sex/Gender Identity", February 15, 2018. Accessed March 27, 2020. https://www.passports.govt.nz/what-you-need-to-renew-or-apply-for-a-passport/information/.

Vincent, Ben, and Ana Manzanzo. "History and Cultural Diversity". In *Genderqueer and Non-Binary Genders*, edited by Christina Richards, Walter Pierre Bouman and Meg-John Barker (London: Palgrave, 2017).

Whittle, Stephen. "The Opposite of Sex Is Politics—The UK Gender Recognition Act and Why It Is Not Perfect, Just Like You and Me: FORUM" *Journal of Gender Studies* 15, no 3 (2006): 267–271.

Wong, Curtis M. "Arkansas Has Been Offering a Nonbinary Gender Option on State IDs for Years" *HuffPost*, October 17, 2018. https://www.huffingtonpost.com/en-try/arkansas-gender-neutral-state-idoption_us_5bc79f75e4b0d38b58 74a669.

Queering the Queer/Non-Queer Binary: Problematising the "I" in LGBTI+

Fae Garland and Mitchell Travis

1 Introduction

"Intersex" is an umbrella term that refers to individuals who are born with chromosomal, hormonal or genital variations in sex characteristics that mean they fall outside of commonplace understandings of male or female. This chapter draws upon the findings of a small-scale empirical project which interviewed intersex rights activists to consider, first, how "intersex" is being constructed by and to policymakers and legislators and, second, who is responsible for constructing the terms of this political debate. By considering how this construction impacts upon legislative reform, this chapter argues that a more nuanced approach is required by law in relation to the intersex movement and that queer or LGBT+ framing may be an ineffective mechanism alone through which to incorporate the intersex experience. Moreover, this chapter reveals underlying tensions in the strategies that outsiders are using to instigate legal change relating to the narratives of inclusion/exclusion and queer/non-queer. Such tensions have resulted in an increasingly polarised

F. Garland
Centre for Social Ethics and Policy,
University of Manchester, Manchester, UK
e-mail: fae.garland@manchester.ac.uk

M. Travis (✉)
Centre for Law and Social Justice, School of Law,
University of Leeds, Leeds, UK
e-mail: m.travis@leeds.ac.uk

S. Raj and P. Dunne (eds.), *The Queer Outside in Law*, Palgrave Socio-Legal Studies,
https://doi.org/10.1007/978-3-030-48830-7_7

schism within the intersex community that threatens to destabilise reform progress.

Before expanding on our methodology and results, it is first important to stress that our engagement with "queer" is largely informed by the understandings of our participants and situated predominantly within the context of activism rather than theory. Whilst some of these views may be contrary to dominant understandings of queer, they represent the lived experiences of intersex activists as they navigate the complexity of social, legal, medical and activist spaces and apparatus. Problematically, queer was often used interchangeably with LGBT+ in activist spaces, which means this research is unable to distinguish assimilationist political narratives and potentially more radical queer agendas. Whilst this collapsing of queer and LGBT+ is problematic in terms of queer theory, it is important to engage with this conflation as a practical issue in the utility of queer theory and its translation outside of the privileged academic sphere. One of the reasons for this and a key finding from this study is that queer activism is still perceived by our participants to coalesce around single-issue politics related to sexuality despite the critical interventions of theorists, such as Warner,[1] Berlant and Freeman[2] and Cohen[3] with the potential effect of limiting "the comprehensive and transformational character of queer politics."[4]

Our participants were divided, therefore, as to those who identified with (or approved of) queer either as an identity or political stance and those who were not willing to engage with queerness. Those that did identify as queer were able to articulate that their queerness emanated from their bodies (their genetic, hormonal or congenital make-up) which destabilise institutionally established societal, legal and medical understandings of sex, gender and sexuality. For these people, intersex acts as an interpellation of normativity and, as a result, embodies the disruptive element of queer. For others, however, it was important for them to be distinguished from queer. For these individuals, queer is a "'doing' rather than a 'being'"[5] and as such they felt that many intersex people are not in fact performing queer but rather conform (and

[1]Michael Warner, "Introduction," in *Fear of a Queer Planet: Queer Politics and Social Theory*, ed. Michael Warner (Minneapolis: University of Minnesota Press, 1993), i–xxviii.

[2]Lauren Berlant and Elizabeth Freeman, "Queer Nationality," in *Fear of a Queer Planet: Queer Politics and Social Theory*, ed. Michael Warner (Minneapolis: University of Minnesota Press, 1993), 193–229.

[3]Cathy Cohen, "Punks, Bulldaggers, and Welfare Queens: The Radical Potential of Queer Politics?" *GLQ: A Journal of Lesbian and Gay Studies*, 3, no 4, (1997): 437–465.

[4]Ibid., 441.

[5]Noreen Giffney and Myra Hird, *Queering the Non/human*, 1st ed. (Aldershot: Ashgate Publishing Ltd., 2008), 5.

indeed wish to conform) to normative expectations associated with gender and sexuality. Consequently, many intersex people do not identify with the queer or LGBT+ community and instead specifically desire to be excised from that community in both policy decisions and/or legislative change.

For those that understood queer as an activist (or wider) community, those people largely rejected association with queer politics. In some ways, this is not surprising. The intersex movement's overwhelming focus on non-therapeutic medical interventions has meant that, whilst they are critical of legal and medical institutions, their political goals have necessitated working largely within the system rather than destabilising the gender binary or rejecting or creating new societal or political infrastructures. As a result, this research highlights how intersex embodied people navigate their status as outsiders in terms of both law and activism. For many, this space as outsider, whilst by no means ideal, was necessary in order to communicate their needs without being co-opted or misconstrued by queer and LGBT+ activists or policymakers.

2 Methodology

As aforementioned, this chapter draws on results from a small-scale empirical project that was funded by the Socio-Legal Studies Association to examine first, whether intersex people are "doing queer" and second, whether the legal responses to intersex campaigns are being appropriately informed by activist parties. This project accordingly complied with the SLSA's ethical guidelines[6] and consisted of 17 semi-structured telephone interviews carried out between 2014 and 2016 with intersex rights activists and organisations from across the globe.[7] The interviews examined perceptions of differing contemporary

[6]See "Statement of Principles of Ethical Research Practice." *Socio-Legal Studies Association*, Last modified: January 2009. http://www.slsa.ac.uk/images/slsadownloads/ethicalstatement/slsa%20ethics%20statement%20_final_%5B1%5D.pdf. Information sheets with details of the project and consent forms were given to participants prior to the interview to ensure that consent was fully informed. Participants were made aware that they could withdraw from the process at any time, and all data has had any identifying information removed to maintain the participants' anonymity. Only the authors have encrypted access to any non-anonymised data. Moreover, given the sensitive nature of the topic, two independent intersex organisations reviewed the interview schedule and information sheets. All respondents were also directed to links for support groups via the information sheets.

[7]These were telephone interviews. However, three submitted responses via e-mail as they did not wish to be interviewed. Respondents came from a number of different jurisdictions, including the UK, Denmark, USA, Sweden, Australia, Germany, Malta and Iceland. Given that respondents were internationally campaigning for intersex rights, they were each aware of the differing legislative responses to intersex in other jurisdictions. Thus, they were able to draw on this knowledge and compare it to their own experience within their jurisdiction.

legal reforms aimed at increasing the resilience of intersex individuals. We used theoretical thematic analysis,[8] generating themes by analysing the data through a Queer Theory lens.[9] Tensions were revealed around attaching the label "intersex" to the wider lesbian, gay, bisexual and transgender (LGBT) or queer umbrella throughout this analysis. The responses encouraged us to think critically about the way in which the intersex community engages with or resists notions of "Queer" in spaces of law in the pursuit of legal reform. Accordingly, we have structured the results in this paper simply into three overarching themes: Intersex People as Queer; Intersex People as not Queer: Individuals; and Intersex People as not Queer: Activism.

3 Intersex People Are Queer

Conceptually, many activists and commentators view Queer Theory as a politically powerful tool for intersex embodied people in terms of achieving social and legal recognition and reform. Participants that engaged with this approach were more likely to engage with the idea that intersex people have a "queering effect" on established institutional understandings of sex and gender:

> … intersex people have always existed throughout time and space and have fed into some sort of intra male or female biological space for millennia … (Respondent 1)

> Sex is a spectrum from male to female (or vice versa) and intersex is a blend of both. (Respondent 2)

Despite the benign nature of the vast majority of these variations,[10] the medical profession considers these "queer bodies"[11] to be states of medical

---

[8]Virginia Braune and Victoria Clarke, "Using Thematic Analysis in Psychology," *Qualitative Research in Psychology*, 3 (2006): 77–101, 87.

[9]Thematic analysis involves a six step process as set out by Braune and Clarke (2006): familiarisation with the data; generating initial codes; searching for themes; reviewing themes; defining and naming themes; and then producing the report. Theoretical thematic analysis involves the generation of themes informed by a particular theory. In this instance, themes were generated through the lens of Queer Theory.

[10]Georgiann Davis, *Contesting Intersex: The Dubious Diagnosis* (New York: New York University Press, 2015).

[11]Morgan Carpenter, "Australia Can Lead the Way for Intersex People." *The Guardian*, June 18, 2013. https://www.theguardian.com/commentisfree/2013/jun/18/intersex-people-australia.

emergency in need of "fixing."[12] Consequently, intersex embodied infants are routinely subjected to unnecessary and non-consensual gender-normalising medical interventions[13] to ensure their "unnatural" bodies can be placed into the "natural" male/female binary. This not only rigidly constructs sex as a binary, but it results in a medical invisibilisation of intersex people that forcibly places them into a sex.[14]

The results are manifold: not only do many individuals face long-term negative consequences of non-consensual and unnecessary gender-normalising medical treatments (the majority of which lack any evidence-base in terms of successful outcomes),[15] but their "erasure" by the medical profession, compounded by the degree of individual and family shame and secrecy associated with such variations, has led to a cultural and legal "disappearing" of intersex embodied people in order to undo the institutional "queering effects" of intersex bodies.[16] The themes of unnecessary and non-consensual "medical harm" and "invisibility" were, unsurprisingly, prominent in our empirical data:

[12]Katrina Karkazis, *Fixing Sex: Intersex, Medical Authority and Lived Experience* (London: Duke University Press, 2008); Fae Garland and Mitchell Travis, "Temporal Bodies: Emergencies, Emergence, and Intersex Embodiment." In *Jurisprudence of the Body*, edited by Chris Dietz, Michael Thomson and Mitchell Travis (London: Palgrave, 2020).

[13]Committee on Bioethics of the Council of Europe. *The Rights of Children in Biomedicine: Challenges Posed by Scientific Advances and Uncertainties*, by Kavot Zillén, Jameson Garland and Santa Slokenberga. Last modified 2017. https://rm.coe.int/16806d8e2f at 40–42.

[14]Anne Fausto-Sterling, *Sexing the Body: Gender Politics and the Construction of Sexuality* (New York: Basic Books, 2000), 54; Mitchell Travis, "Accommodating Intersexuality in European Union Anti-Discrimination Law." *European Law Journal*, 21, no 2 (2015): 180–199, 183.

[15]Our empirical data also revealed this concern: "...there aren't enough studies that really track the longitudinal effect of intersex people who don't have their reproductive organs ... I think that's what the medical community should actually invest in given that they're doing these surgeries, and in a way, it's leaving people out in the cold ..." (Respondent 15). See also Julie Greenberg, *Intersexuality and the Law: Why Sex Matters* (London: New York University Press, 2012), 21; Sarah Creighton, "Surgery for Intersex." *Journal of the Royal Society of Medicine*, 94, no 5 (2001): 218; Morgan Holmes, "Distracted Attentions: Intersexuality and Human Rights Protections." *Cardozo Journal of Law and Gender*, 12 (2005): 127. For discussions on why early interventions have no benefit and should be delayed until puberty. See e.g. Naved Alizai and others. "Feminizing Genitoplasty for Congenital Hyperplasia: What Happens at puberty?" *Journal of Urology*, 161 (1999): 1588–1591 and Sarah Creighton et al., "Objective Cosmetic and Anatomical Outcomes at Adolescence of Feminizing Surgery for Ambiguous genitalia Done in Childhood." *Lancet*, 358 (2001): 124–125; Committee on Bioethics of the Council of Europe. *The Rights of Children in Biomedicine: Challenges Posed by Scientific Advances and Uncertainties*, by Kavot Zillén et al., Last modified, 2017. https://rm.coe.int/16806d8e2f, 43–45.

[16]Fae Garland and Mitchell Travis, "Legislating Intersex Equality: Building the Resilience of Intersex People Through Law." *Legal Studies*, 38, no 4 (2018): 587–606, 590.

> ... [The Medical profession] changes something which is a natural variation of humanity through to illness. They are created as patients that have a medical problem and they didn't have one in the first place... (Respondent 7)[17]

> That's what they're told from day one. 'You have to hide it and if anybody finds out your world will collapse, and this will be the end.' So, they always try to hide it ... this secrecy and being hidden [means] it's very difficult to make the people understand what it's all about. (Respondent 6)

These queering effects around sex and gender have led to allyship with academic and activist groups concerned with queer or LGBT+ issues. Indeed, many of our respondents emphasised that intersex groups and LGBT+ groups had "overlapping concerns ... to do with the binary ideologies around sex, gender and sexuality" (Respondent 13) and thus had parallel struggles that required similar strategies to fight cultural and institutional norms[18]:

> ... when I am talking about on a trans and intersex platform ... of course there are differences, but the commonality is like bodily autonomy, that people get to choose what they want to do with their bodies ... (Respondent 15)

> ... the root of our [parallel] problems comes from homophobia and transphobia and you can say non-binary phobia. (Respondent 4)

Thus, framing intersex lives as "Queer" has been a source of empowerment and a means for highlighting and reflecting upon such invisiblising experiences. Queer theory, at least at a philosophical level, enables individuals to challenge the authenticity of the medical narrative in this area by questioning the naturalness of the sex binary[19] allowing intersex embodied people a voice:

> ... it's giving intersex voices. It has centralised intersex voices. ... definitely the queer community has really given intersex people, intersex activists a platform in which to address these sort of human rights violations. (Respondent 15)

---

[17]This narrative of the medical profession *creating* medical problems is reflected in the literature, see e.g. Sharon Preves, *Intersex and Identity: The Contested Self* (New Brunswick: Rutgers University Press, 2013).

[18]See also Fae Garland and Mitchell Travis, "Legislating Intersex Equality: Building the Resilience of Intersex People Through Law." *Legal Studies*, 38, no 4 (2018): 587, 599–600.

[19]Michael Warner, *The Trouble with Normal: Sex, Politics, and the Ethics of Queer Life* (Cambridge: Harvard University Press, 1999); Judith Butler, *Gender Trouble: Feminism and the Subversion of Identity* (London and New York: Routledge, 1990).

By deconstructing the norms surrounding sex and gender, Queer Theory can work to dismantle (and redistribute) medical power/knowledge so that intersex embodied people can move away from this historical site of oppression and understand their bodies in new and different ways. In the activist arena, "Queer" has been seen as a politically potent term increasingly used to raise political and social awareness of (intersex) lives.[20] Thus, its use often has a political intent behind it, "based in part on a decision to confront what is experienced as discrimination and to commit to a collective identity based on being marginalized ...."[21]

By building strategic alliances and finding points of common ground with other marginalised groups, particularly through inclusion within queer and LGBT+ groups, intersex activists have been able to make the intersex community more vocal and simultaneously use collective action to precipitate social and legal change. This pressure from such groups has certainly had an effect in instigating legal reform and we are beginning to see a global shift towards some form of legislative response that attempts to bring intersex inside the protective remit of law. For example, in 2015, Malta introduced groundbreaking legislation for intersex embodied people that prohibited gender-normalising surgeries and also introduced a series of provisions that protected intersex embodied people from discrimination.[22] The development of this legislation can in part be traced back to a hugely successful International Intersex Conference, funded by ILGA-Europe (International Lesbian, Gay, Bisexual, Transsexual and Intersex Association), which offered a platform for dialogue to take place between intersex activists and Maltese policymakers.[23] Certainly, then, our respondents recognised the need for queer and LGBT alliances in order to access funding to make such campaigning possible and therein achieve the broader intersex community's goals. As one participant explains "...the [LGBTI] alliance is really useful

---

[20]Annamarie Jagose, *Queer Theory: An Introduction* (New York: New York University Press, 1996), 105.

[21]Patrick Dilley, "Queer Theory: Under Construction." *Qualitative Studies in Education*, 12 (1999): 457–472, 461.

[22]This narrative of the medical profession *creating* medical problems is reflected in the literature, see e.g. Sharon Preves, *Intersex and Identity: The Contested Self* (New Brunswick: Rutgers University Press, 2013).

[23]The Third International Intersex Forum was held in Malta in 2013 and issued the *Maltese Declaration* 2013, a document aimed at legislators and policymakers that highlighted the demands of the international intersex community. This event was supported by ILGA and ILGA-Europe and fed into the long collaborative process between policymakers, activists and stakeholders in Malta that eventually led to the development and introduction of the Gender Identity, Gender Expression and Sex Characteristics Act 2015. The introduction of this Act was greatly helped by the role that Ruth Baldacchino, ILGA's co-secretary general, had in the Maltese Government; working at the Ministry for Social Dialogue, Consumer Affairs and Civil Liberties.

to us because it's really our only source of funding." (Respondent 1). Such alliances are therefore seen as a necessary and practical strategy by many intersex activists to ensure that intersex falls inside rather than outside of law's protective sphere.

However, the impact of this interaction by the intersex community with the concept of "Queer" has yet to be critically examined. This is particularly important given that the relationships with and reliance upon queer and LGBT+ allies and narratives have a structuring effect on the way that law understands and constructs experiences. Thus, it is crucial to ask whether the current political co-opting and mobilising of intersex people is adequate for framing the understandings and constructions of intersex experiences: does it meet the broader goals of intersex embodied people or do these alliances continue to leave intersex embodied people as law's outsiders?

4 Intersex People Are Not Queer: Individuals

"Queer" has been used to identify a positionality against the normative rather than a positivity; a sense of "'doing' rather than a 'being'"[24] where "doing" encompasses a "diverse range of critical practices and priorities."[25] Many of our intersex respondents and many intersex people who have contacted us since, have not identified with the term queer. Rather the sex and gender binary is often reaffirmed by intersex embodied people:

> ... the vast majority of people do not identify, intersex people, do not identify as gender queer or outside of the gender binary. (Respondent 13)

> The grand majority of intersex people in the world, the grand majority meaning 80-90% of people, who are born intersex, who have a gender assigned to them at birth, either surgically or just with a pen and paper, are fine with the gender identities they were assigned with. They're fine. The grand majority... (Respondent 4)

> ... the belief that intersex means bi-gendered, the belief that all intersex people have a neutered gender expression or identity... it's simply not true. (Respondent 3)

[24]Noreen Giffney and Myra Hird, *Queering the Non/human*, 1st ed. (Aldershot: Ashgate Publishing Ltd., 2008), 5.

[25]Tamsin Spargo, *Foucault and Queer Theory (Postmodern Encounters)* (Cambridge: Icon Books Ltd., 1999), 8.

This is in part because some individuals may not know, nor ever know, of their intersex variation.[26] For those who have received some form of medical diagnosis, their lived experiences remain under-researched. However, the few studies that have explored sex assignment of intersex embodied people at birth and comparatively in adulthood corroborate these findings: most intersex individuals identify as either male or female and this is true even where sex is ambiguous at birth and thus medically "assigned."[27] Furthermore, findings also suggest that most intersex embodied people who were incorrectly assigned a sex at birth and have since reassigned have done so within the male/female binary (although it must be noted that these may have been the only options available to respondents in the studies).[28] If queer is a "doing" then, these people are not doing queer in the sense of challenging or destabilising existing gender (and other) binaries. Their day-to-day lives, their sex-lives, their engagements with the workplace, their families, their governments reaffirm the gender binary.

This chapter, however, is by no means suggesting that all intersex embodied people gladly fall within the male/female binary. Certainly, some studies have shown that significant minorities of individuals identify outside of the binary in some form. Jones et al.,[29] for example, found that 19% of 292 respondents with atypical sex characteristics selected an "X"/"other" marker rather than m/f, and six per cent were unsure as to which marker they would use. Furthermore, Schweizer et al. found that 18% of individuals were unsatisfied with their current gender allocation and some studies indicate that a small

[26]Intersex variations are not always apparent at birth: "[I]ntersex people are diagnosed visually, at birth, or via amniocentesis, by chromosome, and other blood tests... Intersex differences may also be determined during infancy, at puberty, when attempting to conceive, or through random chance." Consequently, some individuals may have a variation but may never become aware of this fact; The Australian Senate Community Affairs Committee Secretariat, "The Involuntary or Coerced Sterilisation of Intersex People in Australia" (Parliament House, Canberra: Senate Printing Unit 2013), para. 1.7.

[27]Research conducted in Australia found that 75% of 292 respondents with atypical sex characteristics applied either the male or female sex marker. Tiffany Jones et al., *Intersex: Stories and Statistics from Australia* (Cambridge: Open Book Publishers, 2016). Schweizer and others found that only seven per cent of individuals with intersex variations chose gender roles other than male or female. Katinka Schweizer et al., "Gender Experience and Satisfaction with Gender Allocation in Adults with Diverse Intersex Conditions (Divergences of Sex Development, DSD)," *Psychology & Sexuality* 5 (2014): 56.

[28]Cohen-Kettenis found between 39 and 64% of children with certain intersex traits changed from their assigned gender. The change was typically to either a male/female gender role. Peggy Cohen-Kettenis, "Gender change in 46, XY persons with 5α-Reductase-2 Deficiency and 17β-Hydroxysteroid Dehydrogenase-3 Deficiency." *Archives of Sexual Behavior* 34, no 4 (2005): 399.

[29]Tiffany Jones et al., *Intersex: Stories and Statistics from Australia* (Cambridge: Open Book Publishers, 2016).

minority of intersex embodied individuals experience distress as a result of their sex assignment on birth.[30]

Nevertheless, given that the majority of intersex embodied people identify as either male or female, it is far from accurate (or helpful) to assume that all intersex people are "doing" Queer. Recently (as Flora Renz has already noted in Chapter 6 of this edited collection), Germany introduced legislation, which allowed for a "blank space" to be left on birth certificates where the infants' sex was ambiguous.[31] Whilst this reform was meant to give families and clinicians more time to determine the child's "true" sex, it has resulted not only in an increase in gender-normalising surgeries, but in surgeries being performed much earlier, as parents do not want their newborn infant to be seen to fall outside of the male/female binary.[32] Germany's limiting of third genders to intersex people incorrectly implies both that most intersex individuals will identify outside of male and female (because of their experience with body) and that only intersex embodied persons will have a gender identity that stretches beyond male and female.[33] Law reform that attempts to include intersex premised on this queer narrative does not reflect the lived realities of most intersex individuals.[34] As respondent 15 stated: "not all intersex people are queer but some queer people are intersex."

Moreover, presenting intersex embodied individuals as "queer" may also be highly problematic. For many, "Queer" was linked to the stigma and shame associated with a failure to conform to the sex binary. A large proportion of our respondents indicated that not only do the majority of intersex individuals fall within the male/female binary, but that there is a conscious desire to do so: many intersex individuals (and their parents) want to be seen as "normal" and view social acceptance to be intrinsically linked with conformity

[30] Katinka Schweizer et al., "Gender Experience and Satisfaction with Gender Allocation in Adults with Diverse Intersex Conditions (Divergences of Sex Development, DSD)," *Psychology & Sexuality* 5 (2014): 56–82. These figures vary between studies. For example, Furtado et al. (2012) found that 8.5–20% of intersex embodied individuals experienced some sort of distress in relation to their gender identity. In comparison, Callens et al. (2016) found that 3.3% of individuals changed gender and experienced distress about their gender from childhood. Paulo Furtado et al., "Gender Dysphoria Associated with Disorders of Sex Development," *Nature Reviews Urology*, 9, no 11 2012: 620 and Nina Callens et al., "Recalled and Current Gender Role Behavior, Gender Identity and Sexual Orientation in Adults with Disorders/Differences of Sex Development." *Hormones and Behavior*, 86 (2016): 8.

[31] Gesetz zur Änderung personenstandsrechtlicher Vorschriften (Personenstandsrechts-Änderungsgesetz—PStRÄndG) 2013.

[32] Amnesty International. "First, Do No Harm: Ensuring the Rights of Children with Variations of Sex Characteristics in Denmark and Germany" (London: Amnesty International Ltd., 2017); Mitchell Travis, "Accommodating Intersexuality in European Union Anti-Discrimination Law." *European Law Journal*, 21, no 2 (2015): 180–199.

[33] Fae Garland and Mitchell Travis, "Legislating Intersex Equality: Building the Resilience of Intersex People through Law." *Legal Studies*, 38, no 4 (2018): 587–606.

[34] See below.

to the sex binary. To be framed as something "other" than male or female is undesirable, and indeed is viewed as potentially alienating and marginalising:

> ... they don't want to stick out. If they had the possibility, they wouldn't use this opportunity to put an X instead of F or M ... Most intersex people I know, they are really afraid that somebody knows that they are intersex, even in the family... (Respondent 5)

Consequently, individuals and parents may go to extreme lengths to keep their or their child's intersex variance secret,[35] severing contact with friends or family or even "mov[ing] to another town and not [telling] anybody where they went."[36] Indeed, associating "queerness" with intersex could drive parents towards gender-normalising medical interventions and certainly, in the German context, this has been the effect.[37] Framing intersex as "queer" may actually strengthen medical power/knowledge rather than disrupt it as the medical profession and parents are still driven by heteronormativity and the gender binary in a way that law may be moving away from. Laws that position intersex children as "queer" may actually lower their resilience as they encourage parents to "normalise" them—thus, handing more power to healthcare professionals. This raises an interesting concern about the practical limits of a push against the gender binary. To the extent that advocates or academics laud intersex as proof that binary sex is a construct, we must equally acknowledge that (whether real or constructed) binary sex is a social norm and that there are consequences (or at least perceived consequences) for failing to conform to that social norm. Putting children at the forefront of challenges to the gender binary does result in physical and psychological harm. A view confirmed by our participants:

> ...if people were forced to fit into any box just because of their biology I would think that would be a case for further discrimination or stigmatisation down the line... (Respondent 1)

> ... parents will even more readily sign the consent form [for compulsory medical treatment]. (Respondent 5)

---

[35]Georgiann Davis, *Contesting Intersex: The Dubious Diagnosis* (New York: New York University Press, 2015).

[36]Peter Hegarty and Cheryl Chase, "Intersex Activism, Feminism and Psychology: Opening a Dialogue on Theory, Research and Clinical Practice." *Feminism & Psychology*, 10, no 1 (2000): 117–132, 128.

[37]Amnesty International. "First, Do No Harm: Ensuring the Rights of Children with Variations of Sex Characteristics in Denmark and Germany" (London: Amnesty International Ltd, 2017); Mitchell Travis, "Accommodating Intersexuality in European Union Anti-Discrimination Law." *European Law Journal*, 21, no 2 (2015): 180–199.

Unsurprisingly, then, most intersex rights activists do not advocate an intersex-specific "third" gender marker for children and have serious concerns over the implications of such a legal device.[38] Not only may it serve to "other" intersex individuals by bringing them "inside" law in a manner that is entirely unsuited to their experiences, but also it may pressurise parents and medical practitioners into performing the very sorts of gender-normalising surgeries that the community is seeking to prohibit by depicting intersex individuals as a queer outsider in law. The medical profession here justifies their practices through an attempt to bring intersex people "inside" the gender binary. Whilst many of our participants were negative about embracing a queer identity or political stance on an individual basis, they also raised significant concerns about their experiences of queer activism.

5 Intersex People Are Not Queer: Activism

As noted earlier, whilst our participants recognised that there are strategic advantages in including "I" to facilitate collective action, there are notable concerns that doing so will further entrench a queer/non-queer binary in law whereby legislators will presume intersex individuals face the same issues as queer or LGBT+ persons. Our respondents felt that this was because, where intersex had been included within Queer and LGBT+ groups, their real needs in fact remained "outside" the remit of these organisations. Consequently, Queer and LGBT+ organisations had fundamentally different priorities from the intersex community that meant that they were failing to understand the needs of intersex embodied people. The consequence of this was to misrepresent intersex-specific issues as relating to identity rather than bodily autonomy. Some of our respondents felt that this misrepresentation was more cynically the result of LGBT+ organisations being motivated by funding concerns rather than shared sympathies with the intersex community:

> When an LGBT charity says, 'We help LGBTI people'... they have no concept of what [intersex] is, or how to help them; it looks really good, and definitely looks good to funders. (Respondent 3)

> There is increasingly money available, but it always goes for discrimination and LGBT issues. In our experience the intersex groups who define themselves

[38]However, most respondents welcomed a third-gender marker for all those who wished to use it. Their main concern was that a third-gender marker should not be used automatically for those with intersex variations.

> as LGBT they get the funding, but groups like us who want a change in the medical practice we get shunned. (Respondent 6)

These concerns about funding are heightened by two factors. First, a context in which intersex organisations receive little to no funding often doing huge volumes of work without financial or administrative support. Second, due to the mismanagement of funds towards groups proclaiming to do intersex work who, in reality, have no real experience with the needs of intersex groups. For example, Zwischengeschlecht draw attention to a funded video made by a Scottish LGBTI organisation that failed to consult intersex people and, thus, at best, lacked some precision and quality and, at worst, may have added to the erasure of, and misinformation around, intersex people.[39]

Regardless of the motivations for including "I," the implications of misrepresentation are both long-reaching and problematic in terms of how intersex is being constructed by and to policymakers and legislators. At the academic and activist level, intersex does much work for the communities it is co-opted into. For example, many LGBT+ groups and queer scholars working in the field of gender have often used the *concept* rather than the *experience* of being intersex as a method of affirming their own views about the fluidity of gender and sex.[40] As a result, these works tend to offer intersex people as confirmation of the instability of sex or gender—without engaging with the harms that are done to intersex people by that system. Certainly, this has been a criticism of queer and LGBT+ activists working at an international level. Intersex activists from Zwischengeschlecht, for instance, have raised concerns over the misappropriation of intersex by larger organisations that then erase intersex issues from the UN agenda by "framing them as trans, LGBT and discrimination issues, for example IGM as '*sex alignment surgeries*', IGM survivors as '*transsexual children*', and intersex NGOs as '*a group of lesbians, gays, bisexuals, transgender and intersex victims of discrimination and violence*'" [emphasis in the original].[41] Zwischengeschlech go on to note that, as a consequence of this reframing, non-therapeutic medical interventions are being commented on less frequently by UN committees.[42] Our participants felt strongly that

[39] Seelenlos. "UK > Misappropriation of Intersex Funding by LGBT Groups, Misrepresentation of Intersex as LGBT Issue." *Stop.Genitalmutilation.org*, accessed April 10, 2019, http://stop.genitalmutilation.org/post/UK-Misappropriation-of-Intersex-Funding-by-LGBT-Groups.

[40] Julie Greenberg, *Intersexuality and the Law: Why Sex Matters* (London: New York University Press, 2012).

[41] Seelenlos. "CEDAW67 Italy > Major Setback for Intersex Human Rights at UN :-(." *Stop.Genitalmutilation.org*, accessed April 10, 2019, http://stop.genitalmutilation.org/post/Major-Setback-for-Intersex-Human-Rights-at-the-UN.

[42] Ibid.

queer and LGBT+ activists are contributing to an erasure of intersex issues from domestic and international policy and legislative agendas.

> I do not engage with academics who want to 'use' intersex people and our experiences without any benefit to us. As a volunteer I don't have time. (Respondent 2)

> Most people who are actually interested about intersex issues come from a gay perspective and they look at this issue through their own lens and recognise something. Then they frame it; that it's about coming out, about acceptance and social recognition, but the mutilation is not part of their own agenda and experience so it doesn't fit into their lens, so they just leave it out. (Respondent 6)

This concern is growing amongst intersex activists because relationships with and reliance on queer and LGBT+ allies and narratives has a structuring effect on the way that law understands and constructs intersex experiences. This structuring effect, respondents fear, is to essentially result in intersex-specific concerns being left outside of queer and LGBT+ platforms. The consequence of this is very real in terms of the law reform that may follow. The danger is that this will prompt legislators to extend identity-based remedies (such as anti-discrimination law or the Gender Recognition Act 2004 in the UK) and overlook the more pressing and specific challenges faced by the intersex community by translating the LGBT+ misrepresentation of "I" into law thus leaving intersex embodied individuals as queer outsiders in law:

> Sometimes policy makers deal with trans issues and believe that by doing so they are covering intersex issues as well, not realising that protections put in place that benefit trans people while they benefit part of our community it's not the grounds or key demands of our community. (Respondent 8)

> … the reference to gender identity and sexual orientation… intersex essentially seems to be tacked on, the way that intersex is tacked on to LGBT… (Respondent 3)

This misrepresentative construction of "intersex" has been adopted by the majority of global legislative reforms seen thus far and is being replicated at the international level. Most state responses have focused on anti-discrimination law and third gender markers that build upon existing narratives within LGBT+ activism, rather than focusing on intersex-specific concerns. These legal approaches have attempted to shift "intersex" from outside to within the zone of legal protection, by introducing "intersex" as a protected characteristic within anti-discrimination/hate crime legislation, and/or using a "third" marker such as an "X" or a blank space to signify intersex on official documents.[43] Whilst such responses have signified a growing legal awareness of "intersex," there has been a lack of legal focus on prohibiting unnecessary, non-consensual gender-normalising medical interventions and, thus far, only two states; Malta and Portugal; have attempted to fully engage with these concerns of bodily autonomy.[44]

Unsurprisingly, our respondents were highly critical of solely identity-focused legislative reform models as they did not address intersex-specific concerns "...anti-discrimination...doesn't mean anything to me. The passport, the X, again, go back to identity" (Respondent 3). Although many respondents recognised a symbolic importance of the "insider" status of legal inclusion at this level through the "recognition of the existence of intersex people, and the ability to reduce discrimination on the basis of our biological variations" (Respondent 2), all our respondents recognised that the failure to address unnecessary and non-consensual gender-normalising surgeries meant that these legislative reforms did not protect intersex embodied people, leaving them as "outsiders." Australia is frequently cited as an example of how ineffectual such reforms are: despite the introduction of intersex as a protected characteristic within anti-discrimination law in 2013,[45] the Family Court of Australia in 2016 later ruled that parents can consent to gender-normalising procedures on their child (even where it results in sterilisation) without seeking the Court's approval.[46]

> This essentially superficial legislation in Australia is still a way of introducing visibility, it's still a way of getting the concept in front of legislators, people who are patently ignorant on the subject, of general sexuality and gender, and not to mention intersex stuff. I think it's important. But if you want to talk

[43]Fae Garland and Mitchell Travis, "Legislating Intersex Equality: Building the Resilience of Intersex People Through Law." *Legal Studies*, 38, no 4 (2018): 587–606.

[44]See Malta's Gender Identity, Gender Expression and Sex Characteristics Act 2015 and Portugal's Law No. 75/XIII/2 2018. These are the only two state-level binding prohibitions. There have been other "soft law" developments in the State of California, USA and also in Columbia's Constitutional Court. In 2018, California introduced a non-binding Senate Concurrent Resolution 110 calling for the medical profession to delay all normalising surgeries until individuals are old enough to consent. Columbia's Constitutional Court issued a series of rulings in the 1990s that restricted parents' and medical practitioners' ability to consent to gender-normalising surgeries: Mary Newbould, "When Parents Choose Gender." *Medical Law Rev*, 24 (2016): 471. At the time of our interviews, only Malta and had legal developments regarding gender-normalising surgeries.

[45]Section 5C Sex Discrimination Act 1984 (Cth).

[46]Morgan Carpenter, "The 'Normalisation' of Intersex Bodies and 'Othering' of Intersex Identities in Australia." *Journal of Bioethical Inquiry*, 15 (2018): 487–495.

> about, 'Is this a watershed moment for intersex people?' in my opinion, it is not. (Respondent 3)

Yet, the administrative ease of just amending anti-discrimination legislation rather than developing law and policy that challenges current medical practice,[47] combined with the dominant (and misrepresentative) LGBT+ narrative of intersex (and global press response), has meant that this type of law reform continues to be the most common state response.[48]

> So, the passport stuff, anti-discrimination stuff, the conflation of gender and sexuality and intersex, aren't the... You've seen it, it garners the most press around the world. (Respondent 3)

Our respondents' critique not only centred on the States' failure to address gender-normalising medical practices, but also on the cyclical effect that such identity-focused legislative reform would have on cultural and institutional misunderstandings: identity-focused reform would perpetuate such misunderstandings and, as a result, leave intersex-specific concerns regarding gender-normalising surgeries outside the protective legal sphere:

> If it's only about registration and nobody's talking about the reality of intersex people, like genital mutilation, then it does more harm...if it's like putting LGBT and it's about registration then...some newspapers [may say that]...intersex can also put an X instead of 'male' or 'female', then most people think even more that intersex is something like gay or trans. The problem with this first registration thing is that there is no talk about genital mutilation. It's like two different topics... (Respondent 5)

This is particularly problematic given that the social mobilisation of an intersex "community" is inherently difficult. Not only does the medical response to intersex variations leave many individuals too traumatised or fearful to "come out" as intersex publicly, but large schisms exist within the "community" itself; indeed, it is not possible to refer to any singular homogenous intersex community at all.

Thus, conceptualising intersex as part of a broader "queer" community may have potentially problematic ramifications for intersex embodied people.

---

[47] Fae Garland and Mitchell Travis, "Legislating Intersex Equality: Building the Resilience of Intersex People through Law." *Legal Studies*, 38, no 4 (2018): 587–606 and Fae Garland and Mitchell Travis, "Making the State Responsible: Intersex Embodiment, Medical Jurisdiction and State Responsibility." *Law and Society*, 47, no 2 (2020): 298–324.

[48] Fae Garland and Mitchell Travis, "Legislating Intersex Equality: Building the Resilience of Intersex People Through Law." *Legal Studies*, 38, no 4 (2018): 587–606.

The cultural and institutional understandings and implications of being labelled "queer" and the political agendas mobilised by queer activists have led many intersex embodied people to wholly reject any notion of "queerness" and ultimately exclude themselves from queer, LGBT+ and intersex activism. A recent example has been DSDfamilies decision to run a guest campaign about their work on "mumsnet"[49]—a website noted for its history of transphobia.[50] The queer/non-queer narrative has resulted in a split within the "community" over the language and narratives used to frame understandings and experiences of intersex variations. Some participants highlight the importance of being "inside" the legal system, even if this is done in a problematic way, in order to have a starting point for further dialogue. Others note that once "inside" the legal system, such dialogue is effectively closed down as uninformed policymakers believe that the issues are resolved. As a result, many of our participants were happy to remain outside the legal system until they could be brought in on their own terms—with a full acknowledgement of the problems of non-therapeutic medical interventions. As such, the majority of our participants saw intersex as not only outside law, but also outside the queer and LGBT+ activist agendas.

The practical repercussions of queer and LGBT+ alliances may not only lie in a weaker mobilisation of collective action to push for legal reform (and therefore ineffective reform). As previously mentioned, the desire to actively reject a "queer" or "intersex" identity may dangerously strengthen medical power/knowledge in this arena and the continued use of unnecessary and non-consensual gender-normalising medical interventions on intersex children. Consequently, our respondents were aware of how identity-focused reforms could further impact upon this schism within the intersex "communities" and thus wanted legal reform to focus on bodily autonomy and prohibiting these non-consensual and unnecessary gender-normalising surgeries to ensure that all intersex embodied people were protected whether or not they identified with an intersex "community."

Malta was presented by respondents as being a "gold standard" (although with imperfections)[51] in this regard. Malta introduced a series of reforms

[49]Anonymous "Guest Campaigns: February 2020." *mumsnet.com*, accessed February 6, 2020, https://www.mumsnet.com/campaigns/guest-campaigns-february-2020.

[50]Amelia Tait, "Mumsnet Moderators Are Struggling to Find the Line Between Free Speech and Transphobia." *wired.co.uk.*, accessed February 6, 2020, https://www.wired.co.uk/article/mumsnet-moderators-trans-rights-debate.

[51]For example, there is nothing in the Gender Identity, Gender Expression and Sex Characteristic Act 2015 that prohibits parents from taking their children abroad to undergo gender-normalising treatments. See Fae Garland and Mitchell Travis, "Legislating Intersex Equality: Building the Resilience of Intersex People Through Law." *Legal Studies*, 38, no 4 (2018): 587, 606.

in its Gender Identity, Gender Expression and Sex Characteristics Act 2015 which makes "sex assignment treatment and, or surgical intervention on the sex characteristics of a minor which … can be deferred until the person to be treated can provide informed consent" unlawful. Simultaneously, the 2015 Act also introduced a self-declaration model of legal gender, as well as anti-discrimination and hate crime provisions that included a person's "sex characteristics" as a protected category. Thus, Malta introduced comprehensive protections that were not fundamentally based on the assumption that intersex embodied people were queer and thus required differential treatment. Rather, Malta's approach to reform protects intersex embodied people, regardless of identity or status, whilst also providing a legal space where intersex embodied people are able to identify as queer if they so wish.

6 Conclusion

In conclusion, this chapter encouraged us to think more critically about intersex individuals' relationships with—and understandings of—queer activism. For us, queer is not a "being" located somewhere in the materiality of our embodiment. Rather, queerness may be created through our relationships with institutions, such as healthcare and law. Intersex embodied people's "outsider" status is determined at an institutional rather than individual level that can be remedied through social, rather than medical, change. Queer can also be a "doing" found in the iterative performances of our social encounters. For many intersex people, therefore, queerness does not form part of their day-to-day lives, which encourages us to think about the experiences of intersex people rather than using them as concepts.

This leads us to think more carefully about the challenges brought through the inclusivity of queer community and LGBT+ allyship. This deeper understanding of intersex people's relationship to queer and LGBT+ activism will be vitally important to policymakers and the way they frame these issues going forward. Whilst many intersex people see the utility of aligning with queer and LGBT+ groups, this is far from unanimous within intersex communities. Insider status, whether in terms of queer or LGBT+ activism or policy and legislation, can be problematic if done without understanding the demands of the intersex community, leading them to retain their position as outsiders (even) in law. For many of our participants retaining a sense of being outsiders was important for preserving their own distinct political agenda until their needs are met.

In a sense, this willingness or desire to work with the State may be what separates intersex activists from queer theorists and activists. In many ways, their requests are to replace one source of power (medical knowledge) with another (law), whilst maintaining the primacy of the State. As a result, we might understand their desires as reifying traditional power structures rather than destabilising them. As such, intersex embodied people and their activism(s) may occupy an uneasy space in relation to queer theory, perhaps highlighting a hitherto unexplored binary at the heart of queer theory, which warrants further investigation as to the increasingly unclear boundaries between queer and non-queer subjects; a place where intersex people continue to reside. For queer theorists, who have long railed against binaries of sex and gender, this may be an important direction for future thought.

References

Alizai, Naved et al. "Feminizing Genitoplasty for Congenital Hyperplasia: What Happens at Puberty?" *Journal of Urology*, 161 (1999): 1588–1591.

Amnesty International. "First, Do No Harm: Ensuring the Rights of Children with Variations of Sex Characteristics in Denmark and Germany" (London: Amnesty International Ltd., 2017).

Australian Senate Community Affairs Committee Secretariat. "The Involuntary or Coerced Sterilisation of Intersex People in Australia." Parliament House, Canberra: Senate Printing Unit, 2013.

Berlant, Lauren and Elizabeth Freeman. "Queer Nationality." In *Fear of a Queer Planet: Queer Politics and Social Theory*, ed. Michael Warner (Minneapolis: University of Minnesota Press, 1993), 193–229.

Braune, Virginia and Clarke, Victoria. "Using Thematic Analysis in Psychology." *Qualitative Research in Psychology*, 3 (2006): 77–101.

Butler, Judith. *Gender Trouble: Feminism and the Subversion of Identity* (London and New York: Routledge, 1990).

Callens, Nina et al. "Recalled and Current Gender Role Behavior, Gender Identity and Sexual Orientation in Adults with Disorders/Differences of Sex Development." *Hormones and Behavior*, 86 (2016): 8–20.

Carpenter, Morgan. "Australia Can Lead the Way for Intersex People." *The Guardian*, June 18, 2013.

Carpenter, Morgan. "LGBTI Sponsorship and the Elimination of Intersex Traits." *International Human Rights Australia*, July 10, 2016. Accessed December 12, 2018. https://ihra.org.au/30555/sponsorship-elimination-intersex-traits/.

Carpenter, Morgan. "The 'Normalisation' of Intersex Bodies and 'Othering' of Intersex Identities in Australia." *Journal of Bioethical Inquiry*, 15 (2018): 487–495.

Cohen, Cathy. "Punks, Bulldaggers, and Welfare Queens: The Radical Potential of Queer Politics?" *GLQ: A Journal of Lesbian and Gay Studies*, 3, no 4 (1997): 437–465.

Cohen-Kettenis, Peggy. "Gender Change in 46, XY Persons with 5α-Reductase-2 Deficiency and 17β-Hydroxysteroid Dehydrogenase-3 Deficiency." *Archives of Sexual Behavior*, 34, no 4 (2005): 399–411.

Committee on Bioethics of the Council of Europe. *The Rights of Children in Biomedicine: Challenges Posed by Scientific Advances and Uncertainties*, by Kavot Zillén, Jameson Garland and Santa Slokenberga. Last modified 2017. https://rm.coe.int/16806d8e2f.

Creighton, Sarah. "Surgery for Intersex." *Journal of the Royal Society of Medicine*, 94, no 5 (2001): 218–220.

Creighton, Sarah, Catherine Minto and Stuart Steele. "Objective Cosmetic and Anatomical Outcomes at Adolescence of Feminizing Surgery for Ambiguous Genitalia Done in Childhood." *Lancet*, 358 (2001): 124–125.

Davis, Georgiann. *Contesting Intersex: The Dubious Diagnosis* (New York: New York University Press, 2015).

Dilley, Patrick. "Queer Theory: Under Construction." *Qualitative Studies in Education*, 12 (1999): 457–472.

Fausto-Sterling, Anne. *Sexing the Body: Gender Politics and the Construction of Sexuality* (New York: Basic Books, 2000).

Furtado, Paulo et al. "Gender Dysphoria Associated with Disorders of Sex Development." *Nature Reviews Urology*, 9(11) (2012): 620–627.

Garland, Fae and Mitchell Travis. "Legislating Intersex Equality: Building the Resilience of Intersex People Through Law." *Legal Studies*, 38, no 4 (2018): 587–606.

Garland, Fae and Mitchell Travis. "Making the State Responsible: Intersex Embodiment, Medical Jurisdiction and State Responsibility." *Law and Society*, 47(2) (2020): 298–324.

Garland, Fae and Mitchell Travis. "Temporal Bodies: Emergencies, Emergence, and Intersex Embodiment." In *Jurisprudence of the Body*, eds. Chris Dietz, Michael Thomson and Mitchell Travis (London: Palgrave, 2020).

Giffney, Noreen and Myra Hird. *Queering the Non/human*, 1st ed. (Aldershot: Ashgate Publishing Ltd., 2008).

Gleeson, Jules. "I'm Intersex and Wish the Gender Recognition Act Was More Inclusive." *Vice.com*, October 15, 2018. https://www.vice.com/en_uk/article/9k7mzv/intersex-experience-gender-recognition-act-reforms.

Greenberg, Julie. *Intersexuality and the Law: Why Sex Matters* (London: New York University Press, 2012).

"Guest Campaigns: February 2020." mumsnet.com. Accessed February 6, 2020. https://www.mumsnet.com/campaigns/guest-campaigns-february-2020.

Halperin, David. *Saint Foucault: Towards a Gay Hagiography* (Oxford: Oxford University Press, 1995).

Hegarty, Peter and Cheryl Chase. "Intersex Activism, Feminism and Psychology: Opening a Dialogue on Theory, Research and Clinical Practice." *Feminism & Psychology*, 10, no 1 (2000): 117–132.

Holmes, Morgan. "Distracted Attentions: Intersexuality and Human Rights Protections." *Cardozo Journal of Law and Gender*, 12 (2005): 127–133.

Jagose, Annamarie. *Queer Theory: An Introduction* (New York: New York University Press, 1996).

Jones, Tiffany et al. *Intersex: Stories and Statistics from Australia* (Cambridge: Open Book Publishers, 2016).

Karkazis, Katrina. *Fixing Sex: Intersex, Medical Authority and Lived Experience* (London: Duke University Press, 2008).

Monro, Surya et al. *Intersex, Variations of Sex Characteristics, and DSD: The Need for Change,* Research Report (University of Huddersfield, 2017).

Newbould, Mary. "When Parents Choose Gender." *Medical Law Rev*, 24 (2016): 471–497.

Preves, Sharon. *Intersex and Identity: The Contested Self* (New Brunswick: Rutgers University Press, 2013).

Schweizer, Katinka et al. "Gender Experience and Satisfaction with Gender Allocation in Adults with Diverse Intersex Conditions (Divergences of Sex Development, DSD)." *Psychology & Sexuality*, 5 (2014): 56–82.

Seelenlos. "CEDAW67 Italy > Major Setback for Intersex Human Rights at UN :-(." *Stop.Genitalmutilation.org*. Accessed April 10, 2019. http://stop.genitalmutilation.org/post/Major-Setback-for-Intersex-Human-Rights-at-the-UN.

Seelenlos. "UK > Misappropriation of Intersex Funding by LGBT Groups, Misrepresentation of Intersex as LGBT Issue." *Stop.Genitalmutilation.org*. Accessed April 10, 2019. http://stop.genitalmutilation.org/post/UK-Misappropriation-of-Intersex-Funding-by-LGBT-Groups.

Socio-Legal Studies Association. "Statement of Principles of Ethical Research Practice." *SLSA.ac.uk*. Accessed April 4, 2019. http://www.slsa.ac.uk/images/slsadownloads/ethicalstatement/slsa%20ethics%20statement%20_final_%5B1%5D.pdf.

Spargo, Tamsin. *Foucault and Queer Theory (Postmodern Encounters)* (Cambridge: Icon Books Ltd, 1999).

Tait, Amelia. "Mumsnet Moderators Are Struggling to Find the Line Between Free Speech and Transphobia." *wired.co.uk*. Accessed February 6, 2020. https://www.wired.co.uk/article/mumsnet-moderators-trans-rights-debate.

Travis, Mitchell. "Accommodating Intersexuality in European Union Anti-Discrimination Law." *European Law Journal*, 21, no 2 (2015): 180–199.

Warner, Michael. "Introduction." In *Fear of a Queer Planet: Queer Politics and Social Theory*, ed. Michael Warner (Minneapolis: University of Minnesota Press, 1993), i–xxviii.

Warner, Michael. *The Trouble with Normal: Sex, Politics, and the Ethics of Queer Life* (Cambridge: Harvard University Press, 1999).

The Best Place on the Planet to Be Trans? Transgender Equality and Legal Consciousness in Scotland

Sharon Cowan

> The tensions between opposing theories and political stances vitalise the feminist dialogue. It may only be combined with respect, partial understanding, love, and friendship that keeps us together in the long run.[1]

1 Introduction

This chapter is based on findings from a four-year, socio-legal study exploring transgender (trans) people's experiences of equality in three jurisdictions: Scotland, Canada and the USA. Equality has been a central focus of government and academic attention in each jurisdiction. The study explores whether similar issues come to the fore for trans people in each location: despite different social, political and legal cultures, Canada, the UK and the USA share a common law tradition and, broadly speaking, a set of human or civil rights-based values that are embodied in their legal systems. It examines the different ways in which trans people's experiences of gender identity and gender expression are intimately connected with other aspects of their

[1] Gloria E. Anzaldúa, "Bridge, Drawbridge, Sandbar, or Island: Lesbians-of-Color *Hacienda Alianzas*," in *Bridges of Power: Women's Multi-cultural Alliances*, ed. Lisa D. Albrecht and Rose Brewer (Santa Cruz: New Society Publishers, 1990), 229.

S. Cowan (✉)
Feminist and Queer Legal Studies, Edinburgh University, Edinburgh, UK
e-mail: s.cowan@ed.ac.uk

S. Raj and P. Dunne (eds.), *The Queer Outside in Law*, Palgrave Socio-Legal Studies,
https://doi.org/10.1007/978-3-030-48830-7_8

lives, including poverty, race, cultural background, physical ability, kinship, nationality, geographical location and immigration status. It also aims to demonstrate how crucial it is that law and policy-makers consider how trans people actually experience (in)equality and discrimination on a daily basis; and acknowledge that the segregated approach often taken to different equality strands is inadequate for a proper understanding of trans people's lives.[2]

In this chapter, I focus on one part of the larger study—the experiences of trans people living in Scotland. Through the lens of legal consciousness and using a "femiqueer" perspective (that is, one that interweaves feminist and queer critical methods of analysis),[3] I will explore the ways in which trans people in Scotland talk about their everyday experiences of discrimination and (in)equality. In so doing, I present original findings that increase our understanding of the lives of trans people in Scotland, but also contribute to socio-legal theoretical literature by suggesting a new strand of "legal consciousness".

Connecting with the theme of this collection, Scotland is very much a country that is inside the UK, and yet has something of an "outsider" identity, "oscillating between independence and in-dependency".[4] Likewise, trans people are both inside and outside, with respect to their relationship to law. Legal rights are the bedrock of any contemporary claim to equality, and yet trans people depend on so much more than the letter of the law for their flourishing, and, sometimes, their very survival. It is their interactions inside

[2]Paisley Currah has undertaken empirical research in the US interviewing trans activists about their choice of legal strategies: "Gender Pluralisms Under the Transgender Umbrella," in *Transgender Rights*, ed. Paisley Currah, Richard Juang and Shannon Price Minter (Minneapolis: University of Minneapolis Press, 2006). The Scottish Trans Alliance has also completed a survey of trans people asking about their experiences of living in Scotland, but not focusing specifically on inequality and discrimination—*Transgender Experiences in Scotland: Research Summary* (Edinburgh: Equality Network, 2008); Sally Hines (Sally Hines, *Gender Diversity, Recognition and Citizenship: Towards a Politics of Difference* [London: Palgrave MacMillan, 2013], 11–57) and Flora Renz (Davina Cooper and Flora Renz, "If the State Decertified Gender, What Might Happen to Its Meaning and Value?" *Journal of Law and Society* 43, no. 4 [2016]) have both conducted research asking trans people in England and Wales about their experiences of encountering the Gender Recognition Act 2004, and, in 2017, Chryssy Hunter completed a doctoral thesis at London Metropolitan University, interviewing trans people about their experiences of the effectiveness of equality legislation in England and Wales. In 2017, Sylvia Morgan completed a PhD thesis examining trans people's experiences of gender identity in Scotland; and, in 2018, Karen Kaufman completed her MRes dissertation on trans people's negotiations around identity in Scotland—neither focus on law but both are illuminating and important studies.

[3]This term has also been used in the humanities in Rachel Lee, *The Exquisite Corpse of Asian America: Biopolitics, Biosociality, and Posthuman Ecologies* (New York: NYU Press, 2014), and in Kendal Broad and Mary K. Bloodsworth, "FemiQueer Pedagogies: 'Lesbian/Gay' Studies in Postmodern Women's Studies," *Feminist Teacher* 13, no. 2 (2001), and in the scientific context, in *Queer Feminist Science Studies: A Reader*, ed. Cyd Cipolla et al. (Washington DC: University of Washington Press, 2017).

[4]Sharon Cowan, Chloe Kennedy and Vanessa E. Munro, eds, *The Scottish Feminist Judgments Project: (Re)Creating Law from the Outside In* (Oxford: Hart Publishing, 2019).

the law and their experiences beyond and outwith the law that this chapter investigates.

Since this research began in Canada in 2013, many legal and social changes have taken place that have changed the rights or social position of trans people. For example, in 2018 Canada passed Bill C-16, which adds gender identity or expression as a protected ground to the Canadian Human Rights Act, and also to the Criminal Code provisions dealing with hate propaganda, incitement to genocide, and aggravating factors in sentencing. In its 2015 Rainbow Map, though Scotland is not marked separately from the rest of the UK, the European Region of the International Lesbian, Gay, Bisexual, Trans and Intersex Association (ILGA Europe) said that, if marked separately, Scotland would have ranked highest in Europe, as the most inclusive for LGBTI equality and human rights legislation (meeting 92% of ILGA Europe's 48-point criteria).[5] Scotland's scores have fallen since other countries have increased the pace of their changes, but Scotland still ranked higher than the rest of the UK in the 2019 figures.[6] Through the Herculean efforts of the TIE campaign, in 2018 Scotland became the first country in Europe to introduce mandatory education about LGBTI equality in schools.[7]

However, it is premature to assume that these changes indicate a linear trajectory of progress and enlightenment across the western world. In January 2019, the American Supreme Court approved Donald Trump's ban, which came into force in April of the same year, on transgender people serving in the military (President Obama only having lifted the ban in 2016).[8] Moreover, a recent Stonewall survey report reveals that, in Scotland, 20% of those identifying as LGBT, and 48% of those identifying as trans, had suffered a hate

[5]"Scotland Rated Best Country in Europe for LGBTI Legal Equality," Equality Network, May 10, 2015, accessed March 20, 2020, https://www.equality-network.org/scotland-rated-best-country-in-europe-for-lgbti-legal-equality. Scottish government policy refers to LGBTI rather than LGBT equality.

[6]The figures are 66% for the whole of the UK and 73% for Scotland. "Scotland Slips Down International LGBT Rankings," *Pink Saltire*, May 13, 2019, accessed March 20, 2020, https://pinksaltire.com/2019/05/13/scotland-slips-down-international-lgbt-rankings.

[7]Libby Brooks, "Scotland to Embed LGBTI Teaching Across Curriculum." *The Guardian*, November 9, 2018, accessed March 20, 2020, https://www.theguardian.com/education/2018/nov/09/scotland-first-country-approve-lgbti-school-lessons.

[8]"Trans Troops Return to Era of 'Don't Ask, Don't Tell' as Trump Policy Takes Effect." *The Guardian*, April 13, 2019, accessed March 20, 2020, https://www.theguardian.com/us-news/2019/apr/12/transgender-ban-military-trump-take-effect-dont-ask-dont-tell. The Trump administration also revoked federal guidance, introduced by President Obama under Title IX, that included trans people within the sex discrimination protections, thereby allowing trans students to use school bathrooms that matched their gender identity; however, this attempt to retreat from trans equality has been challenged in various federal courts: Matt Stevens, "Transgender Student in Bathroom Dispute Wins Court Ruling," *New York Times*, May 22, 2018, accessed March 20, 2020, https://www.nytimes.com/2018/05/22/us/gavin-grimm-transgender-bathrooms.html. See also Susan G. Mezey, *Transgender Rights: From Obama to Trump* (New York; London: Routledge, Taylor & Francis Group, 2020) for in-depth discussion.

crime in the previous 12 months (2017); and in the UK more generally, the Gender Recognition Act 2004 has been the subject of much critique, since the gender recognition process remains one of pathologisation and bureaucracy, and hence exclusionary.[9] Therefore, the coherent "progress" narrative that is often woven through government policy documents is not entirely in keeping with real life experiences.[10]

As Flora Renz has already noted in Chapter 6, in Scotland, and in England and Wales, governments have conducted consultations on how best to reform the 2004 Act, exploring the possibilities of depathologising the gender recognition process and allowing people to self-identify without a psychiatric diagnosis of gender dysphoria.[11] This has resulted in heated debates across not only social media but also in Parliament and in the print media, about access to sex-segregated spaces, and the impact of gender self-identification on the rights of (cis) women and girls.[12] Also across the UK, trans men have been prosecuted for sexual assault when engaging in consensual sexual activity with cis women, without informing them of their gender attributed at birth

[9]Stonewall. 2017. LGBT in *Scotland: Hate Crime and Discrimination* available at http://www.stonewall scotland.org.uk//scotlandcomeoutforLGBT/lgbt-in-britain/hate-crime, accessed March 26, 2020. On critiques of the existing gender recognition process, see for example: Stephen Whittle, "The Opposite of Sex Is Politics—The UK Gender Recognition Act and Why It Is Not Perfect, Just Like You and Me," *Journal of Gender Studies* 15, no. 3 (2006): 267; Sally Hines, "(Trans)forming Gender: Social Change and Transgender Citizenship," *Sociological Research Online* 12, no. 1 (2007), accessed March 23, 2020, https://doi.org/10.5153/sro.1469; Sharon Cowan, Ralph Sandland and Alex Sharpe, "Debate and Dialogue—The Gender Recognition Act 2004," *Social and Legal Studies* 18, no. 2 (2009).

[10]See Matson Lawrence and Yvette Taylor, "The UK Government LGBT Action Plan: Discourses of Progress, Enduring Stasis, and LGBTQI+ lives 'Getting Better'," *Critical Social Policy* 1, no. 22 (2019).

[11]Other jurisdictions have moved to gender self-identification, e.g. Malta, Ireland, Argentina. For discussion see Mitchell Travis and Fae Garland, "Legislating Intersex Equality: Building the Resilience of Intersex People Through Law," *Legal Studies* 38, no. 4 (2018): 587–606; Cooper and Renz, supra note 2.

[12]For discussion of the situation in England and Wales, see Stephen Whittle and Fiona Simkiss, "A Perfect Storm: The UK Government's Failed Consultation on the Gender Recognition Act 2004," in *Research Handbook on Gender, Sexuality and the Law*, ed. Chris Ashford and Alexander Maine (Cheltenham, UK: Edward Elgar, 2020); for Scotland see the article by James Morton, Scottish Trans Manager, Scottish Trans Alliance: James Morton, "Focus on the Facts When Debating Gender Recognition Act." *Herald*, October 20, 2018, accessed March 20, 2020, https://www.heraldscotland.com/opinion/16996220.focus-on-the-facts-when-debating-gender-recognition-act/. The UK government announced in September 2020 that they were no longer proceeding with plans to reform the GRA to allow trans people to self-identify their gender without medical assessment or treatment.

(GAB).[13] In fact, ILGA Europe has reported for the first time in the ten-year history of their Rainbow Index that "countries are moving backwards, as existing laws and policies disappeared".[14]

The timing of this contribution is therefore especially important for the UK, and particularly the Scottish context. Clearly, there is still work to be done to make LGBTQ people safer, and to ensure that laws and policies are inclusive and relevant to LGBTQ people in their everyday experiences and interactions. This chapter adds to our knowledge about the way that trans people themselves understand the role and relevance of law in their lives in achieving these goals. It does so in three ways: by examining how trans people understand and experience equality conceptually and in practice; by contributing to the legal consciousness literature in introducing the new concept of "optimistic legal realism" and by analysing recent shifts in discourse on equality and trans rights in Scotland. This is not a study of identity as such, or of law as such, but of trans people's narratives about equality and discrimination in their lives, as well as how they negotiate living in and outwith the trans and cisgender (i.e. non-trans) communities around them. In light of the particular attention (and much of it not trans positive) currently being given to if and how gender identity and expression should be regulated, and the policing of gendered spaces, it is crucial that we pay attention to trans people's narratives; their intersectional experiences of equality and life generally in Scotland—and elsewhere—require nuanced and sensitive consideration.

Because the interviews for this study were undertaken before the debates on the issue of self-identification through the reform of the Gender Recognition Act 2004 (GRA), this was not covered in our conversations about legal equality, and I do not explore specifically here the impact of the GRA on trans people's lives, except in so far as they are relevant to the discussion in the final section of this chapter, on recent political shifts around what it means to be trans in Scotland. If my interviews had taken place just 18 months later, undoubtedly the context and content of our conversations would have been very different.

Before setting out the methods and ethics in Section 3 and the findings of this study in Sections 4 and 5, I will explain briefly the analytical lens used in this chapter—legal consciousness—and the femiqueer methodological approach taken.

[13] See Alex Sharpe, *Sexual Intimacy and Gender Identity 'Fraud'* (London: Routledge, 2018).

[14] "Rainbow Europe 2019," ILGA Europe, accessed March 20, 2020, https://www.ilga-europe.org/rainboweurope/2019.

2 Theoretical Framework

2.1 Legal Consciousness

Legal consciousness research "traces the ways in which law is experienced and interpreted by specific individuals as they engage, avoid, or resist the law and legal meanings".[15] It explores what Simon Halliday and Sylvia Morgan call the background assumptions about law that structure people's lives, or "the almost invisible life of law in society".[16] The study of attitudes to law is just as important—if not more so—than studying doctrinal law itself.[17]

Patricia Ewick and Susan Silbey[18] suggested three types of legal consciousness (which are conceptually distinct but not mutually exclusive): before the law, with the law and against the law. Briefly, in their schema, "before the law" legal consciousness understands the law as remote, impartial, formal and objective, with lawyers acting as gatekeepers and in control, and law's subjects as compliant and respectful of law—Halliday et al.[19] have termed this law as a "shield". "With the law" (or for Halliday et al.[20] law as a "sword") sees law as part of everyday life rather than formal and remote, and something that is a shared resource, accessible to (at least some of) its subjects, potentially serving as a strategic tool to better one's situation. "Against the law", as is evident from the name, is a legal consciousness that sees law as dangerous and untrustworthy, a site of violence and power, and something to be resisted and struggled against.[21]

In his recent book, "Nobody's Law",[22] Marc Hertogh has further refined legal consciousness to explore how many people are alienated from law, living to a large degree outside its margins even while under its yoke. This approach is particularly helpful for this study; as Zach Richards[23] has

---

[15] Susan S. Silbey, "Legal Culture and Consciousness," in *International Encyclopedia of the Social and Behavioral Sciences*, ed. Neil J. Smelser and Paul B. Baltes (Amsterdam: Elsevier Science, 2001), 8626.

[16] Simon Halliday and Bronwen Morgan, "I Fought the Law and the Law Won? Legal Consciousness and the Critical Imagination," *Current Legal Problems* 66, no. 1 (2013): 2.

[17] Simon Halliday, Celia Kitzinger and Jenny Kitzinger, "Law in Everyday Life and Death: A Socio-legal Study of Chronic Disorders of Consciousness," *Legal Studies* 35, no. 1 (2015): 69.

[18] Patricia Ewick and Susan Silbey, *The Common Place of Law* (Chicago: The University of Chicago Press, 1998).

[19] Halliday et al., supra note 17.

[20] Halliday et al., supra note 17.

[21] Ewick and Silbey's schema has been refined by Halliday and Morgan (supra note 16), who have suggested a new kind of legal consciousness—"collective dissent".

[22] Marc Hertogh, *Nobody's Law* (London: Palgrave MacMillan, 2018).

[23] Zach Richards, "Book Review: Nobody's Law: Legal Consciousness and Legal Alienation in Everyday Life," *The UK Administrative Justice Institute*, October 12, 2018, https://ukaji.org/2018/10/12/book-review-nobodys-law-legal-consciousness-and-legal-alienation-in-everyday-life/. For a full

said, Hertogh's approach helps us to understand better the experiences of marginalised and minority groups. Legal consciousness is an appropriate framework here also because of the "puzzle" of legal hegemony that Silbey sets out: "Why do people acquiesce to a legal system that, despite its promises of equal treatment, systematically reproduces inequality?"[24] More specifically, she queries:

> How could we explain what looks like unrelenting faith in and support for legal institutions in the face of what appeared to be consistent distinctions between ideal and reality, law on the books and law in action, abstract formal equality and substantive, concrete material inequality?[25]

Building on such work, this chapter offers an analysis of the nuances and complexities of trans people's relationships and (dis)connections with law, particularly around their conceptions of equality, and the faith they choose to have (or are obliged to have) in law.

It should be noted that although the initial focus of the main study was legal rights and protections, it quickly became obvious that trans people's lives are structured and regulated as much by medical norms and practices as by law. While neither the pathologisation of trans lives nor access to healthcare are central themes of this chapter, I will refer to these issues where relevant in what follows. First, I turn to explain my methodological choices and challenges.

2.2 Feminist and Queer Research Approaches

Feminist research approaches encourage centring the standpoint and experiences of research participants—that knowledge about a community must begin with that community.[26] However, trans people belong to an already marginalised community, one often left out of much community survey

review essay that examines the field, as well as Hertogh's recent book, see Simon Halliday, "After Hegemony: The Varieties of Legal Consciousness Research," *Social & Legal Studies* 28, no. 6 (2019): 859. See Rosie Harding, *Regulating Sexuality: Legal Consciousness in Lesbian and Gay Lives* (Abingdon: Routledge, 2010) for research with LGBT people that uses the legal consciousness framework and asks how they draw on the concept of equality in relation to same-sex marriage.

[24] Susan Silbey, "After Legal Consciousness," *Annual Review of Law and Social Science* 1 (2005): 323.

[25] Silbey, supra note 24, p. 326.

[26] Sandra Harding, "Introduction: Is There a Feminist Method?" in *Feminism and Methodology*, ed. Sandra Harding (Bloomington: Indiana University Press, 1987); Sandra Harding, *Whose Science? Whose Knowledge?* (Ithaca, NY: Cornell University Press, 1991).

research which does not ask about gender identity,[27] but simultaneously over-researched given the proportionate size of the community. That means being conscious and careful, as a cisgender person, of the dangers of speaking to and for others. I see this research as part of what Sara Ahmed[28] has called "an affinity of hammers"—it is affinity rather than experience that informs my approach to this research.

And what of queer research approaches? Like feminist researchers, queer researchers agree that it is difficult to say with any precision what exactly queer methodology might look like, and that there is no one "quintessential" queer methodology.[29] Rather, it is more intuitive to talk about many queer methodologies,[30] or that all methodologies are open to "queering potentialities"[31] as long as they have a common political and intellectual commitment to challenging heterocentric and ciscentric norms.[32] Daniel Warner suggests two further characteristics of queer methodology. First, he suggests, is an awareness of the way it "constitutes the object it investigates", acknowledging this makes for "more equitable research".[33] Secondly, queer methodology is qualitative, because it "speaks directly to the experience of the oppressed".[34]

Like feminist methodologies, queer methodologies take as their focus the normative structures that produce (and are produced by) our social world; challenge the dogma of grand explicatory narratives; and are reflexive about their own role in knowledge production. Further, both methodologies challenge the researcher/researched and objective/subjective dichotomy. A blend of both approaches can offer what I am calling here a femiqueer lens through which to view the ways in which sex-gender and sexuality remain central disciplining features of contemporary social and political life, and how they

---

[27] "Research and Data Needs," National Center for Transgender Equality, accessed March 20, 2020, https://transequality.org/issues/research-data-needs.

[28] Sara Ahmed, "An Affinity of Hammers," *Transgender Studies Quarterly* 3, no. 1–2 (2016): 22.

[29] Andrea Doucet and Natasha S. Mauthner, "Feminist Methodologies and Epistemologies," in *The Handbook of 21st Century Sociology*, ed. Dennis. L. Peck and Clifton D. Bryant (Thousand Oaks, CA: Sage Publications, 2007); Caroline Fusco, "Critical Feminist/Queer Methodologies: Deconstructing (Hetero)Normative Inscriptions," in *Qualitative Research on Sport and Physical Culture*, ed. Kevin Young and Michael Atkinson *(Research in the Sociology of Sport, Volume 6)* (Bingley: Emerald Group Publishing Limited, 2012), 152.

[30] Daniel Warner, "Towards a Queer Research Methodology," *Qualitative Research in Psychology* 1, no. 4 (2004): 334.

[31] Catherine Nash, "Queer Conversations: Old-time Lesbians, Transmen and the Politics of Queer Research," in *Queer Methods and Methodologies: Intersecting Queer Theories and Social Science Research*, ed. Kath Browne and Catherine J. Nash (London: Routledge, 2010), 133.

[32] Fusco, supra note 29.

[33] Warner, supra note 30.

[34] Warner, supra note 30, p. 335.

are interwoven with other key aspects of material embodiment such as race, class, physical ability, nationality and many others.

3 Methods and Ethical Choices

In this section, I reflect briefly on the ethical choices I made in the practical navigation and management of the research, such as terminology, sampling, interview methods and analysis.

3.1 Terminology

The term "trans" is often used as an "umbrella term" to describe a wide range of people who are gender non-conforming either in their identification, or expression, or both.[35] Recently, non-binary gender identities have been grouped together with, but also referred to separately from, trans people, as a group with distinct claims and interests who do not identify with what they see as an implicit binary in trans(gender).[36]

Though some have pointed out the potential problems of using the term trans, in particular its erasure of the experiences of some transsexual people,[37] ultimately, there may be "no perfect word"; Julia Serrano has suggested that we should, instead, be more attentive to the context and connotation of language, since most terms used, even by trans people themselves, "exist in a perpetual state of debate or dispute" such that there is an inevitable "activist

[35]See for example Stephen Whittle et al., *Engendered Penalties: Transgender and Transsexual People's Experiences of Inequality and Discrimination* (A Research Project and Report Commissioned by the Equalities Review, 2007), http://www.pfc.org.uk/files/EngenderedPenalties.pdf; see also Stephen Whittle, "The Trans-Cyberian Mail Way," *Social and Legal Studies* 7, no. 3 (1998): 389.

[36]Helene Frohard-Dourlent et al., "I Would Have Preferred More Options": Accounting for Non-Binary Youth in Health Research. *Nursing Inquiry* 24, no. 1 (2017), accessed March 25, 2020, https://doi.org/10.1111/nin.12150. Scottish Trans provides a neat description of non-binary: "Non binary People," Scottish Trans, accessed March 20, 2020, https://www.scottishtrans.org/trans-rights/an-intro-to-trans-terms/non-binary-people/. Sometimes intersex people are also included under the trans umbrella (or the LGBTQ banner), for example by the Scottish Government, but this has proved controversial for some intersex people who do not wish to be labelled in such a way. Garland and Travis discuss this at length in Chapter 7 of this edited collection.

[37]Viviane Namaste, *Sex Change, Social Change; Reflections on Identity, Institutions and Imperialism* (Toronto: Women's Press, 2005); see also Judith Halberstam, *In a Queer Time and Place: Transgender Bodies, Subcultural Lives* (New York: New York University Press, 2005), 49, 54; See also Jacob Hale, "Suggested Rules for Non-Transsexuals Writing About Transsexuals, Transsexuality, Transsexualism, or Trans_____," Sandy Stone, Last modified November 18, 2009 https://sandystone.com/hale.rules.html.

language merry go round" of terminology.[38] As my interviews progressed, it became clear that some people had used or currently use more than one term to identify themselves—the same person may refer to themselves as being or having been a trans man, queer, transgender, transsexual and/or gender queer or fluid. I have reflected herein the terms that participants themselves used.

The study's key research terms, "law" and "equality" are also open-ended. Returning to Sibley's puzzle, if we are to understand what trans people's everyday experiences tells us about the place of law in their lives, it is important to highlight their own views of the administrative and legal rules and norms that weigh most heavily upon them, paying particularly close attention to the exclusionary effects of supposedly reforming and progressive rules, processes and legislation. Doing so can shed light upon trans people's experiences of regulatory social norms, and the bureaucratic and routinised administrative functions of law, as well as their interactions with formal state law as it manifests, for example in a court room. For this reason, I am using Brian Tamanaha's pluralistic understanding of law as that which people "identify and treat as law through their social practices".[39] Focusing only on legal issues and rights, and law as a "top down" form of power can also obscure the deeply felt ways in which other decentralised social institutions and material conditions impact upon and mould our lives.[40] Following Carol Smart's warning of many years ago,[41] in this study I tried to avoid centring law as necessarily the sole or most important way of addressing issues of social justice.

Borrowing from critical race activism and scholarship, I wanted also to explore law's "microaggressions".[42] As Peggy Davis has stated, for most of us "it is more efficient to act on the basis of a stereotyping heuristic".[43] Stereotypes can then become "assimilated" as truth. For those who are stereotyped, it can be experienced as "incessant and cumulative assaults", or "microaggressions", that is: "subtle, stunning, often automatic, and non-verbal exchanges

[38]Julia Serrano, *Outspoken: A Decade of Transgender Activism and Trans Feminism* (Oakland: Switch Hitter Press, 2016), 244; see also Julia Serrano, "A Personal History of the 'T-word'," *Whipping Girl*, April 28, 2014, http://juliaserano.blogspot.com/2014/04/a-personal-history-of-t-word-and-some.html#activistlanguage.

[39]Brian Tamanaha, "A Non-Essentialist Version of Legal Pluralism," *Journal of Law and Society* 27, no. 2 (2000): 313.

[40]Dean Spade, *Normal Life* (Brooklyn: South End Press, 2011), 119; see also Namaste, supra note 37.

[41]Carol Smart, *Feminism and the Power of Law (*London: Routledge, 1989).

[42]Peggy Davis, "Law as Microaggression," *Yale Law Journal* 98, no. 8 (1989): 1559; see also Derald Wing Sue, *Microaggressions in Everyday Life: Race, Gender and Sexual Orientation* (Hoboken: John Wiley and Sons, 2010).

[43]Davis, supra note 42, pp. 1561–1562.

which are 'put downs' of blacks".[44] Derald Sue[45] has adapted this framework to explain the manifestation of racial, gender and sexual orientation microaggressions. I suggest that microaggressions are also routinely experienced by trans people.[46]

While some of my interviewees have been arrested, appeared before courts and tribunals, been detained by border guards, reported crimes to the police, or worked in the criminal justice system, some of them have had no direct interaction with the formal mechanisms of law. However, most spoke explicitly of the ways in which regulations, decentralised administrative processes and the arbitrary application of rules by bureaucrats and others, affected their lives in ways that echo Davis' definition of microaggressions. For this reason, the study does not focus narrowly on questions of formal legal rights to gender identity recognition and protection, but instead examines issues of social (in)justice raised in my conversations with trans people, and the microaggressions they experienced, whether or not they were prompted by formal legal interventions in their lives.

3.2 Sampling

Using purposive sampling, the broader study is based on semi-structured interviews with people in Scotland, Canada and the USA, who either currently identify, or at some point in their lives have identified as trans, trans*, transgender or transsexual, to find out about their lived experiences of equality and discrimination. I also interviewed advocates, and people from activist, support and campaign organisations for trans people. In total 39 people were interviewed, 37 of which were face-to-face interviews, one was by telephone and one by email; 11 took place in British Columbia, Canada, 20 in the Bay Area, USA, and eight in Scotland. Interviews were conducted over a four-year period, between 2013 and 2016. This chapter focuses on the 11 interviews conducted with eight participants in Scotland from 2014 to 2016.

As with any non-random snowball sampling, it is hard to reach people who are most different from oneself and one's contacts. Such challenges are compounded in this context by the fact that trans people are not always "out" in the world; trans communities are also over-researched, and receive repeated requests to participate in research, and therefore suffer from research fatigue,

---

[44] Davis, supra note 42, p. 1565, quoting Pierce et al. 1978 p. 66.

[45] Sue, supra note 42.

[46] See also Tiffany Chang and Barry Chung, "Transgender Microaggressions: Complexity of the Heterogeneity of Transgender Identities," *Journal of LGBT Issues in Counseling* 9, no. 3 (2015): 217.

and some have had previous negative experiences of participating in research projects. Consequently, my interviewees certainly cannot be said to be generally representative of all trans people, or representative of the locales in which I was based.

Trans people of colour—and especially trans women of colour—are underrepresented in this study. Although the broader study includes people of colour and people of Indigenous, Latino and Asian origin, in Scotland, I only spoke to white participants. This is an unfortunate effect of living in a disproportionately white country and, as such, this study is limited by the degree to which it replicates these demographics. However, my participants range widely across other characteristics such as age, nationality, gender identity, employment status and class background, though there is an over representation of those living in urban areas as opposed to rural areas, a difficulty of recruiting an already hard to reach population in a country such as Scotland.[47]

The aim of this research is not to produce a coherent narrative of trans experience that rings true for every trans person regardless of class, race, gender identity or geographical place. Nonetheless, in the broader study as a whole, many of those interviewed had direct experience of discrimination, and all too frequently had also experienced trauma, mental health issues, racism and poverty.

3.3 Narrative Interviewing and Analysis

The general importance of recording narratives of marginalised individuals and groups has been recognised by many critical scholars. There is a long feminist history of sharing and documenting stories, and prioritising personal testimony, as a way of valuing and including women's voices and subjectivities and countering claims to universality.[48] Excavating narratives enables people to tell stories that have been silenced because they do not match the dominant cultural memory,[49] and challenges prevailing norms of positivistic knowledge production such as a preference for objectivity, or statistical generalisability. Like Sally Hines in her research with trans people,[50] I eschewed the simple

[47]Sylvia Morgan, "Constructing Identities, Reclaiming Subjectivities, Reconstructing Selves: An Interpretative Study of Transgender Practices in Scotland" (PhD thesis, University of Glasgow, 2017).

[48]Samia Bano and Jennifer Pierce, "Personal Narratives, Social Justice, and the Law," *Feminist Legal Studies* 21, no. 3 (2013): 226.

[49]Alistair Thomson, "Memory and Remembering in Oral History," in *The Oxford Handbook of Oral History*, ed. Donald A. Ritchie (Oxford: Oxford University Press, 2010), 81.

[50]Hines (2007), supra note 9; Hines (2013), supra note 2.

Table 1 Participants (Scotland)

	Name	Gender id	Race-culture	Nationality	Interview locus	EU citizen	GRC	Age	Work
1	Nathan	NB	White	Scottish	Scotland	Y	N	29	Policy adviser
2	Becky	F	White	American	Scotland	N	Y	52	Policy volunteer
3	Gavin	M	White	Scottish	Scotland	Y	Y	40s	Teacher
4	Alex	M (prev GQ)	White	Irish	Scotland	Y	N	62	Unemployed
5	Colette	F	White	Scottish	Scotland	Y	N	60s	Archaeologist
6	Connor	M	White	Scottish	Scotland	Y	N	20	Student
7	Jo	F	White	British	Scotland	Y	Y	65	Playwright
8	Gesche	GF/GN	white-Jewish	German	Scotland	Y	N	35	Artist/writer

M—male (3); F—female (3); NB—non-binary (1); GF—gender fluid (1); GN—gender neutral (1); GQ—gender queer (1) (All participants were given a consent form to sign, and a one-page summary about the project, before the interview, reminding them that they could withdraw from the study at any time for any (or no) reason, up until the point of publication. As well as a right to withdraw, participants were also told that once the interview was transcribed and checked, they would have an opportunity to see the text and to amend or delete any part of that text before it appeared in any publicly presented or published work. Participants were given the opportunity to choose a pseudonym, or if they preferred, for me to choose one on their behalf Some have chosen to use their own names, either because they run an organisation and are happy for that organisation and themselves to be named, and sometimes for political reasons, because they are out and vocal and wish to be a visible trans person and/or ally) "question and answer" style in favour of free-flowing narrative interviewing techniques so that I could "flexibly respond" to the narrator and allow stories to be told.[51] In the tradition of empirical legal consciousness research, I did not begin by asking questions about law, but about participants lives, work and families allowing them to mention law if and when it was relevant to them.[52]

The coding and analysis of the interviews for this chapter was done through NVivo software. Having created over 90 themes and subthemes, interviews were then re-coded and organised to address the overarching questions of this paper—how trans people in Scotland experience formal law and equality initiatives, as well as the more mundane, administrative and routine forms of bureaucracies and regulations that affect their lives.

4 Equality for All? Transgender People's Experiences and Responses to Law

In this section, I explore some of the main findings that relate to the eight participants interviewed in Scotland. As mentioned earlier, I have chosen to focus on this group because of the way that Scotland has recently been seen as a leader in the field of LGBTI equality and human rights, despite current divisive, and in some instances extremely harmful, socio-political conversations in the UK about gender recognition reform. It seems especially important at this time to think through the impact that legal interventions have on trans people's lives, and the degree to which their experiences of equality and discrimination are dependent on particular kinds of legal protections, as well as broader cultural factors.

In this chapter, I will explore four broad themes relevant to these issues: (1) the ways in which participants understood the concept of equality; (2) Ewick and Silbey's idea of being "before" and/or "against" the law (where I introduce the concept of "optimistic legal realism"); (3) participants being strategic about using rules and laws to improve their own situation or that of

[51]Hines (2007), supra note 9, p. 199. Hines was following in the tradition of Ken Plummer's groundbreaking work on the social construction of sexual stories, and political role that storytelling plays in carving out space for new kinds of "intimate citizenship": Ken Plummer, *Telling Sexual Stories* (London: Routledge, 1995), 6.

[52]Ewick and Silbey, supra note 18. In my study a number of questions were asked of all interviewees, such as: "what does the term equality mean to you?"; "Would you say you have faith in law?"; and "What other resources do you feel are available to you, other than law, to address any problems you might encounter in your life?" These questions were, however, left until the end of the interview, so that questions about law did not drive the orientation of the conversation.

others—what Ewick and Silbey call "with the law" and (4) participants' observations about the distinct advantages of being trans in Scotland, as opposed to elsewhere in the world. In that final section, I will reflect on contemporary debates about gender identity in Scotland, triggered by the Scottish government's ongoing process of consultation on reform of the Gender Recognition Act 2004, to allow for self-determination of gender.

4.1 Equality

In Great Britain, equality law has been consolidated by the Equality Act 2010, under which there are nine protected characteristics, including sex, sexual orientation and gender reassignment. Individuals are protected from discrimination on the grounds of those characteristics when accessing housing, goods, services, facilities and employment. Several participants mentioned this legislation explicitly and unprompted (I did not mention the 2010 Act in my questions), recognising its role in safeguarding against discrimination. With respect to two of the participants, this is not particularly surprising as both worked in the equalities sector. Becky, an equalities activist, referred to the Equality Act 2010 as a "brilliant piece of legislation", saying:

> The equalities discourse in this country is very much driven by the Equality Act 2010... The fact that every public body has an equalities officer is a direct result of that law. And most people are aware of that. So, I think there is an awareness that the law is behind that, and I think that there's a general understanding that the letter of the law is designed to help and protect us.

Issues relating to the law in practice will be explored below, but Becky's comments are echoed even by those not working in that sector. Colette, employed in the public sector, referred to the legislation as providing protections against discrimination "that may or may not have happened anyway but certainly accelerated them and made it obligatory... That didn't really exist before, it would have been a little bit hit and miss". Gavin, a teacher, also described a situation with his employer where he had to invoke the 2010 Act's reasonable adjustment provisions as a way of ensuring that he was not given work that he was unable to do; and Jo, a writer, while not referring specifically to the statute, mentioned the work of the Equality Network, a charity campaigning for the human rights of LGBTI people in Scotland. This shows a relatively high level of awareness of equality-related law and policy development, though these particular respondents were middle class and well educated, and in that sense may not be representative of the trans population as a whole, or indeed the population generally. However, as Morgan has pointed out, "it has been widely documented that trans people are acutely aware of and well-read in the previous research"[53]; it would not be particularly surprising, then, if trans people were equally knowledgeable about legal—and medical—processes. It is worth noting, however, that none of the participants commented on the fact that the wording of the protected characteristic is "gender reassignment" rather than "gender identity", an issue that was picked up in recommendations for reform of the Equality Act, made by, for example the House of Commons Select Committee on Women and Equalities in their 2016 report, "Transgender Equality".[54]

Near the end of the interviews, when participants were asked to say what equality meant to them, their responses were as follows: equality of opportunity (Nathan, Alex and Jo); to be treated with respect (Colette); to be treated the same or not inferior (Becky and Alex); freedom of expression to be who you are (Colette and Jo); equality of outcome (Connor) and being wanted (Nathan). While academic discussions about equality can tend towards the abstract (especially the "equality of what?" question much discussed amongst traditional legal theorists[55]), or can become reduced to a diluted and oversimplified discussion of sameness versus difference, the trans participants in this study had a real sense of what they understood equality to be, and the role it should and did play in their lives, regardless of the formal legal requirements and protections of the Equality Act 2010.

Nonetheless, as legal consciousness scholars tell us, people often draw on ideas of law and legal concepts to make sense of their lives, and therefore it is unsurprising that participants' comments reflect different facets of the legal concept of equality, or non-discrimination. That is, Connor's "equality of outcome" resonates with the notion of substantive equality; Becky and Alex's

---

[53]Morgan, supra note 47, p. 102.

[54]House of Commons Women and Equalities Committee, *Transgender Equality* (London: The Stationery Office Limited, 2016), 26–27. https://publications.parliament.uk/pa/cm201516/cmselect/cmwomeq/390/390.pdf—though note that the Equality Act's definition of gender reassignment does not mirror the narrower and more medicalised GRA requirements of gender reassignment.

[55]See e.g. Ronald Dworkin, *Sovereign Virtue: The Theory and Practice of Equality* (Cambridge: Harvard University Press, 2000); Thomas Nagel, *Equality and Partiality* (Oxford: Oxford University Press, 1991). Of course the "Equality of What" question has also been open to feminist critique—see for example Catharine MacKinnon, *Women's Lives, Men's Laws* (Cambridge: Harvard University Press, 2005); Martha Nussbaum, *Sex and Social Justice* (Oxford: Oxford University Press, 1999); Amartya Sen, *Inequality Re-examined* (Oxford: Oxford University Press, 1992); Iris Marion Young, *Justice and the Politics of Difference* (Princeton: Princeton University Press, 1990). For feminist analysis of various different approaches to the question, see Davina Cooper, "'And You Can't Find Me Nowhere': Relocating Identity and Structure Within Equality Jurisprudence," *Journal of Law and Society* 27, no. 2 (2000): 249.

"being treated the same" accords with the idea of formal equality, and "not as inferior" with the idea of non-discrimination; Colette's desire for "respect" has been argued to be an essential part of the acceptance of difference, and a corollary of equality of legal recognition,[56] (though Hines argues that the actual process of gender recognition in the UK inhibits respect)[57]; and Jo's "being free to express one's authentic self" and Nathan's "being wanted" are also aspects of social visibility and acknowledgment, and reflect a desire for equal recognition, and resistance to misrecognition.[58]

Of course, not everyone wants to live "under the law" or celebrates the ways in which dominant heteronormative discourses of "equality for all" have played out in practice. As I will illustrate in the next section, many of the trans people interviewed here were deeply sceptical about law's ability to deliver social justice, particularly regarding the implementation on the ground of legislation, such as the Equality Act 2010, and especially where there were intersecting inequalities at play. In other words, an attachment to the idea of equality did not inhibit people from acknowledging the practical complexities of their embodied lives, or indeed the lives of others. For example, several participants explicitly acknowledged the differential treatment people experience, depending on the social, cultural and political position of the person aiming to access the law, and most particularly with respect to class and race. For instance, Gavin, commented on the impact of how someone presents, which is also influenced by their background and upbringing, on how they are treated in society:

> I think this is just true in life, how you present influences people's response...we didn't go to private school but my parents had money for holidays and the nice things and we lived in a nice house and we were taught to talk properly...And then working in a bank and in a professional environment I think if you present as relatively intelligent...and sadly it probably is true to say if you are white also, then I think people's response is different. But I don't just think that's true for trans people, I think that is a general statement of society.

Colette also reflected on the uneven impact of law, depending on the relative advantages that individuals have with which to negotiate with law:

[56] For discussion: see Diane Richardson, *Sexuality and Citizenship* (Cambridge: Polity Press, 2017), Chapter 6.

[57] Hines (2013) supra note 2, p. 24.

[58] Hines (2013) supra note 2, p. 11.

> Whether (law) is always practised properly is another matter… there must be lots of people who are in if you like, who are not … privileged middle-class white people, who are then, who must get picked on a lot.

The issue of implementation is explored in more detail in the next section, but here Gavin and Colette touch on a sense of privilege that other participants also mentioned, acknowledging that even if the letter of the law offered a "shield" against discrimination, or even a "sword" to be wielded against those who discriminate, not all people are treated equally under the law in practice. Several commented that they themselves might be treated with respect, but that this was often down to having the privilege of being middle class and/or white. As Colette put it:

> Yes, I mean there are people I am sure, I know there are, people who get in trouble, bother, they're not living in nice safe environments like me and are not living in, they don't have all these white middle-class privileges that I do.

Connor similarly acknowledged his racial privilege, but both he and Gavin also mentioned a sense of privilege in contrast to trans women. Connor said:

> I mean I am very aware of the fact that trans women are always going to have it way worse than trans guys will, and you know the fact that I am white as well obviously plays a massive factor into the privilege I have.

On the other hand, Becky reflected on her mixed experience of losing the freedoms associated with the privileges of being a heterosexual male, while still having the benefit of racial and class privilege:

> Prior to transition, I may have had horrible conflicts in my head, but as a middle-class white male, you know, living as heterosexual… can you say privileged?… I had it, you know, I gave it up. I don't regret giving it up, what I do regret is that (privilege) exists. And it's my mission to get rid of it.

These moments of reflection on the uneven impact of law depending on the trans person's intersecting characteristics, such as race, class and gender, clearly connect to the ways in which the law was experienced as arbitrary and discretionary, as will be discussed shortly.

What is interesting here, however, is the conscious efforts that some trans people made to emphasise their relative security and freedom under equality legislation, particularly in Scotland (a point I will return to in the final section), rather than align themselves with discourses of victimhood and tragedy. This is despite the fact that seven of the eight people interviewed had experienced abuse, harassment and/or violence as a trans person; three of the eight discussed at length the impact of living in poverty, with Alex saying of poverty, "it eats the soul away"; and seven of the eight also mentioned mental health difficulties of varying degrees including breakdowns and suicidal thoughts or attempts.[59]

These are very serious challenges that trans people face in their daily lives when negotiating law and medical treatment, as well as every day administrative and bureaucratic microaggressions. But the fact that most participants tried to manage, contain or minimise their difficulties illustrates both their resilience, as well as the strategies of self-protection that can often come into play when battling against routinised marginalisation and discrimination. For some, this took the form of an insistence that not every instance of discrimination or harassment was tied to the experience of being trans. As Becky put it: "I have a whole laundry list in my head of reasons, logical reasons, why things might happen that other people might perceive as being harassment". Similarly, Gavin said:

> There is a tendency for a victim attitude, that I don't actually think is helpful… to particularly tell new people that, oh you must stick to the trans community because no one else will understand, you know, you will be victimised, and you will get people taking against you, you know. Sometimes these things will happen, and unfortunately some people do have very bad experiences with that, and when that happens that needs to be dealt with. But actually a lot of the world is okay, you know. And I think we need to be telling that story more.

This echoes the findings of Morgan's study of Scottish trans people's gender identity construction and performance; most of her participants also demonstrated "agentic belief" rather than engaging in "victim stories", even in the face of "extreme adversity" while also showing vulnerability, especially in discussing previous trauma and loss.[60] This agency was also evidenced to

[59]See also: Louis Bailey, Sonja Ellis, and Jay McNeil, "Suicide Risk in the UK Trans Population and The Role of Gender Transition in Decreasing Suicidal Ideation and Suicide Attempt," *Mental Health Review Journal* 19, no 4 (2014): 209–220; and Jay McNeil et al., *Trans Mental Health Study 2012* available at: https://www.gires.ord.uk/wp-content/uploads/2014/08/trans_mh_study.pdf, accessed March 25, 2020.

[60]Morgan, supra note 47, pp. 157, 159, 255; see also Karen Kaufman, "Transgender Voices: How Transgender People Across the Central Belt of Scotland Negotiate Their Identities as Human Beings in the Face of Perceived Disadvantage and Imposed Norms" (Thesis submitted for MRes, University of Glasgow, 2018).

varying degrees in the ways that participants talked about whether they had faith in the legal system, as we will now see.

4.2 Before the Law, Against the Law and Optimistic Legal Realism

Some participants showed a strong acceptance of and commitment to following the law, and a belief that the law does fulfil a protective function—or "shield".[61] Being "before" the law in this way means accepting law as a stabilising force. For example, Connor suggested that the law is "just a thing that has to happen". When speaking about the possibility of prosecution for sexual assault if he did not tell a sexual partner of his gender history, he said:

> I'd rather everybody was taught about consent, and even to the point where as a trans person that I have to tell a partner that I am trans. I would rather that and people were more safe than people relaxing laws on what consent for sexual relationships is.

No doubt many people would agree that the principles of sexual autonomy and consent are important, and therefore Connor's statement here does not necessarily exemplify a broader or deeper commitment to law per se. His view is also related to his experience, which he described, of beginning to learn about feminism and the importance of gender politics, as well as exploring his own trans identity. However, he did on several occasions profess a more generalised belief that the law is there to protect and benefit us, and in that sense, we are, he said, "lucky" in the UK as compared with other countries, even though the law here is "not perfect".

Likewise, Colette stated that without laws, people would continue to discriminate; with an equality-focused legal framework operating as a shield, however, things would get better, gradually:

> By setting that framework then the law, it creates a space for other people who, for folk to think no, no I shouldn't do that. And once you say I shouldn't do that, I won't do that, then they get used to it, people become more accustomed to it.

This confidence in—and deference towards—the legal framework resonates with Hines' findings in her study of trans people's attitudes to and experiences of the Gender Recognition Act 2004. Some of her participants

[61] Halliday et al., supra note 17.

similarly believed that the legislation provided a protective shield, and would prompt a "'trickle-down' effect, which would enhance trans people's cultural value",[62] and that investment in legal recognition was necessary for practical purposes.[63] It also links closely to the strong faith that some participants in this study had in the power of law to afford and protect rights, particularly when compared with the law in other countries. For instance, Jo took a positive view of law's potential to address inequalities; when asked at the end of the interview whether she had faith in law, she answered:

> Yes I do. Because legislation is in place that is there to end discrimination… the law is now on my side. And I am aware of how incredibly lucky I am and when I go to countries which are much more difficult … I was in Poland last year, Brazil, last year… and I speak to trans women there and they live in fear, they are afraid of the law as well as their fellow citizens.

As this quote from Jo illustrates, linear progressive narratives around change in social and legal practice across time, as well as comparative differences across jurisdictions, also formed part of participants' explanations for contemporary "faith" in law. For instance, Alex, who had a complex gender history (he began to transition to male in his 20s, reverted to living as a radical lesbian feminist, then identified as gender queer for a decade before completing his transition in his 50s), spoke about how much better things were now for people transitioning than they had been in the past:

> I realise I talk like an old war veteran saying 'in my day' and so on, 'people don't know they are born' and it's true, I hear young people now and they moan and moan about things and I think... I think to myself, you know you don't know how lucky you are, you have nice doctors and nice supportive people, endless groups to go to, lovely LGBT centre, no end of paid, there's an army of paid workers now whose job it is to be nice and support you.

In contrast to the idea of law as a progressive force in creating a better life for trans people, some participants had no or limited faith in law. For example, when asked if they had faith in law, artist and writer Gesche said:

> Do I believe in law, if I have faith? No… I am Jewish, believing in the law to treat us right killed millions in Nazi Germany. I learned from that.

---

[62] Hines, supra note 2, pp. 22–23.

[63] Hines, supra note 2, p. 57.

This was apparent even where the participant was an equality activist or campaigner, and where the person had played a part in achieving equality-based policy or legal reform. Nathan, a policy adviser in the third sector said:

> No (laughing). I'd have to say not. [Why not?] Because I think it depends so much on who's hands it's left in, who's applying it, who is putting it into practice, I think that makes such a massive difference... that leaves so much wiggle room... I think there's still so many decisions that seem so arbitrary that I don't have a lot of faith. Certainly, in equality law and things.

When probed on the apparent conflict between this and their organisational role, which included working towards law reform, Nathan went on:

> How can you have faith in a system when it leaves you with no remedy? [And yet you work for this organisation?] Yeah, because you've got to keep trying. And also, a lot of what we do isn't actually working with the law, it's changing people's perceptions and minds, and it's working on changing policy and things like that, which can be more effective.

Resonating with the findings of Kathleen Hull,[64] a "before the law" legal consciousness was sometimes expressed alongside this scepticism. For instance, when asked whether she thought laws were supportive of trans people's rights, Becky, a trans activist, was clear about the potential power of law to ameliorate the worst sorts of inequality and injustices, but was just as emphatic about the possible failures of execution:

> Broadly, yes. Specifically, no. The Equality Act is a brilliant piece of legislation, especially having the perspective of living in the US for so long... With the Equality Act, it's proactive. Yes, there's provisions for punishing people if they violate people's rights, but there's also an obligation to educate, there's an obligation to train, there's an obligation to establish equalities functions... And because of that, that law is brilliant in its grand scale. In its day to day implementation on the ground level, it's still flawed.

Acknowledging the gap between the law in the books and the law in action, Becky described her feeling, that she thought was shared by other trans people and other activists, that it would be almost impossible to ensure universal and consistent compliance with, or enforcement of, the law:

[64] Kathleen E. Hull, "The Cultural Power of Law and the Cultural Enactment of Legality: The Case of Same-Sex Marriage," *Law & Social Inquiry* 28, no. 3 (2003): 629–657.

> The law and the structure of the law says one thing, and what happens on a day to day basis is often quite different… the legal system can only go so far. Unless you're going to put a policeman every ten feet down the street to enforce every law, ultimately it goes, it's on the obligation of individual citizens to obey the law and to behave civilly.

Gavin agreed with this assessment:

> I think the intention is there to make the law as robust as possible for trans people. But as with many things, the intention at the top doesn't always lead to implementation at the bottom.

The issue of arbitrariness as to quality of treatment within legal—and medical—processes was identified by most of the participants in this study as an ongoing challenge that had to be navigated. The discretion exercised by individuals within routine legal and administrative processes, such as changing names on bank accounts, or on mobile phone accounts, was thought to be particularly problematic, and a good example of the microaggressions that trans people commonly face. Becky described it as "the luck of the draw" as to who was dealing with you on the day and "what kind of day were they having".

Gavin, who was very wary of the police as a result of various interactions with them, further suggested that the arbitrariness in administrative processes described by Becky is also enshrined within the criminal justice system:

> My understanding is that under the common law, to some extent, the police have an element of discretion as to what they do. And again, that is fine if you have confidence that the police will in every single occasion, every single officer, would say, oh yes we must follow that to its conclusion. But I can't believe for a second that was happening or we wouldn't have had the need for specific legislation to be drafted in the first place.

Similarly, Nathan stated:

> It just, it doesn't come down to… you know, who's in the right, it comes down to whose version of events the Sheriff happens to believe on that particular day. And I think depending on the Sheriff, you know, if he's willing to come down on one side or the other. And so often you get discriminated against, but you can't prove it, and there's nothing you can do.

The gap between the letter of the law and the law in practice means that trans people are both inside, but simultaneously and continually at risk of being outside the protective shield of law—of being misrecognised, treated unfairly or ignored completely. The lack of "follow-through" from law to practice was also attributed to a lack of sufficient resources to call those flouting laws and regulations to account, or a lack of education or knowledge about how to access those resources, particularly in the civil justice system, as Nathan describes:

> We get a lot of people calling us up, having faced discrimination. And I think trans people are some of the most discriminated against people, trans women in particular… And there's so little, often, that we can do about it… Now the EHRC [Equality and Human Rights Commission] has been trimmed back as much as it has, their capacity to take cases forward is so limited… the Citizens Advice Bureau can help, but again they're so overstretched. They so often can't. Unless it's employment issues they can't really represent people… people know that the discrimination legislation exists, they feel wronged when they've been discriminated against, but there's a lack of in-depth understanding of what exactly that means, how they go about dealing with it, all those sorts of issues…

Although none of the participants expressed outright resistance to, or rejection of, law as such, comments such as these show a deep distrust that the enforcement of regulations and laws can be undertaken fairly by those entrusted to do so; they also highlight the structural impediments to accessing legal advice and representation that would allow those experiencing inequality to challenge it through the civil courts.

Unlike Rosie Harding,[65] but similarly to Hull,[66] I found that, other than Gesche, who voiced very strong resistance to the idea that law is always a force for good, and a strong rejection of gender binaries (i.e. identifying and presenting as both gender fluid, and/or gender neutral but also sometimes eschewing gendered language altogether by identifying as fruit salad or an alien rock star who doesn't give any fucks), my participants were unlikely to show strong signs of active resistance or rejection of law or legal norms. In other words, they were not entirely what Ewick and Silbey termed "against the law".

Nor was there evidence of what Halliday et al.[67] described as "collective dissent" against an oppressive legal system. However, in this study participants showed what I would describe as *optimistic legal realism* rather than legal dissidence or resistance. Optimistic legal realism is a complex interwoven

---

[65] Harding, supra note 23.

[66] Hull, supra note 66.

[67] Halliday et al., supra note 17.

blend of cautious, equivocal but also passionate acceptance and/or rejection of the power of law to achieve true equality. It looks somewhat similar to what Halliday and Morgan[68] describe as an oscillation between protest and fatalism, but they are describing a purer form of "against the law"; the optimistic realism expressed by my participants is inherently more positive given that it also has a seam of hope and confidence that law *could* provide real protection—for example, Nathan's statement that they have no faith in law, but they have to "keep trying".

Likewise, while optimistic legal realism seems to overlap with the concept of legal alienation developed by Hertogh,[69] and more specifically, his category of legal "cynics", again his is a form of "against the law", or what Halliday[70] has called an exploration of counter hegemony. Hertogh's cynics "generally do not feel that those norms and values which they themselves consider important are sufficiently reflected in the law".[71] This certainly does not describe my participants, all but one of whom professed a deep attachment to the idea of a distinctly Scottish, progressive approach to trans equality law, as we will see in section 4, even while they were simultaneously pessimistic about the prospect of the full implementation of those laws in specific circumstances.

It is more likely that what I am calling "optimistic legal realism" is what Ewick and Silbey have described as the dynamic relationship between the hegemonic ("before the law" and "with the law") and the counter-hegemonic ("against the law") types of legal consciousness. In other words, my participants experience both pessimism and optimism, scepticism and hope *at the same time*, that these experiences "co-exist in a permanent state of tension".[72] This means that they were both inside—optimistically embracing the promise of law—but also outside, observing what the law can realistically deliver.

For example, Nathan displayed this form of optimistic legal realism, stressing the gap between top-level legal interventions, for example in the form of legislation, which they did feel made a difference, at the same time as doubting the successful implementation of those changes on the ground:

> And obviously there are laws which do make a difference. But I think there's a difference between recognising that and having genuine faith in it. Because I think if you've got faith in it, then you believe that these laws are there and

---

[68] Halliday and Morgan, supra note 16.
[69] Hertogh, supra note 22.
[70] Halliday, supra note 23, p. 871.
[71] Hertogh, supra note 22, p. 59.
[72] Halliday, supra note 23, p. 872.

> so everything will be okay, and so they will always be effective... they will get employed in the right way, whereas I don't think that's the case.

Hines[73] found that some of her participants were also distrustful of the notion that legal change could affect real social change on the ground. As such, further law reform to enhance trans people's rights is not necessarily the solution. Indeed, one participant in this study, Connor, had more faith in social media, as a basis for activism and change, as where the "next big revolutions are going to be... to change people's perceptions and make differences"; and as a more democratising platform that can include those who might not be able to physically attend an activist rally or march.

However, like Nathan and Gavin, Connor also emphasised the importance of having law that protected trans people's safety, such as hate crime laws, and laws on sexual consent. The views of these participants illustrate that given the practical complexities of everyday life, and the difficulties in ensuring a smooth transition from the law in the books to the law in action, it is not necessarily contradictory to believe optimistically in the idea of law as a means of achieving equality and social justice, even while remaining sceptical about the realistic prospect of change. Unsurprisingly then, their scepticism was often accompanied not only by a "before the law" legal consciousness as explored above, but also at times by a "with the law" legal consciousness, as demonstrated by participants' strategic use of and investment in law as a means to advance their position or that of others—in other words, *optimistic legal realism.*

4.3 With the Law

Halliday et al.'s 2015 study suggested that some see law as a sword, a weapon that can be wielded to achieve justice, either individually or collectively; this is what Ewick and Silbey have termed "with the law". The participants here certainly saw law not as something to be resisted but as a mechanism for justice, and one that could readily be put to use—although not by everyone. For example, Becky explained her approach in this way:

> I've always been a believer that systems are best changed from within. That overtly resisting is counterproductive... the fact that I play by the rules might not necessarily help me, but if somebody points out that I don't play by the rules it can definitely hurt me... the system definitely needs to be changed, the

[73]Hines, supra note 2, p. 23.

> system is flawed… But I've learned to play the system… I believe that I will always be treated fairly, not because the system is inherently fair, but because I know enough about the system to be able to catch its unfairness in time, and I also know people in positions.

However, Becky acknowledged that not everyone was able to "play the system" in this way, saying that if you don't have the resources (whether financial or in terms of knowledge and energy) to do so, the system can "eat you up". Her faith therefore did not rest on the law, but her own skills and abilities to navigate powerful and complex systems and processes—skills and abilities that not everyone has.

Participants might also choose their legal forum carefully. For instance, Nathan made a distinction between the criminal law and civil law, perhaps in part due to the supportive and professional response from the police they had received after suffering a serious physical assault:

> I think I've got more faith in the criminal justice system than I do in the civil side of things. And just having seen how much work the police are doing on hate crime, and how committed a lot of them are, I know some really good officers and stuff. And knowing how seriously they take it.

Unsurprisingly, given the costs (emotional and financial) of initiating a civil claim, and the diminishing legal aid available for civil justice,[74] some trans people might find the criminal justice system more accessible. It might also be the case that the government in Scotland, and its criminal justice agents, take violence against and harassment of trans people more seriously than ever before. Nonetheless, Dean Spade and others have argued that neither police officers nor the criminal law have historically been a friend to queers, and that the road to transformative social justice is not paved with increased criminalisation and punishment.[75] This does not mean that we should not address violence against trans people. Nor does it mean that the criminal law can never provide some redress. Rather, we might want to exercise caution

---

[74] In Scotland, excepting those relating to employment, discrimination claims made to tribunals (such as those related to goods or services) are not covered by legal aid. See "Help with Legal Costs," Citizens Advice Scotland, accessed March 20, 2020, https://www.citizensadvice.org.uk/scotland/law-and-courts/legal-system-s/taking-legal-action-s/help-with-legal-costs-s/#Civillegalaid.

[75] Spade, supra note 40; Sarah Lamble, "Queer Necropolitics and the Expanding Carceral State: Interrogating Sexual Investments in Punishment," *Law and Critique* 24, no. 3 (2013); see also Angela Dwyer, "'It's Not Like We're Going to Jump Them': How Transgressing Heteronormativity Shapes Police Interactions with LGBT Young People," *Youth Justice* 11, no. 3 (2011) on the policing of young queer communities.

in turning to the criminal law, particularly as a first resort, and keep the increasingly carceral state in our sights as a target of queer protest.

Sometimes participants made their decisions on whether or not to use law on the basis of how strong the case was, and the potential consequences of doing so. Nathan's decision to turn to civil law to solve a legal dispute with a bar in Glasgow that denied entry to them and their partner—who was in wheelchair—was specifically described by them as strategic:

> There's another reason why we've decided to take this case… because we are discriminated against all the time. [So tell me why you chose to do it this time?] Because of how dramatic and clear cut it was in terms of them saying, you know… I was saying we can't come in because [partner] is a wheelchair user? and they said yes. We had another person with us, so I know that we've got a witness to it. So I guess, yeah we are pretty strategic, but I think you have to be. Because otherwise you'd just be taking cases all of the time which would be exhausting.

The sense of discrimination as pervasive and ongoing that Nathan, who is also disabled, had, was one reason for not engaging with law—because to do so is exhausting. Burn-out was mentioned specifically by both participants working in the equalities sector, as well as by others who had helped to run trans support and information groups, or Pride events.

The other reason that Nathan gave for not pursuing cases on other occasions was the impact of calling attention to the discrimination. For example, they talked about their concern that reporting even overtly discriminatory recruitment or employment practices would have a negative effect on their ability to get a job, despite being a university graduate and a highly trained professional. In contrast, Connor, who is a student, said, "that's why I would turn to [law] because if I went to an employer and they weren't listening then they are breaking the law and I would grab them and slap them in the face with it you know". Unlike Nathan, however, Connor was not at that time aiming to be employed in a professional, specialised context, and in comparison, has no investment in trying to build a reputation with potential employers. Rather, as a queer activist he enjoyed making "as much noise as possible". Knowing when to "go to law"—and when not to—was therefore very much contingent upon what was at stake for individuals when entering the legal system; only those who desire to and can afford to use the law—financially and psychologically—can do so.

For some, this question of whether participants would "go to law" often also turned on issues of discrimination relating to other protected characteristics, such as disability. Of the eight interviewees, one was a frequent wheelchair or stick user, one had Asperger's and one had ME. All three discussed the problems of negotiating being trans alongside their disability. As intimated earlier, participants also discussed the impact of mental ill-health, of past or current poverty, and the impact of being, or being perceived as, gay as well as trans. For instance, Gavin talked about the connection between him being trans and having a disability, and his disability being the driver for a potential discrimination claim rather than being trans:

> Ironically, my biggest worry, and the one I would see myself using the law for, is through work, as things stand, would be disability issues, not trans… I'm well aware that if I'd transitioned 20 years ago I would not be making this statement, but as it stands, I've actually received far more discrimination for having ME than I have for being trans… And I do accept that life could change, and I could get into other circumstances where that wasn't the case and someone did have an issue, with me being trans. But no, it's the [disability] of late… So yeah, I've had to basically say "Equality Act", by saying reasonable adjustment. But not over being trans.

Nathan also relayed a very serious physical assault they had experienced at the hands of a group of young people, but not knowing whether it was on the basis of being read as trans, or gay:

> I was beat up really badly when I just came out as trans. And I think it was because I was read as a very camp guy… I was sitting on a bench with a friend, who is also a trans guy. I think they thought we were together, and they beat me up really badly. I think they were like 14, 15, and there was like four of them… And then, so when I went in [to the police] to give a full statement a couple of days later, they said, you know, I heard that you said you were trans, do you think the assault was because of that. And they were really sensitive, and really good and stuff. But I said I thought it was more likely a sexual orientation thing. But you know – who knows.

Both Gavin and Nathan were willing to use the law to protect their rights, but this is not always possible, especially where the trans person experiences intersecting and compounding inequalities. For instance, for Alex, being poor was connected to periods of depression and mental ill health, as well as identifying as gender queer, which made certain kinds of jobs impossible; as a consequence Alex has received state benefits for most of his life, a situation that equality law is not best placed to resolve.

Clearly the intersections of class, gender, physical ability and mental health impact upon a trans person's desire or capacity to use law as a means of trying to achieve just and equitable outcomes. Strategic decisions about "going to law" or using law as a "sword" are therefore always mediated through the complex realities of lived experiences, where even the best equality legislation, implemented perfectly, is not the solution.[76] The comments of my participants here illustrate the difficulties also of applying law in a properly intersectional way, one that recognises interwoven axes of oppression. As Spade has said, law often "only provide(s) access to the sought after right for those who do not have other intervening vectors of marginality."[77] This raises the question of whether law is in fact the appropriate mechanism to achieve social justice for those for whom it is most required—are queers better off outside law?[78] However, what is clear is that trans people *do* sometimes go to law, even when sceptical about its potential to achieve its own aims. In the next section, I look more closely at why my participants might be so heavily invested in Scottish equality law.

5 Scotland: The Best Place on the Planet to Be Trans?

One of the most strikingly common themes in this study was the sense that all but one participant had that things were different—that is, better—in Scotland than in the rest of the world. Alex, for example felt strongly that Scotland compared very favourably to the rest of the UK with respect to equality:

> You think god, it's like a fantasy come true you know just amazing isn't it? Because Scotland is at the vanguard, who knew yes! Amazing. And we ended up with a much better equal marriage Act than in England and Wales. I mean, it takes lots of hard work obviously, but yes you just think crikey how did all this happen it's astounding, you could just cry you know just astounding… because the Scottish parliament is designed so well you know and designed by

[76]Although none of my participants expressed a desire for gender dysphoria to be classed as a disability, this has been hotly debated in the US where the federal disability law was recently held to include gender dysphoria. See "Breakthrough: Americans with Disabilities Act Can't Exclude Gender Dysphoria," Transequality, accessed March 20, 2020, https://transequality.org/blog/breakthrough-americans-with-disabilities-act-can-t-exclude-gender-dysphoria; and Katy Steinmetz, "Being Transgender Is Not a Mental Disorder: Study," *Time*, July 26, 2016, accessed March 20, 2020, https://time.com/4424589/being-transgender-is-not-a-mental-disorder-study.

[77]Spade, supra note 40, p. 160.

[78]Sharon Cowan, "Sex/Gender Equality: Taking a Break from the Legal to Transform the Social," in *Exploring the Legal in Socio-Legal Studies*, ed. David Cowan and Daniel Wincott (London: Palgrave MacMillan, 2015), 121–146.

good people, liberal people to be much more open than the UK so on paper at least it seems much more approachable.

Both Connor and Gavin agreed:

I think in terms of the laws about trans rights in Scotland are much better than the rest of the UK. And that is obviously fantastic. [Connor]

I think we are very, very lucky in terms of intention, with the law in this country at the current time. Because we've not only got the UK law, we've got the Scottish law as well, in terms of the Scottish Parliament. So my understanding, unless the English law has changed since, is that we actually have like the strongest hate crime legislation, in terms of trans people, in the UK. So it's actually stronger than other parts of the UK. [Gavin]

Jo and Colette went further to compare Scotland with other parts of the world:

The fact that I can now be true to myself feels like a huge gift and I am incredibly lucky because I live in Scotland where that is possible, and I am aware of so many countries in the world where I couldn't. I would be in terror of my life. [Jo]

Actually, you probably know, I am not aware of a country that is a better place to be trans than Scotland. I think this is the best place on the planet. [Colette]

Gesche, who is of German origin, also suggested that Scotland was an easier place to be gender fluid, even when coming into contact with legal actors:

I never was treated so friendly when I mentioned my identity to an authority. I wouldn't mention it to German police, never. I would present as straight female to get the most support from them, but in the UK I feel I can. At least up here in Scotland.

Nathan explained excitedly that the Scottish Trans Alliance had the first properly funded trans specific role in the UK, ahead of anything that has yet to be introduced in England:

It's the first government funded, which is fantastic. And they still don't have a government funded post down south, like we do here. And you can really tell in the way things have developed strategically and policy wise.

Connor specifically focused on his feeling that transphobia would not be tolerated in Scotland and (speaking in 2015) that the media, too, would be supportive of trans rights:

> Yes, over here I think we are very lucky to have good laws about it. I don't know whether that is, I think it is because of the kind of hype around trans issues at the moment, I think if you were to go to court about something that was trans related, and like if you were to get a bad outcome due to stigma or transphobia then you know the newspapers would pick up on it like that [snaps fingers] and immediately they would be oh we'll fix this.

These comments illustrate a palpable feeling of pride and faith in the Scottish legal and political system, especially the symbolic force that apparently progressive law has for those inside the Scottish legal and political system, and those outside looking in.

However, some participants did call attention to some of the problems particular to Scotland. For instance, Nathan highlighted the hurdles for some of those attempting to access legal advice, given the very dispersed rural population in most parts of Scotland and cut-backs to funding for the Equality and Human Rights Commission. Most participants also talked in detail about lengthy waiting lists for medical referral and treatment due to there being limited treatment options for those living in Scotland, and Becky talked in particular about the difficulties faced by trans men in accessing breast reduction surgery, and trans women in accessing breast augmentation, if they did not meet the stringent BMI requirements of some of the medical professionals involved in their treatment. Nonetheless, there was a generally high level of awareness of, and satisfaction with, Scotland's NHS Gender Reassignment Protocol, which governs all procedures relating to gender reassignment, particularly when compared to medical processes in England and Wales. Recently, however, it has been said that lengthy delays have become even lengthier, due to understaffing as a result of recruitment and retention problems.[79]

A couple of participants were also more cautious about the permanence of any legal gains, and even where they were positive about the current regime of rights and protections, a few showed concern that the political tides could

[79] Scottish Trans Alliance, personal communication, July 24, 2019. For the Gender reassignment NHS Scotland protocol 2012, see: Health and Social Care Directorate, The protocol is under review but there is interim guidance from 2017 available in Health Performance and Delivery Directorate, *Gender Reassignment Protocol: Interim Guidance* (Edinburgh: Scottish Government, 2017). For information on waiting lists and survey of gender identity services in 2017, see Scottish Public Health Network, *Health Care Needs Assessment of Gender Identity Services* (Glasgow: SPHN, 2017).

turn just as easily against trans people, where rights could be stripped away or undermined. For instance, Alex said:

> I'm very aware that things could change again, I don't take anything for granted and you know things are really wonderful now and getting more wonderful and that's, obviously we all love that, and if you're a young person now you've no idea how bad things could be, but... I think gosh, this could all change again and I feel very strongly, I read loads of history so I know what people are like and how things can change for good and ill, very easily...

Similarly, Gesche said:

> Do I believe in law, if I have faith? No. Not at all, there are a few good laws to protect people like me, especially here in Scotland, but I am very aware that they might get taken away again, depending on who runs the government.

These comments, made in interviews in 2015 and 2016, are prescient; following the House of Commons Select Committee on Women and Equalities' 2016 report on "Transgender Equality",[80] in 2017 the Scottish and UK governments announced a review of the Gender Recognition Act 2004 to investigate the possibility of allowing gender self-identification, thereby depathologising the gender recognition process. This has resulted in vocal and vehement push back against trans equality, particularly where "trans rights" are portrayed as being in conflict with "women's sex-based rights". What has been described as a "hurricane"[81] has overtaken the process, although Ahmed[82] has pointed out that these are not new attacks on trans people, only that the volume has been turned up in recent times. The Scottish Government, whose consultation period on the GRA ended in March 2018, delayed any proposals for reform until a further round of consultation and review could take place.[83] Eventually, as Flora Renz has discussed in this volume, a new Bill and consultation document were published on 17 December 2019, with a closing date of 17 March 2020.[84] However, in the intervening period, some feminists and others loudly questioned the rights of trans women and girls to participate and be present in sex/gender-segregated spaces, especially

[80] House of Commons Women and Equalities Committee, supra note 56.

[81] Whittle and Simkiss, supra note 12, pp. 211–231.

[82] Ahmed, supra note 28, p. 27.

[83] "Review of the Gender Recognition Act 2004," The Scottish Government, accessed March 24, 2020, https://www2.gov.scot/Topics/Justice/law/17867/gender-recognition-review.

[84] Justice Directorate, *Gender Recognition Reform (Scotland) Bill: Consultation* (Edinburgh: The Scottish Government, 2019).

in hospitals, changing rooms, toilets, the girl guides and prisons, as well as trans individuals in women's sports and on women-only shortlists.[85] These heated debates have filled our news and social media streams, and have spilled over into university campuses, where conflicts have arisen—framed as questions of freedom of expression—over whether or not "gender critical" feminist events should be allowed to go ahead. Ahmed points to the exercise of power that is evident when those who are trying to express protest over the—often explicitly hateful—speech of event participants are themselves labelled as stiflers of free speech:

> We learn that free speech has become a political technology that is used to redefine freedom around the right of some to occupy time and space. Whenever people keep being given a platform to say they have no platform, or whenever people speak endlessly about being silenced, you not only have a performative contradiction; you are witnessing a mechanism of power.[86,87]

More recently, the Scottish Prison System has come under pressure to review some of the more progressive aspects of their policy on housing trans inmates in the prison most appropriate to their self-identified gender, and a separate consultation on these issues is underway.[88] Notably, these debates focus on questioning the impact of the inclusion of trans women, and only very rarely do they mention trans men.[89]

Finally, processes to finalise the questions of the next Scottish census in 2021 have prompted fierce debates over whether or not there should be a

---

[85]Peter Dunne and Tara Hewitt, "Gender Recognition, Self-Determination and Segregated Space," *Oxford Human Rights Hub*, January 16, 2018, https://ohrh.law.ox.ac.uk/gender-recognition-self-determination-and-segregated-space/.

[86]Ahmed, supra note 28, p. 27.

[87]This was most recently at issue for the University of Edinburgh, and one that prompted the whole of the University's Staff Pride Committee to resign: Hilary Mitchell, "Entire Edinburgh University LGBT committee Quit in Dramatic Protest Against 'Anti Trans' Julie Bindel Talk" *Edinburgh Live*, June 6, 2019, accessed March 24, 2020, https://www.edinburghlive.co.uk/news/edinburgh-news/entire-edinburgh-university-lgbt-committee-16389812. I have deliberately chosen not to cite the mainstream broadsheet newspaper reporting of this event in e.g. The Guardian or Telegraph because, under the story's headline, they printed a photograph of Julie Bindel, focusing the story on her and her accusation of assault against one of the protesters outside her event at Edinburgh University, rather than on the committee's resignation—and reasons for it.

[88]Newsroom Reporter, "Scottish Government Accused of Putting Women in Scottish Prisons at Risk," *The Scotsman*, May 30, 2019, accessed March 24, 2020, https://www.scotsman.com/news/politics/scottish-government-accused-of-putting-women-in-scottish-prisons-at-risk-1-4937495. Similar discussions have been taking place in England and Wales – see Whittle and Simkiss, supra note 12.

[89]Some writers do express incredulity as to the claim that trans men are "really" men—see e.g. Julian Vigo, "How to Stage a Study: The Transgender Lobby in British Academia." *Medium*, July 30, 2019, accessed March 24, 2020, https://medium.com/@julian.vigo/how-to-stage-a-study-the-transgender-lobby-in-british-academia-f196f4f686f1.

question that disaggregates sex from gender, with gender critical feminists (and some others) arguing that a two-part question that distinguishes "biological" sex from gender would be the appropriate way to capture data, while others argue that this forces trans people to distinguish between sex and gender in a way that does not accord with their lived experience.[90] Nonetheless, National Records of Scotland who produce the Census, released a statement in January 2020 confirming that, while they recommend keeping a binary sex question, they also recommend a single question to which trans people can respond according to their "lived sex".[91]

The main basis for questioning trans women's rights to inhabit the world as women is the notion that under a system of self-identification, even if a person changes their gender, not only can they not change their sex (where sex is narrowly understood as biological, binary and chromosomal[92]), they are under no obligation to change their physiology. Thus appears the "male-bodied" and "male-sexed" threat to women's spaces. The problem is, therefore, sometimes represented as the dangers of cisgender male infiltration rather than the dangers of including "real" trans women,[93] but it is trans women rather than cisgender men who are currently experiencing the pain, humiliation and anger of having their rights not to be discriminated against put at risk.

Of course, since the Gender Recognition Act 2004 does not require trans people to have surgery, there are some trans women, who have a penis, who are already accessing all of these segregated spaces without incident. It also worth highlighting that all of the women's services in Scotland—Rape Crisis

[90]See the Culture, Tourism, Europe and External Affairs Committee, *Stage 1 Report on the Census (Amendment) (Scotland) Bill* (Edinburgh: The Scottish parliament, February 7, 2019). https://sp-bpr-en-prod-cdnep.azureedge.net/published/CTEEA/2019/2/7/Stage-1-Report-on-the-Census--Amendment---Scotland--Bill/CTEEAS052019R1.pdf, particularly the conclusion, where it is confirmed that the Census will not include a non-binary option in the sex/gender question. For discussion of the Census, as well as the interaction between the Equality Act 2010 and gender recognition processes, see Sharon Cowan et al., "'UK Sex and Gender Equality in Law and Policy: A response to Murray and Hunter Blackburn," *Scottish Affairs* (forthcoming); and Alex Sharpe, "Will Gender Self-Declaration Undermine Women's Rights and Lead to an Increase in Harms?," *Modern Law Review* 83, no 3, (2020): 539.

[91]National Records of Scotland, *Scotland's Census 2021: Sex Question Recommendation Report* (Edinburgh, December 2019), 28 and 32. https://www.scotlandscensus.gov.uk/documents/Scotland's%20Census%202021%20-%20%20Sex%20question%20recommendation%20report%20(2).pdf.

[92]In *Goodwin v. UK* [2002] ECtHR (App. no. 28957/95) 35 ECtHR 447, *I v. UK* [2002] ECtHR (App. No. 25680/94), the European Ct Human Rights held that the UK's legal test for sex as gonadal, genital and chromosomal, as set forth in *Corbett v. Corbett* [1970] 2 All ER 33, was no longer appropriate for determining sex for the purposes of marriage, and that gender—as experienced and identified by the individual themselves—should play an important if not central role. In response to *Goodwin*, the UK introduced the Gender Recognition Act 2004. For discussion see Cowan, Sandland and Sharpe, supra note 9.

[93]Whittle and Simkiss, supra note 12.

Scotland, Scottish Women's Aid, Shakti Women's Aid and Engender—are trans inclusive and have been for some years.[94] While the Scottish government have stated more than once that the protections of the Equality Act 2010—as they apply both to trans and cis women—will not be affected, the uncertainty over the future of their legal gender,[95] as well as the damage that the toxicity of the current debate is causing, is hugely detrimental to all trans and non-binary people's well being.[96] It has caused deep division within the Scottish Nationalist Party's government itself, with the First Minister showing strong support for allowing self-identification, even while some of her cabinet ministers are clearly not in agreement.[97] This is despite the fact that at LGBTI hustings in 2016, before the last Scottish elections, all the leaders of the main parties in Scotland (SNP, Labour, Lib Dems, Greens and even the Conservatives), all pledged a manifesto commitment to reforming the GRA 2004 to allow for self-identification.

And while it cannot be denied that some cisgender men will take advantage of women's vulnerabilities for their own gain, there appears to be no evidence from the countries where self-identification has been introduced that this has caused a significant problem. It is certainly not a problem for which trans people, or trans women in particular, should be made to suffer. Nor is there any evidence currently that shifts in Scotland towards recognition of self-identification at a policy level, for example with respect to trans women's placement in women's prisons, has caused serious concerns, partly because the Scottish Prison System continues to operate on the basis of case conferences that are oriented towards the needs and risk assessments of individuals, notwithstanding the top-level gender identity and gender reassignment policy

---

[94] See Close the Gap, "Scottish Women's Sector response to the consultation on proposed changes to the Gender Recognition Act" (February, 2018): [24], available at https://www.closethegap.org.uk/content/resources/Scottish-Womens-Sector-response-to-the-consultation-on-proposed-changes-to-the-Gender-Recognition-Act.pdf.

[95] For a fuller discussion of the future of legal gender, see website "The Future of Legal Gender: A Critical Law Reform Project", accessed March 25, 2020. https://futureoflegalgender.kcl.ac.uk/.

[96] BBC Reporter, "Scottish Transgender Reforms Put on Hold," *BBC News*, June 20, 2019, accessed March 25, 2020, https://www.bbc.co.uk/news/uk-scotland-scotland-politics-48702946; Anne Fazackerley, "UK Universities Struggle To Deal With 'Toxic' Trans Rights Row." *The Guardian*, October 30, 2019, accessed March 25, 2020. https://www.theguardian.com/education/2018/oct/30/uk-universities-struggle-to-deal-with-toxic-trans-rights-row.

[97] See, for example, Libby Brooks, "Scottish Government Reaffirms Support for Trans Rights," *The Guardian*, April 18, 2019, accessed March 25, 2020, https://www.theguardian.com/politics/2019/apr/18/minister-reaffirms-scottish-governments-support-for-trans-rights and the subsequent statement from the Cabinet Secretary for Social Security and Older People, Shirley-Anne Somerville: Scottish Government, *Statement on gender Recognition* (Edinburgh: Scottish Government, 2019), accessed March 26, 2020, https://www.gov.scot/publications/statement-gender-recognition/.

that requires trans people to be accommodated in the prison that reflects the gender in which the person is living.[98]

The attempts of trans activists (and others) to reform current laws to introduce less intrusive legal processes and easier access to treatment, and to bring practice into line with international best practice[99] have been cast, through what Ahmed[100] has called "an inflammatory mechanism", as the lobbying of so called "powerful transgender interest groups".[101] Given the "relentless nature of the harassment against trans people",[102] and given that trans people are a marginalised and oppressed minority in the UK and elsewhere, this kind of language is both unhelpful and disingenuous.

Gesche expressed fear that rights would be rolled back as a result of a change in government. That is not the explanation for the kinds of regressive discourses and practices that we are currently seeing around trans people's inclusion. But if Scotland is to continue to be one of the best places to be trans, whatever that means, the Scottish government has an obligation over the coming months and years to ensure that equality law is clear, accessible and fair—in letter and in implementation—in order for us all to benefit from it, regardless of gender identity.

6 Conclusion

Using a femiqueer analysis, through the lens of legal consciousness, this chapter has explored trans people's experiences of equality in Scotland. Participants in this study had a high level of awareness of equality laws and norms, and the rights they were or should be entitled to in contemporary Scotland. Other than Gesche, my participants were unlikely to show signs of active resistance to law or legal norms, or what Ewick and Silbey called being

[98]Scottish Prison Service, *Gender Identity and Gender Reassignment Policy for Those in Our Custody* (Edinburgh: Scottish Prison Service, 2014); see also Cowan et al., supra note 90.

[99]See for example Vic Valentine, "Self-declaration Would Bring Britain into Line with International Best Practice," *The Economist*, July 3, 2018, accessed March 25, 2020, https://www.economist.com/open-future/2018/07/03/self-declaration-would-bring-britain-into-line-with-international-best-practice.

[100]Ahmed, supra note 28, p. 29.

[101]See for example "The GRA Consultation and the Fair Play for Women Campaign," Fair Play for Women, July 27, 2018, accessed March 25, 2020, https://fairplayforwomen.com/full_guide/. See also Kath Murray, Lucy Hunter Blackburn and Lisa MacKenzie, "Losing Sight of Women's Rights: The Unregulated Introduction of Gender Self-identification as a Study of Policy Capture in Scotland," *Scottish Affairs* 28, no. 3 (2019): 285, which describes policy making in this area as being "vulnerable" to "single-minded ideologically driven lobbying."

[102]Ahmed, supra note 28, p. 28.

"against the law", or manifesting what Halliday et al.[103] described as "collective dissent". However, while expressing faith in the *idea* of law, or the *promise* of law, many of them simultaneously expressed limited or no faith in law's ability to secure social justice, and as such could be described as demonstrating a new form of legal consciousness—what I have called *optimistic legal realism.*

At the same time, participants often talked about the law as a strategic tool, and as having strong symbolic influence that could have a trickle-down effect upon cultural change. Those who did express views that could be described as "against the law" (for example, against the current gender recognition regime) also adopted strategies for using the law to their own advantage where possible, and fall into the category of being "with the law" where the pervasive power of law, while potentially oppressive, provided mechanisms for resistance against legal rules, as well as more petty administrative bureaucracies.[104]

However, it was clear that participants were cognisant of the differential and arbitrary ways that law is implemented, and the consequences of this for those who were not middle-class, educated, white, heterosexual males. Some were also wary of particular legal frameworks (such as Nathan's trust in criminal rather than civil law) or of particular legal agents (for example, Gavin's distrust of the police). Many said that they felt lucky to live in a country with strong legal protections, but whether or not participants would use the law as an instrument for change or to challenge discrimination they had experienced was very much a matter of context, and a question of the type of legal setting, as well as what was at stake in "going to law". Trans people, in this study at least, were very aware of their status as both legal insiders and outsiders, protected by the letter of the law, but not necessarily through its implementation.

Finally, while participants celebrated the progressive cultural and legal shifts across their lifetimes, particularly in Scotland, and in comparison to the rest of the UK, there was a note of caution sounded regarding the transient and fickle nature of human nature and history, and recognition of the ease with which the winds of change can bring what Stephen Whittle and Fiona Simkiss have called a "hurricane".[105] Recent conversations—in parliament, in the media, in universities and beyond—about the extent to which "trans rights" conflict with "women's sex-based rights" illustrate the

[103]Halliday et al., supra note 19.

[104]Anna-Maria Marshall and Scott Barclay, "In Their Own Words: How Ordinary People Construct the Legal World," *Law and Social Inquiry* 28, no. 3 (2003): 618.

[105]Whittle and Simkiss, supra note 12.

ways in which battles, which we might think had been fought and won, are subject to shifts in political allegiances and socio-cultural priorities. Some of my participants had limited or no faith in law, or they demonstrated deep legal scepticism about the arbitrariness of law; consequently, some may not feel that better laws would make a substantive difference to their everyday lives. However, in this time of increased intolerance of the very idea of being trans, particularly of being a trans woman in sex-segregated spaces, the importance of the Scottish government signalling a commitment to trans equality by following through on their own manifesto pledge of reforming the GRA 2004 cannot be understated, especially given current levels of fear and vulnerability within the trans community.[106] At this moment, perhaps more than any other, we need, as the Gloria Anzaldúa quote at the start of this chapter suggests, to combine the necessary and vitalising tensions in our feminist and queer politics with respect, understanding, love and friendship.

The terms and tone of the "debate" in Scotland (and in the rest of the UK) illustrate a regressive shift that is devastating for many trans people who feel as if their very existence is being fundamentally challenged, but it is also profoundly challenging to feminism: as Ahmed has said, "The policing of the boundaries of 'women' has never *not* been disastrous for feminism".[107] While Scotland may still be a good place to be trans relatively speaking, sadly, Whittle and Simkiss[108] may not be correct in their recent analysis that the Scottish Government will provide a clear, smooth road map for change for England and Wales, or elsewhere.

Acknowledgments I'd like to thank the inordinately patient editors who invited me to be part of this incredible collection and encouraged me when I was faltering; and my research assistant Shy Zvouloun for helping with references. I have given versions of this paper at many conferences in the last few years and would particularly like to thank the organisers and audiences at the following universities: Birmingham, Newcastle, Edinburgh, Durham and Bristol universities in the UK; Victoria, Dalhousie, McGill and York Universities in Canada and UTS, Australia. I have benefited from funding from the Carnegie Trust for the Universities of Scotland and from the University of Edinburgh to complete the field work for this project; and from the generosity of the University of Victoria, Canada, and the Centre for the Study of Law and Society, UC Berkeley, who accepted me as a visiting Professor during fieldwork. I am eternally grateful to my very dear and kind friends Mike Adler and Sue Fyvel who gave me quiet time and space to write in their lovely

[106]Morton, supra note 12; for a critique of the unreflective "progress" narrative of the UK government's policy on LGBTQI+ equality, see Lawrence and Taylor, supra note 10.

[107]Ahmed, supra note 28, p. 31.

[108]Whittle and Simkiss, supra note 12.

London flat in the summer of 2018. Countless thanks of course are due to those who read early drafts, or with whom I have talked incessantly over the last decade about these issues: Justina Molloy, Helen Buxton, Gillian Calder and the inimitable David Sibbering. Simon Halliday gave me time and space and loaned me parts of his brain when needed. I am also eternally grateful to Jess Penrose and Mel Talyor who stepped in with editorial assistance at the last minute! The biggest debt of gratitude I owe is to the people who agreed to be interviewed for this project, who were incredibly open with me, and trusted me to treat their stories with integrity. Without them, none of this research would be possible. I apologise it has taken me so long to tell these stories, and I hope I have done them some semblance of justice.

References

Ahmed, Sara. "An Affinity of Hammers." *Transgender Studies Quarterly* 3, no. 1–2 (2016): 22–34.

Anzaldúa, Gloria E. "Bridge, Drawbridge, Sandbar, or Island: Lesbians-of-Color *Hacienda Alianzas.*" In *Bridges of Power: Women's Multi-cultural Alliances*, edited by Lisa Albrecht and Rose Brewer, 216–233. Santa Cruz: New Society Publishers, 1990.

Bailey, Louis, Sonja Ellis and Jay McNeil. "Suicide Risk in the UK Trans Population and the Role of Gender Transition in Decreasing Suicidal Ideation and Suicide Attempt." *Mental Health Review Journal* 19, no. 4 (2014): 209–220.

Bano, Samia and Jennifer Pierce. "Personal Narratives, Social Justice, and the Law." *Feminist Legal Studies* 21, no. 3 (2013): 225–239.

BBC Reporter. "Scottish Transgender Reforms Put on Hold." *BBC News*, June 20, 2019. https://www.bbc.co.uk/news/uk-scotland-scotland-politics-48702946.

"Breakthrough: Americans with Disabilities Act Can't Exclude Gender Dysphoria." *Transequality*. Accessed March 20, 2020. https://transequality.org/blog/breakthrough-americans-with-disabilities-act-can-t-exclude-gender-dysphoria.

Broad, Kendal and Mary K. Bloodsworth. "FemiQueer Pedagogies: 'Lesbian/Gay' Studies in Postmodern Women's Studies." *Feminist Teacher* 13, no. 2 (2001): 108–124.

Brooks, Libby. "Scotland to Embed LGBTI Teaching Across Curriculum." *The Guardian*, November 9, 2018. https://www.theguardian.com/education/2018/nov/09/scotland-first-country-approve-lgbti-school-lessons.

Brooks, Libby. "Scottish Government Reaffirms Support for Trans Rights." *The Guardian*, April 18, 2019. https://www.theguardian.com/politics/2019/apr/18/minister-reaffirms-scottish-governments-support-for-trans-rights.

Cabinet Secretary for Social Security and Older People, Shirley-Anne Somerville: Scottish Government, *Statement on Gender Recognition* (Edinburgh: Scottish Government, 2019). https://www.gov.scot/publications/statement-gender-recognition/.

Chang, Tiffany and Barry Chung. "Transgender Microaggressions: Complexity of the Heterogeneity of Transgender Identities." *Journal of LGBT Issues in Counseling* 9, no. 3 (2015): 217–234.

Cipolla, Cyd, Kristina Gupta, David A. Rubin and Angela Willey, eds. *Queer Feminist Science Studies: A Reader*. Washington DC: University of Washington Press, 2017.

Close the Gap, "Scottish Women's Sector Response to the Consultation on Proposed Changes to the Gender Recognition Act" (February, 2018): para 24, available at https://www.closethegap.org.uk/content/resources/Scottish-Womens-Sector-response-to-the-consultation-on-proposed-changes-to-the-Gender-Recognition-Act.pdf.

Cooper, Davina. "'And You Can't Find Me Nowhere': Relocating Identity and Structure Within Equality Jurisprudence." *Journal of Law and Society* 27, no. 2 (2000): 249–272.

Cooper, Davina and Flora Renz. "If the State Decertified Gender, What Might Happen to Its Meaning and Value?" *Journal of Law and Society* 43, no. 4 (2016): 483–505.

Cowan, Sharon. "Sex/Gender Equality: Taking a Break from the Legal to Transform the Social." In *Exploring the Legal in Socio-Legal Studies*, edited by David Cowan and Daniel Wincott, 121–146. London: Palgrave MacMillan, 2015.

Cowan, Sharon, H.G. Giles, Rebecca Hewer, Becky Kaufman, Meryl Kenny, Sean Morris and Katie Nicoll Baines. ""UK Sex and Gender Equality in Law and Policy: A Response to Murray and Hunter Blackburn." *Scottish Affairs* (forthcoming).

Cowan, Sharon, Chloe Kennedy and Vanessa E. Munro, eds. *The Scottish Feminist Judgments Project: (Re)Creating Law from the Outside In*. Oxford: Hart Publishing, 2019.

Cowan, Sharon, Ralph Sandland and Alex Sharpe. "Debate and Dialogue—The Gender Recognition Act 2004." *Social and Legal Studies* 18, no. 2 (2009): 241–263.

Culture, Tourism, Europe and External Affairs Committee. *Stage 1 Report on the Census (Amendment) (Scotland) Bill*. SP Paper 47, 1st Report, 2019 (Session 5). Edinburgh. 2019. https://sp-bpr-en-prod-cdnep.azureedge.net/published/CTEEA/2019/2/7/Stage-1-Report-on-the-Census--Amendment---Scotland--Bill/CTEEAS052019R1.pdf.

Currah, Paisley, Richard Juang and Shannon Price Minter, eds. *Transgender Rights*. Minneapolis: University of Minneapolis Press, 2006.

Davis, Peggy. "Law as Microaggression." *Yale Law Journal* 98, no. 8 (1989): 1559–1577.

Doucet, Andrea and Natasha S Mauthner. "Feminist Methodologies and Epistemologies." In *The Handbook of 21st Century Sociology*, edited by Dennis. L. Peck and Clifton D. Bryant (Thousand Oaks, CA: Sage Publications, 2007).

Dunne, Peter and Tara Hewitt. "Gender Recognition, Self-Determination and Segregated Space." *Oxford Human Rights Hub*, January 16, 2018. https://ohrh.law.ox.ac.uk/gender-recognition-self-determination-and-segregated-space/.

Dworkin, Ronald. *Sovereign Virtue: The Theory and Practice of Equality*. Cambridge: Harvard University Press, 2000.

Dwyer, Angela. "'It's Not Like We're Going to Jump Them': How Transgressing Heteronormativity Shapes Police Interactions with LGBT Young People." *Youth Justice* 11, no. 3 (2011): 203–220.

Ewick, Patricia and Susan Silbey. *The Common Place of Law: Stories from Everyday Life*. Chicago: The University of Chicago Press, 1998.

Fazackerley, Anne. "UK Universities Struggle To Deal With 'Toxic' Trans Rights Row." *The Guardian*, October 30, 2019. Accessed March 25, 2020. https://www.theguardian.com/education/2018/oct/30/uk-universities-struggle-to-deal-with-toxic-trans-rights-row.

Frohard-Dourlent, Hélène, Sarah Dobson, Beth Clark, Marion Doull, and Elizabeth Saewyc. "I Would Have Preferred More Options": Accounting for Non-binary Youth in Health Research. *Nursing Inquiry* 24, no. 1 (2017). https://doi.org/10.1111/nin.12150.

Fusco, Caroline. "Critical Feminist/Queer Methodologies: Deconstructing (Hetero)Normative Inscriptions." In *Qualitative Research on Sport and Physical Culture (Research in the Sociology of Sport, Volume 6)*, edited by Kevin Young and Michael Atkinson, 151–166. Bingley: Emerald Group Publishing Limited, 2012.

Halberstam, Judith. *In a Queer Time and Place: Transgender Bodies, Subcultural Lives*. New York: New York University Press, 2005.

Hale, Jacob. "Suggested Rules for Non-Transsexuals Writing About Transsexuals, Transsexuality, Transsexualism, or Trans_____," Sandy Stone, Last modified November 18, 2009 https://sandystone.com/hale.rules.html.

Halliday, Simon. "After Hegemony: The Varieties of Legal Consciousness Research." *Social & Legal Studies* 28, no. 6 (2019): 859–878.

Halliday, Simon and Bronwen Morgan. "I Fought the Law and the Law Won? Legal Consciousness and the Critical Imagination." *Current Legal Problems* 66, no. 1 (2013): 1–32.

Halliday, Simon, Celia Kitzinger and Jenny Kitzinger. "Law in Everyday Life and Death: A Socio-legal Study of Chronic Disorders of Consciousness." *Legal Studies* 35, no. 1 (2015): 55–74.

Harding, Rosie. *Regulating Sexuality: Legal Consciousness in Lesbian and Gay Lives*. Abingdon: Routledge, 2010.

Harding, Sandra. "Introduction: Is There a Feminist Method?" In *Feminism and Methodology*, edited by Sandra Harding, 1–14. Bloomington: Indiana University Press, 1987.

Harding, Sandra. *Whose Science? Whose Knowledge? Thinking from Women's Lives*. Ithaca, NY: Cornell University Press, 1991.

Health and Social Care Directorate. *Gender Reassignment Protocol.* https://www.sehd.scot.nhs.uk/mels/CEL2012_26.pdf. Edinburgh. Scottish Government, 2012.

Health Performance and Delivery Directorate. *Gender Reassignment Protocol: Interim Guidance.* https://www.ngicns.scot.nhs.uk/wp-content/uploads/2015/07/Gender-Reassignment-Interim-Guidance-2.pdf. Edinburgh. Scottish Government, 2017.

"Help with Legal Costs." Citizens Advice Scotland. Accessed March 20, 2020. https://www.citizensadvice.org.uk/scotland/law-and-courts/legal-system-s/taking-legal-action-s/help-with-legal-costs-s/#Civillegalaid.

Hertogh, Marc. *Nobody's Law: Legal Consciousness and Legal Alienation in Everyday Life.* London: Palgrave MacMillan, 2018.

Hines, Sally. "(Trans)forming Gender: Social Change and Transgender Citizenship." *Sociological Research Online* 12, no. 1 (2007). https://doi.org/10.5153/sro.1469.

Hines, Sally. *Gender Diversity, Recognition and Citizenship: Towards a Politics of Difference*. London: Palgrave MacMillan, 2013.

House of Commons Women and Equalities Committee. *Transgender Equality.* The Stationery Office Limited. London. 2016.

Hull, Kathleen E. "The Cultural Power of Law and the Cultural Enactment of Legality: The Case of Same-Sex Marriage." *Law & Social Inquiry* 28, no. 3 (2003): 629–657.

Justice Directorate. *Gender Recognition Reform (Scotland) Bill: Consultation.* The Scottish Government. Edinburgh. 2019. https://www.gov.scot/publications/gender-recognition-reform-scotland-bill-consultation-scottish-government/.

Kaufman, Karen. "Transgender Voices: How Transgender People Across the Central Belt of Scotland Negotiate Their Identities as Human Beings in the Face of Perceived Disadvantage and Imposed Norms" (Thesis submitted for MRes, University of Glasgow, 2018).

Lamble, Sarah. "Queer Necropolitics and the Expanding Carceral State: Interrogating Sexual Investments in Punishment." *Law and Critique* 24, no. 3 (2013): 229–253.

Lawrence, Matson and Taylor, Yvette. "The UK Government LGBT Action Plan: Discourses of Progress, Enduring Stasis, and LGBTQI+ Lives 'Getting Better'." *Critical Social Policy* 1, no. 22 (2019). https://doi.org/10.1177/0261018319877284.

Lee, Rachel. *The Exquisite Corpse of Asian America: Biopolitics, Biosociality, and Posthuman Ecologies.* New York: NYU Press, 2014.

MacKinnon, Catharine. *Women's Lives, Men's Laws.* Cambridge: Harvard University Press, 2005.

Marshall, Anna-Maria and Scott Barclay. "In Their Own Words: How Ordinary People Construct the Legal World." *Law and Social Inquiry* 28, no. 3 (2003): 617–628.

McNeil, Jay, Louis Bailey, Sonja Ellis, James Morton and Maeve Regan. *Trans Mental Health Study 2012.* https://www.gires.ord.uk/wp-content/uploads/2014/08/trans_mh_study.pdf.

Mezey, Susan. *Transgender Rights: From Obama to Trump*. New York and London: Routledge, 2020.

Mitchell, Hilary. "Entire Edinburgh University LGBT Committee Quit in Dramatic Protest Against 'Anti Trans' Julie Bindel Talk." *Edinburgh Live*, June 6, 2019. Accessed March 24, 2020. https://www.edinburghlive.co.uk/news/edinburgh-news/entire-edinburgh-university-lgbt-committee-16389812.

Morgan, Sylvia. "Constructing Identities, Reclaiming Subjectivities, Reconstructing Selves: An Interpretative Study of Transgender Practices in Scotland." PhD thesis, University of Glasgow, 2017.

Murray, Kath, Lucy Hunter Blackburn and Lisa MacKenzie. "Losing Sight of Women's Rights: The Unregulated Introduction of Gender Self-identification as a Study of Policy Capture in Scotland." *Scottish Affairs* 28, no. 3 (2019): 262–289.

Nagel, Thomas. *Equality and Partiality*. Oxford: Oxford University Press, 1991.

Namaste, Viviane. *Sex Change, Social Change; Reflections on Identity, Institutions and Imperialism*. Toronto: Women's Press, 2005.

Nash, Catherine. "Queer Conversations: Old-time Lesbians, Transmen and the Politics of Queer Research." In *Queer Methods and Methodologies: Intersecting Queer Theories and Social Science Research*, edited by Kath Browne and Catherine J. Nash, 129–142. London: Routledge, 2010.

National Records of Scotland. *Scotland's Census 2021: Sex Question Recommendation Report*. https://www.scotlandscensus.gov.uk/documents/Scotland's%20Census%202021%20-%20%20Sex%20question%20recommendation%20report%20(2).pdf. (Edinburgh, December 2019).

Newsroom Reporter. "Scottish Government Accused of Putting Women in Scottish Prisons at Risk." *The Scotsman*, May 30, 2019. https://www.scotsman.com/news/politics/scottish-government-accused-of-putting-women-in-scottish-prisons-at-risk-1-4937495.

Nussbaum, Martha. *Sex and Social Justice*. Oxford: Oxford University Press, 1999.

Plummer, Ken. *Telling Sexual Stories*. London: Routledge, 1995.

"Research and Data Needs." National Center for Transgender Equality. Accessed March 20, 2020. https://transequality.org/issues/research-data-needs.

"Review of the Gender Recognition Act 2004." Scottish Government. Accessed March 24, 2020. https://www2.gov.scot/Topics/Justice/law/17867/gender-recognition-review.

Richards, Zach. (2018). *Book Review: Nobody's Law: Legal Consciousness and Legal Alienation in Everyday Life*. Available at: https://ukaji.org/2018/10/12/book-review-nobodys-law-legal-consciousness-and-legal-alienation-in-everyday-life/.

Richardson, Diane. *Sexuality and Citizenship*. Cambridge: Polity Press, 2017.

"Scotland Rated Best Country in Europe for LGBTI Legal Equality." Equality Network. Last modified May 10, 2015. https://www.equality-network.org/scotland-rated-best-country-in-europe-for-lgbti-legal-equality/.

"Scotland Slips Down International LGBT Rankings." Pink Saltire. Last modified May 13, 2019. https://pinksaltire.com/2019/05/13/scotland-slips-down-international-lgbt-rankings/.

Scottish Prison Service. *Gender Identity and Gender Reassignment Policy for Those in our Custody* (Edinburgh: Scottish Prison Service, 2014).

Scottish Public Health Network. *Health Care Needs Assessment of Gender Identity Services,* by Rachel Thomson, Jessica Baker and Julie Arnot. https://www.scotphn.net/wp-content/uploads/2017/04/2018_05_16-HCNA-of-Gender-Identity-Services.pdf. Glasgow: SPHN, 2017.

Sen, Amartya. *Inequality Re-examined*. Oxford: Oxford University Press, 1992.

Serrano, Julia. *Outspoken: A Decade of Transgender Activism and Trans Feminism.* Oakland: Switch Hitter Press, 2016.

Sharpe, Alex. *Sexual Intimacy and Gender Identity 'Fraud'*. London: Routledge, 2018.

Sharpe, Alex. "Will Gender Self-Declaration Undermine Women's Rights and Lead to an Increase in Harms?" *Modern Law Review* 83, no 3 (2020): 539–557.

Silbey, Susan. "Legal Culture and Consciousness." In *International Encyclopedia of the Social and Behavioral Sciences,* edited by Neil Smelser and Paul Baltes, 8623–8629. Amsterdam: Elsevier Science, 2001.

Silbey, Susan. "After Legal Consciousness." *Annual Review of Law and Social Science* 1 (2005): 323–368.

Smart, Carol. *Feminism and the Power of Law.* London: Routledge, 1989.

Somerville, Shirley-Anne. Cabinet Secretary for Social Security and Older People: Scottish Government, *Statement on Gender Recognition* (Edinburgh: Scottish Government, 2019). https://www.gov.scot/publications/statement-gender-recognition/.

Spade, Dean. *Normal Life.* Brooklyn: South End Press, 2011.

Steinmetz, Katy. "Being Transgender Is Not a Mental Disorder: Study." *Time,* July 26, 2016. https://time.com/4424589/being-transgender-is-not-a-mental-disorder-study.

Stevens, Matt. "Transgender Student in Bathroom Dispute Wins Court Ruling." *New York Times,* May 22, 2018. https://www.nytimes.com/2018/05/22/us/gavin-grimm-transgender-bathrooms.html.

Stonewall. 2017. LGBT in *Scotland: Hate Crime and Discrimination.* Available at http://www.stonewallscotland.org.uk//scotlandcomeoutforLGBT/lgbt-in-britain/hate-crime.

Sue, Derald Wing. *Microaggressions in Everyday Life: Race, Gender and Sexual Orientation.* Hoboken: John Wiley and Sons, 2010.

"Suggested Rules for Non-Transsexuals Writing About Transsexuals, Transsexuality, Transsexualism, or Trans_____," Sandy Stone, Last modified November 18, 2009. https://sandystone.com/hale.rules.html.

Tamanaha, Brian. "A Non-Essentialist Version of Legal Pluralism." *Journal of Law and Society* 27, no. 2 (2000): 296–321.

The Future of Legal Gender: A Critical Law Reform Project. Accessed March 25, 2020. https://futureoflegalgender.kcl.ac.uk/.

Thomson, Alistair. "Memory and Remembering in Oral History." In *The Oxford Handbook of Oral History*, edited by Donald A. Ritchie, 77–95. Oxford: Oxford University Press, 2010.

"Trans Troops Return to Era of 'Don't Ask, Don't Tell' as Trump Policy Takes Effect." *The Guardian*, April 13, 2019. https://www.theguardian.com/us-news/2019/apr/12/transgender-ban-military-trump-take-effect-dont-ask-dont-tell.

Garland, Fae and Mitchell Travis. "Legislating Intersex Equality: Building the Resilience of Intersex People Through Law." *Legal Studies* 38, no. 4 (2018): 587–606.

Valentine, Vic. "Self-declaration Would Bring Britain into Line with International Best Practice." *The Economist*, July 3, 2018. https://www.economist.com/open-future/2018/07/03/self-declaration-would-bring-britain-into-line-with-internati onal-best-practice.

Vigo, Julian. "How to Stage a Study: The Transgender Lobby in British Academia." *Medium.* July 30, 2019. Accessed March 24. 2020. https://medium.com/@jul ian.vigo/how-to-stage-a-study-the-transgender-lobby-in-british-academia-f196f4 f686f1.

Warner, Daniel. "Towards a Queer Research Methodology." *Qualitative Research in Psychology* 1, no. 4 (2004): 321–337.

Whittle, Stephen. "The Trans-Cyberian Mail Way." *Social and Legal Studies* 7, no. 3 (1998): 389–408.

Whittle, Stephen, "The Opposite of Sex Is Politics—The UK Gender Recognition Act and Why It Is Not Perfect, Just Like You and Me." *Journal of Gender Studies* 15, no. 3 (2006).

Whittle, Stephen and Fiona Simkiss. "A Perfect Storm: The UK Government's Failed Consultation on the Gender Recognition Act 2004." In *Research Handbook on Gender, Sexuality and the Law*, edited by Chris Ashford and Alexander Maine, 211–231. Cheltenham: Edward Elgar 2020.

Whittle, Stephen, Lewis Turner, and Maryam Al-Alami. *Engendered Penalties: Transgender and Transsexual People's Experiences of Inequality and Discrimination* (A Research Project and Report Commissioned by the Equalities Review, 2007). http://www.pfc.org.uk/files/EngenderedPenalties.pdf.

Young, Iris Marion. *Justice and the Politics of Difference*. Princeton: Princeton University Press, 1990.

Coming Inside and/or Playing Outside: The (Legal) Futures of LGBTIQ Rights in the United Kingdom

Senthorun Raj and Peter Dunne

1 Introduction

This collection is about making space for queer outsiders, both in UK LGBTIQ law reforms and activist-scholarly discussions of those reforms. To do this, the chapters that we have assembled for this project take the organising concepts of *queer*, *law*, *inside* and *outside*, and subject them to critical scrutiny. We do not seek to romanticise the terms of queering law or remaining outside the scope of legal recognition, nor are we attempting to reject the possibilities of law reform or the value that comes from being inside the space of legal recognition. *The Queer Outside in Law* does not resolve the tensions of being queer and inside/outside law. As we noted in the Introduction, citing the work of queer scholars Cynthia Weber, Eve Sedgwick and Mariana Valverde, the chapters in this collection conceptualise queerness and legality across multiple registers: queerness captures gender and sexual

S. Raj
Keele University, Newcastle-Under-Lyme, UK
e-mail: s.raj@keele.ac.uk

P. Dunne (✉)
University of Bristol, Bristol, UK
e-mail: pd17563@bristol.ac.uk

S. Raj and P. Dunne (eds.), *The Queer Outside in Law*, Palgrave Socio-Legal Studies,
https://doi.org/10.1007/978-3-030-48830-7_9

dissidence, both inside and/or outside states, and it does not signify dissident genders and sexualities monolithically across different sites of law.[1] This heterogeneity is how we come to assess LGBTIQ[2] law reform.

In concluding the collection, we take inspiration from Davina Cooper, who invites us to reconceptualise the State around notions of responsibility and heterogeneity. Cooper notes that pluralising conceptions of "the state" (as a condition of governance) and foregrounding "playing" (as a provisional and pleasurable strategy of governance) can enable us to realise progressive social agendas.[3] This lets us—as scholars, activists, and advocates—grasp how diffuse legal practices, functioning at different scales, shape state interactions with (and between) subjugated communities.[4]

What is especially timely for us about Cooper's theoretical intervention is how reimagining the State, as an affective set of relations that make public governance possible, enables us to think more carefully about what different modalities of law (legislation, judicial review, street-level decision-making) are doing in the process of recognising, protecting and/or punishing LGBTIQ people in the United Kingdom. In doing so, we can begin to explore how we might play around with those modalities at grassroots levels to support the lives of those (queer outsiders) who are cast beyond the remit of legal recognition and/or denied social affirmation. Playing, according to Cooper, is a "creative" and "open-ended" strategy that does not seek to make possessive claims about subjects (people, legal issues, state institutions) nor does it require coercive legal sanctions (criminal penalties, economic sanctions).[5]

In this concluding chapter, we take up Cooper's invitation to "play" with(in) the state by exploring four case studies—each of which is at a different stage of development in the United Kingdom. These contemporary examples have been chosen to illustrate how we (as LGBTIQ people) might come inside for rights while also playing outside the law as *queer outsiders*. The four case studies focus on: (I) self-determination as a means of obtaining legal gender recognition (currently proposed reform); (II) intersex

[1]Cynthia Weber, *Queer International Relations* (Oxford: Oxford University Press, 2016), 16; Eve Sedgwick, *Tendencies* (Durham: Duke University Press, 1993), 8; Mariana Valverde, *Chronotopes of Law: Jurisdiction, Scale and Governance* (Abingdon: Routledge, 2015), 66.

[2]In this chapter, we alternate between using "LGBTIQ", "LGBTI", "LGBT", and "LGB" to be precise (without being tokenistic) about the content of statutes, cases, policies, and submissions being discussed.

[3]Davina Cooper, *Feeling Like a State: Desire, Denial, and the Recasting of Authority* (Durham: Duke University Press, 2019), 24–25.

[4]Ibid., 55.

[5]Ibid., 116.

experiences with medicine and rights (subject of a recent Government Equalities Office Call for Information); (III) the adjudication of LGBT asylum claims (under Home Office review); and (IV) LGBT-inclusive relationships and sex education (RSE) in schools (policy to be implemented in England no later than the start of the summer term 2021).[6] Taken together, the case studies reflect the myriad legal, cultural and political challenges which confront queer populations in modern UK society. They interrogate key questions posed by the various chapters in this edited collection and invite the reader to think more broadly about the complexities of LGBTIQ law reform. In exploring these four case studies, we are: (a) drawing both from and together the core themes and insights identified by those who have contributed to this book; and (b) seeking to locate current and proposed LGBTIQ laws within existing discourses on rights, identity and effective social movement building. Ultimately, we address our discussions and concluding remarks to three fundamental questions that we hope will be the subject of further socio-legal work: (I) why do LGBTIQ people seek to come inside law? (II) what has happened to LGBTIQ people who have come inside the law? and (III) what can be gained from staying or playing outside?

2 Case Study I. Defining Identity: Autonomy, Control and the Gender Recognition Act 2004

> ...it is humiliating to have your gender assessed by someone else. You are the only person who can come to that realisation, not a panel...I do not feel it necessary to have my gender looked at by a group of people.[7]

Since April 2005, individuals in the United Kingdom have been able to access formal acknowledgement of their self-identified gender.[8] Under the terms of

---

[6] Department of Education, *Communication to Schools on the Implementation of Relationships Education, Relationships and Sex and Health Education*, 1 (June 2020).

[7] House of Commons Select Committee on Women and Equalities, *Transgender Equality* (London: The Stationery Office Limited, 2016), [41] per Ashley Reed.

[8] See generally: Peter Dunne, "Ten Years of Gender Recognition in the United Kingdom: Still a 'Model for Reform'?", *Public Law* (October 2015): 530; Alex Sharpe, "Endless Sex: The Gender Recognition Act 2004 and the Persistence of a Legal Category", *Feminist Legal Studies* 15, no 1 (2007): 57; Stephen Whittle, "The Opposite of Sex Is Politics—The UK Gender Recognition Act and Why It Is Not Perfect, Just Like You and Me: FORUM", *Journal of Gender Studies* 15. no 3 (2006): 267; Emily Grabham, "Governing Permanence: Trans Subjects, Time, and the Gender

the Gender Recognition Act 2004 (GRA 2004), where an applicant successfully obtains a Gender Recognition Certificate (GRC), that "person's gender becomes for all purposes the acquired[9] gender (so that, if the acquired gender is the male gender, the person's [legal] sex becomes that of a man and, if it is the female gender, the person's [legal] sex becomes that of a woman)."[10] As Flora Renz notes in Chapter 6, the GRA 2004 was a landmark moment for human rights—both in this jurisdiction and across Europe. In England and Wales, the legislation represented an explicit, statutory repudiation of the (in)famous *Corbett*[11] case law[12]—under which trans persons had been denied validation of their lived identity. For Europe, and farther afield, the Gender Recognition Act 2004 stood as a key point of departure—a national framework, which showed that self-identified gender could be acknowledged without requiring an applicant to undertake a process of sterilisation.[13]

In the years preceding the GRA 2004, there had been an increasing domestic campaign advocating for gender recognition rights in the United

---

Recognition Act", *Social & Legal Studies* 19, no 1 (2010): 107; Ralph Sandland, "Feminism and the Gender Recognition Act 2004," *Feminist Legal Studies* 13, no 1 (2005): 43.

[9]Section 1(2) of the Gender Recognition Act 2004 states that, "[i]n this Act 'the acquired gender', in relation to a person by whom an application under subsection (1) is or has been made, means—(a) in the case of an application under paragraph (a) of that subsection, the gender in which the person is living, or (b) in the case of an application under paragraph (b) of that subsection, the gender to which the person has changed under the law of the country or territory concerned." Thus, when referring to a person's self-identified gender (as opposed to their Birth Assigned Gender), the GRA 2004 specifically speaks of a person's "acquired gender". It is important to acknowledge that there is no universally preferred terminology when referring to gender, and that many individuals may find the idea of an "acquired" gender (i.e. an identity which the Gender Recognition Act 2004 creates, but which has no prior existence) as both offensive and as inconsistent with their lived experience.

[10]*Gender Recognition Act 2004*, s. 9(1). It is important to note that sub-sections 9(2) and (3) qualify the general right set out in s. 9(1) of the GRA 2004. Section 9(2) provides that "[s]ubsection (1) does not affect things done, or events occurring, before the certificate is issued; but it does operate for the interpretation of enactments passed, and instruments and other documents made, before the certificate is issued (as well as those passed or made afterwards)." Furthermore, according to s. 9(3), "[s]ubsection (1) is subject to provision made by this Act or any other enactment or any subordinate legislation."

[11]*Corbett v Corbett (Otherwise Ashley) (No 1)* [1971] 2 All ER 33.

[12]See Sharon Cowan, "That Woman Is a Woman!" the Case of Bellinger v. Bellinger and the Mysterious (Dis) appearance of Sex: Bellinger v. Bellinger [2003] 2 All ER 593; [2003] FCR 1; [2003] 2 WLR 1174; [2003] UKHL 21", *Feminist Legal Studies* 12, no 1 (2004): 79; Anne Barlow, "A New Approach to Transsexualism and a Missed Opportunity?", *Child and Family Law Quarterly* 13, no 2 (2001): 225; Stephen Gilmore, "Bellinger v Bellinger—Not Quite Between the Ears and Between the Legs—Transsexualism and Marriage in the Lords", *Child and Family Law Quarterly* 15, no 3 (2003): 295.

[13]For a comparative discussion of the legal gender recognition laws post-2004, see *The Legal Status of Transsexual and Transgender Persons*, edited by Jens M. Scherpe (Cambridge: Intersentia, 2015). In particular, see generally: Jens M. Scherpe and Peter Dunne, "The Legal Recognition of Transsexual and Transgender Persons—Comparative Analysis and Recommendations": 615.

Kingdom.[14] Although scholars, such as Gonzalez-Salzberg have noted the queer potential of trans populations playing outside the realms of formal acknowledgement—particularly where, as in the United Kingdom, individuals often had diverging genders on multiple, state-issued documents[15]—a strong catalyst for change emerged with the historic judgment of the European Court of Human Rights (ECtHR) in *Goodwin v United Kingdom.*[16] In its decision, the ECtHR found that withholding official validation of self-identified gender (at least for individuals who had undertaken a process of surgical transition) was incompatible with art. 8 of the European Convention of Human Rights (ECHR).[17]

The *Goodwin* litigation brought into sharp relief the many reasons why trans and non-binary individuals might seek acknowledgement of their lived identity and why an existence "outside" the sphere of legal recognition can be experienced as a dignitary injury. The absence of legal validation means that, as in *Goodwin*, trans and non-binary individuals are frequently denied key benefits (e.g. social advantages, social protection, etc.).[18] Christine Goodwin, for example, could not enter into a marriage with a male partner because English law deemed her to be legally male, and it did not yet sanction same-sex marital unions.[19]

Refusing to acknowledge self-identified gender may also expose individuals both to allegations of fraud and to heightened levels of abuse. Where trans and non-binary persons lack legal recognition, which is congruent with

---

[14]Evelyn Ellis, "The Gender Recognition Bill", *Public Law* (Autumn 2004): 467, who notes, when speaking about the GRA 2004 (when in Bill form) [at 467–468] that "[t]he Bill, which had Government backing, was introduced into the House of Lords. It received the approval of the Commons at a Second Reading in February this year, and completed its Commons Committee stage in mid-March. It is a detailed and carefully crafted instrument *whose subject-matter was first considered by an Interdepartmental Working Group in 1999*" (emphasis added). See, in particular, the important campaigning work of the organization, Press for Change, during the 1990s and the early 2000s.

[15]Damian A. Gonzalez-Salzberg, "The Accepted Transsexual and the Absent Transgender: A Queer Reading of the Regulation of Sex/Gender by the European Court of Human Rights", *American University International Law Review* 29, no 4 (2013): 797, 810–811, 814.

[16][2002] 35 EHRR 18.

[17]Ibid., [93].

[18]In *Goodwin,* the European Court of Human Rights observed, [76], that withholding gender recognition "has had, and continues to have, effects on the applicant's life where sex is of legal relevance and distinctions are made between men and women, as, inter alia, in the area of pensions and retirement age. For example, the applicant must continue to pay national insurance contributions until the age of 65 due to her legal status as male. However as she is employed in her gender identity as a female, she has had to obtain an exemption certificate which allows the payments from her employer to stop while she continues to make such payments herself. Though the Government submitted that this made due allowance for the difficulties of her position, the Court would note that she nonetheless has to make use of a special procedure that might in itself call attention to her status."

[19]Ibid., [94]–[104].

their public expression of identity, they are frequently subject to social and institutional gender questioning, including accusations that they are misrepresenting their identity for self-gain.[20] This lived reality can substantially limit trans and non-binary access to basic services, such as transportation, education, healthcare and the postal system.[21] In addition, these conflicts between public expressions of gender and legal status may also increase risks of discrimination and violence. Where incongruence exists between self-identified and legal gender, there is a greater likelihood that an individual's trans history will be publicly revealed and that the person may experience the consequences of transphobia.[22]

Finally, for many individuals—although acutely aware of the practical impact of withholding formal acknowledgement—their primary focus in advocating for gender recognition is the symbolic injury, which they experience as a result of legal exclusion. Where jurisdictions, such as the United Kingdom, refuse to validate gender, this implicitly undermines trans identities and legitimatises unequal treatment motivated by disrespect for trans personhood.[23] Of course, subjecting such argument to a queer lens of analysis, one might question, as Renz suggests, why the value and legitimacy of gender should depend either upon state approval or on an individual coming within prescribed narratives of acceptable gender. There is a compelling argument that, by seeking to come inside inherently defective structures of identity regulation, queer individuals will only reinforce the very gender institutionalism, which is the source of their oppression. From this perspective, there may be greater merit in queers choosing to play outside the scope of legal recognition, working creatively to radically reshape how law, gender and the State interact. Yet, what symbolism-focused concerns do reveal is that, within a context where social and legal privilege *are* still contingent

---

[20] Michael Silverman, "Issues in Access to Healthcare by Transgender Individuals", *Women's Rights Law Reporter* 30, no 2 (2009): 347, 349; Jordan Alkan, "Promoting an Integrated Approach to Ensuring Access to Gender Incongruent Health Care", *Berkeley Journal of Gender, Law and Justice* 31, no 1 (2016): 1, 33.

[21] *Report of the Independent Expert on Protection Against Violence and Discrimination Based on Sexual Orientation and Gender Identity* (May 12, 2018) UN Doc No. A/HRC/38/43, [43], where the Independent Expert observes that "[i]naccurate or inadequate identity documents may result in greater levels of violence and extortion, *exclusion from school and the official labour market, housing, health…and access to other social services, and in being able to cross borders*" (emphasis added).

[22] Ibid., [43], where the Independent Expert notes that "[t]rans persons are particularly vulnerable to human rights violations when their name and sex details in official documents do not match their gender identity or expression."

[23] In *Goodwin*, Christine Goodwin argued that "[t]he lack of legal recognition of her changed gender had been the cause of numerous discriminatory and humiliating experiences in her everyday life", [2002] 35 EHRR 18, [60].

upon status, many trans and non-binary individuals experience both tangible and intangible disadvantage when excluded from official acknowledgement.

The Gender Recognition Act 2004 was an attempt to address the problems (both practical and symbolic) created by the legal invisibility of trans populations in the United Kingdom. It established a framework for acknowledging trans identities—centred around core supervisory pillars, including the required invention of medical officers, the oversight of a Gender Recognition Panel and an obligation to live in one's "acquired" gender for two years before applying.[24] Although the GRA 2004 was broadly welcomed as a milestone in domestic human rights protections, it was also subject to critique.[25] In 2016, the House of Commons Select Committee on Women and Equalities recommended fundamental changes to the existing statutory regime,[26] and the Government Equalities Office subsequently issued a public consultation on reform (although the Minister for Women and Equalities, Liz Truss MP, has recently confirmed that no substantive amendments will be made to the requirements for a GRC).[27] In 2019, the Scottish Government went one step further, seeking public comments on a draft amending bill, the Gender Recognition Reform (Scotland) Bill.[28]

There are a number of objections which have been raised against the Gender Recognition Act 2004. While the legislation was striking for the absence of a sterilisation requirement (common in other European laws at the time), it remains a fundamentally medicalised framework. In order to obtain a Gender Recognition Certificate, applicants must show that they have, or have had, a diagnosis of "gender dysphoria"—requiring verification from at least two medical practitioners or psychologists.[29] This "diagnosis requirement", as it has come to be known, is strongly opposed by many trans individuals and their allies.[30] Mandating a diagnosis assumes that all trans individuals see their gender identity in medical terms[31] and that all applicants for gender recognition will feel distress related to their internal experience of

[24] *Gender Recognition Act 2004,* s. 2(1).

[25] Dunne, "Ten Years of Gender Recognition"; Alex Sharpe, "Gender Recognition in the UK: A Great Leap Forward", *Social & Legal Studies* 18, no 2 (2009): 241, 244–245.

[26] Select Committee on Women and Equalities, *Transgender Equality,* [44]–[45], [70]–[71].

[27] "Reform of the Gender Recognition Act 2004", accessed March 29, 2020, https://www.gov.uk/government/consultations/reform-of-the-gender-recognition-act-2004.

[28] "Gender Recognition Reform (Scotland) Bill: Consultation", accessed March 29, 2020, https://www.gov.scot/publications/gender-recognition-reform-scotland-bill-consultation-scottish-government/.

[29] *Gender Recognition Act 2004*, s. 2(1) and s. 3.

[30] The House of Commons Select Committee on Women and Equalities observed that "[t]he current process of applying for a GRC was described to us as 'bureaucratic', 'expensive' and 'humiliating'. Witnesses told us that it required the collection and submission of substantial quantities of evidence of a type which ought to have no bearing on the granting of gender recognition." Select Committee on Women and Equalities, *Transgender Equality*, [33].

[31] This is a general phenomenon that many scholars, across jurisdictions, have noted—in relation to physical and mental health gender affirmative care. See e.g. Sana Loue, "Transsexualism in Medicolegal

gender. This is not only untrue for many applicants (who may be comfortable with their gender identity and, thus, possibly excluded from a diagnosis of gender dysphoria); it also reproduces an historic trope that trans identities are pathological.[32] Rather than upholding a core human right, access to a Gender Recognition Certificate would be seen as merely one element in a wider protocol for "curing" trans populations.[33] While seeking to avoid ableist norms, which frame mental health as inevitably stigmatised,[34] linking the GRA 2004 to requirements of diagnosis encourages cultural perceptions of trans individuals as confused, incapable and needing protection.

The current structures of the Gender Recognition Act 2004 are also highly exclusionary—failing to acknowledge (either explicitly or implicitly) core demographics.[35] In order to come within the statutory framework, an applicant must have achieved the age of majority.[36] At present, it is not possible for children or adolescents, under 18 years, to apply for a Gender Recognition Certificate. In recent times, the status, and appropriate response to, trans and non-binary youth, both in law and in medicine, has become a source of political, media and social debate.[37] Among those who oppose affirmative interventions,[38] there is concern that trans youth are insufficiently mature to

Limine: An Examination and a Proposal for Change", *Journal of Psychiatry and Law* 24, no 1 (1996): 27, 34; Dean Spade, "Documenting Gender", *Hastings Law Journal* 59 (2007): 731, 756.

[32]Scherpe and Dunne, "The Legal Recognition of Transsexual and Transgender Persons", 653–654. Pieter Canoot writes that it is "striking that the Court continues to allow the requirement of providing evidence of the existence of the 'syndrome of transsexuality', sex reassignment therapy, and the possibility for the State to order the performance of a medical expert examination, considering its recognition that the psycho-pathologisation of gender identity reinforces stigmatization of trans* persons", see Pieter Canoot, "The pathologisation of Trans* Persons in the ECtHR's Case Law on Legal Gender Recognition", *Netherlands Quarterly of Human Rights* 37, no 1 (2019): 14, 23.

[33]Ibid.

[34]Dean Spade, "Resisting Medicine, Re/modelling Gender", *Berkeley Women's Law Journal* 18 (2003): 15, 34.

[35]Select Committee on Women and Equalities, *Transgender Equality*, [31] and [64]–[71].

[36]*Gender Recognition Act 2004*, s. 1(1). See Peter Dunne, "Transgender Children and the Law", *Family Law* 47 (January 2017): 123.

[37]Janice Turner, "Cult of Gender Identity Is Harming Children", *The Sunday Times*, September 21, 2019, https://www.thetimes.co.uk/article/cult-of-gender-identity-is-harming-children-pjvbkjzxq; Leyla Sanai, "The Danger of Letting Children Transition Too Early", *The Spectator*, May 13, 2019, https://www.spectator.co.uk/article/the-danger-of-letting-children-transition-gender-too-early; Vic Parsons, "Trans Kids Are as Sure of Their Gender as cis Kids at a Young Age, According to Science", *Pink News*, December 27, 2019, https://www.pinknews.co.uk/2019/12/27/transgender-children-study-gender-identity-cis-children-washington-university/; Julian Norman, "'Shifting Sands' Six Legal Views on the Transgender Debate", *The Guardian*, October 19, 2018, https://www.theguardian.com/society/2018/oct/19/gender-recognition-act-reforms-six-legal-views-transgender-debate.

[38]See e.g. Heather Brunskell-Evans, "The Medico-Legal 'Making' of the Transgender Child", *Medical Law Review* 27, no 4 (2019): 640.

understand the full complexity of their identity,[39] and there are increasing claims that patriarchal social norms pressure young cisgender girls to transition.[40] Opposition to trans affirmation has manifested itself in high-profile campaigns to maintain age restrictions in the GRA 2004[41] and a judicial review seeking to limit access to reversible, puberty blocking medication.[42]

Much of the disagreement surrounding trans and non-binary youth stems from a comparative lack of medical and social research. There are legitimate questions as to whether young individuals, who were previously identified as trans, ultimately persist with that identification into adulthood.[43] Yet, there are equally question marks relating to the present data on persistence/desistence,[44] and an increasing body of scholarship indicates the

[39] Keira Bell, who is acting as an applicant in a judicial review of the gender affirmative care protocols adopted by the NHS Gender Identity Development Service (Gids), located within the Tavistock and Portman NHS Trust, states that: "I have become a claimant in this case because I do not believe that children and young people can consent to the use of powerful and experimental hormone drugs like I did. I believe that the current affirmative system put in place by the Tavistock is inadequate as it does not allow for exploration of these gender dysphoric feelings nor does it seek to find the underlying causes of this condition. Hormone changing drugs and surgery does not work for everyone and it certainly should not be offered to someone under the age of 18 when they are emotionally and mentally vulnerable. The treatment urgently needs to change so that it does not put young people, like me, on a torturous and unnecessary path that is permanent and life changing." Mrs A, who is also an applicant in the judicial review, states: "I have deep concerns that the current clinical approach at GIDS means that my daughter will be subjected to an experimental treatment path that is not adequately regulated, where there are insufficient safeguards, where her autism will not be properly accounted for and where no-one (let alone my daughter) understands the risks and therefore cannot ensure informed consent is obtained." See "Legal Case to Protect Children from Experimental Medical Treatment", *Crowd Justice*, accessed March 29, 2020, https://www.crowdjustice.com/case/protect-children/.

[40] Emma Hartley, "Why Do So Many Teenage Girls Want to Change Gender?", *Prospect*, March 3, 2020, https://www.prospectmagazine.co.uk/magazine/tavistock-transgender-transition-teenage-girls-female-to-male.

[41] For example, Transgender Trend is a UK-based organisation, which has recently emerged as an opponent of reforms to the GRA 2004. Here is their recent submission on the Gender Recognition Reform (Scotland) Bill; Transgender Trend, "Transgender Trend Submission to the Gender Recognition Reform (Scotland) Bill Consultation", accessed March 29, 2020, https://www.transgendertrend.com/transgender-trend-submission-gender-recognition-reform-scotland-bill/.

[42] *R(ota) Mrs A, and Sue Evans v. Tavistock and Portman NHS Foundation Trust* (due for full hearing in late 2020).

[43] Herbert J. Bonifacio and Stephen M. Rosenthal, "Gender Variance and Dysphoria in Children and Adolescents", *Paediatric Clinics of North America* 62, no 4 (2015): 1001, 1004; Stephen Rosenthal, "Approach to the Patient: Transgender Youth: Endocrine Considerations", *The Journal of Clinical Endocrinology and Metabolism* 99, no 12 (2014): 4379, 4384.

[44] Kristina Olson, "Prepubescent Transgender Children: What We Know and What We Do Not Know", *Journal of the American Academy of Child and Adolescent Psychiatry* 55, no 3 (2016): 155, 155; "Statement on Gender Affirmative Approach to Care from the Paediatric Endocrine Society Special Interest Group on Transgender Health", accessed March 29, 2020, https://www.pedsendo.org/members/members_only/PDF/TG_SIG_Position%20Statement_10_20_16.pdf; Randall D. Ehrbar et al., "Clinician Judgment in the Diagnosis of Gender Identity Disorder in Children", *Journal of Sex and Marital Therapy* 34(5) (2008): 385, 388; Brynn Tannehill, "The End of the Desistence Myth",

benefits of affirmation.[45] Furthermore, it is also unclear where one can locate the voice of transgender children and adolescents within these ongoing political and social discussions. If a queer approach to law is one, which centres lived or subjective experiences, is it not troubling that contemporary dialogue on these issues, particularly arguments which oppose positive interventions, frequently omit the perspectives of trans and non-binary youth?

A preferable approach would be to adopt a case-by-case analysis, centred on the particular needs and development of individual children.[46] While legal gender recognition will not be appropriate for many persons under 18 years, the law must be responsive to, and accommodate, those children for whom a GRC would be beneficial. A queer lens on gender recognition would also, as Sharon Cowan encourages in Chapter 8, accurately disaggregate the various modes of transition which individuals can choose—understanding that different factors are relevant where a minor considers medical and legal transition pathways, and acknowledging that conflating these separate choices obstructs, rather than promotes, the welfare of the child.

The Gender Recognition Act 2004 also excludes non-binary individuals. Section 1 of the GRA 2004 speaks of a person of "either" gender who has been "living in the other gender". The current statutory framework clearly envisages only requests where an applicant, who is either male or female, wishes to legally transition to another binary gender. For those who do not fit within traditional gender classifications, and who do not self-identify as either "man" or "woman", the GRA 2004 fails to accommodate their lived experiences, nor are there other identity documents (e.g. passport, etc.)[47] which would accurately reflect their internal understanding of gender.

The current UK position largely conforms to peer gender recognition structures across Europe.[48] Although, as Renz observes, there are a small number of European jurisdictions, such as Germany and Austria, which provide for alternative legal gender options, these countries largely restrict

Huffington Post, January 1 2016, http://www.huffingtonpost.com/brynn-tannehill/the-end-of-the-desistance_b_8903690.html.

[45] Annelou de Vries et al., "Young Adult Psychological Outcome After Puberty Suppression and Gender Reassignment", *Paediatrics* 134, no 4 (2014): 696; Kristina R. Olson et al., "Mental Health of Transgender Children Who Are Supported in Their Identities", *Paediatrics* 137, no 3 (2016): 1.

[46] Such an approach appears to be possible in a number of other European jurisdictions, such as Malta, Norway and Ireland (although Ireland and Norway do have lower age limits under which a child cannot be formally acknowledged in their self-identified gender), see Peter Dunne and Marjolein van den Brink, *Trans and Intersex Equality Rights in Europe: A Comparative Analysis* (Luxembourg: Publications Office of the European Union, 2018), 65–66.

[47] *Elan-Cane v Home Secretary* [2020] EWCA Civ 363 (currently on appeal to the United Kingdom Supreme Court).

[48] Dunne and van den Brink, *Trans and Intersex Equality Rights in Europe,* 66–67.

non-binary recognition to persons who experience intersex variance.[49] In their contribution, Fae Garland and Mitchell Travis critique such restrictions—observing how they mispresent intersex experiences of gender, while simultaneously excluding vast numbers of non-binary individuals.

Although the Gender Recognition Act 2004 mirrors European practice, it is inconsistent with recent results from the Government's National LGBT Survey—which reveal that a growing number of queer persons in the UK self-identify beyond male or female.[50] For these individuals, the GRA 2004 presents a stark decision: continue to inhabit an incorrect identity status involuntarily assigned to you at birth, or embrace an alternative gender classification, which inaccurately reflects your internal understanding of self. As the facts in *R (on the application of Christie Elan-Cane) and Secretary of State for the Home Department* lay bare, such impossible choices place significant practical and emotional burdens upon non-binary populations.[51] A queer approach to law reform would acknowledge this dignitary injury and, even within the constraints of a binary legal system, seek to validate the multiple ways in which individuals experience gender, even if through alternative recognition procedures[52] (such as the issue of "X" passports, as requested in the *Elan-Cane* litigation[53]).

In light of the current defects within the Gender Recognition Act 2004, what might a queer reform agenda look like for this area of law? Even if we choose to validate state regulation of gender identity, are there ways that we, as queers, can playfully work, inside the gender recognition frameworks, to redesign how such regulation operates?

In an increasing number of European jurisdictions, including Ireland, Portugal and Belgium, legislatures are adopting affirmation models grounded

[49]Peter Dunne, "Acknowledging or Erasing Intersex Experiences? Gender 'Diversity' in German Law", *Northern Ireland Legal Quarterly* 70, no 1 (2019): 163.

[50]Government Equalities Office, *National LGBT Survey: Summary Report (June 2018)*, 8, accessed March 29, 2020, https://assets.publishing.service.gov.uk/government/uploads/system/uploads/attachment_data/file/722314/GEO-LGBT-Survey-Report.pdf.

[51]*Elan-Cane v Home Secretary* [2020] EWCA Civ 363 (Court of Appeal Decision); [2018] EWHC 1530 (Admin) (High Court Decision).

[52]See Select Committee on Women and Equalities, *Transgender Equality*, where the Committee recommends, at [299], that "[t]he Government should be moving towards 'non-gendering' official records as a general principle and only recording gender where it is a relevant piece of information. Where information on gender is required for monitoring purposes, it should be recorded separately from individuals' personal records and only subject to the consent of those concerned."

[53]The option of an "X" passport is available in Malta, see Peter Dunne and Stephen Clark, *Comparative Legal Overview of Gender Recognition Laws across the Commonwealth* (London: Equality and Justice Alliance, 2019), 40.

in the principle of self-determination.[54] This means that individuals are entitled to access official validation based upon their own personal experience of gender rather than on compliance with externally imposed pre-conditions.[55] For many trans individuals, self-determination is a preferable system of recognition, acknowledging that applicants themselves, rather than state-appointed third parties, should be the arbiter of personal gender. While many trans and non-binary persons are anxious that they should still have appropriate access to medical transition pathways,[56] self-determination does remove the obligation to comply with the stigmatising, often inaccessible diagnosis requirements, which some believe should not form part of legal structures.

In this jurisdiction, both the English and Scottish governments have mooted the possible introduction of self-determination.[57] However, these proposals have been criticised as compromising the rights and safety of cisgender woman—with the strongest critiques often originating from "gender-critical" individuals.[58] While any queer reform project should be sensitive (and attentive) to the ways in which law reproduces systemic, gender-based violence, opposition to self-determination in the United Kingdom relies upon a number of questionable assumptions. To the extent that observers fear that self-determination will aid cisgender men to fraudulently access single-sex spaces, this misunderstands the relationship between the GRA 2004 and the Equality Act 2010.[59] More fundamentally, as Cowan observes in this collection, it suggests, that the rights of trans individuals in the United Kingdom should be contingent upon the behaviour of cisgender peers (a standard not applied to any other protected group). Rather, a preferable, queer approach to legal recognition would be one, which acknowledges the multifarious ways in which gender-based oppression impacts all

[54]Dunne and van den Brink, *Trans and Intersex Equality Rights in Europe,* 59.

[55]Pieter Canoot offers an interesting discussion relating to self-determination in "The pathologisation of Trans*". Jens T. Theilen has also discussed the depathologisation of legal gender recognition in "Depathologisation of Transgenderism and International Human Rights Law" *Human Rights Law Review* 14 (2014): 327.

[56]Chris Dietz, "Governing Legal Embodiment: On the Limits of Self-Declaration", *Feminist Legal Studies* 26 (2018): 185.

[57]"Gender Recognition Reform (Scotland) Bill: Consultation", accessed March 29, 2020, https://www.gov.scot/publications/gender-recognition-reform-scotland-bill-consultation-scottish-government/; UK Government, "Reform of the Gender Recognition Act 2004", accessed March 29, 2020, https://www.gov.uk/government/consultations/reform-of-the-gender-recognition-act-2004.

[58]See e.g. Kathleen Stock, "Why Self-Identification Should Not Legally Make You a Woman", *The Conversation,* October 1, 2018, https://theconversation.com/why-self-identification-should-not-legally-make-you-a-woman-103372.

[59]See generally: Alex Sharpe, "Will Gender Self-Declaration Undermine Women's Rights and Lead to an Increase in Harms?", *Modern Law Review* 83, no 3 (2020): 539.

individuals; this would allow us to heed Cooper's call, to creatively re-reimagine how we validate gender, while working in coalition to counteract all discrimination, violence and abuse, which arises from repressive gender norms.[60]

A queer approach to law might also look beyond gender recognition. As noted, there are cogent arguments for questioning the confirmatory powers which we locate (both explicitly and implicitly) within state validation, and to explore the emancipatory potential of playing outside state-sanctioned gendered borders. Can a system—however accessible—which conditions the legitimacy of gender upon state approval ever be anything other than disempowering for trans and non-binary populations? Perhaps, rather than seeking to improve legal recognition frameworks, a queerer methodology would interrogate the necessity of legal gender or seek to reimagine the role which gender plays within the law.

Even for those who are reticent about the potential of a de-gendered legal system (and there are compelling reasons to adopt such position[61]), it is not clear that legal gender recognition is actually an optimal strategy for incorporating trans and non-binary experiences into UK laws. As Renz's and Cowan's contributions illustrate, legal approaches to gender recognition, both in this jurisdiction and across Europe, typically emphasise the private aspects of gender identity—foregrounding personal entitlements to develop one's identity without interference. There has been, however, less substantive consideration of the public dimensions of gender, or of how state policy towards gender creates (or enshrines) systemic discrimination.[62] In the United Kingdom, greater focus on equality-based remedies, including a movement towards "gender identity" and "gender expression" (rather than "gender reassignment")[63] and an expanded understanding of reasonable accommodation, might ultimately have a greater impact in enhancing the well-being and lived experiences of trans populations.

---

[60] Davina Cooper, "A Very Binary Drama: The Conceptual Struggle for Gender's Future", *feminists@law* 9, no 1 (2019): 1.

[61] Peter Dunne and Jule Mulder, "Beyond the Binary: Towards a Third Sex Category in Germany?", *German Law Journal* 19, no 3 (2018): 627, 645–646.

[62] See e.g. Iina Sofia Korkiamäki, "Legal Gender Recognition and (Lack of) Equality in the European Court of Human Rights", *The Equal Rights Review* 13 (2014): 20.

[63] Dunne and van den Brink, *Trans and Intersex Equality Rights in Europe,* 46–47, where the authors talk about the potential benefit of the language of "gender identity" rather than relying upon "sex" or "gender reassignment". Under s. 7 of the *Equality Act 2010,* "gender reassignment" is currently the specific protected characteristic in UK law. This reflects EU case law, such as *P v S and Cornwall* Case C-13/94 [1996] ECR I-2143, and secondary legislation, such as Directive 2006/54.

3 Case Study II. Intersex in the United Kingdom: Invisibility, Bodily Integrity and Owning How You Come "Inside"

> ...In essence, as a result of surgeries or other sex-altering medical interventions, intersex people are denied their right to physical integrity as well as their ability to develop their own gender identity, as an a priori choice is made for them. Additionally, these interventions often disrupt their physical and psychological well-being, producing negative impacts with lifelong consequences, which include sterilisation, severe scarring, infections in the urinary tract, reduced or complete loss of sexual sensation, removal of natural hormones, dependency on medication, and a deep feeling of violation of their person...[64]

On 17 January 2019, the Government Equalities Office (GEO) launched a "call for information," seeking to provide "everyone in the United Kingdom, especially people with variations in sex characteristics, with an opportunity to engage with Government and to tell us in detail about their experiences."[65] The announcement—which controversially used the term "variations in sex characteristics" rather than "intersex"—did not seek feedback on a specific policy or proposal; rather, it commenced an "information gathering process" where a range of relevant stakeholders, including those with experience of being intersex, could securely and confidentially communicate their insights and perspectives to policymakers.[66]

As Garland and Travis note in Chapter 7, "intersex" is an umbrella term that refers to individuals who are born with chromosomal, hormonal or genital variations in sex characteristics that mean they fall outside of commonplace understandings of male or female. In recent years, both within activist dialogue and human rights adjudication, experiences of intersex have been increasingly (but not unproblematically[67]) linked with wider political debates on sexual orientation and gender identity.[68] The acronym "LGBTQ"

---

[64]Council of Europe Commissioner for Human Rights, *Human Rights and Intersex* (Strasbourg: Council of Europe, 2015), 14.

[65]Government Equalities Office, "Variations in Sex Characteristics Call for Evidence", accessed March 29, 2020, https://www.gov.uk/government/consultations/variations-in-sex-characteristics-call-for-evidence.

[66]Ibid.

[67]Fae Garland and Mitchell Travis, "Legislating Intersex Equality: Building the Resilience of Intersex People through Law", *Legal Studies* 38, no 4 (2018): 587, 598–599.

[68]See e.g. the high-profile report of the UN High Commissioner for Human Rights on "Discrimination and violence against individuals based on their sexual orientation and gender identity" which consistently refers to "intersex" throughout even though nominally relating to only to sexual

has expanded to embrace gay, lesbian, bisexual, trans, *intersex* and queer populations, and key civil society organisations have reframed their advocacy work to encompass sex characteristics.[69] Yet, in many ways, the GEO's call for information—rather than evidence of a logical step in a unidirectional arc-of-queer-progress (what Sharon Cowan refers to as the "coherent 'progress' narrative" in this collection)—actually exposes the dangerous simplicity of many contemporary "LGBT*I*Q" narratives.

First, and perhaps most obviously, if one accepts that experiences of intersex fall within the wider LGBTQ movement, they reveal a significant lacuna "inside" the UK's LGBT rights framework. At present, there are few, if any, UK protections, which specifically address the unique position of intersex populations.[70] This is true both in terms of guarantees against unwanted physical interventions (guarantees, which although imperfect, are secured for trans applicants through the GRA 2004) and accurate non-discrimination entitlements. It is not so much that intersex complicates the arc-of-queer-progress narrative. Rather, the striking invisibility of intersex perspectives in UK human rights frameworks, and the position of intersex populations as distant strangers to UK law, requires us to fundamentally rethink whether any broad statement about unidirectional queer progress can legitimately be made.

Second, intersex experiences also complicate what coming "inside" the law involves—or, at least, they challenge us to reflect upon what meaningful inclusion requires for queer individuals. Is it possible that, as queers, we may find greater inclusion within the community-devised structures that we playfully construct for ourselves outside the law than through the potentially rigid, imposed norms which are a pre-condition for obtaining insider status? In considering what it might mean to bring intersex lived experiences into UK law, there is a range of potential strategies.

Across Europe, a number of jurisdictions have sought to acknowledge intersex lives through expanding sex discrimination frameworks or by adopting alternative gender categories.[71] These policies may be superficially welcome as a basic acknowledgement of intersex experiences, and they

---

orientation and gender identity concerns, United Nations High Commissioner for Human Rights (UNHCHR), "Discrimination and Violence Against Individuals Based on Their Sexual Orientation and Gender Identity" (4 May 2015) UN Doc No. A/HRC/29/23.

[69] See e.g. ILGA-Europe, "Intersex", accessed March 29, 2020, https://www.ilga-europe.org/what-we-do/our-advocacy-work/trans-and-intersex/intersex.

[70] Garland and Travis, "Legislating Intersex Equality". The UK approach is largely reflective of the legislative approach throughout Europe, see generally: Dunne and van den Brink, *Trans and Intersex Equality Rights in Europe.*

[71] See e.g. Germany and Austria.

may often conform with broader LGBTQ movement demands. Yet, such strategies are also potentially misrepresentative of, and may even supplant, actual intersex advocacy goals. In addition, they risk reproducing historic assumptions around intersex self-identification outside the binary.[72]

While, as Renz outlines, countries, such as Germany, are expanding gender options for intersex populations, many intersex persons actually do identify as male or female.[73] The Declaration of the Third International Intersex Forum explicitly recommends "register[ing] intersex children as females or males"[74] and many individuals find descriptions of intersex as outside the gender binary to be "othering".[75] Indeed, within both UK and international intersex communities, there is considerable frustration that LGBTQ advocates (particularly within the sphere of gender recognition) frequently use intersex as a tool to challenge binary logics, without having to confront the involuntary shame, invisibility and physical violations, which are often common for intersex populations.[76] This frustration may, in some instances, run deeper, with Garland and Travis noting scepticism that mainstream LGBTQ activism has only brought intersex inside wider policy agendas in order to access additional funding sources. Whatever the truth in that regard, it is clear that, to the extent one considers non-discrimination and non-binary legislative responses as constitutive of greater legal inclusion, that approach is unlikely to satisfy the needs of intersex populations. In the United Kingdom, this may result in intersex communities voluntarily remaining as strangers to the law—preferring instead (as Garland and Travis suggest) to stay outside until they can control how the games of inclusion are played.

For many intersex individuals, coming "inside" the law requires institutional respect for bodily integrity and an end to unnecessary surgical interventions upon intersex youth.[77] Such procedures, which became increasingly common in the latter half of the twentieth century, but which are

[72]Lena Holzer, "Sexually Dimorphic Bodies: A Production of Birth Certificates", *Australian Feminist Law Journal* 45, no 1 (2019): 91, 100, who writes that "the majority of intersex persons identify with a binary gender/sex, mostly with the one assigned at birth, and only a minority identifies with a category other than female or male."

[73]Garland and Travis, "Legislating Intersex Equality", 598.

[74]ILGA Europe, "Public Statement by the Third International Intersex Forum", accessed March 29, 2020, https://www.ilga-europe.org/what-we-do/our-advocacy-work/trans-and-intersex/intersex/events/3rd-international-intersex-forum.

[75]Holzer, "Sexually Dimorphic Bodies", 100.

[76]In the Australian context, see Morgan Carpenter, "The Normalization of Intersex Bodies and Othering of Intersex Identities in Australia", *Bioethical Inquiry* 15 (2018): 487, 492.

[77]Intersex NGO Coalition UK, "NGO Report (for PSWG) to the 8th Report of the United Kingdom on the Convention on the Elimination of All Forms of Discrimination Against Women (CEDAW)", accessed March 29, 2020, https://tbinternet.ohchr.org/Treaties/CEDAW/Shared%20Documents/GBR/INT_CEDAW_ICO_GBR_31475_E.pdf. The Coalition writes (page 4) that "[t]he United Kingdom

now subject to considerable critique, compromise the physical autonomy of intersex populations.[78] They are performed in circumstances where intersex infants—the individuals who will live with the consequences of surgery—have no opportunity to provide informed consent,[79] where their parents may feel compelled by problematic societal norms[80] and where too little weight is placed upon the absence of medical necessity. These are interventions, which, at least historically, have been motivated by questionable understandings of body and a belief that sex characteristics define gender status.[81] To the extent that the supposed adequacy of an infant's penis may determine what legal gender is assigned (or what surgical procedures are performed), there is legitimate doubt as to whether such reasoning benefits either the young person or society more generally.[82] It is also uncertain whether the supposed "social emergency" occasioned by intersex justifies interventions which may rob individuals of their fertility or the capacity for future sexual sensation.[83] For many advocates, it to those questions, which, irrespective of broader LGBTQ agendas, an intersex inclusive UK legal system must turn. And, indeed, if a queer reform movement really does seek to prioritise personal voice and experience, it is only by addressing concerns relating to bodily integrity that a queer framework, which is inclusive of intersex lives, can be achieved.

There are, however, valid questions as to how prominent a role law can (and should) play in the sphere of intersex, and how a queer response to the

is in breach of its obligations under the Convention on the Elimination of All Forms of Discrimination against Women to (a) take effective legislative, administrative, judicial or other measures to prevent involuntary, non-urgent surgery and other medical treatment and harmful practices of intersex persons based on prejudice, and (b) to ensure access to redress, and the right to fair and adequate compensation and rehabilitation for victims (CEDAW Arts. 1 and 5(a), General Recommendations No. 19 and 31)."

[78]Jameson Garland and Santa Slokenberga, "Protecting the Rights of Children with Intersex Conditions from Non-consensual Gender-Conforming Medical Interventions: The View from Europe", *Medical Law Review* 27, no 3 (2019): 482; Mary Newbould, "When Parents Choose Gender", *Medical Law Review* 24 (2016): 474.

[79]Peter Dunne, "Towards Trans and Intersex Equality: Conflict or Complementarity?" in *The Legal Status of Intersex Persons*, edited by Jens Scherpe, Tobias Helms and Annatol Dutta (Cambridge: Intersentia, 2018), 229.

[80]Jurg C. Streuli et al., "Shaping Parents: Impact of Contrasting Professional Counseling on Parents' Decision Making for Children with Disorders of Sex Development", *Journal of Sexual Medical* 10 (2013): 1953, 1958; Georgiann Davis and Erin L. Murphy, "Intersex Bodies as States of Exception: An Empirical Explanation for Unnecessary Surgical Modification", *Feminist Formations* 25, no 2 (2013): 129, 144–145.

[81]Myra Hird, "Gender's Nature: Intersexuality, Transsexualism and the 'Sex'/'Gender' Binary", *Feminist Theory* 1, no 3 (2000): 347, 351.

[82]Julie Greenberg, "Defining Male and Female: Intersexuality and the Collision Between Law and Biology", *Arizona Law Review* 41, no 2 (1999): 265, 271.

[83]Commissioner for Human Rights, *Human Rights and Intersex*, 33.

medicalisation of intersex youth might employ alternative, extra-legal strategies. By playing outside, can intersex individuals achieve solutions, which the limited scope and vision of law cannot accommodate?

Beyond (the perhaps overstated) concerns that criminal prohibitions against surgical interventions on intersex bodies might deter other medically necessary treatments, there is the broader consideration of whether—if non-therapeutic procedures are motivated by binary social norms (what Fausto-Sterling famously termed the desire to "control those bodies that are so unruly as to blur the borders"[84])—any remediating policy, which fails to challenge societal attitudes towards bodily diversity, might have only surface impact in terms of changing key stakeholder (e.g. doctors, parents, policy-makers) approaches to intersex. This is not to suggest that law reform is irrelevant. There are coherent reasons why intersex advocates favour legal safeguards against unnecessary medical procedures. Indeed, as Garland and Travis observe in this collection, Malta's Gender Identity, Gender Expression and Sex Characteristics Act 2015 serves as an example of how statutory intervention can positively advance intersex autonomy—directly interrogating the social factors which drive so-called "normalising" surgeries.[85]

Yet, a playfully queer perspective on law must not only seek to change the applicable rules; it must engage with those social and cultural factors which initially encourage problematic practices. To the extent that ignorance or prejudice over intersex variance motivates continued medicalised responses to physical diversity, these phenomena require a broader consciousness-raising exercise. It is interesting that, in its landmark Concluding Observations to Germany in 2011, the United Nations Committee Against Torture (UNCAT) not only recommended "legal provisions in order to provide redress to the victims" of intersex surgeries administered without effective consent.[86] The Committee also explicitly called upon the German authorities to "[e]ducate and train medical and psychological professionals on the range of sexual, and related biological and physical, diversity."[87] In

[84]Anne Fausto-Sterling, *Sexing the Body* (New York: Basic Books, 2008), 8.

[85]Gender Identity, Gender Expression and Sex Characteristics Act 2015. Article 15(1) of the 2015 Act provides that "[i]t shall be not be lawful for medical practitioners or other professionals to conduct any sex assignment treatment and, or surgical intervention on the sex characteristics of a minor which treatment and, or intervention can be deferred until the person to be treated can provide informed consent." Article 15(2) goes on to clarify that "[i]n exceptional circumstances treatment may be effected once there is an agreement between the Interdisciplinary Team and the persons exercising parental authority or tutor of the minor who is still unable to provide consent: [p]rovided that medical intervention *which is driven by social factors without the consent of the individual concerned will be in violation of this Act*" (emphasis added).

[86]Committee against Torture, "Concluding Observations of the Committee Against Torture" (December 12, 2011) UN Doc No. CAT/C/DEU/CO/5, [20].

[87]Ibid.

2016, the United Nations Committee on the Rights of the Child (UNCRC) made similar comments to the United Kingdom, calling upon this jurisdiction to "[e]ducate medical and psychological professionals on the range of sexual, and related biological and physical, diversity and on the consequences of unnecessary interventions for intersex children."[88] The UNCAT and CRC observations are not a repudiation of law, nor do they suggest that the vindication of key human rights can be achieved through solely extra-legal means. Rather, they are an honest assessment that, if state authorities (including officials in the United Kingdom) are going to bring intersex populations within the realm of required legal protection, this may necessitate interrogating what key actors understand that protection to mean for intersex individuals. A queer reform movement should embrace this opportunity for structural change, ensuring that, when intersex lives are brought inside UK law, this is a process which accurately reflects and foregrounds the lived experiences of those who are affected.

4 Case Study III. Que(e)rying the Hostile Environment of Asylum

> So nothing happened in your life which made you feel like you prefer men to girls?[89]

The importance of foregrounding the lived experiences of those cast as queer outsiders to law also resonates with discussions around how to make it easier for LGBT people to claim asylum in the United Kingdom. Laws criminalising homosexuality exist in at least 68 countries while laws limiting family recognition, restricting LGBT associations, and denying people the ability to legally change gender persist in many others.[90] Over the past two decades, the United Kingdom has made space in law for the recognition and protection of some LGBT people, who flee such state-sanctioned

[88] Committee on the Rights of the Child, "Concluding Observations on the Fifth Periodic Report of the United Kingdom of Great Britain and Northern Ireland" (July 12, 2016) UN Doc No. CRC/C/GBR/CO/5, [47].

[89] UKLGIG, "Still Falling Short: The Standard of Home Office Decision-Making in Asylum Claims Based on Sexual Orientation and Gender Identity", *UKLGIG website*, July 2018, 19, accessed March 28, 2020, https://uklgig.org.uk/wp-content/uploads/2018/07/Still-Falling-Short.pdf.

[90] See ILGA, "State Sponsored Homophobia: Global Legislation Overview Update", 9–28, accessed March 28, 2020, https://ilga.org/downloads/ILGA_World_State_Sponsored_Homophobia_report_global_legislation_overview_update_December_2019.pdf.

homo/transphobic persecution and serious discrimination to seek asylum. In 1999, the United Kingdom recognised the possibility of sexual and gender minorities constituting a "particular social group" (a category mentioned by the UN Refugees Convention 1951) for the purposes of protection.[91] In 2010, the UK Supreme Court expanded the reach of this protection by ruling that administrative expectations that gay and lesbian people could be "discreet" about their sexuality to avoid persecution were unlawful.[92] More recently, jurisprudence from the Court of Justice of the European Union has affirmed the UK Supreme Court's rejection of discretion as a requirement and limited the use of stereotypes in decision-making (including the prohibition on sexually explicit material as evidence).[93]

These progressive moves in the United Kingdom to bring LGBT people within refugee law, however, have emerged alongside new modes of state surveillance and scrutiny. The legal landscape facing LGBT(IQ) people who seek asylum in the United Kingdom is structured by competing vulnerabilities that inhibit the accommodation of queer sexualities and gender identities that cannot be indexed against stereotypes of what it means to be gay/lesbian or bi or trans. LGBT people who seek asylum typically demonstrate their vulnerability to human rights abuses by showing a "well-founded fear of persecution" as part of a "particular social group."[94] Status determination processes make LGBT refugees vulnerable to removal if they cannot account for their experiences through rigid categories. Bureaucratic scrutiny of LGBT asylum claims also points to the vulnerabilities of an adjudication system plagued with anxieties about "bogus" claims that threaten the integrity of the state.[95] Political vulnerabilities shape the legal architecture that governs the adjudication of such claims. Screening interviews, strict statutory or jurisprudential criteria on persecution, detention practices, and limited judicial review expose underlying state fears that "opening the floodgates" will compromise the integrity of the refugee system.

Political vulnerabilities, expressed as fears or anxieties for protecting the integrity of state borders and legal process, materialise as a product of state immigration policy. In 2012, the UK government embarked on a process

---

[91] *Islam (A.P) v Secretary of State for the Home Department of Regina v Immigration Appeal Tribunal and Another Ex Parte Shah* (1999) 2 All ER 545 at 452 (Steyn LJ).

[92] *HJ (Iran) and HT (Cameroon) v Secretary of State for the Home Department* (2010) UKSC 31.

[93] *Joined Cases C-199/12 to C-201/12 X (C-199/12), Y (C-200/12), Z (C-201/12) v Minister voor Immigratie en Asiel* [2013] *ECR* I and *Joined Cases C-148/13 to C-150/13 A (C-148/13), B (C-149/13), C (C-150/13) v Staatssecretaris van Veiligheid en Justitie* [2014] ECR I.

[94] Sharalyn Jordan, "Un/Convention(al) Refugees: Contextualizing the Accounts of Refugees Facing Homophobia or Transphobic Persecution", *Refuge* 26 (2011): 165.

[95] Didier Faissin, "The Precarious Truth of Asylum", *Public Culture* 25, no 1 (2013): 39.

of creating a "hostile environment" for people who remained in the country without a regularised migration status. This was made possible through a series of policy, legislative and regulatory measures that "showed contempt" towards migrants.[96] As S Chelvan details in Chapter 4, for individuals like Aderonke Apata, a hostile immigration bureaucracy—one that defaults to suspicion, disbelief, and scrutiny when faced by people who make asylum claims—creates hurdles for queer outsiders to overcome in order to gain asylum. The Home Office's statistics on sexual orientation claims reveal the scale of how many people fail to overcome such hurdles: only about 30% of asylum applications on the basis of sexual orientation were accepted at first instance.[97]

In the United Kingdom, the progressive willingness to consider LGBT asylum claims "inside the law" has also led to the reproduction of sexual and gender stereotypes. While the scale of rejected LGB asylum claims is largely consistent with non-sexuality-based asylum claims, queer people seeking asylum in the United Kingdom are faced with a pernicious "culture of disbelief" when it comes to demonstrating the veracity of their sexuality and the depth of the harm that they face if returned.[98] The UK Lesbian and Gay Immigration Group has documented how this functions in practice. In one case, a gay man who described how his "schoolboy friendship" developed into a romantic relationship was dismissed because he failed to remember the exact dates of its beginning and anniversaries (this relationship happened 20 years earlier).[99] In another case from August 2016, a bisexual man disclosed that he wished to remain in the United Kingdom and marry his male partner despite his family wishing for him to return and marry a woman. Rather than recognise the unique situation faced by bisexual persons, the Home Office interviewer queried the "issue" of persecution (presumably assuming that a

---

[96]Frances Weber, "On the Creation of the UK's 'Hostile Environment'", *Race & Class* 60, no 4 (2019): 76, 77.

[97]UK Home Office, "Experimental Statistics: Asylum Claims on the Basis of Sexual Orientation: August 2019)", accessed March 28, 2020, https://www.gov.uk/government/publications/immigration-statistics-year-ending-june-2019/experimental-statistics-asylum-claims-on-the-basis-of-sexual-orientation. The Home Office also notes that 38% of asylum appeals in relation to a negative decision are allowed.

[98]UKLGIG, "Missing the Mark: Decision Making on Lesbian, Gay, Bisexual, Trans, and Intersex Asylum Claims", accessed March 28, 2020, https://uklgig.org.uk/wp-content/uploads/2014/02/Missing-the-Mark.pdf; Moira Dustin, "Many Rivers to Cross: The Recognition of LGBTQI Asylum in the UK", *International Journal of Refugee Law* 30, no1 (2018): 104; Jenni Millbank, "From Discretion to Disbelief: Recent Trends in Refugee Determinations on the Basis of Sexual Orientation in Australia and the United Kingdom", *The International Journal of Human Rights* 13, no 2–3 (2009): 391; Senthorun Raj, "A/Effective Adjudications: Queer Refugees and the Law", *Journal of Intercultural Studies* 3, no 4 (2017): 453.

[99]UKLGIG, "Still Falling Short", 18.

bisexual man could be "safe" if they married someone of a different sex).[100] In February 2017, a lesbian woman had her claim refused because she could not provide corroborating evidence of her relationship with a woman (such as evidence that they had lived together) because it was secret.[101] A trans woman was questioned about whether she had surgery (which assumes surgical intervention is what it means to be trans—a concept which UK law had already abandoned as part of the GRA 2004).[102]

The above encounters with immigration officers in the United Kingdom evince how the uses of sexual and gender stereotypes in asylum law in the UK police the boundaries of what counts as "authentic" homosexuality, bisexuality and being trans. This administrative policing situates "inauthentic" queers with contested or complicated accounts of their sexuality or gender identity outside the zone of protection. As Jenni Millbank documents in her work, LGBT people's experiences of lodging an asylum claim expose their unique vulnerabilities to degrading processes that both define and confine their sexualities and gender identities according to scripts of genital activity, public visibility, pop culture and medical transitions while dismissing as "self-serving" those who hew too closely to those stereotypes.[103] One individual who, in May 2016, was told that he did not need to be in a relationship or belong to an LGBT social group to prove the veracity of his sexuality, was subsequently asked whether he had done anything to "enhance" his claim.[104] It is a Catch-22; state bureaucrats demand that a person produce evidence of their claim for the purpose of inclusion while also excluding (as incredible) evidence that seems too neat or scripted. LGBT people are coerced to subscribe to harmful evidentiary practices (when "performing gayness").

---

[100]Ibid., 19.

[101]Ibid., 30.

[102]Ibid., 31.

[103]See generally Jenni Millbank, "Fear of Persecution or a Just a Queer Feeling? Refugee Status and Sexual Orientation in Australia", *Alternative Law Journal* 20, no 6 (1995): 261; Jenni Millbank, "Imagining Otherness: Refugee Claims on the Basis of Sexuality in Canada and Australia", *Melbourne University Law Review* 26, no 7 (2002): 144; Jenni Millbank, "Gender, Sex and Visibility in Refugee Claims on the Basis of Sexual Orientation", *Georgetown Immigration Law Journal* 18 (2003): 71; Jenni Millbank, "A Preoccupation with Perversion: The British Response to Sexual Orientation Refugee Claims, 1989–2003", *Social & Legal Studies* 14, no 1 (2005): 115; Jenni Millbank, "The Ring of Truth: A Case Study of Credibility Assessment in Particular Social Group Refugee Determinations", *International Journal of Refugee Law* 21, no 1 (2009): 1; Jenni Millbank, "From Discretion to Disbelief: Recent Trends in Refugee Determinations on the Basis of Sexual Orientation in Australia and the United Kingdom", *The International Journal of Human Rights* 13, nos 2-3 (2009): 391; See Laurie Berg and Jenni Millbank, "Developing a Jurisprudence of Transgender Particular Social Group" in *Fleeing Homophobia: Sexual Orientation, Gender Identity and Asylum,* edited by Thomas Spijkerboer (Abingdon: Routledge, 2013), 121.

[104]UKLGIG, "Still Falling Short", 18.

It is understandable, then, that advocates (like UKLGIG) and scholars (like Chelvan) have offered some prescriptive suggestions as a way of creating a more "open and reassuring environment" for LGBT people to tell their stories of displacement.[105] UKLGIG's recent submission to the review of this process suggests that improved policy is insufficient and that decision-makers require ongoing training on these issues to improve the practice of adjudicating LGBT asylum claims.[106] Chelvan suggests that improving practice requires an institutional shift in approach: moving away from identity-based narratives to make room to accommodate accounts of "difference". In Apata's case, her claim for asylum—and recognition as a lesbian—was ultimately successful when she could articulate her desires, discuss her previous marriage to a man, and explain her delayed disclosure about her sexuality. Creating a welcome, rather than hostile, environment for people to come into is essential for queer claims that do not fit linear and stereotypical accounts of sexuality or gender. Making space for queers seeking asylum to come inside both the country and its legal system—to tell their stories—enables greater recognition of protection claims. The process of making space is not simply about securing administrative convenience or improving legal integrity. These legal interventions are important as the material consequences of rejecting an asylum claim (and forced removal) are dire for those who face persecution on return to their country of origin.

However, displacing the anxiety-laden legal architecture that scaffolds the UK's asylum adjudication space with the "welcoming of differences" risks limiting queer disruptions to the integrity of the space itself. Eddie Bruce-Jones' account of "death zones" and "comfort zones" in Chapter 3 aptly articulates how coming inside the ambit of legal (refugee) protection individualises what is a structural, cross-border problem of homophobia and transphobia. This is not to say that individual litigation and casework should be rejected but Bruce-Jones suggests that we need to rethink the political consequences of the "progressive" legal claims we make for inclusion. This means moving away from the "comfort" provided by human (refugee) rights discourse that situates some states as "better" than others and confronting how violence materialises for displaced people on the peripheries of a racist, xenophobic state that purports to care for them. This violence is acutely apparent in the ways in which LGBT people who seek asylum have sexual

[105]Ibid., 18–10. See also S. Chelvan's contribution in Chapter 4 of this edited collection.

[106]UKLGIG, "Submission to the Independent Chief Inspector of Borders and Immigration Inspection of the Home Office's Presenting Officers' Function", accessed March 20, 2020, https://uklgig.org.uk/wp-content/uploads/2020/02/UKLGIG-submission-to-ICIBI-inspection-of-presenting-officers-Jan-2020-FINAL.pdf.

and gender categories imposed on their stories and are made to conform to them. This is also evident in British political rhetoric that casts migrants as intolerant and a source of homo/transphobia while state institutions (such as the Home Office) dismiss the veracity of LGBT people who flee such "homo/transphobic migrants."[107]

Queer outsiders to refugee law invite us (as scholars and advocates) to play with legal categories that force people to subscribe to static, essentialist and transhistorical ideas of sexuality and gender. For Moira Dustin and Nina Held, a bureaucratic insistence on establishing clear accounts of persecution and linear narratives about sexuality is incongruous with individual experiences which are largely fluid and contested.[108] To address this tension—and foreground fluidity—means advocates, lawyers, and decision-makers need to consider playing around with individualised assessments of gender and sexuality and to engage with queer (refugee) outsiders in less harmful ways. This process of playing with law could allow for self-determination of sexuality/gender but require scrutiny over the scope of the protection/persecution claim or it could result in undoing the process of verification altogether and allow people to self-determine both their sexuality/gender and need for protection. But, as Bruce-Jones makes clear in his chapter, we also need to look outside law and beyond borders to a world where formal citizenship is not the key to safety or visibility. Those queers who literally remain "outside" the ambit of state refugee law (such as people who are internally displaced) require forms of engagement that are political, social and economic rather than legal to address their human rights violations. Queering international (refugee) law involves disrupting the existence of borders and recognising

[107]Theresa May, while acknowledging the colonial legacy of anti-gay laws, moralised about the importance of protecting LGBT people who seek asylum from the "terrible suffering" they face elsewhere and how the UK stands as a beacon for the protection of LGBT rights. These claims were made while the Home Office continued to remove a number of LGBT people who had sought asylum. See Nick Duffy, "Prime Minister Theresa May Challenged over Deportation of LGBT Asylum Seekers", *PinkNews*, October 25, 2017, https://www.pinknews.co.uk/2017/10/25/prime-minister-theresa-may-challenged-over-deportation-of-lgbt-asylum-seekers/. Jasbir Puar describes this political use of LGBT inclusion as a barometer of state progress as "homonationalism", see Jasbir Puar, "Homonationalism as Assemblage: Viral Travels, Affective Sexualities", *Jindal Global Law Review* 4, no 2 (2013): 23, 24. Kay Lalor elaborates in Chapter 2 on how this rhetoric functions to promote the political "progressiveness" of the UK in relation to LGBT rights. This also relates to the way migrants are positioned in discussions about including LGBT content in sex and relationships education.

[108]Moira Dustin and Nina Held, "In or Out: A Queer Intersectional Approach to 'Particular Social Group' Membership and Credibility in SOGI Asylum Claims in Germany and the UK", *Genius* 2 (2018): 74, 1.

collective forms of (irregular) citizenship that do not conform to nationalistic notions of (homo)sexual and (trans)gender belonging.[109]

5 Case Study IV. The Queer Politics of LGBT Education

> It would have meant a great deal to me to have had LGBT issues as part of the curriculum when I was growing up. I went through a great deal of self-loathing then, and began to self-harm. Seeing people like me, who were queer and Muslim, would have been very empowering and made my life easier.[110]

Que(e)rying the politics of belonging and protection in relation to people who seek asylum or seek legal gender recognition also connects to recent attempts in England to protect the well-being of young LGBT people through a new national curriculum dealing with sex and relationships. In 2019, Parliament voted to adopt a new LGBT-inclusive Relationships and Sex Education (RSE) curriculum that would make LGBT content compulsory in secondary schools and voluntary in primary schools.[111] The adoption of these regulatory measures generally, and the proposed implementation of LGBT content specifically, generated heated public debates.[112] These debates were largely caricatured by media outlets and protestors as a conflict between state-mandated inclusion of LGBT content, on one hand, and the undermining of parental authority, particularly of religious and ethnic minorities, on the other.[113] Most sensationally, the protests against similar content at a primary school in Birmingham generated a legal conflict about the extent to which the inclusion of LGBT experiences in school curricula could be

[109] Bina Fernandez, "Queer Border Crossers: Pragmatic Complicities, Indiscretions and Subversions", In *Queering International Law: Possibilities, Alliances, Complicities, Risks*, edited by Dianne Otto, (Abingdon: Routledge, 2017), 211.

[110] Saima Mir, "'I Feel Caught in the Middle': Queer Muslims on the LGBTQ Lessons Row", *The Guardian,* March 27, 2019, https://www.theguardian.com/education/2019/mar/27/caught-in-middle-queer-muslims-lgbtq-lessons-schools-protests.

[111] *Relationships Education, Relationships and Sex Education and Health Education (England) Regulations 2019.*

[112] Benjamin Butterworth, "MPs for LGBT Inclusive Sex and Relationship Education from Primary School", *iNews,* March 28, 2019, accessed March 28, 2020, https://inews.co.uk/news/education/lgbt-sex-relationship-education-mps-support-504670.

[113] Nazia Parveen, "Parents Complain to Manchester Schools About LGBT Lessons", *The Guardian,* March 19, 2019, https://www.theguardian.com/education/2019/mar/19/fresh-complaints-about-lgbt-lessons-at-greater-manchester-primary-schools.

objected to, and what (if any) legal sanctions could be used by the State to block such objections.[114]

Before unpacking these debates, it is necessary to contextualise how policy and legal responses in the United Kingdom to matters of LGBT wellbeing in schools capture the movement of queer children as outsiders (ignored and feared in law) to insiders (protected and supported in law). In 1988, the British government legislated to prevent local authorities from funding school content that "promoted" homosexuality as a "pretended family relationship" (commonly referred to as Section 28).[115] LGBT content, specifically homosexuality, was positioned as outside the zone of both legal relationship validity and social acceptability. Queer children were rendered absent through this law.

In the last two decades, successive UK governments have remedied this absence and expressed greater interest in, and willingness to include, discussions of homosexual and trans identities in the classroom. The UK government's sex and relationship guidance just prior to Section 28's repeal (published in 2000) suggested that teachers should deal "honestly" and "sensitively" with questions about sexuality.[116] The newly revised sex and relationship guidance (published in 2019) goes much further and recognises the importance of progressing discussions of LGBT intimacies and identities (at staged levels of complexity and depth) across all school years.[117] Stonewall's advocacy and research on this topic has been of particular importance in achieving law reform. As its recent report on the nature of bullying in schools points out, inclusion matters because it provides young LGBT people with affirmation of their desires and interests, visibility to counter their erasure and isolation, access to information to improve their sexual health, and awareness of diversity to counter the hate, stigma and discrimination they face.[118] When approached in light of equality law in England, these LGBT-inclusive measures in schools aim to increase understanding of the intersection between law and people's lives, particularly in relation to public sector obligations to

---

[114] "Parkfield Community School: Ofsted Says LGBT Lessons Are 'Appropriate'", *BBC News*, March 2, 2019, https://www.bbc.co.uk/news/uk-england-birmingham-47536752.

[115] *Local Government Act 1988* (UK), s. 28.

[116] UK Department for Education, "Sex and Relationship Education Guidance".

[117] UK Department for Education, "Relationships Education, Relationships and Sex Education (RSE) and Health Education Statutory Guidance".

[118] See Stonewall UK, "School Report: The Experiences of Lesbian, Gay, Bi and Trans Pupils in Britain's Schools", *Stonewall website,* November 2017, accessed March 28, 2020, https://www.stonewall.org.uk/system/files/the_school_report_2017.pdf. Stonewall was founded by activists campaigning against Section 28.

"foster good relations" and "eliminate discrimination".[119] Despite these statutory changes, the expansion of religious schools and parental objections to sex education, coupled with political anxieties over "cultural sensitivity", have exposed the limits of existing legal measures of inclusion: some (religious) schools can be dismissive, and parents can withdraw their children (under the age of 15) from the discussion of LGBT lives, even though schools must include some discussion of them.[120]

This confusing form of inclusion—naming LGBT people as a group to proactively include in classroom discussions and then rendering that inclusion conditional (on religious sensitivities)—resonates with what Kay Lalor refers to in Chapter 2 as an impasse or paradox. In her contribution, Lalor traces how recent legislative recognition of Britain's responsibility to promote LGBT rights, including acknowledgement of how Britain is implicated in existing laws criminalising homosexuality, creates hierarchies of inclusion/exclusion and home/elsewhere. Lalor discusses how a "Global LGBT Rights Debate" in Westminster rendered the "outside" (of the United Kingdom) as a space of continuing violence against LGBT people while implicitly claiming the "inside" (of the United Kingdom) as a space of relative safety and comfort. The inside/outside emerged as co-constituting positions in an elastic temporal and spatial relationship. In other words, the British Empire's seemingly former history as a homophobic regime that exported its homophobia outside its (even at the time contested) borders was redressed through a contemporary obligation for the British government/parliament to use the resources inside its jurisdiction (such as a parliamentary debate) to challenge homo/transphobic outsiders (such as postcolonial governments) in other countries. Yet, as Lalor maintains, a colonial register structures the ways in which MPs use diplomatic engagement to assume a kinship with other LGBT people while distancing their experiences of structural violence from those who they claim are "more seriously" oppressed. This coloniality re-emerges in the current debates about including LGBT content in schools. Here, the British government recognises its historical ignorance or marginalisation of LGBT people and then positions itself as a contemporary bearer of pro-LGBT inclusion values. These inclusion values are realised by a mandated cultivation in the curriculum, even if state values position Muslims or minority ethnic communities as (homo/transphobic) outsiders.

[119] *Equality Act 2010* (UK), s. 149.

[120] Paul Johnson and Robert Vanderbeck, *Law, Religion and Homosexuality* (Abingdon: Routledge, 2014), 190–197; UK Department for Education, "Relationships Education, Relationships and Sex Education (RSE) and Health Education Statutory Guidance", 15, 17–18.

The limits of inclusion are a productive space to think about what is gained from legally mandating LGBT inclusive-curricula and how exemptions or withdrawals from these programmes prompt alternative interventions by activists, particularly those from minority ethnic and religious backgrounds. This is exemplified in the High Court's recent decision to bar certain anti-LGBT protestors from a school in Birmingham. In *Birmingham City Council v Afsar* (2019), the High Court had to consider whether to uphold an injunction against parents/guardians who had engaged in relentless protests just outside the school gates about the inclusion of LGBT content at Anderton Park Infant and Junior School. It is important to note that the protests that gave rise to this litigation do not deal with the new RSE curriculum (due to be implemented no later than the start of the summer term 2021) but rather were concerned with school measures (such as books with LGBT content in the library) aimed at promoting the inclusion of LGBT people. These measures, erroneously linked to a related programme called "No Outsiders", became the subject of intense animosity among a select group of parents and local community members who felt the school was engaging in "LGBT sexual education."[121]

The case raises a number of procedural and technical issues, which we do not address here. What is particularly useful for us to draw out in this jurisprudence is the way in which space functions both literally and metaphorically in the argument between parties to determine the extent to which the law accommodates pro-LGBT content and parental rights to protest that content. In their submissions, the defendants essentially argued that "the teaching of LGBT issues" unlawfully discriminated against British Pakistani Muslim children (and their parents) to the extent that they could not preserve their cultural values that are "centred on heterosexual relationships in marriage."[122] For them, the school's inclusion of LGBT content alienated some children and parents—made them outsiders to the school (as many were literally protesting outside the school gates). To the school, these outsiders (many of whom were not connected to the school) became an enduring "nuisance".[123] Their abusive conduct had detrimental impacts on the wellbeing of staff and the noise generated by the protests inhibited

[121] *Birmingham City Council v Afsar (No 3)* [2019] EWHC 3217 (QB), [3]. "No Outsiders" was a programme that was taught at another school in Birmingham, where primary school pupils were taught about equalities, rights, and differences. The programme was discontinued at the school following the withdrawal of Muslim students from the school. See Nazia Parveen, "Birmingham School Stops LGBT Lessons After Parents Protest", *The Guardian*, March 4, 2019, https://www.theguardian.com/education/2019/mar/04/birmingham-school-stops-lgbt-lessons-after-parent-protests.

[122] *Birmingham City Council v Afsar (No 3)* [2019] EWHC 3217 (QB), [37] (Warby J).

[123] Ibid., [40] (Warby J).

teaching at the school.[124] In issuing a permanent injunction against some of the protestors, the Court literally demarcated the boundaries that they could occupy. The individuals concerned were still allowed to protest but they were pushed outside the gates onto a nearby park and blocked from using a megaphone to amplify their messages.[125]

As this case makes apparent, inclusion was a polarising flashpoint for two marginalised communities in the United Kingdom (LGBT people and Muslims). Legal address (via judicial review) presented this polarisation as a conflict of rights: religious expression and cultural identity placed in opposition to LGBT rights and lives. Judicial review was invoked to mediate between protestors' demands that the school withdraw LGBT content (such as books), along with their threats to withdraw children from the school if this was not done, and the school's (legally mandated) interest in promoting equality. But here, an injunction to permanently exclude is impossible. On one hand, some parties are required to be inside the school when it comes to their children. On another hand, parties with children at the school are not able to block parts of the curriculum that deal with LGBT people. As Cooper notes, these "conflicts over withdrawal" involve generative contact between various parties (the school, the local Council, protestors, parents, LGBT people/activists) and stitch them together both inside (the school) and outside (the protest).[126]

Some LGBTIQ Muslims note, however, that framing the protest as a conflict between religion and sexuality (where one must cede to the other) is unproductive because it erases their experiences of both. Ferhan Khan suggests that we "need to give queer Muslims a voice. Let us go into the schools and talk to the children. Give us the brief, the resources and the platform – if you really care."[127] Khan's words speak to being queer on the outside of a debate that prioritises white LGBT voices and straight Muslim perspectives. Rather than subscribe to law's spatialising tendency to create an inside/outside or religion/sexuality binary in resolving complaints of discrimination—a tendency that is deeply racialised as Lalor and Bruce-Jones indicate in their respective chapters—Khan's words gesture to why it is important to highlight what queer outsiders can offer. Specifically, the State giving resources to queer Muslims to come inside schools might provide a route to build solidarity between LGBT people and Muslims. New statutory guidance relating to RSE might be an avenue to enable this as it provides an infrastructure

[124]Ibid., [90]–[95] (Warby J).
[125]Ibid., [120] (Warby J).
[126]Cooper, *Feeling Like a State,* 99–100.
[127]Mir, "'I Feel Caught in the Middle'".

to both affirm LGBT young people and address intersecting experiences of bullying, harassment and discrimination. Yet, legal regulation alone is insufficient to address or mediate between minoritarian differences that arise between and within communities (as the protests in Birmingham make clear). We need to think creatively from outside law about how we might resource cross-cultural dialogues outside the curriculum—outside mandated requirements—using alternative educational platforms (such as social media) and occupying non-school spaces (such as places of worship or community halls).

Moreover, we might want to pause and consider how inclusion of LGBT content in the curriculum strengthens state institutionalisation of norms relating to "proper" or "good" sexuality, intimacy, and gender. Much like norms governing the adjudication of asylum claims that Chelvan and Bruce-Jones critique, and the recognition of trans and non-binary identities as illustrated by Renz and Cowan, state governance of sexuality and gender risk reproducing racialised, ableist and heteronormative ideas. As Felicity Adams and Fabienne Emmerich argue in Chapter 5 about LGBTIQ incarceration, prisons exemplify the consequences of state control over the sex, gender, and sexuality of outsiders (prisoners) through the exclusion of trans people, isolation of vulnerable queers, and intense scrutiny of queer relationships. They discuss how recent prison policies, for example, insist that trans prisoners undergo a permanent gender transition and perform a binary gender identity to be institutionally accommodated. Further, they outline how caring and consensual (not always sexual) interactions between those in the prison estate threaten the "equilibrium" of prison by allegedly making other (heterosexual) prisoners feel hostile about their inability to engage in relationships. As Grietje Baars notes, heterosexual people also face the "distributive effects" of a state control of outsiders that render their (heterosexual) intimacies impossible.[128]

While the new RSE curriculum to be implemented in England accommodates a much broader range of sexual interactions and relationship statuses, the British government's "respect" for different kinds of intimacies and identities is circumscribed. The guidance reifies those relationships that are "committed" and "stable" while affirming why "marriage is an important choice."[129] When it comes to sex, echoing prison policy, the guidance for secondary schools emphasises safeguarding and risk management by teaching pupils to manage the "harms" present in online spaces, understand legal

[128]Grietje Baars, "Queer Cases Unmake Gendered Law, Or, Fucking Law's Gendered Function", *Australian Feminist Law Journal* 45, no 1 (2019): 15, 47.

[129]UK Department for Education, "Relationships Education, Relationships and Sex Education (RSE) and Health Education Statutory Guidance", 27.

penalties for the sharing of self-produced sexually explicit material, engage with criminal law relating to sexual assault, and grasp the consequences of sexually transmitted infections.[130] Young people are encouraged on one hand to respect platonic and other relationships while encouraged to defer the sexual kind.

These examples show us why remaining outside law is a productive way to challenge the state's policing functions in relation to transgressions of sexual and gendered morality. In both prisons and schools, even if to differing degrees, queer pleasures and relationship pluralities remain outside the scope of state inclusion. From this outside vantage point, we can take account of the relationship between regulation of RSE and other laws to recognise the divergences between state education that encourages relationship plurality (even if only to the extent of long-term committed relationships), and other laws that police or refuse relationship plurality. This is evident in how marriage (and to a lesser extent civil partnerships) are privileged (in-law) at the expense of other meaningful caring, non-dyadic or non-sexual relationships (outside of law).[131] Law should make room for LGBTIQ people to pursue their intimacies from the outside, too.

6 Confronting Queer Outside(r)s

The case studies discussed above show how expanding the "inside" of law to reach new individuals, issues, and institutions can "colonise" the generative possibilities of a queer outside. Our critical engagements with the case studies above show that queer outsiders coming in, seeking inclusion in legal spaces, have redefined the spatiality and operation of particular laws in divergent ways. The case studies we have discussed point to how state control over sexuality and gender (in legal gender recognition, intersex, asylum law, and education policy) make protection and affirmation conditional on the performance of authenticity—obliging queer individuals to frame, shape and (even) contort their understandings of identity and body into rigid, inflexible norms of gender and sexuality.

The chapters in our collection point out that queer analysis can risk objectifying people and the materiality of their experiences by treating people as

[130] Ibid., 28–29.

[131] For a discussion on same-sex relationship recognition and relationship diversity, see Alexander Maine, "The Hierarchy of Marriage and Civil Partnerships: Diversifying Relationship Recognition" in *Same-Sex Relationships, Law and Social Change*, edited by Frances Hamilton and Guido Noto La Diega (Abingdon: Routledge, 2020), 209.

conceptual categories. Intersex rights and activism, as outlined in Garland's and Travis' interviews, contest the queer "othering" of their bodies and identities in law. As Adams and Emmerich observe both in case law and existing policies, prisons are not romantic spaces of queer intimacy or sites for reform to improve upon. Chelvan and Bruce-Jones use immigration bureaucracy to show how people who seek asylum are, and should not be, made queer to legal mechanisms of protection. Renz details how the proliferation of gender categories may enable the "queering" of a binary as a conceptual matter, but it does not address the structural realities or embodied experiences of oppression that non-binary people face. In Cowan's discussions with trans people, equality cannot be dismissed as a concept in critique because it is a central material and embodied claim of optimism, particularly for trans people who seek social belonging and affirmation. Lalor captures how talking about (in abstract terms), rather than talking with, marginalised LGBTIQ people reproduces colonial hierarchies of insider/outsider, saviour/victim and safety/oppression.

LGBTIQ reforms expose how legal systems can open up ways of imagining sex, gender and sexuality theoretically or conceptually, while foreclosing them in practice. There is much to be gained by rendering the investment law has in certainty less secure (making space for fluidity, anxiety and uncomfortability). For us, the queer analyses of legal interventions assembled in this collection are not about romanticising specific modes of analysis or using experiences of injustice to develop a theoretical agenda. Instead, each contributor engages with the material and normative consequences of staying inside and/or playing outside law. Taken together, they navigate how this involves withdrawal from particular sites of legal recognition and protection, while seeking inclusion in others. As Baars suggests, withdrawal of our lives from the inside of law—to engender a strike—is a way to contest the state institutionalisation of gender and sexuality.[132] Cooper, in a different vein, observes that we can also think about the drama of withdrawal as a form of relation and refiguration: withdrawing involves contact between parties who withdraw (legal protection or social services) from others (LGBTIQ people) and this reshapes how these parties are governed by that withdrawal.[133] Queers can come inside and play outside law, in different arenas and subdisciplines of law, at the same time.

Playing with queerness outside law—and withdrawing from specific legal interventions—is a way to pursue activism and solidarity (whether it involves global LGBTIQ rights, intersex autonomy, refugee protection or dismantling

[132] Baars, "Queer Cases Unmake Gendered Law", 21.

[133] Cooper, *Feeling Like a State,* 31.

prisons). Intersex remains outside both law and queer (activist) agendas—to refuse "disciplining" by legal, medical and academic knowledges. Queer decolonial and migration activisms contest the punitive impacts of legal recognition or incorporation/inclusion that reify xenophobic state politics while demonising those who migrate from "elsewhere." Queer abolition speaks to the importance of legally withdrawing from carceral systems to avoid the premature death and systemic harms faced by racialised and poor populations. Alternatively, intersex and non-binary activisms point to the possibility of removing (legal) gender as a site of (legal) governance.

The different forms of play imagined in this collection also carry productive risks. We urge scholars, activists and advocates to pursue further questions in projects of LGBTIQ law reform and political activism. We think it is important for our legal futures to keep interrupting with critical questions. What would it mean to queer the legal insistence in some areas of defining sex/gender or relationships? What might be gained by refusing borders? What alternatives to recognition and punishment can we create for accountability? How might we come together, as disparate and intersecting demographics, to do this work? In responding to these sorts of questions, we are better placed to support LGBTIQ people both inside and outside the law.

References

Aikan, Jordan. "Promoting an Integrated Approach to Ensuring Access to Gender Incongruent Health Care", *Berkeley Journal of Gender, Law and Justice* 31, no 1 (2016): 1–59.

Baars, Grietje. "Queer Cases Unmake Gendered Law, Or, Fucking Law's Gendered Function", *Australian Feminist Law Journal* 45, no 1 (2019): 15–62.

Barlow, Anne. "A New Approach to Transsexualism and a Missed Opportunity?", *Child and Family Law Quarterly* 13, no 2 (2001): 225–240.

Berg, Laurie and Jenni Millbank. "Developing a Jurisprudence of Transgender Particular Social Group." In *Fleeing Homophobia: Sexual Orientation, Gender Identity and Asylum,* edited by Thomas Spijkerboer, 121–153. Abingdon: Routledge, 2013.

Bonifacio, Herbert J. and Stephen M. Rosenthal. "Gender Variance and Dysphoria in Children and Adolescents", *Paediatric Clinics of North America* 62, no 4 (2015): 1001–1016.

Brunskell-Evans, Heather. "The Medico-Legal 'Making' of the Transgender Child", *Medical Law Review* 27, no 4 (2019): 640–657.

Butterworth, Benjamin. "MPs for LGBT Inclusive Sex and Relationship Education from Primary School", *iNews*, March 28, 2019. https://inews.co.uk/news/education/lgbt-sex-relationship-education-mps-support-504670.

Canoot, Pieter. "The Pathologisation of Trans* Persons in the ECtHR's Case Law on Legal Gender Recognition", *Netherlands Quarterly of Human Rights* 37, no 1 (2019): 14.

Carpenter, Morgan. "The Normalization of Intersex Bodies and Othering of Intersex Identities in Australia", *Bioethical Inquiry* 15 (2018): 487–495.

Cooper, Davina. *Feeling Like a State: Desire, Denial, and the Recasting of Authority.* Durham: Duke University Press, 2019.

Council of Europe Commissioner for Human Rights, *Human Rights and Intersex* (Council of Europe, 2015).

Cowan, Sharon. "'That Woman Is a Woman!' the Case of Bellinger v. Bellinger and the Mysterious (Dis) appearance of Sex: Bellinger v. Bellinger [2003] 2 All ER 593;[2003] FCR 1;[2003] 2 WLR 1174;[2003] UKHL 21", *Feminist Legal Studies* 12, no 1 (2004): 79–92.

Crowd Justice. "Legal Case to Protect Children from Experimental Medical Treatment." Accessed March 29, 2020. https://www.crowdjustice.com/case/protect-children/.

Davis, Georgiann and Erin L. Murphy. "Intersex Bodies as States of Exception: An Empirical Explanation for Unnecessary Surgical Modification", *Feminist Formations* 25, no 2 (2013): 129–152.

Dietz, Chris. "Governing Legal Embodiment: On the Limits of Self-Declaration", *Feminist Legal Studies* 26 (2018): 185–204.

de Vries, Annelou, et al. "Young Adult Psychological Outcome After Puberty Suppression and Gender Reassignment". *Paediatrics* 134, no 4 (2014): 696–704.

Duffy, Nick. "Prime Minister Theresa May Challenged over Deportation of LGBT Asylum Seekers." *PinkNews*, October 25, 2017. https://www.pinknews.co.uk/2017/10/25/prime-minister-theresa-may-challenged-over-deportation-of-lgbt-asylum-seekers/.

Dunne, Peter. "Ten Years of Gender Recognition in the United Kingdom: Still a 'Model for Reform?", *Public Law* (October 2015): 530–539.

Dunne, Peter. "Transgender Children and the Law", *Family Law* 47 (January 2017): 123–124.

Dunne, Peter. "Towards Trans and Intersex Equality: Conflict or Complementarity?" In *Legal Status of Intersex Persons*, edited by Jens Scherpe, Tobias Helms and Annatol Dutta, 217–240. Cambridge: Intersentia, 2018.

Dunne, Peter. "Acknowledging or Erasing Intersex Experiences? Gender 'Diversity' in German Law", *Northern Ireland Legal Quarterly* 70, no 1 (2019): 163–169.

Dunne, Peter and Jule Mulder. "Beyond the Binary: Towards a Third Sex Category in Germany?", *German Law Journal* 19, no 3 (2018): 627–648.

Dunne, Peter and Marjolein van den Brink, *Trans and Intersex Equality Rights in Europe: A Comparative Analysis* (Luxembourg: Publications Office of the European Union, 2018).

Dunne, Peter and Stephen Clark, *Comparative Legal Overview of Gender Recognition Laws across the Commonwealth* (Equality and Justice Alliance, 2019).

Dustin, Moira. "Many Rivers to Cross: The Recognition of LGBTQI Asylum in the UK", *International Journal of Refugee Law* 30, no 1 (2018): 104–127.

Dustin, Moira and Nina Held. "In or Out: A Queer Intersectional Approach to 'Particular Social Group' Membership and Credibility in SOGI Asylum Claims in Germany and the UK", *Genius* 2 (2018): 74–87.

Ehrbar, Randall D., et al. "Clinician Judgment in the Diagnosis of Gender Identity Disorder in Children", *Journal of Sex and Marital Therapy* 34, no 5 (2008): 385–412.

Faissin, Didier. "The Precarious Truth of Asylum", *Public Culture* 25, no 1 (2013): 39–63.

Fausto-Sterling, Anne. *Sexing the Body.* New York: Basic Books, 2008.

Fernandez, Bina. "Queer Border Crossers: Pragmatic Complicities, Indiscretions and Subversions." In *Queering International Law: Possibilities, Alliances, Complicities, Risks,* edited by Dianne Otto, 193-211. Abingdon: Routledge, 2017.

Garland, Fae and Mitchell Travis. "Legislating Intersex Equality: Building the Resilience of Intersex People through Law", *Legal Studies,* 38, no 4 (2018): 587–606.

Garland, Jameson and Santa Slokenberga. "Protecting the Rights of Children with Intersex Conditions from Non-consensual Gender-Conforming Medical Interventions: The View from Europe", *Medical Law Review* 27, no 3 (2019): 482–508.

"Gender Recognition Reform (Scotland) Bill: Consultation", *Scottish Government website,* December 17, 2019. Accessed March 29, 2020, https://www.gov.scot/publications/gender-recognition-reform-scotland-bill-consultation-scottish-government/.

Gilmore, Stephen. "Bellinger v Bellinger—Not Quite Between the Ears and Between the Legs—Transsexualism and Marriage in the Lords", *Child and Family Law Quarterly* 15, no 3 (2003): 295–311.

Gonzalez-Salzberg, Damian A. "The Accepted Transsexual and the Absent Transgender: A Queer Reading of the Regulation of Sex/Gender by the European Court of Human Rights", *American University International Law Review* 29, no 4 (2013): 797–829.

Government Equalities Office. *National LGBT Survey: Summary Report (June 2018).* Accessed March 29, 2020. https://assets.publishing.service.gov.uk/government/uploads/system/uploads/attachment_data/file/722314/GEO-LGBT-Survey-Report.pdf.

Government Equalities Office. "Variations in Sex Characteristics Call for Evidence." Accessed March 29, 2020. https://www.gov.uk/government/consultations/variations-in-sex-characteristics-call-for-evidence.

Grabham, Emily. "Governing Permanence: Trans Subjects, Time, and the Gender Recognition Act", *Social & Legal Studies* 19, no 1: (2010): 107–126.

Greenberg, Julie. "Defining Male and Female: Intersexuality and the Collision between Law and Biology", *Arizona Law Review* 41, no 2 (1999): 265–328.

Hartley, Emma. "Why Do So Many Teenage Girls Want to Change Gender?" *Prospect*, March 3, 2020. https://www.prospectmagazine.co.uk/magazine/tavistock-transgender-transition-teenage-girls-female-to-male.

Hird, Myra. "Gender's Nature: Intersexuality, Transsexualism and the 'Sex'/'Gender' Binary", *Feminist Theory* 1, no 3 (2000): 347–364.

Holzer, Lena. "Sexually Dimorphic Bodies: A Production of Birth Certificates", *Australian Feminist Law Journal* 45, no 1 (2019): 91–110.

House of Commons Select Committee on Women and Equalities, *Transgender Equality* (London: The Stationery Office Limited, 2016).

ILGA-Europe. "Intersex." Accessed March 29, 2020. https://www.ilga-europe.org/what-we-do/our-advocacy-work/trans-and-intersex/intersex.

ILGA Europe. "Public Statement by the Third International Intersex Forum." Accessed March 29, 2020. https://www.ilga-europe.org/what-we-do/our-advocacy-work/trans-and-intersex/intersex/events/3rd-international-intersex-forum.

ILGA. "State Sponsored Homophobia: Global Legislation Overview Update (December 2019)." Accessed March 28, 2020. https://ilga.org/downloads/ILGA_World_State_Sponsored_Homophobia_report_global_legislation_overview_update_December_2019.pdf.

Intersex NGO Coalition UK. "NGO Report (for PSWG) to the 8th Report of the United Kingdom on the Convention on the Elimination of All Forms of Discrimination Against Women (CEDAW)." Accessed March 29 2020. https://tbinternet.ohchr.org/Treaties/CEDAW/Shared%20Documents/GBR/INT_CEDAW_ICO_GBR_31475_E.pdf.

Jens M. Scherpe (ed), *The Legal Status of Transsexual and Transgender Persons.* Cambridge: Intersentia, 2015.

Johnson, Paul and Robert Vanderbeck. *Law, Religion and Homosexuality.* Abingdon: Routledge, 2014.

Jordan, Sharalyn. "Un/Convention(al) Refugees: Contextualizing the Accounts of Refugees Facing Homophobia or Transphobic Persecution", *Refuge* 26 (2011): 165–182.

Korkiamäki, Iina Sofia. "Legal Gender Recognition and (Lack of) Equality in the European Court of Human Rights", *The Equal Rights Review* 13 (2014): 20–50.

Loue, Sana. "Transsexualism in Medicolegal Limine: An Examination and a Proposal for Change", *Journal of Psychiatry and Law* 24, no 1 (1996): 27–51.

Maine, Alexander. "The Hierarchy of Marriage and Civil Partnerships: Diversifying Relationship Recognition." In *Same-Sex Relationships, Law and Social Change*, edited by Frances Hamilton and Guido Noto La Diega, 209–220. Abingdon: Routledge, 2020.

Millbank, Jenni. "Fear of Persecution or a Just a Queer Feeling? Refugee Status and Sexual Orientation in Australia", *Alternative Law Journal* 20, no 6 (1995): 261–265.

Millbank, Jenni. "Imagining Otherness: Refugee Claims on the Basis Of Sexuality in Canada and Australia", *Melbourne University Law Review* 26, no 7 (2002): 144–177.

Millbank, Jenni. "Gender, Sex and Visibility in Refugee Claims on the Basis of Sexual Orientation", *Georgetown Immigration Law Journal* 18 (2003): 71–110.

Millbank, Jenni. "A Preoccupation with Perversion: The British Response to Sexual Orientation Refugee Claims, 1989–2003", *Social & Legal Studies* 14, no 1 (2005): 115–138.

Millbank, Jenni. "The Ring of Truth: A Case Study of Credibility Assessment in Particular Social Group Refugee Determinations", *International Journal of Refugee Law* 21, no 1 (2009): 1–33.

Millbank, Jenni. "From Discretion to Disbelief: Recent Trends in Refugee Determinations on the Basis of Sexual Orientation in Australia and the United Kingdom", *The International Journal of Human Rights* 13, no 2–3 (2009): 391–414.

Mir, Saima. "'I Feel Caught in the Middle': Queer Muslims on the LGBTQ Lessons Row." *The Guardian,* March 27, 2019. https://www.theguardian.com/education/2019/mar/27/caught-in-middle-queer-muslims-lgbtq-lessons-schools-protests.

Newbould, Mary. "When Parents Choose Gender", *Medical Law Review* 24 (2016): 471–496.

Norman, Julian. "'Shifting Sands' Six Legal Views on the Transgender Debate." *The Guardian,* October 19, 2018. https://www.theguardian.com/society/2018/oct/19/gender-recognition-act-reforms-six-legal-views-transgender-debate.

Olson, Kristina, et al. "Mental Health of Transgender Children Who Are Supported in Their Identities", *Paediatrics* 137, no 3 (2016): 1–8.

Olson, Kristina. "Prepubescent Transgender Children: What We Know and What we Do Not Know", *Journal of the American Academy of Child and Adolescent Psychiatry* 55, no 3 (2016): 155–156.

"Parkfield Community School: Ofsted Says LGBT Lessons Are 'Appropriate'", *BBC News,* March 2, 2019. Accessed March 28, 2020, https://www.bbc.co.uk/news/uk-england-birmingham-47536752.

Parsons, Vic. "Trans Kids Are as Sure of Their Gender as cis Kids at a Young Age, According to Science." *Pink News,* December 27, 2019. https://www.pinknews.co.uk/2019/12/27/transgender-children-study-gender-identity-cis-children-washington-university/.

Parveen, Nazia. "Birmingham School Stops LGBT Lessons After Parents Protest." *The Guardian,* March 4, 2019. https://www.theguardian.com/education/2019/mar/04/birmingham-school-stops-lgbt-lessons-after-parent-protests.

Parveen, Nazia. "Parents Complain to Manchester Schools About LGBT Lessons." *The Guardian,* March 19, 2019. https://www.theguardian.com/education/2019/mar/19/fresh-complaints-about-lgbt-lessons-at-greater-manchester-primary-schools.

Puar, Jasbir. "Homonationalism as Assemblage: Viral Travels, Affective Sexualities", *Jindal Global Law Review* 4, no 2 (2013): 23–43.

Raj, Senthorun. "A/Effective Adjudications: Queer Refugees and the Law", *Journal of Intercultural Studies* 3, no 4 (2017): 453–468.

Rosenthal, Stephen. "Approach to the Patient: Transgender Youth: Endocrine Considerations", *The Journal of Clinical Endocrinology and Metabolism* 99, no 12 (2014): 4379–4389.

Sanai, Leyla. "The Danger of Letting Children Transition Too Early." *The Spectator*, May 13, 2019. https://www.spectator.co.uk/article/the-danger-of-letting-children-transition-gender-too-early.

Sandland, Ralph. "Feminism and the Gender Recognition Act 2004", *Feminist Legal Studies* 13, no 1 (2005): 43–66.

Scherpe, Jens M. and Peter Dunne. "The Legal Recognition of Transsexual and Transgender Persons—Comparative Analysis and Recommendations." In *The Legal Status of Transsexual and Transgender Persons,* edited by Jens M Scherpe, 615–633. Cambridge: Intersentia, 2015.

Sharpe, Alex. "Endless Sex: The Gender Recognition Act 2004 and the Persistence of a Legal Category", *Feminist Legal Studies* 15, no 1 (2007): 57–84.

Sharpe, Alex. "Gender Recognition in the UK: A Great Leap Forward", *Social & Legal Studies* 18, no 2 (2009): 241–245.

Sharpe, Alex. "Will Gender Self-Declaration Undermine Women's Rights and Lead to an Increase in Harms?", *Modern Law Review* 83, no 3 (2020): 539–557.

Sedgwick, Eve. *Tendencies*. Durham: Duke University Press, 1993.

Silverman, Michael. "Issues in Access to Healthcare by Transgender Individuals", *Women's Rights Law Reporter* 30, no 2 (2009): 347–351.

Spade, Dean. "Resisting Medicine, Re/modelling Gender", *Berkeley Women's Law Journal* 18 (2003): 15–37.

Spade, Dean. "Documenting Gender", *Hastings Law Journal* 59 (2007): 731–842.

"Statement on Gender Affirmative Approach to Care from the Paediatric Endocrine Society Special Interest Group on Transgender Health." Accessed March 29, 2020. https://www.pedsendo.org/members/members_only/PDF/TG_SIG_Position%20Statement_10_20_16.pdf.

Stephen, Whittle. "The Opposite of Sex is Politics—The UK Gender Recognition Act and Why it is Not Perfect, Just Like You and Me", *Journal of Gender Studies* 15, no 3 (2007): 267–271.

Stock, Kathleen. "Changing the Concept of 'Woman' Will Cause Unintended Harms." *The Economist,* July 6, 2018. https://www.economist.com/open-future/2018/07/06/changing-the-concept-of-woman-will-cause-unintended-harms.

Stock, Kathleen. "Why Self-Identification Should Not Legally Make You a Woman." *The Conversation,* October 1, 2018. https://theconversation.com/why-self-identification-should-not-legally-make-you-a-woman-103372.

Stonewall UK. "School Report: The Experiences of Lesbian, Gay, Bi and Trans Pupils in Britain's Schools."Accessed March 28, 2020. https://www.stonewall.org.uk/system/files/the_school_report_2017.pdf.

Streuli, Jurg C., et al. "Shaping Parents: Impact of Contrasting Professional Counseling on Parents' Decision Making for Children with Disorders of Sex Development", *Journal of Sexual Medical* 10 (2013): 1953–1960.

Tannehill, Brynn. "The End of the Desistence Myth." *Huffington Post,* January 1, 2016. http://www.huffingtonpost.com/brynn-tannehill/the-end-of-the-desistance_b_8903690.html.

Theilen, Jens T. "Depathologisation of Transgenderism and International Human Rights Law", *Human Rights Law Review* 14 (2014): 327–342.

Transgender Trend. "Transgender Trend Submission to the Gender Recognition Reform (Scotland) Bill Consultation." Accessed March 29, 2020. https://www.transgendertrend.com/transgender-trend-submission-gender-recognition-reform-scotland-bill/.

Turner, Janice. "Cult of Gender Identity Is Harming Children." *The Sunday Times,* September 21, 2019. https://www.thetimes.co.uk/article/cult-of-gender-identity-is-harming-children-pjvbkjzxq.

UK Government. "Reform of the Gender Recognition Act 2004." Accessed March 29, 2020, https://www.gov.uk/government/consultations/reform-of-the-gender-recognition-act-2004.

UK Home Office. "Experimental Statistics: Asylum Claims on the Basis of Sexual Orientation (August 2019)." Accessed March 28, 2020. https://www.gov.uk/government/publications/immigration-statistics-year-ending-june-2019/experimental-statistics-asylum-claims-on-the-basis-of-sexual-orientation.

UKLGIG. "Missing the Mark: Decision Making on Lesbian, Gay, Bisexual, Trans, and Intersex Asylum Claims (September 2013)." Accessed March 28, 2020. https://uklgig.org.uk/wp-content/uploads/2014/02/Missing-the-Mark.pdf.

UKLGIG. "Still Falling Short: The Standard of Home Office Decision-Making in Asylum Claims Based on Sexual Orientation and Gender Identity (July 2018)." Accessed March 28, 2020. https://uklgig.org.uk/wp-content/uploads/2018/07/Still-Falling-Short.pdf.

UKLGIG. "Submission to the Independent Chief Inspector of Borders and Immigration Inspection of the Home Office's Presenting Officers' Function." Accessed March 20, 2020. https://uklgig.org.uk/wp-content/uploads/2020/02/UKLGIG-submission-to-ICIBI-inspection-of-presenting-officers-Jan-2020-FINAL.pdf.

Valverde, Mariana. *Chronotopes of Law: Jurisdiction, Scale and Governance.* Abingdon: Routledge, 2015.

Weber, Cynthia. *Queer International Relations.* Oxford: Oxford University Press, 2016.

Weber, Frances. "On the Creation of the UK's 'Hostile Environment'", *Race & Class* 60, no 4 (2019): 76–87.

Index

S. Raj and P. Dunne (eds.), *The Queer Outside in Law*, Palgrave Socio-Legal Studies,
https://doi.org/10.1007/978-3-030-48830-7

The manufacturer's authorised representative in the EU is Springer Nature Customer Service Centre GmbH, Europaplatz 3, 69115 Heidelberg, Germany. If you have any concerns regarding our products, please contact ProductSafety@springernature.com

Printed and bound by CPI Group (UK) Ltd, Croydon, CR0 4YY
30/09/2026
02225704-0010